History of Botswana

Thomas Tlou and Alec Campbell

© T. Tlou and A. Campbell 1984

All rights reserved. No part of this publication may be reproduced or transmitted in any form or by any means, without permission.

First published 1984

Published by
Macmillan Botswana Publishing Co (Pty) Ltd
P.O. Box 1155
Gaborone
Botswana

ISBN 0 333 36531 3

Printed in Hong Kong

Contents

Preface	v	16 The Batswana after the Difaqane	115
1 Introduction to History	1	17 Trade and Changes in the Economy	119
2 The First People	4	18 The Missionaries	129
3 Climate and Environment	8	19 British Rule in Botswana: The Beginning	142
4 The Stone Age	12	20 New Threat to the Protectorate	154
5 San and Khoe, Hunters and Pastoralists	20	21 Administrative and Political Developments in the Protectorate	175
6 The Arrival of Bantu-speaking Farmers	29	22 Economic and Social Developments	188
7 The Iron Age	34	23 Two Important Events	209
8 Early Mining and Smelting	42	24 Nationalism and Independence	220
9 The Beginning of the Kingdoms AD 1000-1250	46	25 The Independence Period: Government and Politics	229
10 Botswana and the Zimbabwe Empire 1200-1350	51	26 Economic and Social Developments	238
11 Origins of the Batswana and Bakgalagadi	57	27 Botswana and the World	256
12 Life of the Batswana before the Difaqane	71	Select Bibliography	267
13 Origins of the Bakalanga	81	Abbreviations	269
14 Northern Botswana 1600-1850	89	Terminology	270
15 Difaqane, a Time of Troubles: The 1820s	101	Glossary of Non-English Terms	271
		Index	273

Acknowledgements

The authors and publishers wish to acknowledge, with thanks, the following photographic sources:
ACP Secretariat, Brussels; Africana Museum, Johannesburg; anglo-America Corporation; C.J. Andersson; BBC Hulton Picture Library; Charles Bewlay; Botswana Defence Force; Botswana Democratic Party; Botswana Independence Party; Botswana People's Party; Department of Information and Broadcasting, Botswana; Botswana National Archives; Ministry of Agriculture, Botswana; National Museum and Art Gallery, Botswana; Alec C. Campbell; Cape Archives, Cape Town; Council for World Mission; Educational Resources Centre, University of Botswana; Foreign and Commonwealth Office, London; Sandy Grant; Illustrated London News; Michael Kahn; Moeding College, Botswana; D. Mongwa; Rhodes Memorial Museum; Struan Robertson; Roberts photo; Royal Commonwealth Society; School of Oriental and African Studies, London; LMS Archives; Mrs R.O. Sekgororoane; Mrs L.S. Ketlogetswe; Isaac Schapera; Thomas Tlou; United Nations; WHO; Zimbabwe National Archives, Harare.

The authors and publishers have also used material from the following sources: *Australian Women's Weekly*; T. Baines, *Explorer and Artist 1820-1875*; T. Baines, *Explorations in South-West Africa*; Baldwin, *African Hunting*, 1894; J.T. Brown, *Among the Bantu Nomads*, 1926, photographs taken by A.M. Duggin-Cronin; W.J. Burchell, *Travels in the Interior of Southern Africa*, 1824; S. Daniel, *South African Scenery and Animals*: W. Ellerton Fry; D. Livingstone, *Missionary Travels and Researches in Southern Africa*, 1857; Andrew Smith, *Journal of an Expedition into the Interior of Southern Africa*, 1834-1836.

S.M. Gabatshwane; Lady Ruth Khama; S.M. Molema, *Montshiwa 1815-1896, Barolong Chief and Patriot, 1966*; Aurel Schulz and August Hammar, *The New Africa — A journey up the Chobe and Down the Okavango Rivers. A Record of Exploration and Sport, 1897*; S.M. Gabatshwane, *Tshekedi Khama of Bechuanaland*, 1961; Evangelical Lutheran Mission.

Cover: By kind permission of the National Museum of Botswana, photograph Alec C. Campbell.

The authors and publishers have made every effort to trace the copyright holders, but if they have inadvertently overlooked any, they will be pleased to make the necessary arrangement at the first opportunity.

Preface

'A nation without a past is a lost nation and a people without a past is a people without a soul.'

Sir Seretse Khama,
Daily News, 19 May 1970.

Over many years a number of excellent books have been ·published which cover selective aspects of the history of Botswana. These were however neither normally available nor suited to the secondary school student, or general reader.

This book seeks to fill the gap by providing the reader with the history of Botswana from the origins of mankind to the present. Naturally, within the confines of a single volume such as this, to deal in full depth, or with every aspect of the rich and diverse history of the country, would prove impossible.

In our selection of material we have tried to cover the experiences of almost every group within the population of Botswana. We must point out that where omissions occur this is partly due to the lack of existing information. Considerable research is taking place at present, and new information is being uncovered almost daily. We have also had to select on the basis of the material that we consider significant. The reader may not necessarily agree with us. We are presenting our interpretation of the history of Botswana with our perspective, and the reader should not regard ours as the only one.

We have tried to present history as a whole, taking into account social, political, cultural and economic factors in the pre-colonial, colonial and indepedence periods. Our sources are the most up to date at the time of writing, being based on the latest research. This is of particular significance with regard to the Iron Age in Botswana which we now believe to be considerably older than was previously thought.

Many people who read the manuscript deserve special thanks, in particular Ralph Manyane, Maleshoane Makunga, Busisiwe Mosiieman, Keba Mophuting, Neil Parsons, Jim Denbow, Bob Hitchcock, Professor Revil Mason and Alison Brooks for their constructive criticism and suggestions. We would also like to show our gratitude to Charles Bewlay and Clare Eastland of Macmillan without whom this book would not have been the same.

Our wives and families deserve special thanks for bearing with us while we laboured through the manuscript, and it is to them that we dedicate this book.

Thomas Tlou and Alec Campbell
Gaborone
May 1983

1 Introduction to History

We all know something about our own past, the history of our own families. Our parents and grandparents tell us about themselves and about their parents. We usually know where our parents and grandparents were born. We know whether they worked for themselves at home, or went away to work. Our parents tell us something about the group to which we belong, for instance, 'Great Grandfather came to Botswana in 1871 with the Bakgatla and settled at Mochudi.'

Before the Whites came to Botswana we learned our history from our old people and in the initiation schools, *bogwera* and *bojale*. At these schools, the young were taught the history of their groups and leaders by learning long poems known as praise poems, *maboko*, which tell of great events.

Both these kinds of history, passed down from our parents and grandparents, or through praise poems, are known as oral history. They were passed down by word of mouth and not written down.

Written history

Written history contains facts, the story of what has happened in the past. But it cannot contain the whole story because that would require thousands of books. Also, much of early history was forgotten before writing started.

The person who writes a history book collects information from different sources. He has to choose his facts and join them together to make his story. In doing this he often has to use his imagination because all the facts are not available. Sometimes the evidence is conflicting and he has to make a choice. This is called interpreting. Remember that no two people who have seen an event will describe it in the same words. Also, two people writing the same history might choose different facts and interpret them in different ways. Every piece of information must be checked in case the source has left something out or wrongly interpreted the facts.

Historical sources

Historians use as many sources as they can and compare the evidence from each. The five main sources used are:

1 Oral history

This is the story of our past handed down from generation to generation by word of mouth. It is now becoming confused and is disappearing. There is still much knowledge in the minds of the old people which should be written down immediately, before they die and it is forgotten.

It is important to record oral history in the language of the person who describes it, the informant. Ideally, the recorder should be able to speak the language and know the customs of the people concerned. Everything said should be recorded either in a notebook or on a tape recorder. As many informants as possible should be used. The information given by one can then

Fig. 1 Recording oral history. Notice the tape recorder that S. Petere and his wife are using

be checked against that given by another. The best informants are those people who still practise their traditional culture. Women are just as good at being informants as men.

2 Archaeology

This is studying the past by digging up the remains that people have left behind them. What is found at one place is compared with what is found at another. Archaeology tells us much about history which has been completely forgotten. It also helps us to confirm oral history and put it in its proper order.

The archaeologist finds a place (*lerotobolo*) where there are cultural remains: stone tools, pottery, ash, hut floors, stone walls, etc. He marks a pattern of squares with string. Each square has sides of a metre long. This pattern, or grid, covers the area to be dug and helps the archaeologist to mark everything he finds on a map. He digs each square down a little at a time and collects and maps everything he finds. Sometimes he finds one layer of remains on top of another. He knows that these are different settlements: the lower the layer, the earlier the settlement or time of occupation.

There are various ways to find out the date of settlements. The best and most commonly used in Africa is to send some organic material (things which once had life, such as plants, shell, bone, etc.), usually charcoal, for testing in a laboratory. During their lives animals and plants contain a small amount of carbon. When they die some of the carbon breaks down slowly, at a speed which can be measured. Unfortunately, for anything older than 40 000 years there is too little carbon left to make an accurate measurement.

From the things they find, archaeologists can tell us a lot about the way people lived. They can

Fig. 2 An archaeological excavation. The area has been marked in squares with string and levels show different periods

Fig. 3 The skeleton of a Toutswe woman buried about AD 1100 with pottery. How do we know the age?

tell what people ate by the plant and bone remains, whether they kept cattle and small livestock, whether they used iron or traded. They can even tell us how large the population was and the size of the country it occupied.

3 Eye-witness accounts

These are mainly the diaries and drawings of the first white travellers to come to Botswana. For example, Samuel Daniell visited Batlhaping in 1802 and made many beautiful drawings and paintings of what he saw. There were many visitors during the early 19th century: travellers such as Daniell, missionaries such as Moffat and Livingstone, hunters such as Baldwin, scientists such as Burchell and Smith, and traders such as Bain and Andersson. Each one recorded what was most interesting to him. Unfortunately, much that we would like to know now did not really interest them. Even so, their accounts help us to reconstruct how people lived over 150 years ago.

4 Official records

These were written by missionaries, businessmen and administrators. They can be very helpful, particularly because the people who wrote them were not writing about themselves but about administrative matters. However, missionary records have to be treated carefully as missionaries were closely involved in trying to change the whole way of life of the Batswana. They criticised things which appeared unChristian. The records of business and mining concerns also need to be looked at carefully since the writers were most interested in making money.

5 Other history books

These are a valuable source, but they must be read critically. Most of the histories written about Southern Africa were recorded by non-Africans, people from Europe and America. They were trying to record the history of a land where written records were scarce or did not exist. They were also writing about people with a different culture and language from their own. What may be important to a foreign historian may not be important to the people about whom he writes. Because these historians did not always understand what was involved many history books about Southern Africa make us angry today. When reading them we should try to find the truth and separate it from what is false. We should not condemn them all as useless. The very few early records of Southern Africa were mostly made by the Portuguese. Then, in the 1600s, the Dutch arrived and more was recorded. However, nothing was written about Botswana until the early 1800s. There are many gaps in our history. Some of them may be filled in the future but many of them may never be filled.

Questions

1. List the five main sources in the study of history. Which of these sources do you think is most important when we want to study the very early history of Botswana?
2. The class should choose a recent school event. Write down the six most important facts about that event. Compare your list with those of the rest of the class. Are there many differences? Does this tell you something about the study of history?

2 The First People

Evolution and natural selection

The different races on the Earth today are not all the same. Some people have black skins and some people have white skins. Some have curly hair and some have straight hair. People belonging to some races are generally larger than those belonging to other races. Even within a racial group all people are not the same. Some are taller than others, some darker in complexion (skin colour) and so on.

This range of different characteristics in different individuals is entirely natural. It exists in all populations of plants and animals. These characteristics are determined by a combination of the information inherited from the individual's parents and factors in the environment (surroundings). The environment in which a population lives is always changing, though often extremely slowly. At a given time some individuals in a population will be better suited than others to the environmental conditions at that time. For example, when the climate in Africa grew drier and the vegetation gradually changed from forest to plains, some apes were better suited to this than others. Many animals, such as leopards and lions, could move unseen through the long grass and catch and eat the apes. Those apes which were able to stand upright were better adapted (suited). They could spend more time looking over the grass for their enemies, and so survived. Those which did not adapt (change) in this way, died out or survived only in the forests. This whole process of change and adaptation is called evolution and is the result of natural selection. As a result of natural selection all populations of plants and animals alter. The fittest (best adapted) survive and the least well adapted do not.

Physical characteristics also develop as the result of our environment and way of life. A child who has a good diet will often grow taller, and have bigger bones than a child fed on a bad diet. People who do heavy work usually have bigger muscles than those who do light work. If a family has a history of heavy work, going back many generations, then the children usually inherit the very well-developed bodies of their ancestors.

Both individual people and whole races can change their shape and colour as a result of the environment in which they live and the type of life they lead. In other words, we are changing very slowly all the time. Even a thousand years ago we may not have looked exactly the same as we do today. Perhaps we were slightly smaller in body size and height.

It is not only people who change. Animals and plants also change for the same reasons. One of the best examples to take is that of cattle. Today we breed our cows to get the best animals, selecting bulls which will produce the type of calves we want. We value the cows which produce a calf every year and which do not die during the drought. This is also a form of selection, it is artificial (man-made) selection. We see the results quickly because we deliberately choose the best. Long ago people valued certain types of cattle. The Bangwaketse valued white animals and the Bakalanga valued black. The Bangwaketse crossed white bulls with white cows and the Bakalanga black bulls with black cows to produce the colour of animal they most wanted.

Everything: humans, animals and plants, slowly changes by evolution. Millions of years ago there were no humans as we know them today, but there were monkeys which had tails and apes which looked like monkeys but had no tails. We are all descended from the apes. It has taken about seven million years for us to evolve gradually from apes to humans. Look at Fig. 4 on page 6, which shows our family tree.

Monkeys and baboons move around by walking on both feet and hands at the same time. But sometimes they stand up on their back legs, usually to try to see something in the distance. Also, their feet and hands are more or less the same shape because they use their feet as well as their hands to hold on to branches when climbing trees. They sleep in trees and spend much of their time above the ground. Their bodies are adapted to their environment and life in the trees.

Environmental change and adaptation

We believe that about seven million years ago the forests were shrinking and open plains of grassland began to appear. The ape population became too large for its forest environment. Perhaps there was no longer sufficient food for all the animals who lived in the forest. Over hundreds of thousands of years some of the apes were slowly forced to move from the forest to the open plains. Some of the apes adapted to suit their new environments. Those that did this survived, whilst others did not. Those that adapted no longer needed to spend all their time in the trees. They now needed to be able to move across the grass-covered plains searching for food. The danger from other animals meant that they began to spend more time standing upright looking over the grass for their enemies. Also their feet began to change so that they were more suited to walking on the ground than climbing trees.

The food they ate also changed. When they lived in the forest they ate mostly fruit and young, soft shoots. Their jaws were longer and narrow with teeth like a dog. They tore bits from their food and swallowed them without chewing. On the plains their food consisted of hard seeds, roots, bulbs and tubers which had to be chewed. Slowly their teeth changed so that they were more suited to grinding and chopping.

Australopithecines

The apes moved away from the trees and began to live on the plains walking upright (although probably bent forward and sometimes dropping on all fours again). At the same time our earliest ancestors broke away from the ape family and began to develop into human beings. These apes are known as *Australopithecines* (which means 'Southern Ape'). See Fig. 4 on page 6.

The remains of *Australopithecines* were first found at Taung in the Northern Cape not far from Vryburg. The earliest remains have been found in East Africa, southern Ethiopia, Kenya and Tanzania. They consisted of bones, bits of skull, skeletons and teeth which had, over time, been turned into stone. Scientists can tell that the remains did not belong to apes because of the shape of the bones. The joint where the thigh bone fits into the pelvis shows that the animal spent some of its time walking upright. The teeth are flat-topped and adapted for grinding rather than pointed for tearing. The skull is different: the skull cavity is larger and more dome-shaped than that of a monkey.

There were differences among the *Australopithecines* and scientists have divided them into two types or families. These are *Australopithecus gracilis* or Slender *Australopithecine* and *Australopithecus robustus*, or Robust *Australopithecine*. They were given these names because the Gracilis (Slender) were lighter and less powerful than the Robustus. Although scientists have divided them there is not much evidence and they may have all belonged to one family.

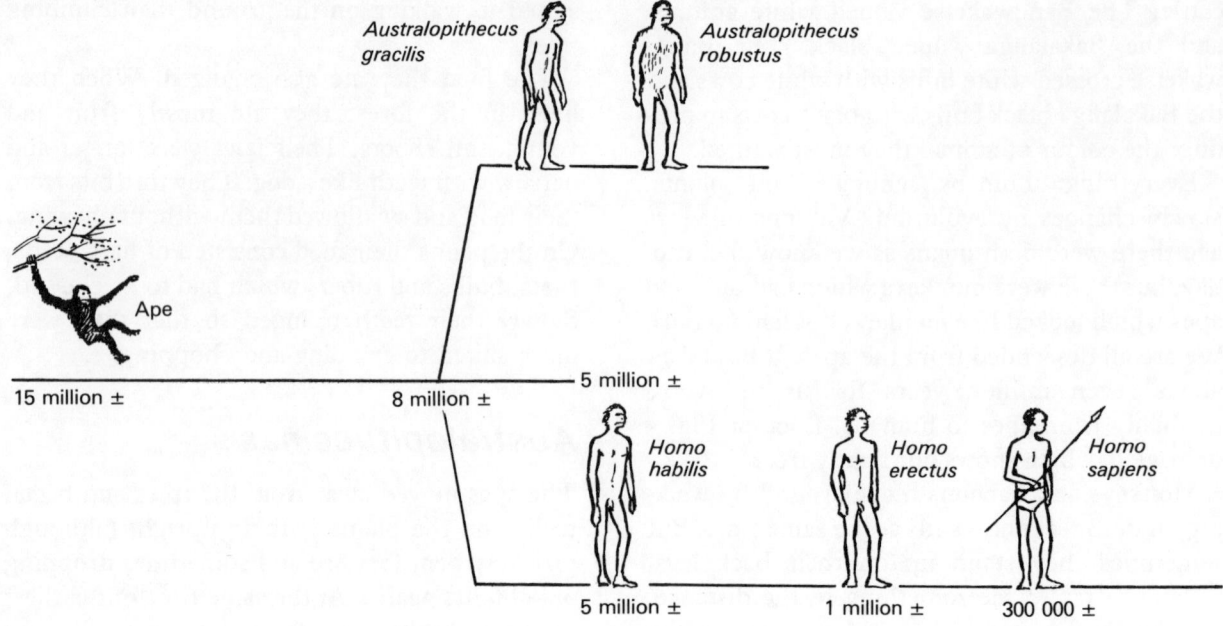

Fig. 4   Our family tree: from apes to *Homo sapiens*

Australopithecus gracilis

The earliest *Australopithecines* found in Southern Africa, in the Transvaal, are about two and a half million years old and are all of the Gracilis type. The Gracilis were probably the height of a modern eight-year-old child and weighed about 25 kilogrammes. They were probably omnivorous (eating both vegetables and meat) but mainly ate softer vegetable foods. At this time the climate was wetter and there were probably more forests providing more fruits and soft shoots.

Australopithecus robustus

By 1.5 million years ago *Australopithecus gracilis* had disappeared and *Australopithecus robustus* had replaced them. They were heavier, weighing about 45 kilogrammes. It is not known whether the Gracilis type developed into the Robustus, or whether natural selection resulted in the Robustus surviving from an earlier time and the Gracilis vanishing.

Probably *Australopithecines* never made tools for themselves. But, like modern apes they would pick up sticks, stones and bones to defend themselves or get ants out of a hole. No shaped tools have been found which definitely belong with their remains.

Homo habilis

About one million years ago *Homo habilis* or Handy Man began to appear. Probably they were a form of evolved Australopithecine which developed human characteristics more quickly than the others. The main differences between them and the Australopithecines were bigger heads, smaller teeth and the ability to shape tools.

Tools, which have been deliberately chipped to form a sharp edge, have been found with the earliest remains of *Homo habilis*. The *Homo habilis* people are important because they were the first tool makers.

Homo erectus

The *Homo habilis* people developed into *Homo erectus* (Erect or Upright Man). Look at Fig. 5. At the same time *Australopithecus robustus* disappeared. This may have been because of competition from the *Homo erectus* people who lived in the same environment and ate the same food, but who could also make tools.

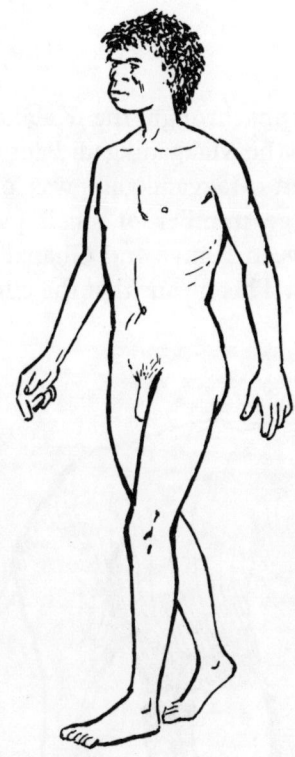

Fig. 5 *Homo erectus*

Homo sapiens

By about 300 000 years ago, scientists believe, the *Homo erectus* people had developed into an early form of ourselves. They were called *Homo sapiens* or Knowledgeable Man. They were 1.5 metres tall, walked upright, had heads the same size as ours, could talk and make plans. They continued to develop until about 40 000 years ago when they probably looked more or less like us.

The remains of these early people have not been found in Botswana. However they have been found just west of Pretoria so it is almost certain that they roamed eastern and north-eastern Botswana.

Questions

1. Use the word 'evolution' in a complete sentence to show its meaning.
2. Give two possible reasons why apes began to walk upright.
3. Complete the following sentences using the correct name for a type of early man. Then rearrange the sentences in the right order.
    (a) By about 300 000 years ago_____ was more than 1.5 metres tall.
    (b) About 40 000 years ago_____ probably looked like us.
    (c) _____began to appear two and a half million years ago.
    (d) The earliest remains of_____have been found in East Africa.

3 Climate and Environment

When the climate of an area changes, the species of trees and grasses also change. Then the species of animals which feed on the vegetation also change. These changes take thousands or tens of thousands of years.

Look at a map of Botswana. The dry river beds which run through the Kalahari Desert (Kgalagadi) to the Makgadikgadi Pans once flowed with water. Makgadikgadi was once a big lake. The large number of small pans in the Kalahari between Kanye and Ghanzi once held shallow water. This means that the climate must

Fig. 6 Some prehistoric animals: a giant hartebeest, an ancestral elephant, a giant buffalo and a sabre-toothed tiger

Fig. 7 Trees similar to those found in prehistoric Botswana. Today they grow in better rainfall areas only

have been much wetter and cooler. It is even possible to tell how deep Lake Makgadikgadi was, by finding the old beaches and then measuring how high these are above the present pan floor. These beaches are now ridges of stones, rounded by rolling in the waves of the lake shore. The bones of animals which have survived from long ago can also tell us about the climate. Many of the animals have died out completely but from their surviving relatives we know what they ate and what type of country they lived in. Some of the ancient animals are shown in Fig. 6.

The changes in climate must have had a great effect on the people then living in Botswana. During wetter, cooler periods, when rivers flowed in the Kalahari and there was more forest, people probably lived throughout the whole country. In drier, hotter times they probably moved to those areas which still had water. As the climate changed their way of life also changed. Some food plants must have disappeared and others grown. Forests changed to open plains and lakes to dry pans. The animals they hunted also changed.

Look at Fig. 8 on page 10 which gives a rough guide to the changes in climate and vegetation experienced in Botswana in the past. The major changes were as follows.

1. A million years ago it was probably four times as wet as it is today and much cooler. The Kalahari, though sandy, was covered in forest and dotted with small lakes. Rivers ran into the huge Makgadikgadi Lake. There were a few plains animals such as gemsbok *(kukama)*, hartebeeste *(kgama)*, and springbok *(tshephe)*. The most common animals were buffalo *(nare)*, kudu *(tholo)*, sable *(kwalata)*, impala *(phala)*, and elephant *(tlou)*. There were also animals which have disappeared today, such as giant zebra, giant buffalo, gogops or lake hippopotamus.

2. 200 000 years ago it was much drier and warmer. The forests began to disappear giving way to open grassland. By 100 000 years ago the rainfall was about the same as it is today. Many small lakes and rivers dried up and Lake Makgadikgadi got smaller. The forest animals disappeared and plains animals took their place.

3. By 80 000 years ago rainfall had increased again. It was again four times as wet as it is today. Lakes filled and new ones were formed. Rivers flowed and forest covered the country. The species of wild animals also changed.

4. By 40 000 years ago the rainfall had decreased to about today's level or even less. The country was very dry again.

5. By about 25 000 years ago rainfall had increased to about one and a half times what we get today. It was slightly cooler. Areas of the Kalahari were well wooded, although other areas were still fairly dry. Forest animals lived along the rivers and lakes, and in most of the north and east. In drier areas plains animals were found in large numbers.

6. By 10 000 years ago it was drier and warmer than it is today. Probably much of the vegetation in the south-west disappeared leaving bare sand dunes. There were a few trees like boscias *(mopipi* and *motlopi)* and acacias *(mogotlo, mooka, mosu* and *mongana)*.

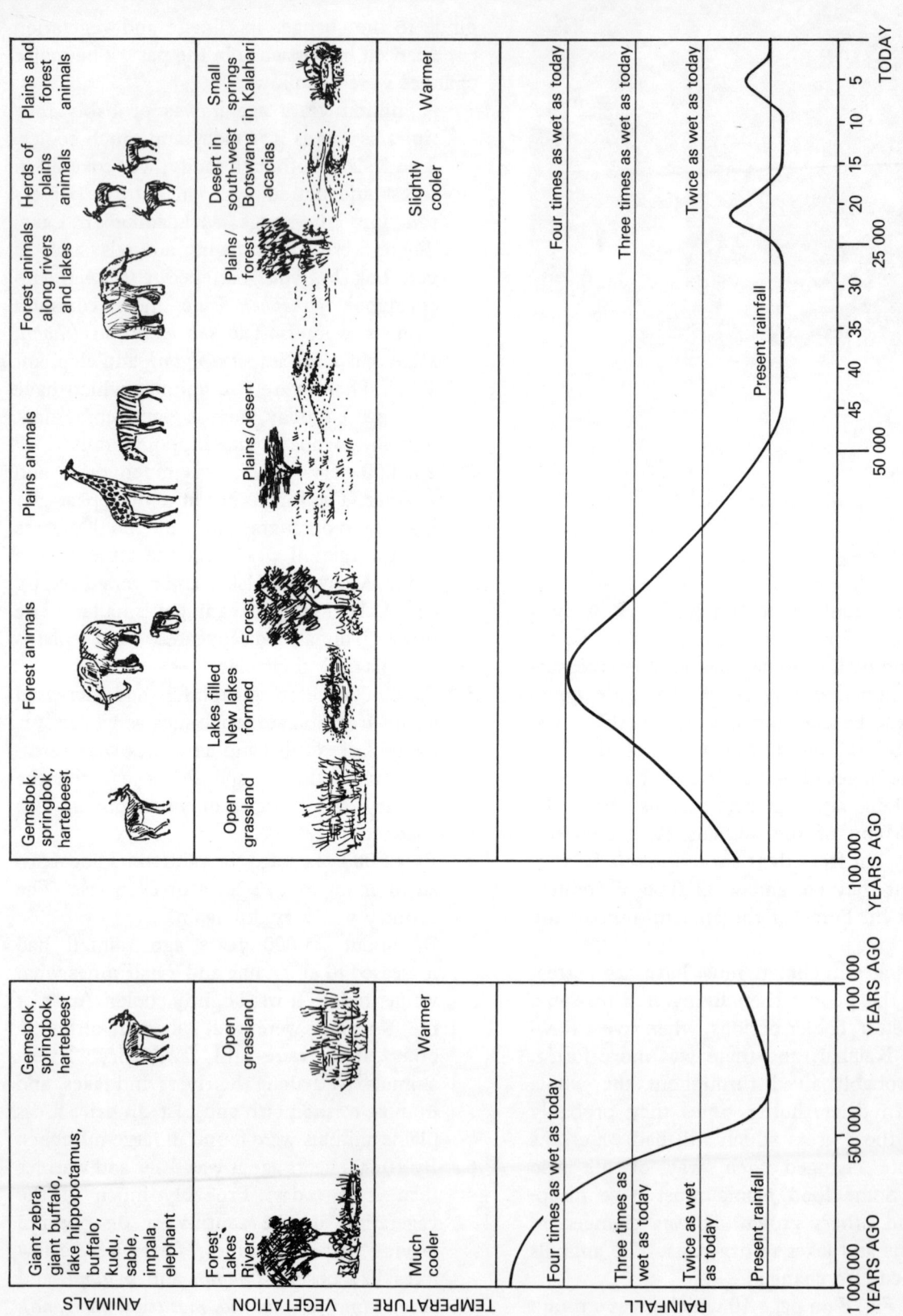

Fig. 8 Time chart to show changes in climate, vegetation and animals in Botswana

Note: The period from 1 million to 100 000 years ago has been telescoped. If it was drawn to the same scale it would be approximately ten times the width of the page. Draw your own time chart from 1 million years to today all on the same scale using a very large piece of paper

7 Around 5 000 years ago the rainfall increased again until it was well above today's level. There were permanent small springs in the Kalahari. Although plains animals were most common, forest animals such as elephant and buffalo could be found at Ghanzi, Matsheng and Letlhakeng. This lasted for about 4 000 years when the rainfall fell again to today's level.

8 Rainfall has remained fairly constant for the last 1 000 years. There was a slight increase 500 years ago which lasted for 200 years.

Questions

1 Why did changes in climate in early Botswana cause the movement of people?
2 Study the diagram Fig. 8 on page 10 and answer the following questions.
   (a) When was there four times as much rainfall as today?
   (b) When was there *less* rainfall than today?

4 The Stone Age

We have seen that our earliest ancestors broke away from the apes about seven million years ago. We call them our earliest ancestors because they began to walk upright and their teeth grew to look more like ours than those of a monkey.

Today, scientists study monkeys, apes and baboons and record their behaviour. Baboons, in particular, live in large groups, while apes tend to live in smaller families. We can guess that when our ancestors broke away from the apes they probably behaved much as apes and baboons behave today. But something changed them and this was probably the use of tools.

We do not know for certain when they began to make tools to help them get food. We think it was between two and three million years ago. We do not know which came first: whether they walked upright and this allowed them to use their hands to hold tools, or whether they started by using tools and then, because their hands were full, began to walk upright. Modern apes such as chimpanzees will pick up sticks and stones to defend themselves. They will also use a thin stick to draw termites from a hole. If there is no thin stick available they will take a stick and strip the leaves off it. This is the start of making tools.

Scientists have learned much about group behaviour from watching baboons. They know how individual animals treat each other, feed together, defend themselves, breed and even communicate. The more we study apes and baboons the more we learn about the probable behaviour of our ancestors.

We also study their skulls and teeth in relation to our own. By using tools the earliest people developed their brains so that they could make more and better use of tools. As the brain developed, so apparently did the need for speech. We do not know when people began to be able to communicate well through speech, but it was probably a very long time ago.

Walking on two feet (known as bipedalism), making tools and speech all developed together. As they developed, so the brain became larger and able to perform more varied and different functions. We tend to measure progress through the Stone Ages by the skill used in making tools because little else remains to guide us.

The time chart on pages 14 and 15 shows developments from early man to the present day.

The Early Stone Age

The earliest certain tools were made by our ancestors about 1.8 million years ago. These tools are called *Oldowan* because they were first found at Olduvai in Tanzania. They were very crude but several different types were made for different purposes. This shows that people had already developed a long way from their ancestors who just picked up things to use as tools.

By 1.5 million years ago some very beautiful tools were being made, showing that people's brains had begun to develop.

Later still, about a million years after the Oldowan tools, much better tools were being made. These are called *Acheulian* because they were first found at the village of St Acheul in France. Acheulian tools have been found all over eastern and parts of northern Botswana. They continued to be made until about 70 000 years ago.

Look at Fig. 9 and compare the earliest stone tools (Oldowan) with those called Acheulian. See how much better the Acheulian tools look.

Tools got better because people had developed new ways to make them. To shape the earliest tools people took a hard rock. Then they chipped pieces off this rock using another hard rock like a hammer. This is known as trimming.

· This period, when tools were made from stone, is known as the Early Stone Age. By this time people were living in groups of more than one family, were able to talk, understood how to make and use fire. They cooperated in hunting, built shelters and made tools including hand

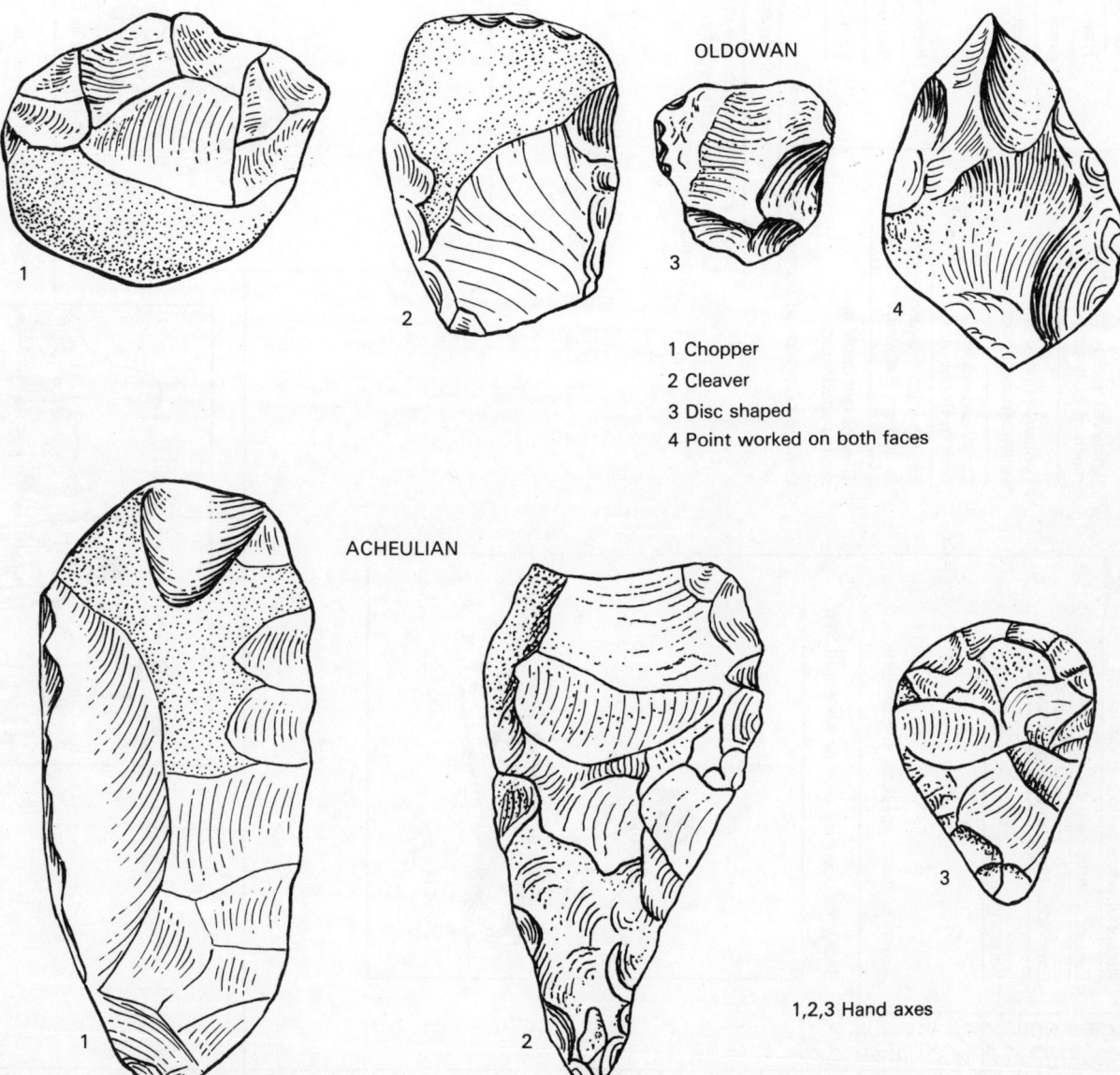

Fig. 9 Early Stone Age tools

Fig. 10 Time chart from Early Man to the present day

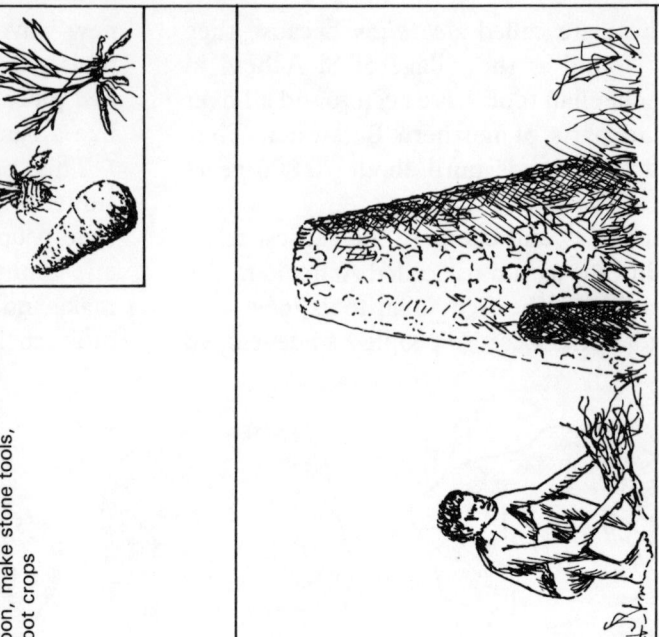

- Independence
- Bechuanaland Protectorate
- Arrival of white people in Botswana
- Bakwena settle near Molepolole
- Bangologa begin to occupy Kalahari
- Barolong occupy area around Zeerust

- Arrival of Bantu speakers in Botswana

- Botswana occupied only by Khoe and San

- Barozvi Empire
- Torwa Empire
- Great Zimbabwe Empire
- Mapungubwe

- Broederstroom occupied
- Bantu speaking peoples in Zimbabwe
- Bantu speaking peoples in Eastern Africa

- Batswana spread to occupy much of Botswana
- Toutswemogola: large, cattle-herding societies
- Cattle herders in eastern Botswana
- Khoe herders possibly settled in nothern Botswana
- They obtain cattle and spread southwards
- General expansion of Bantu speaking peoples
- Iron smelting reaches Bantu speakers
- Bantu speaking peoples live in area around Cameroon, make stone tools, grow root crops

- Discovery of iron smelting in Fertile Crescent
- Domestication of animals and crops in Fertile Crescent

LATE IRON AGE
EARLY IRON AGE
LATE STONE AGE
STONE AGE

Today
1 000
2 000
3 000
4 000
5 000
5 000
10 000

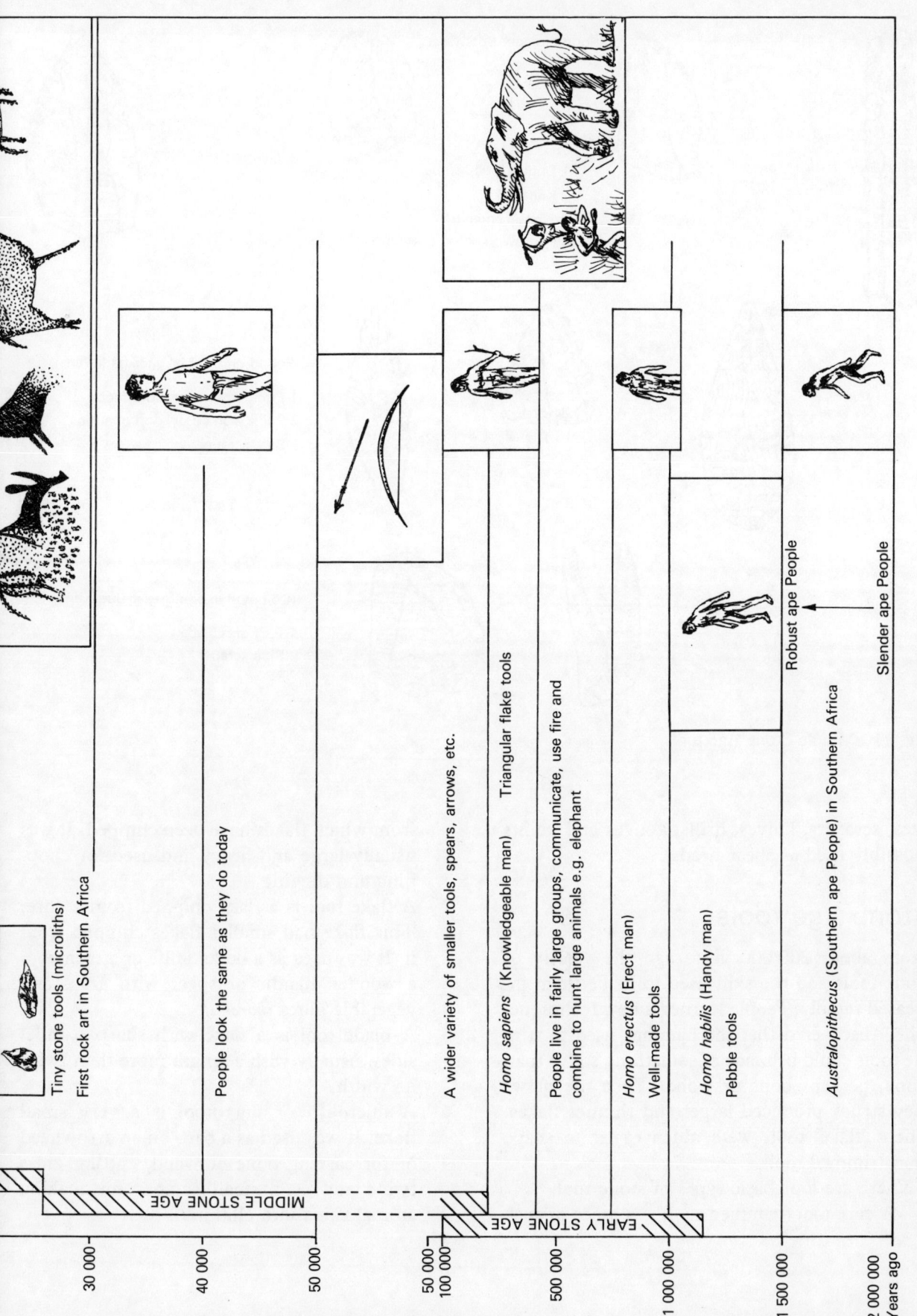

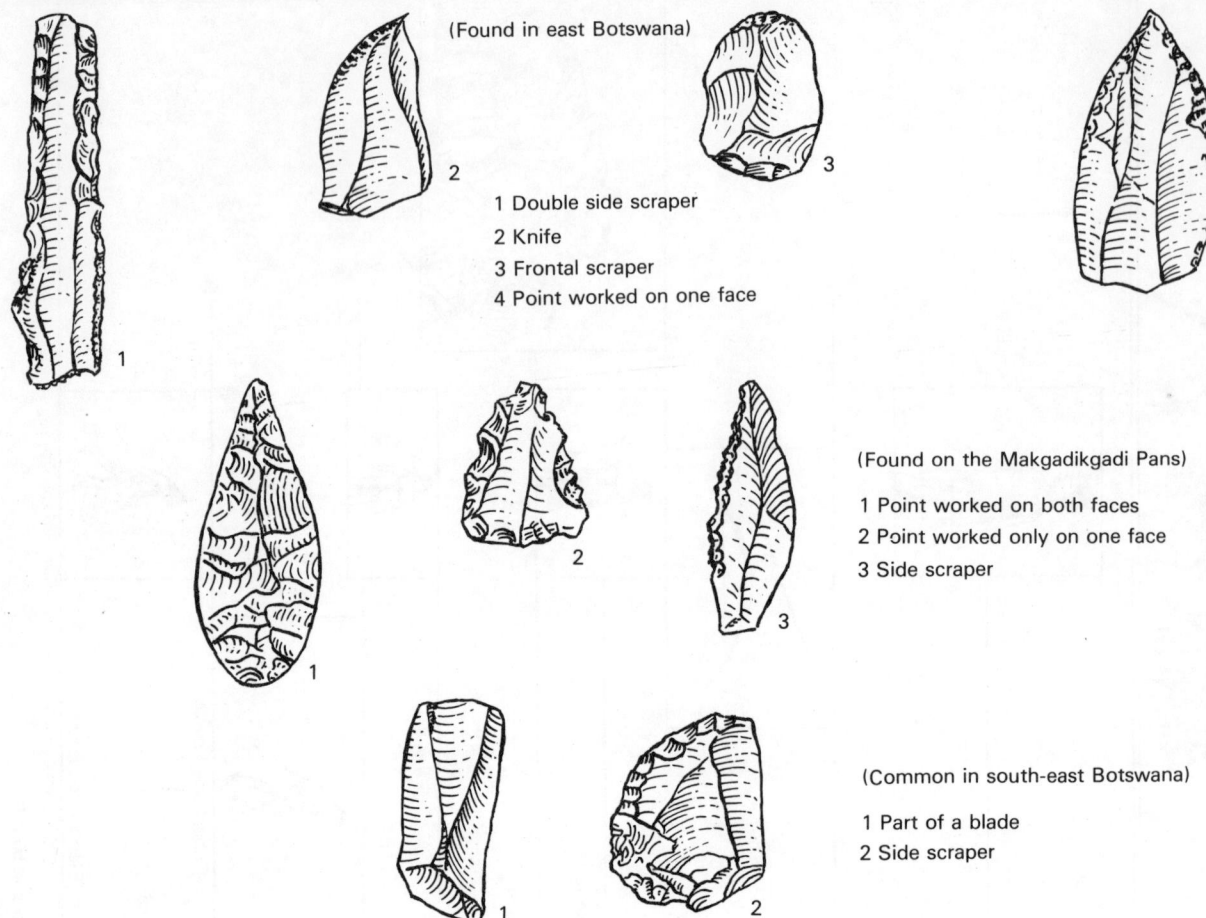

Fig. 11 Middle Stone Age tools

axes, scrapers, knives, drills, gouges and points (possibly used as spear heads).

Stone Age tools

From about 200 000 years ago the variety of stone tools and the skill used to make them increased rapidly. People learned a new technique. They discovered that the hammer used to trim the tools could be made of something softer than stone, perhaps bone or wood. Then the blows they struck produced larger and thinner flakes. These 'flake' tools were much easier to shape than trimmed tools.

There are four basic types of stone tool.

1. A core tool (trimmed tool) is a piece of rock from which flakes have been chipped. It was usually large and heavy and used for chopping and digging.
2. A flake tool is a flake chipped from a core. This flake had smaller flakes chipped from it. It was used as a bulky knife or attached to a wooden handle or spear with grass and vegetable glues *(boreku)*.
3. A blade tool is a flake with sharp parallel sides, usually with a length more than twice its width.
4. A microlith or microtool is a very small flake. It was used as a barb on an arrowhead or for carving bone or wood, cutting grass twine and as a small scraper for making animal skins into clothing.

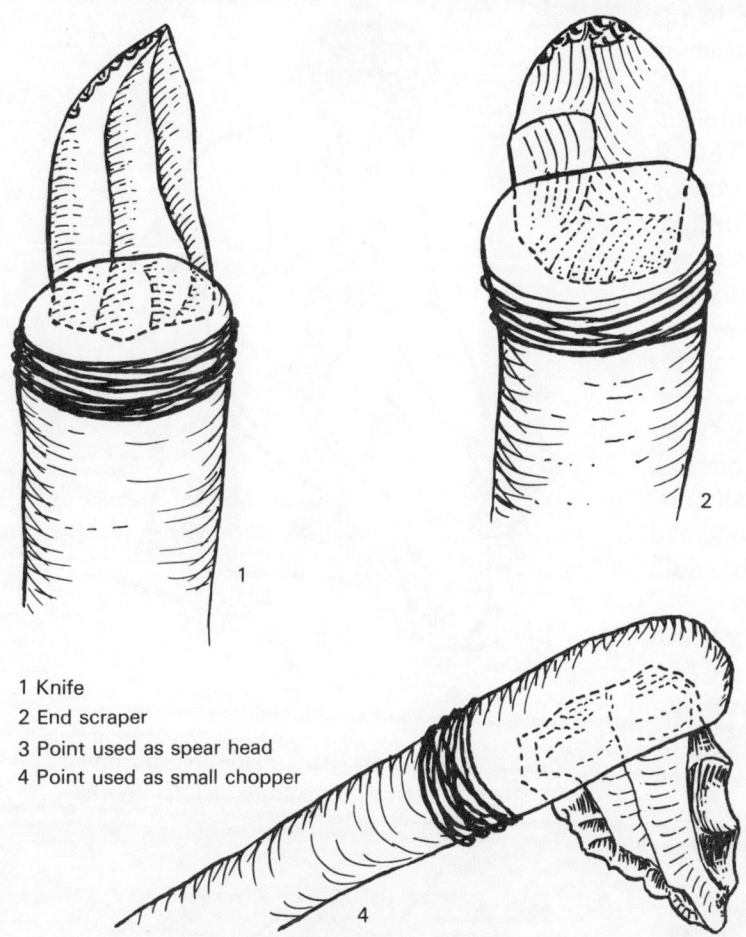
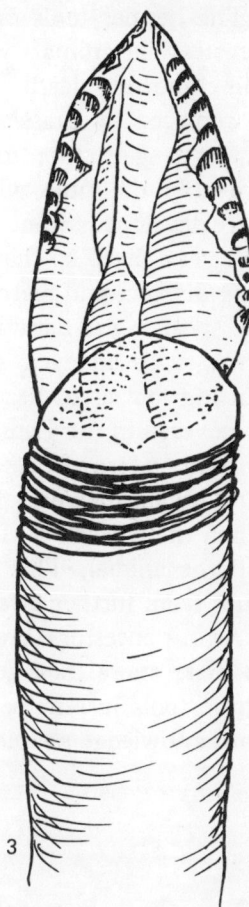

1 Knife
2 End scraper
3 Point used as spear head
4 Point used as small chopper

Fig. 12 A possible method for hafting stone tools

Core tools and flake tools were used throughout the Stone Age. Blade tools were first used in the Middle Stone Age. Microliths were first used in the Late Stone Age.

Look at the diagrams, Figs. 11 and 12 above, and see how these tools were properly hafted (attached to a handle).

The Late Stone Age

The Late Stone Age began about 25 000 years ago. All the tools were very small and usually made from hard rocks. Many were hafted and sometimes one haft carried many small tools fitted together to form a saw or a sickle. The makers of these tools were the ancestors in Botswana of the San or 'Bushmen' (*Basarwa*) and the Khoe or 'Hottentots' (*Bakgothu*) some of whom still live in Botswana today. These people probably made wooden and bone tools as well but they have not survived because of decay. We call this period, from about two million years ago until quite recent times, the Stone Age because stone tools are the most common remains we find. Fig. 13 on page 18 shows stone tools being made.

The different types of tool tell us how people lived. Often the shape of the tools tells us how they were used. Scientists examine the marks of wear on their cutting edges. They can often work out the way the tool was held and how the cutting edge was used.

The heavier tools probably suited life in the forest. Wild animals were cornered or trapped and clubbed to death. As the forest was gradually replaced by grasslands it became more difficult to get close to wild animals. This is probably the time when spears for throwing were developed. Stone spearheads had to be light and very sharp so that they could be thrown a long distance and pierce the animal's skin. From the spear it was natural to develop the bow and arrow with an even smaller point. Poison for putting on arrowheads may also have been discovered in the Late Stone Age. This was important as arrowheads no longer had to pierce a vital organ, they only had to make a small hole. Then the poison would mix with the blood and kill the animal. This meant that people could hunt from further away from the animal.

As our ancestors' brains developed they began to make more tools for different uses. At first crude tools just helped people to survive. But with knowledge people were able to make them-

Fig. 13 Stone tools being made. Notice how one stone is used as a hammer against another for roughly shaping the tool

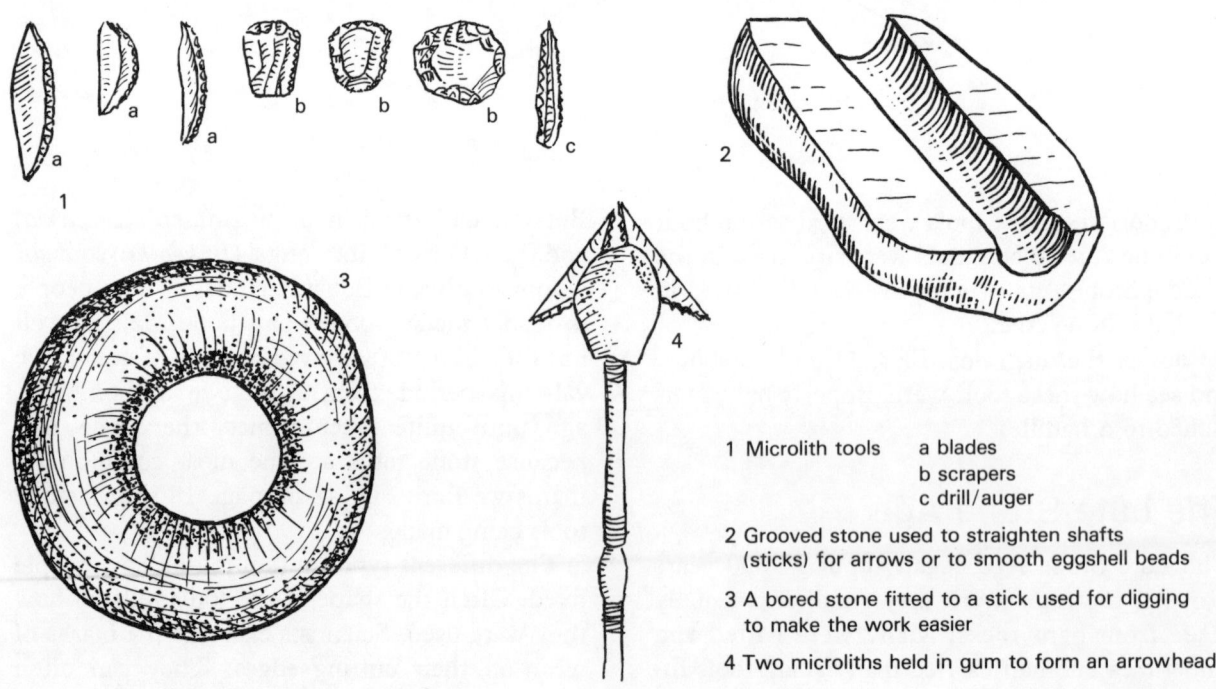

1 Microlith tools   a blades
                             b scrapers
                             c drill/auger

2 Grooved stone used to straighten shafts (sticks) for arrows or to smooth eggshell beads

3 A bored stone fitted to a stick used for digging to make the work easier

4 Two microliths held in gum to form an arrowhead

Fig. 14 Late Stone Age tools

selves more comfortable by making skin clothing to protect them from the cold weather. They were able to decorate themselves with beads and other ornaments. People became more efficient in everything they did. As the number of tools increased and they became more sophisticated (advanced) so these were used to make other tools. Each tool, instead of being used for many jobs, became more specialised. See Fig. 14.

Think of all the tools and skills needed to make a bow and arrow.

1. Knives to cut the skin and sinew to make string.
2. Scrapers to make the shaft smooth.
3. Heat to make the shaft straight.
4. Heat and a container to mix the glue *(boreku)* for fixing the head to the shaft.
5. Containers for poison, carved from wood, using chisels, gouges and axes.
6. The root bark of *mopipi* trees, used to make quivers (containers) for arrows.
7. The skin of a steenbok *(phuduhudu)* made into a bag to carry the bow and arrows over the shoulder.
8. Scrapers to remove the hair, an awl to punch holes and sinew to sew the skin into a bag.

Stone tools were used to make other tools of bone, wood, skin and sinew. Probably such tools have been made for a very long time, but they were not durable (lasting) like stone and most of them have disappeared.

Through time people became more intelligent and able to adapt to a wider range of environments. By the end of the Early Stone Age they lived in widely differing areas; from the ice-covered tundra of northern Europe to the tropical rain forests of Africa.

Questions

1. Find two pieces of hard rock and try to make an Early Stone Age tool like the ones shown in Fig. 9 on page 13.
2. Provide approximate dates for the following.
   (a) The first tools found at Olduvai in Tanzania.
   (b) Acheulian tools ceased to be made in Botswana.
   (c) People understood how to make fire.
   (d) The start of the Late Stone Age.

5 San and Khoe, Hunters and Pastoralists

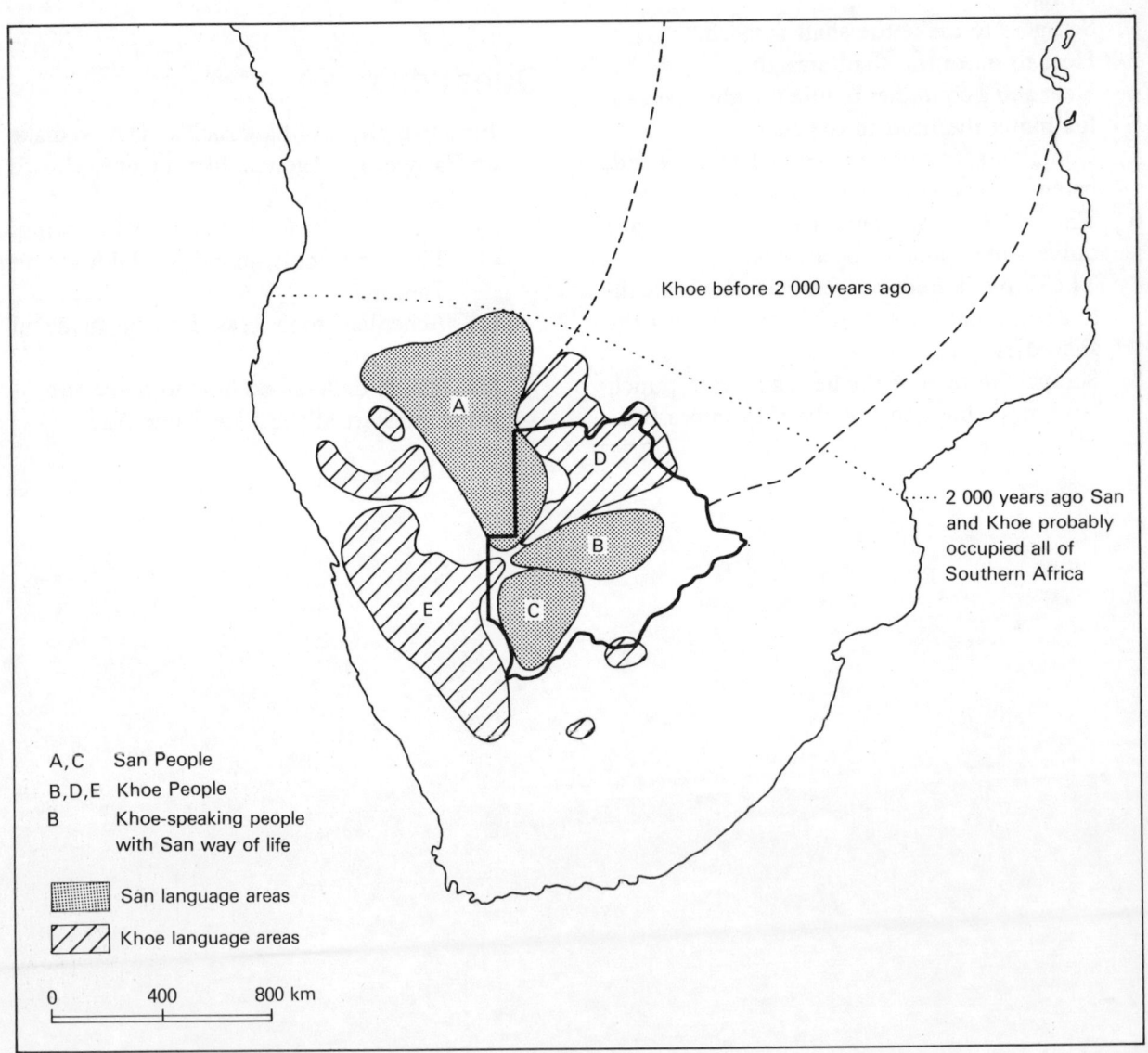

Fig. 15 Map of San and Khoe distribution, 1960

When the Dutch first landed in the Cape and met the modern San (*Basarwa*) and Khoe (*Bakgothu*) people they called the Khoe, who kept cattle and sheep, Hottentots, and the San, who lived by hunting and collecting, Bushmen. The word 'Hottentot' describes the way the Dutch thought they spoke, like stutterers. 'Bushmen' simply meant people who lived in the unoccupied country.

Scientists like to call them Khoe (pronounced 'Khwe') and San after names used by *Bakgothu*. Khoekhoen means 'Men of men', that is 'The real people' and is what the *Bakgothu* called themselves. 'Khoe' means 'man'. San, or Sana, means 'Those who gather (wild food)' and is the name the *Bakgothu* gave to the Basarwa or San. Their languages have some similarities and are characterised by click consonants. However, they are not closely related, some are as different as Setswana is to English. Look at the map, Fig. 15. It is thought by some people that the Khoe lived in the wetter country to the north-east while the San lived in the drier country to the south-west, and that only during recent times have the Khoe pushed their way into the south-west.

Although in the past Khoe were thought to be pastoralists and San hunters, this was probably a mistake. Almost certainly some Khoe have had to live by hunting and collecting, while some San have kept cattle. For example the San living today on the Nata and Boteti Rivers keep cattle, make pots and grow crops.

We know that 3 000 years ago, and possibly

Fig. 16 A rock painting in the Tsodilo Hills, Botswana. The eland and giraffe are ritually highly valued by the San hunters

less, both Khoe and San living in Southern Africa were gatherers and hunters. They did not own stock. Look at the map again. About 3 000 years ago both the D and E groups probably lived in northern Botswana and Zimbabwe. The E group did not move to the south-west until later. Some of the E group obtained sheep (probably from the north) and started moving towards the south-west through Botswana into Namibia and the northern Cape. They may have changed some of their traditional customs as some people became richer and more powerful than others. Some time later more Khoe got cattle (also probably from the north) and began to move south-westwards, although a few remained in northern Botswana. Their descendants are the Banoka who live along the Boteti and Thamalakane Rivers, and possibly the San of the Nata River.

Almost certainly the peoples living in Africa south of the Sahara today were, some 60 000 years ago or a little less, one people. Probably they looked more like San than like the Bantu-speaking peoples of today. Khoesan-type skeletons have been found over much of southern and eastern Africa dating back 15 000 years or more. Bantu-type skeletons only date back about 6 000 years. Probably the Bantu-type people broke away from the Khoesan-type people more than 10 000 years ago in the hot, rain-forest areas of equatorial Africa. They developed differently

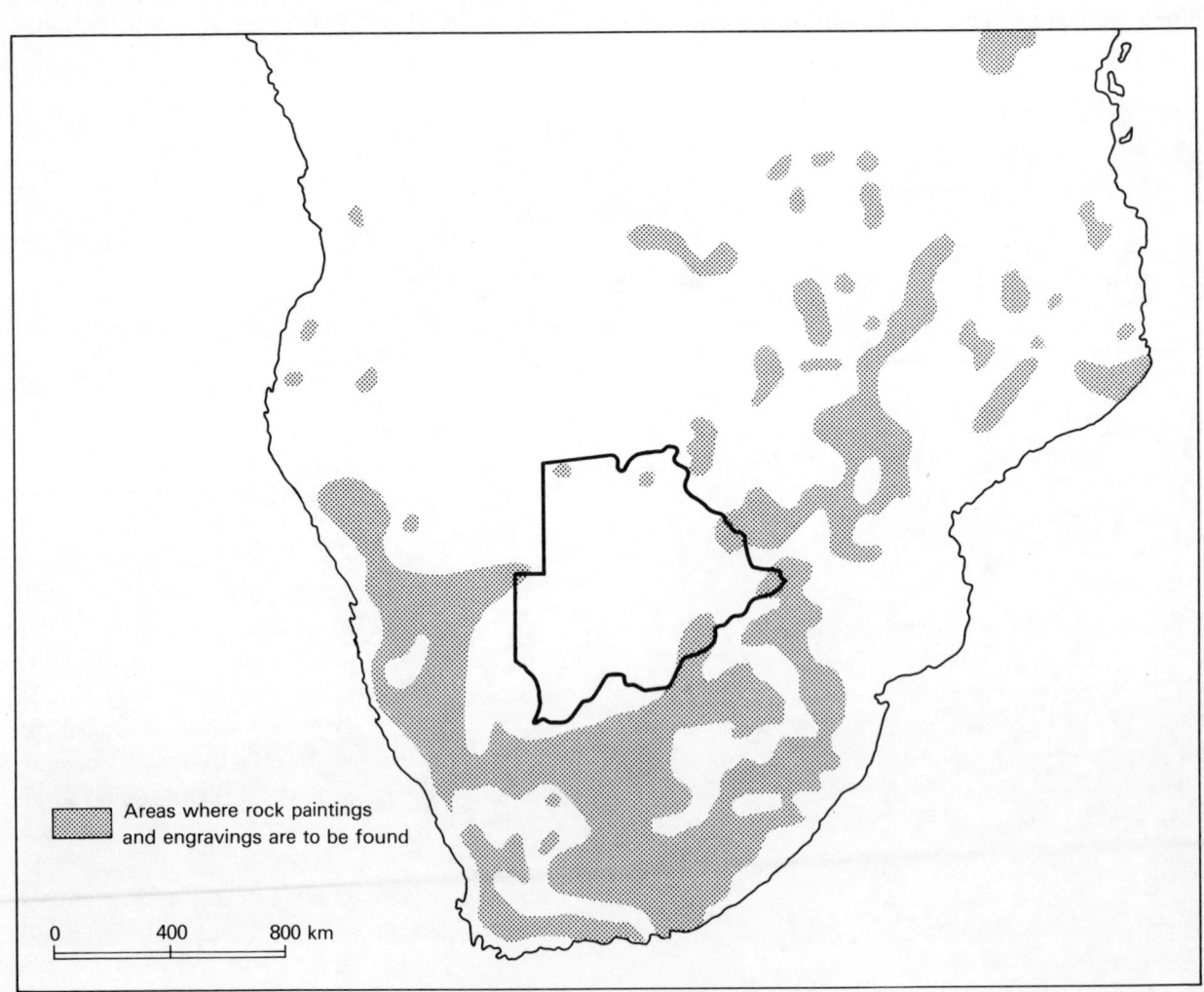

Fig. 17 The distribution of rock paintings and engravings in Southern Africa

Fig. 18 San women suck water from the ground and store it in ostrich eggshells. It takes great skill to find the water

because of their different environment.

We believe the ancestors of the San and Khoe made the paintings of people and animals which are found throughout Eastern and Southern Africa and even in the Sahara Desert. See Fig. 16 on page 21. The earliest of these paintings, found in Namibia, have been dated to nearly 25 000 years ago. They are very important because they show the San have been in Southern Africa for a very long time. They also tell us something about the way these early people lived. Today we study both the paintings and the way of life of the modern San, as well as 19th century records, in order to find out how our ancestors lived thousands of years ago.

The San

The San were grouped into small camps of between 15 to 80 people although sometimes camps contained as many as 120 people. Each camp recognised an area or areas of land where it had rights to live, collect food and hunt. Sometimes these areas overlapped. But usually each camp had its own area and people from neighbouring camps would not hunt or gather in it without permission.

Inside its area a camp moved from place to place seeking food. Sometimes they split up into small groups when food was difficult to find. Each day women and older children would go out to find wild food: tubers, roots, bulbs, fruit, nuts, caterpillars, birds' eggs and tortoises. The youngest children stayed at home with the very old or sick. Regularly the men went out in pairs or threes to hunt with light bows and poisoned arrows. They looked for eland, giraffe, gemsbok, wildebeest and kudu, but they hunted anything they saw.

The San were expert hunters using many different techniques. Their bows were very light, made of *moretlwa*, and the arrows were made from thin reeds. Each arrow was made in three pieces and the shaft behind the point was smeared with poison. The poison was made from the pupa of beetles, from plants such as wild asparagus and euphorbia, and from snake venom. Once the point of the arrow stuck in the animal the main shaft fell to the ground. The poison made the animal's blood clot (become thick) and it was not able to focus its eyes. Soon it fell and was then stabbed with a spear.

The San also used thin sticks, sometimes more than four metres long, with a duiker's horn bound at the end to form a barb or hook. Such a stick was pushed down springhare (*ntlole*) holes and the animals were either pulled out or held while other people dug down to them.

Another method used was to build a small hide at the edge of a pan where animals came to drink. The hide was usually made by digging a hole and covering it with branches. Where the ground was rocky then stones were used to form a small circular wall. Sometimes a pan would be surrounded by such hides. The San hunted in winter. A fire was built in the bottom of the hide during the day. At night it was removed or covered with earth. This kept the hide warm. The San then hid and waited for the animals to come to drink. As they passed the San either shot them from close range with arrows or stabbed them with spears.

The River San or Banoka used different methods. They would fence a long stretch of the river leaving gaps at a few places where game came to drink. In these gaps they dug deep holes and covered them with reeds and earth. When the animals came to drink they fell through the covering into the hole. Often the San put sharpened sticks in the hole facing upwards so the animals were stabbed as they fell.

Along the rivers the San were great fishermen. They used three main ways of fishing.

1. They built a raft of reeds which they pushed slowly through shallow water. Fish swam under it looking for shade. The raft was pushed into very shallow water and as the fish tried to escape they were stabbed with spears.
2. They built stone walls across areas which were flooded. As the floods went down the

Fig. 19 A San hunter. These hunters study and track animals for many hours to choose the best animal to kill

fish were trapped behind the walls.
3. They made baskets for fishing. One type was a trap which was fixed in the stone wall. Fish swimming along the wall would see the open mouth of the basket and swim in. But the mouth was made of sharp points facing inwards so they could not swim out. The San also used a large basket which was drag-

ged along the bottom. When fish entered it the basket was quickly raised above the water.

The main food was the plants the women gathered. This formed about 80 per cent of everything they ate. Each family collected for itself. Small animals also belonged only to the family but large animals were shared amongst the whole camp. Each person knew what he should receive. In this way, meat was more important as a means of linking people together than as food. The act of sharing meat helped to join people and families.

Camps which spoke the same dialect recognised a relationship with each other, but no camp considered another as either senior or junior to itself. Each camp was complete in itself. In areas of permanent water one family might have special rights to a waterhole. These rights were inherited through the eldest male child. Often this person was the leader of the camp, but he had no real legal authority. Generally older people were recognised as leaders and the camp did what they decided, although an expert young hunter might also lead them.

Men went to neighbouring camps to look for wives whom they brought home, although sometimes not until after a child had been born. Inter-camp visiting was very important. To make certain this happened there was a system of gift exchange between members of different camps. Very beautiful ostrich-eggshell, bead jewellery was made and then taken to a particular member of a neighbouring camp. This person had to accept the jewellery and later pass it to somebody else in a different camp, who in turn also passed it on. These people became linked in a gift-giving relationship which ensured that visiting and good relations were maintained between camps.

San religion was and is of great importance. They believe that once everything could talk; the animals, the plants, the wind, the sun and people, but one day this changed. They still recognise a special relationship between people and natural things. They believe that if they kill animals when they do not need the meat or cut down plants unnecessarily they will be punished by long, dry periods with lack of food. They believe in a creator god who now takes little interest in them. He changes the seasons and sends death.

San believe that misfortune results from their own actions, usually being caused by somebody doing something wrong. This has to be put right and this is often done through dance. Women sit round a special fire and sing while the men dance round them. During a dance men may go into a trance *(tsitego ya pelo)* several times. While in a trance they receive power from the supernatural which helps them to heal, bring rain and strengthen hunters.

These people had no possessions except what they could make from plants and animals. Their way of life was well suited to their difficult

Fig. 20 San hunters use light bows and poisoned arrows. They get very close before shooting

environment. Their small camps moved often so they had no effect on the wild animals they hunted and they could follow the plants as they ripened. They became expert hunters and very knowledgeable about plants. They could find moisture in bulbs and tubers underground during the driest season. They even learned how to dig a hole in the sand, pack the bottom of it with soft grass, insert a hollow grass into it and then, by sucking, draw the moisture out of the surrounding sand into the grass and so up the straw. If the camps had been large they could never have lived in one area for long. The resources of food, animals and water would have been destroyed.

The Khoe

The Khoe were also once hunters and gatherers but they acquired stock. Recent finds of sheep bones near Kimberley dating back about 3 000 years suggest they had stock long before the Bantu-speaking farmers arrived in Southern Africa.

When the Dutch first saw the Khoe they lived in groups with a leader who ruled loosely over them. Each group split up into smaller units called 'clans' each under its own headman. These clans came together only in times of stress or war.

They owned stock which provided milk, but hunted for meat. Stock was only killed on important occasions. The women also gathered wild food. They grew no crops.

Clans lived separately, although in the same area. The leader normally kept a large village in which the head of each clan also lived. Inheritance took place from father to son. Men took their wives from a different clan to their own and brought them to live in their village. These villages consisted of a large thorn fence built in a circle, inside which each family built its house. In the middle of the village were small enclosures for sheep and calves. Look at the plan of a Khoe village in Fig. 21. Khoe houses were made of mats laid over a wooden framework. When they moved they took their houses to pieces, rolled up the mats and carried them on the backs of their cattle (see Fig. 22, page 28). Little is known about the religious beliefs of these pastoralists. They believed in a supreme being and other important spirits to whom they prayed and occasionally sacrificed their stock. Some of their beliefs were similar to those held by the San, possibly coming from the time before they acquired stock.

Water was very important in the dry land in which they lived. They dug wells in the floors of pans, deepening natural waterholes so that they held water long after the rains were finished. Each group and each clan owned waterholes and recognised exclusive rights (keeping out all other people) to these. Like the San, the Khoe stayed in one area, that surrounding their wells, and moved from place to place following the grazing within their area. In times of drought when water and grazing were scarce there was sometimes fighting between groups over water. At such times each clan in a group sent men to fight.

A comparison of the San and Khoe

The San and Khoe looked much the same, although the Dutch say the Khoe were bigger than the San when they first saw them in about 1600. This may be because Khoe children drank milk when young. They both hunted and collected wild food and neither grew crops. The big difference lies in the ownership of stock. Some Khoe could become rich through owning stock and therefore powerful and able to control others. Because San generally did not own stock nobody became rich. Property remains after a person dies and this means that someone will inherit it. Property also means a society must have laws to ensure that ownership is respected. Property also provides the means for an economy involving exchange and work. The stock belonging to the Khoe changed their society, producing leaders and complicated laws. Without stock the San did not need the same leaders and laws. For each people, their culture fitted their way of life.

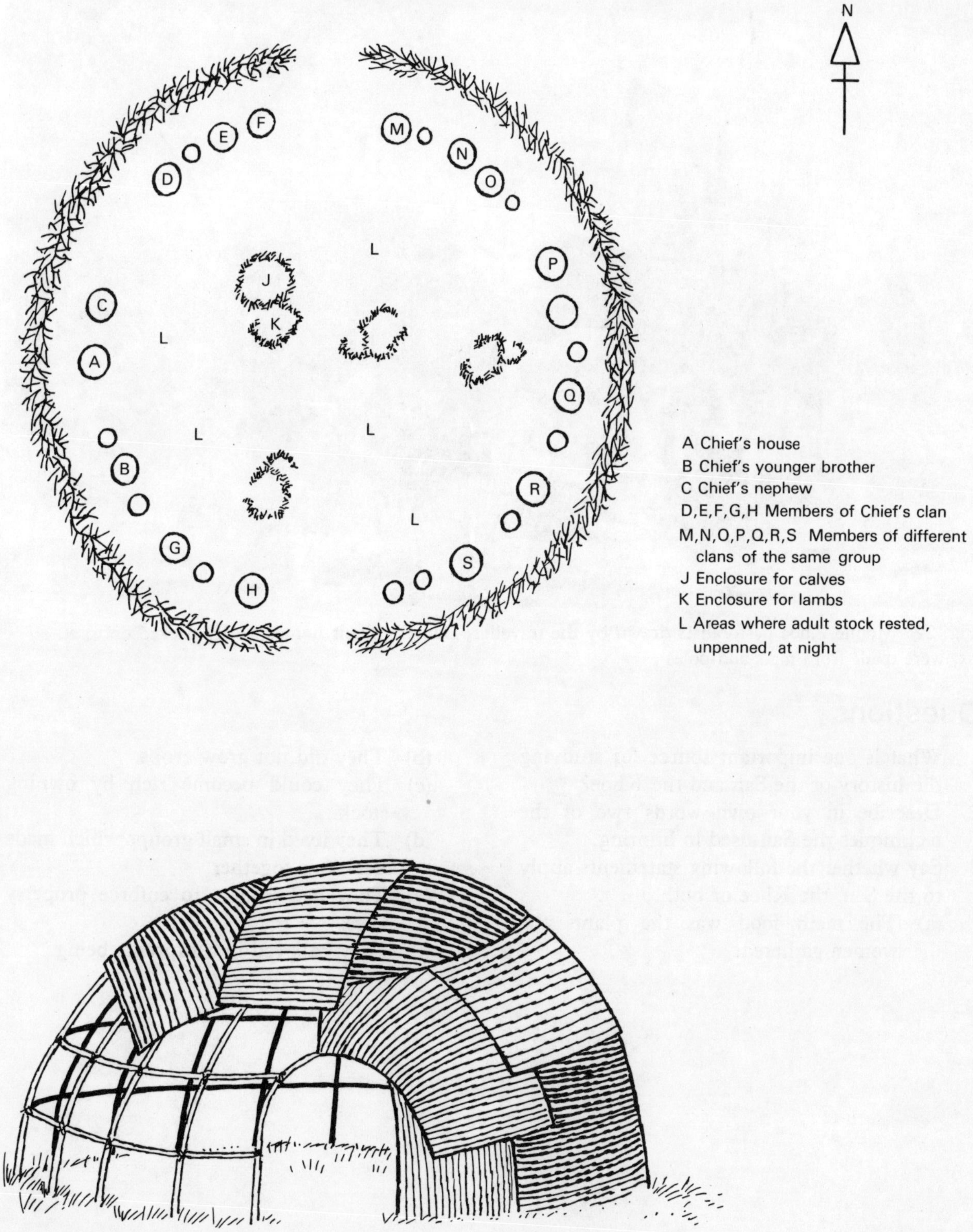

A Chief's house
B Chief's younger brother
C Chief's nephew
D,E,F,G,H Members of Chief's clan
M,N,O,P,Q,R,S Members of different clans of the same group
J Enclosure for calves
K Enclosure for lambs
L Areas where adult stock rested, unpenned, at night

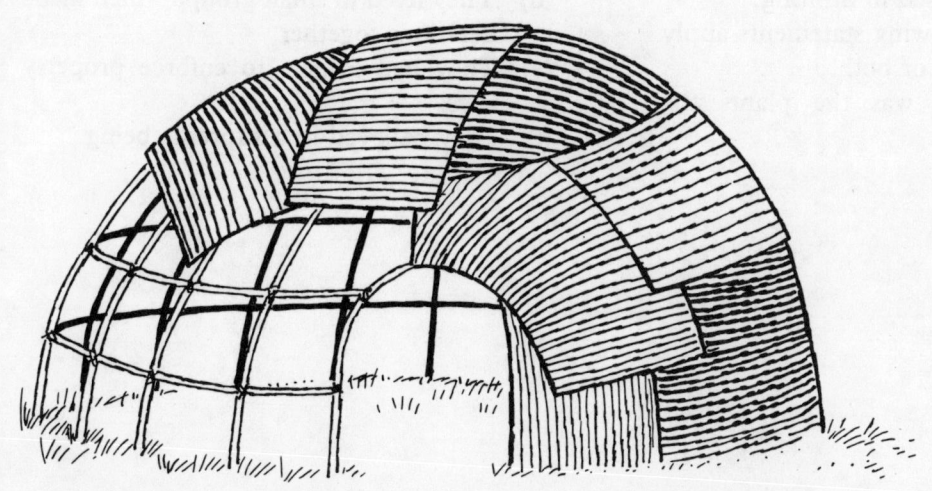

Fig. 21 Plan of a Khoe village and a Khoe house under construction

Fig. 22 Mobile Khoe pastoralists drawn by the traveller, Daniell. Their homes, easily packed on to an ox, were made from mats and poles

Questions

1. What is one important source for studying the history of the San and the Khoe?
2. Describe in your own words two of the techniques the San used in hunting.
3. Say whether the following statements apply to the San, the Khoe or both.
   (a) The main food was the plants the women gathered.
   (b) They did not grow crops.
   (c) They could become rich by owning stock.
   (d) They lived in small groups which made decisions together.
   (e) They had leaders to enforce property laws.
   (f) They believed in a supreme being.

6 The Arrival of the Bantu-speaking Farmers

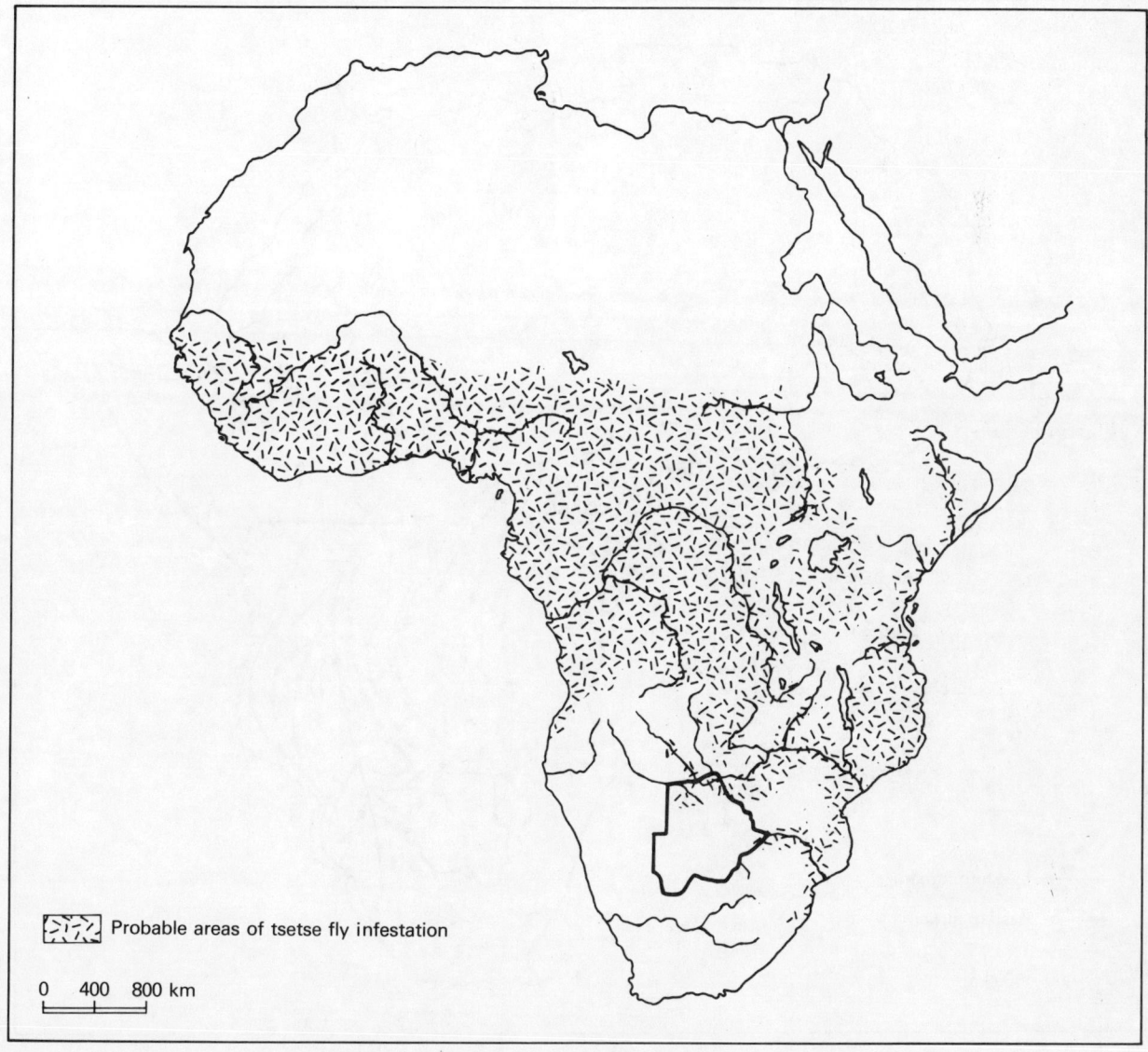

Fig. 23 Probable distribution of tsetse fly in prehistoric times

The origins of the Bantu-speaking farmers

The Bantu-speaking peoples are believed to have originated in the rain-forest areas around modern Cameroon about 4 000 years ago. The name 'Bantu-speaking' today refers to most of the Negroid peoples of Southern, Eastern, Central and parts of Western Africa. They speak languages which are related through some common word stems and a common form of grammar.

Archaeological excavations in West Africa have shown that until about 2 500 years ago the ancestors of the Bantu-speakers made stone tools and grew some root crops. About that time knowledge of iron smelting reached the area of modern Nigeria having been taken from Egypt through the Sahara. It is thought they also owned goats, which were able to resist the disease carried by the tsetse fly which infested the area.

It is believed that the earliest farmers to arrive in Southern Africa spoke Bantu languages, but we cannot be absolutely certain of this. It is

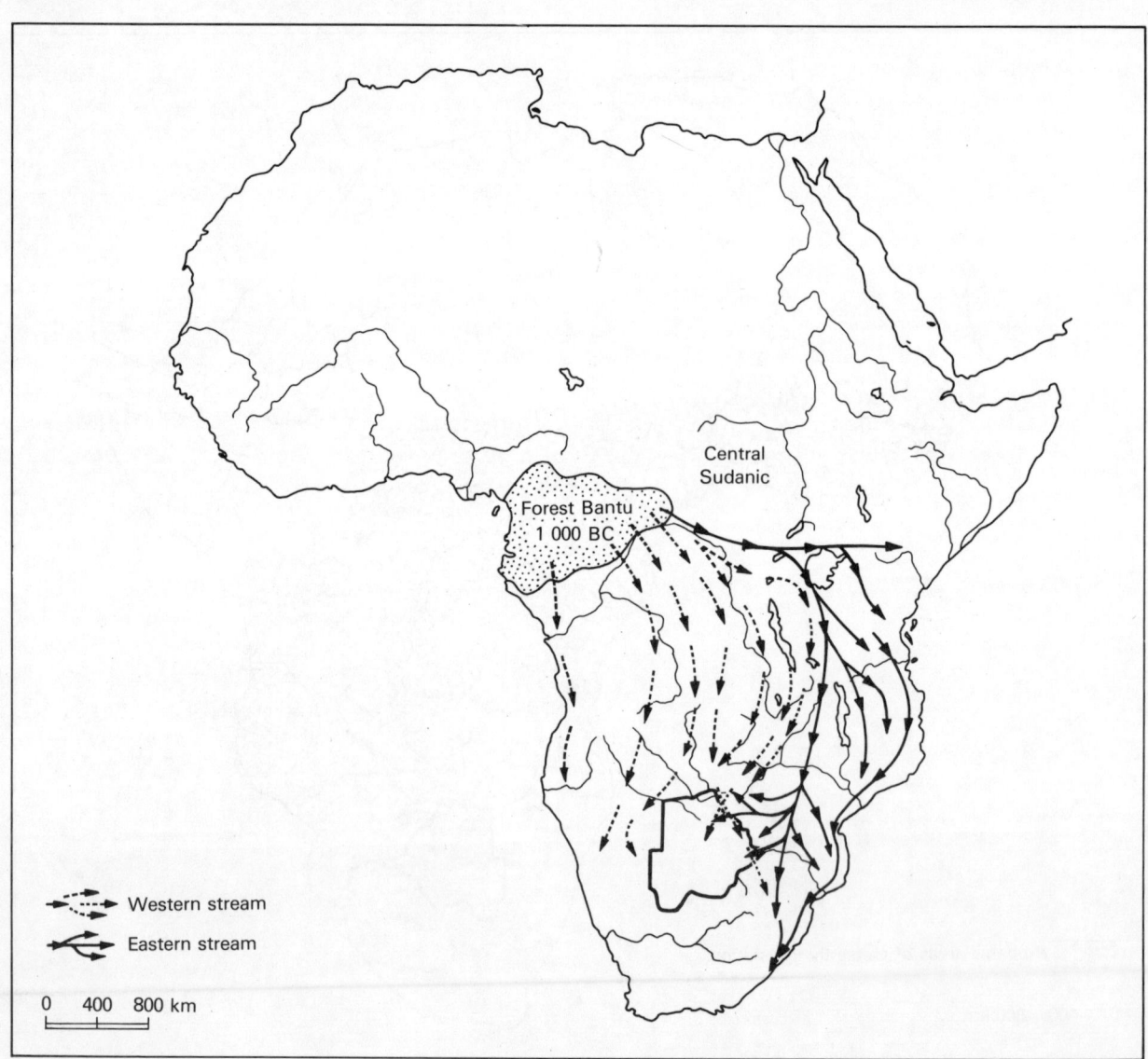

Fig. 24 Probable southward migration routes of Forest Bantu-speakers

Fig. 25 A tsetse fly. These limited the spread of people (see Fig. 23) since their bite kills cattle, and sometimes humans also

possible that they were Negroid peoples from the general area of Southern Sudan, Uganda and Northern Kenya who spoke what are today known as Nilotic languages. This is, however, not likely to be correct.

From about 2 500 years ago rapid expansion took place. 500 years later some of them had spread eastwards to the area of the Great Lakes in East Africa. 200 years after that they lived in modern Zimbabwe and on the Natal Coast. Look at the maps, Figs 23 and 24. The movements south have been divided into two streams called the 'eastern' and 'western' streams. The eastern stream arrived in Southern Africa first, with some people working their way southwards down the long corridor between the areas infested with tsetse fly, a few of them bringing stock with them. Others travelled down the coast, mainly living off shell fish and probably not having any stock. The western stream first appeared in the area of modern Zambia about 200 years later, probably also bringing some cattle and small stock with it.

Lifestyle of the Bantu-speaking farmers

These first farmers probably did not look like we do today. They inter-married with the hunter-gatherers they found living here. Also they probably practised different forms of subsistence, even at this early time. Some people grew crops such as sorghum and millet and worked iron. Others probably lived mainly by hunting and keeping some stock. Others may have been primarily iron-workers and some may have just hunted and gathered wild food. It is fairly certain that they all made pots of clay and used some iron tools, even if they traded for these.

These new arrivals are generally known as the people of the Iron Age because they brought this new technology with them. Those who kept stock settled in the higher, open grasslands which were free from tsetse fly and stock diseases. Those who grew crops settled in areas where the rainfall was more than 500 mm a year. Look at Fig. 26 on page 32 which shows the areas most suitable for cultivation in Botswana. They also had to be within reach of iron-bearing rocks.

They came in small groups and the earliest arrivals must have lived in little communities far from each other. In all their journeys, they came into contact with the San and Khoe who were already living in the land. We know little about this first contact. Probably it was peaceful as there would have been too few farmers to make any difference to the general way of life of the hunter-gatherers. When excavating the farmers' early village sites we find stone tools and grooved stones for making beads which we know belonged to the San. Probably some San came to live with the farmers who married their daughters. Also, earlier rock paintings in Zimbabwe and South Africa do not show any fighting.

Evidence in Botswana

In Botswana we are beginning to find traces of the early farmers. The earliest remains come from the area around Francistown, the Chobe, Thamalakane and Boteti Rivers. Although we have not yet been able to date our earliest sites, in Zimbabwe and Zambia similar sites have been dated to about 1 500 years ago. On the Boteti

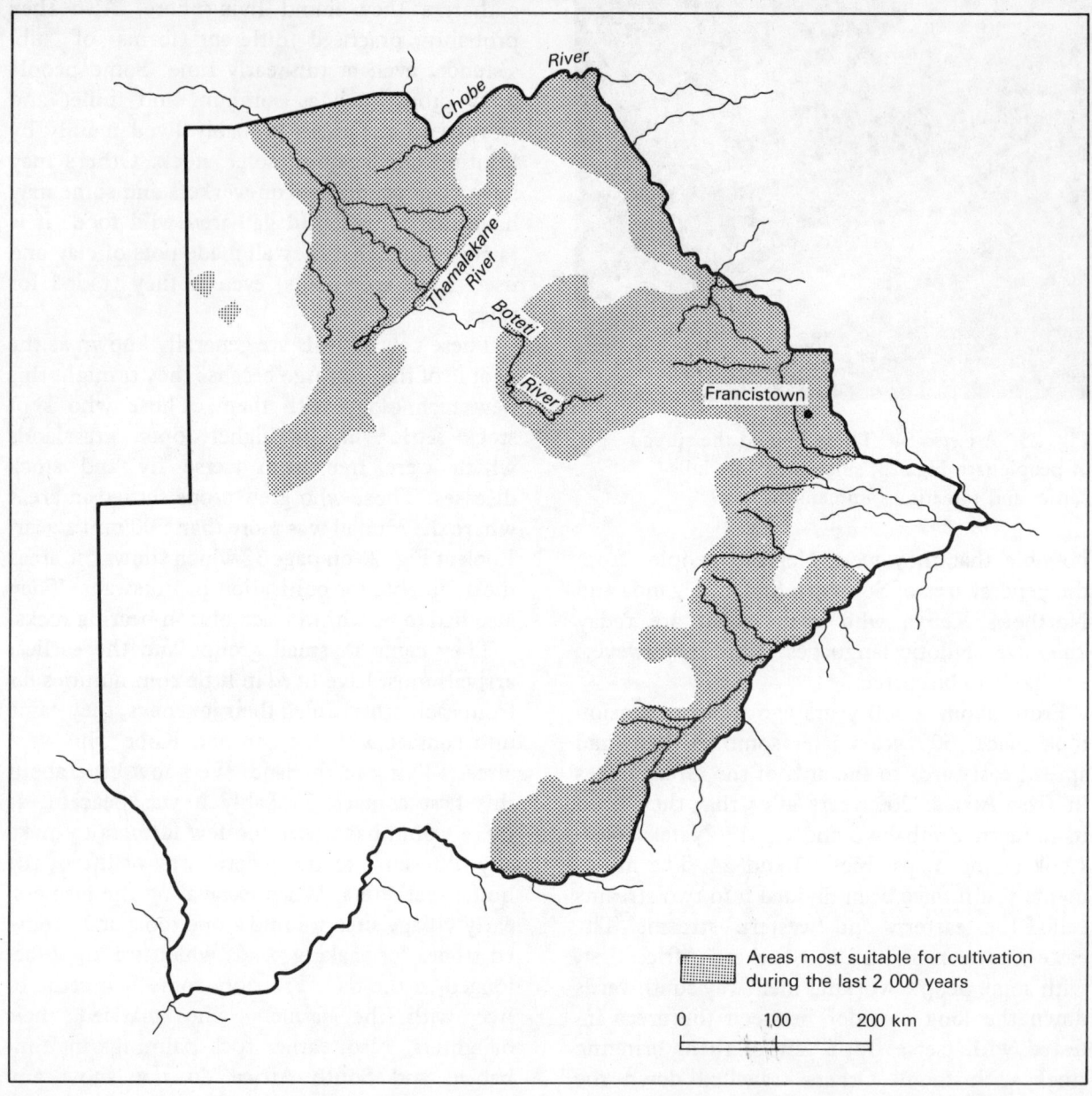

Fig. 26 The areas most suitable for cultivation during the last 2 000 years, taking into account soil and rainfall

River two different types of pottery have been found. One is similar to that made by early Bantu-speakers while the other type is like that made by the historic Khoe. It has lugs (projections or handles) on the sides and a pointed bottom. There are still Khoe (the Bateti) living on the Boteti. Possibly the first farmers found them there already owning some stock, probably sheep, and came to trade with them.

By AD 650 in the Central District there was a large farming population settled on the upper Motloutse River and stretching southwards to Shoshong. These people built quite large villages on hilltops with smaller settlements scattered around them. They kept large herds of cattle, smelted iron and grew crops.

Another place of early settlement is at Tsodilo where an Early Iron Age site has been found high in the hills. The site is rich in pottery, iron, cattle and small-stock bones. A skeleton of a Negroid person was also found there. The hills have rock paintings, mostly of wild animals, but there are some of cattle drawn in two colours and many schematic designs (patterns). See Fig. 16, page 21. In Zambia similar designs are attributed (thought to belong) to early farmers rather than to the San. The date of the Iron Age settlement at Tsodilo is about AD 800. We know there was contact between farmers and San because of the paintings of cattle. Also, in some of the rock shelters, we have found pottery and iron mixed with tools of the Late Stone Age.

Questions

1. What stages in the expansion of the Bantu-speaking peoples occurred at the following times?
   (a) 4 000 years ago (b) 2 500 years ago
   (c) 2 000 years ago (d) 1 800 years ago
   (e) 1 600 years ago
2. What two things did all the different groups of Bantu-speaking peoples probably have in common?
3. Where in Botswana have the earliest remains of Bantu-speaking farmers been found? What are the remains? What do we call the people who have found these remains?

7 The Iron Age

The discovery of how to smelt iron and make it into tools took place in the north of the Fertile Crescent about 7 000 years ago. The Fertile Crescent is a name given by historians to the area which stretches from the Nile Delta north-eastwards through modern Israel and then south-eastwards between the Euphrates and Tigris Rivers to the Persian Gulf. See Fig. 27. It was here also that people first learned to grow crops and domesticate wild animals. At first the secret of iron smelting was carefully guarded, but by about 2 700 years ago it had spread to Egypt. It may have been taken across the Sahara about the same time by Phoenicians who were trading and mining copper in Mauritania.

Certainly, within a hundred years of reaching Egypt the knowledge had travelled more than 1 400 kilometres up the Nile River to Meroe in modern Sudan. Shortly afterwards it also appeared in Nigeria. The first farmers to arrive in Southern Africa brought the knowledge with them and by AD 200 mining of both iron and

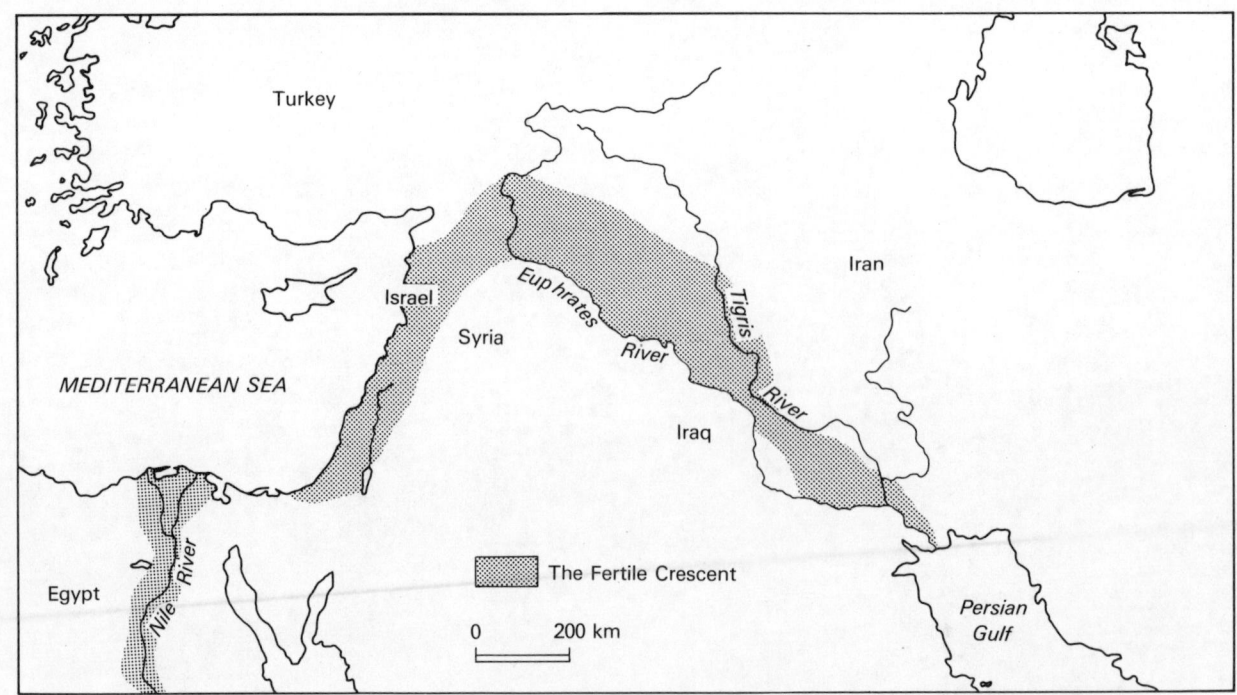

Fig. 27   The Fertile Crescent where people first learned to grow crops and domesticate wild animals

Fig. 28 Early Iron Age, approximately AD 600, pot and bowl. Notice the characteristic decorations

copper was taking place.

What is known as the 'Iron Age' lasted in Southern Africa until the introduction of manufactured goods from Europe. In Botswana this occurred about 1850 when it became easier to barter with foreign traders for metal. Then the difficult process of smelting rock to get iron was abandoned (stopped). Smithing continued for some time and traditional methods are still practised in a few remote areas of the Okavango to this day.

The Early Iron Age

The Early Iron Age lasted from the time of the arrival of the farmers in Southern Africa until approximately AD 1000. A large number of Early Iron Age remains have been found, particularly in Zimbabwe and South Africa, and more recently in Botswana. But still little is known about the identity of these early people.

It is likely they were Bantu-speaking people, but this has not been conclusively (completely) proved. We do know they came from the north, made pottery, mined iron and copper to make tools and ornaments, kept stock, grew some crops and hunted.

Pottery, because it is made of clay, lasts in the ground almost indefinitely (forever), whereas iron and copper tend to disappear slowly, destroyed by the acids in the soil. So pottery is the main item made by the people of the Early Iron Age which we can still find today. Their pottery is often fairly thick, grey to buff coloured and has characteristic decorations. See Fig. 28.

Early Iron Age sites

The earliest sites have been found in Zimbabwe and South Africa. Probably these early farmers sought out the most fertile areas first and later expanded into drier Botswana. Look at the map,

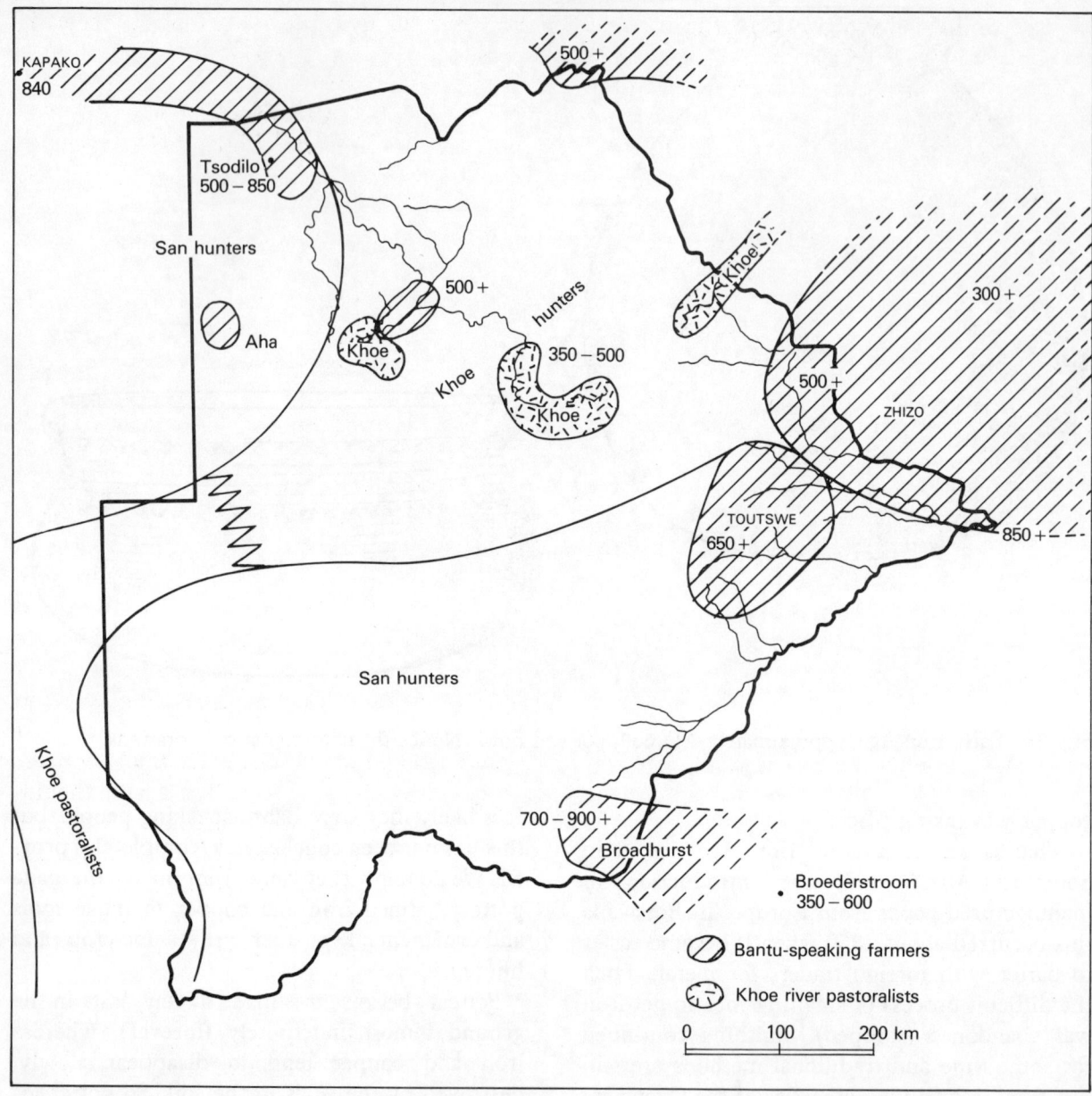

Fig. 29 Settlement in Botswana about 1 000 years ago

Fig. 29 which shows the distribution of the earliest farming populations. One of the best studied groups lived at a place now called Broederstroom, about 50 kilometres west of Johannesburg. Other sites dating from the same period have been found, but they are very few in number. This suggests that the first farmers lived in very small, widely scattered groups.

Some may have relied on crops and remained in one area, while others kept stock and relied heavily on hunting and foraging for food. Some of them probably mined iron, while others may have traded it from those who did the mining.

Broederstroom

People lived at Broederstroom from about AD

350 to 600 in a village which covered an area of about 25 hectares. The site may not have been occupied the whole time. The people probably moved away and returned later. At any time of occupation there were probably about 10 huts, suggesting between 40 and 60 people. Some burials have been found in the village. The skeletons are of Negroid-type people with some San features. The method of burial and the removal of front teeth suggested the practice of various forms of ritual. The huts were small, round, made of wood plastered with mud and raised on stones above the ground. Amongst the huts iron ore had been smelted in clay furnaces. Waste food included bones of cattle, sheep or goats and wild animals. Only grindstones were found, no crop remains, but this does suggest that crops were grown. Quantities of grooved stones and ostrich-eggshell beads were also found on the site. This suggests that they were living either with or in close association with Khoesan who still make beads in this way. The quantities of beads were far more than would be needed by that small community; possibly they were being made for trade. The whole area was littered with broken pottery with bold designs which changed little during the 250 years of occupation.

Although no sites of a comparable date have been found in south-eastern Botswana, some pottery remains have been found near Lobatse and west of Molepolole which are fairly similar to the most recent of the Broederstroom pottery. This probably indicates that similar people were living here before AD 600.

Sites in Botswana

There are seven areas in Botswana where Early Iron Age pottery has been found. The early farmers arrived at different times and from different directions. They did not come as a wave of people moving into Botswana all at the same time, but rather as small isolated communities. Some expanded into large societies, while others remained small. One group may not have settled at all but merely traded from a distance. These early remains have been found in the following areas.

The Francistown area about AD 500.
The Chobe River area about AD 600.
The Boteti River area about AD 350-500.
The Serowe to Shoshong area about AD 650.
The northern Limpopo Valley area about AD 850.
The Tsodilo Hills (and Aha Hills) about AD 500-850.
The Gaborone to Molepolole area about AD 700-900.
The Thamalakane River area about AD 700.

The Francistown area

At some time a little before AD 300 the farmers were populating Zimbabwe. They are known by the name of the place where their remains were first identified, Gokomere in north-eastern Zimbabwe. These people probably lived widely scattered in small communities, smelting iron and copper, keeping a very few cattle, sheep and goats, growing crops such as millet, beans and melons, and hunting. They made thick, not particularly well-fired pottery, bowls and shouldered jars with concave necks decorated with lines of channelling, raised bands and stamped or incised patterns which occasionally reached over the rim. They had probably spread into Botswana by AD 500, but never penetrated far beyond the Shashe River.

The Boteti area

At about the same time or a little earlier other Early Iron Age peoples had gone as far into the Kalahari as the Boteti River. The pottery they left behind them is similar to Bambata ware. This is named from the place in the Matopo Hills in Zimbabwe where it was first identified. Although this pottery has been found at a number of sites stretching from Tsienyane to Lake Xau, no proper village remains have been discovered. The pottery is found among Late Stone Age tool remains. It is coarse, not well fired and often has stamped decoration over a thickened rim. In the past it has been associated with the Late Stone Age, but it has many similarities to Gokomere and must have been made by Negroid people. It is also similar to early pottery found at Matlapaneng near Maun. No village remains have been found but this does not mean that the people who made the pottery did not live on the Boteti. However they may have gone there just to trade with the Khoe, or the Khoe may have obtained the pottery on trading expeditions.

The Serowe to Shoshong area

Remains of one society have been found stretching from Shoshong to north of the Motloutse River, and from Mmashoro in the west to Tobane in the east. About AD 650 some of the

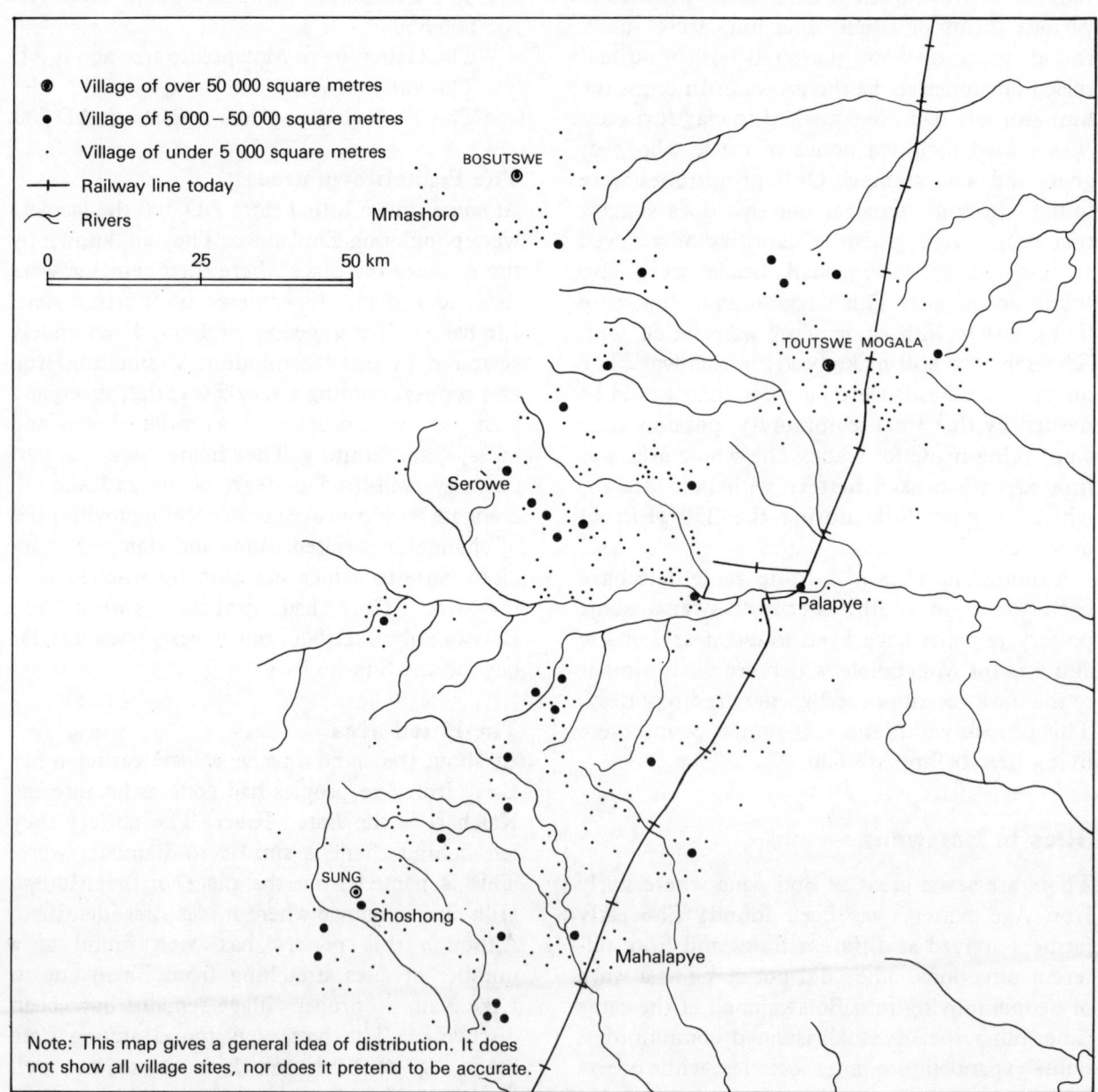

Fig. 30 Toutswe society settlement pattern

Zhizo people who were living in Zimbabwe, began to spread south-westwards to settle in this fairly dry area, possibly because it was very suitable for cattle raising. At first they lived in small scattered villages, but as time passed some villages began to grow. By about AD 1050 there appear to have been a few very large villages each situated on a hilltop and occupying six or more hectares. (So far three have been located at Toutswemogala, Bosutswe and Shoshong.) Surrounding these and fairly close to them were a number of smaller hilltop settlements. They were in turn surrounded by a very large number of much smaller settlements, some on hills and others on the plain. See the sketch map, Fig. 30.

This organisation suggests important central villages, probably the homes of rich ruling families surrounded by those of their headmen. The much smaller, scattered homesteads belonged to their subjects. Such a pattern indicates a large society split into three or more self-ruling groups, each with its own hierarchy (ladder) of social levels, including commoners, rulers and their assistants. Today we call them the Toutswe people after the hill Toutswemogala, about 40 kilometres north of Palapye where their remains were first excavated.

All these villages contain a central stock kraal, some 20 metres across, encircled by houses and granaries, all surrounded by a thorn fence. In the bigger villages the stock area is sometimes 70 metres across and the deposit of dung as much as one and a half metres deep, bigger than any other known sites in Southern Africa. From this it has been concluded that the Toutswe people were rich in cattle, much richer than other contemporary (at the same time) societies, and that their hierarchical system was mostly based on cattle-ownership.

The northern Limpopo Valley area
The same people who had expanded from Zimbabwe to reach the Toutswe area by about AD 650 were also expanding south-eastwards down the Shashe River to where it joins the Limpopo and beyond. It is thought that they must have been very like the Toutswe people because their pottery styles were so similar. They may even have spoken a related language. However, they never evolved quite the same hierarchical system. They are known as the Zhizo people. Living side by side with the Toutswe people they prevented the Toutswe from expanding eastwards. As the years passed and populations increased without sufficient room for expansion, settlements must have become more and more dense. This must have resulted in poor agricultural land and over-grazing of grasslands.

The Tsodilo Hills and the north-west
It is believed that farmers were settled along the Chobe River at a very early date. Excavations made near Serondela, about 20 kilometres west of Kasane, tell us that between about AD 600 and AD 750 farmers living there were similar to others then living in Zambia. Probably they had first arrived about 200 years earlier. Excavations at Matlapaneng about 12 kilometres north of Maun suggest that other farmers were also living there as early as about AD 700. These same people probably lived all along the Thamalakane and Nchabe Rivers as far as Lake Ngami, as we have found similar remains at Toteng.

Excavations at Tsodilo have been dated to about AD 850. Similar pottery to that found at Tsodilo has also been found in the Aha Hills about 200 kilometres to the south-west. The finds at the Aha Hills are Late Stone Age and have been dated to about AD 500. In other words Iron Age pottery has been found in Stone Age sites such as the Aha Hills. However no Iron Age settlements have been found there. They may exist, or the pottery may have been traded from elsewhere.

The people who lived at Tsodilo came from Zambia and perhaps Angola. Their pottery was hardened with charcoal and decorated with thickened rims and occasional false-relief chevron, herring-bone, cross-hatching and bands of comb-stamping. See Fig. 28. They smelted iron and worked it into tools and ornaments. However, the iron ore may have been brought from north of Shakawe more than 70 kilometres away. A short piece of copper chain has been found which suggests that they traded with people from the copper-rich areas in the south-east. Cowry shells and glass beads also suggest very early trade networks which reached the east coast.

There are more than 2 000 rock paintings in the hills. Many of these are patterns which, in Zambia, have been attributed to Early Iron Age peoples. There are also San paintings in red, purple and white of cattle and people herding or driving them. In rock shelters in the hills Iron Age pottery has been found associated with stone tools. This means these people also lived in close association with the San. A similar site has been found at Kapako in Namibia, about 300 kilometres to the west on the Okavango River.

It appears that small groups of stock owners were moving into north-western Botswana about AD 850. Although they appear to have remained in the area for a long time, there is no suggestion that their settlements remained anything but small.

The Gaborone to Molepolole area
The first Bantu-speaking farmers probably settled in south-eastern Botswana about AD 600-700. We know that in the 10th century small groups of stock owners were settled over most of the rocky area of the south-east. These people lived in small villages often on hilltops. We will call them the Moritsane people (their remains have been excavated on Moritsane Hill near Gabane). Their sites are also found in the Transvaal from where they must have expanded into Botswana.

In their middens, *thutubudu* (the places where they threw their ash and rubbish) we have found signs of iron smelting and bits of iron, bones of cattle, sheep, goats and wild animals, what appear to be the remains of granaries, and iron, shell and copper beads. One burial site has produced several hundred tiny glass beads which came from Persia or India.

Most of the sites found contain the remains of cattle kraals, but these villages and kraals never reached any large size. These people had a fairly similar way of life to those in the Tsodilo area. They lived in small, widely spread settlements without any strong hierarchical structure. Certainly they never achieved an organisation such as that of the Toutswe people further to the north.

Early Iron Age to Late Iron Age
Looking at Botswana as a whole in about AD 1000 we see that farmers had surrounded the Kalahari in the north and east and even settled on its edges. At present we have found no definite village remains in the Boteti area, only a few pieces of their pottery. Since the area is so suitable for livestock we assume they did not settle there because it was already occupied by the pastoral Khoe with whom they traded. Probably most of the Kalahari was occupied by the San foragers, Nharo, G/wi, G//ana and Shuakhwe. Many of them were coming into contact with the farmers who were steadily moving further and further into San country.

Considerable changes had taken place since the farmers had first settled in Zimbabwe and built a village at Broederstroom. In the early days they spent much of their time hunting and collecting wild foods. It is probable that their herds were extremely small, some may only have owned goats or no stock at all. Domestic animals were only occasionally killed, possibly just for ritual purposes such as deaths, births, marriages and religious ceremonies. As time passed the populations increased, spreading out into drier areas. There cattle thrived (lived well). We can see from the size of their kraals that their herds were growing bigger. By about AD 1000 they were eating more domestic than wild animals.

Trading had also increased. Beads from India and Persia as well as sea shells were being traded through a network of villages all the way from the coast of the Indian Ocean (see Fig. 31). We are not certain what was traded in exchange, but probably the Zhizo people of the upper Limpopo were trading ivory and furs as early as AD 850. Perhaps cattle and specularite (*sebilo*) were also going east.

Society was becoming much more organised, particularly for the Toutswe people. Rulers and

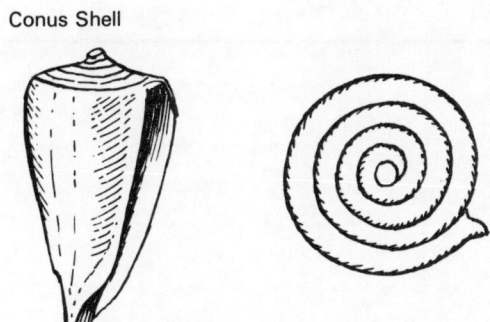

Conus Shell

The part of the shell usually found – the end of the shell with a hole drilled through its centre. This was possibly worn around the neck on a leather thong

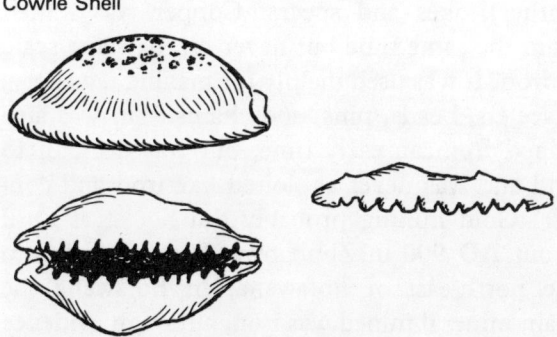

Cowrie Shell

Whole cowrie shells are sometimes found, but more usually only a piece. Often the back of the shell had been drilled twice to take a thread for sewing it onto leather or threading it on a string

Fig. 31 Shells from the Indian Ocean used as trade goods and made into prestige ornaments

headmen grew rich through tribute (*sehuba*) paid in cattle and probably grain, iron and furs. They grew crops which they stored in village granaries and during the rains took their cattle to western pans where grazing was better, not returning until surface water dried up during the winter.

On the fringes of this society lived the San foragers some of whom joined the farmers, probably looking after stock, acting as servants and hunting for skins. Some of the women may have been taken as wives or concubines (*dinyatsi*). We find traces of the San in the form of stone tools in the middens of the smaller, outlying villages, although only rarely in the larger hilltop settlements.

This then was the position in about AD 1000 when Botswana, and other areas already occupied by the farmers, saw the arrival of new people who settled amongst them and, apparently, in most areas rapidly took over. These new arrivals heralded the end of the Early Iron Age and the rise of large kingdoms and empires, although the way of life of the average farmer probably remained much the same. These later Iron Age developments are explained in Chapter 9.

Questions

1. For approximately how many years did the 'Iron Age' last in Southern Africa?
2. Answer the following questions about the Iron Age settlement of Broederstroom.
    (a) When were people living there?
    (b) How many people lived there?
    (c) What kind of huts did they live in?
    (d) How do we know they used iron?
    (e) Why do we think they grew crops?
    (f) Why do we think they traded with other communities?
3. To which of the areas of Botswana do the following statements apply?
    (a) The people probably spread into Botswana by AD 500.
    (b) Bambata pottery has been found.
    (c) The people lived in large central villages each situated on a hilltop with smaller settlements around.
    (d) The people owned many cattle.
    (e) The people expanded down the Shashe River to the confluence with the Limpopo.
    (f) The people came from Zambia and perhaps Angola.
    (g) They settled in small villages, usually on hilltops.

8 Early Mining and Smelting

Some people continued to make stone tools in Southern Africa until very recently, possibly only 200 years ago in the north-west of Botswana. However the last 2 000 years is generally known as the 'Iron Age'. Knowledge of the manufacture and use of iron helped to create many changes in the lifestyle of our ancestors.

Iron smelting and smithing (changing raw iron into tools) was a very great technological achievement involving a great variety of skills. Its users were well on the road to the start of modern industry more than a thousand years before traders from outside Africa began to introduce other manufactured goods.

The earliest mines in Southern Africa, dated to about 33 000 years ago, were being exploited by Stone Age peoples long before the arrival of the iron-working farmers. They dug red ochre, known as haematite (*letshoku*), and a glittering black iron ore known as specularite (*sebilo*). These ores that they mined were ground into powder and mixed with fat, blood, white-of-egg or honey to make paint. This could be used both for drawing pictures on the rocks and for decorating the human body.

Knowledge of mineral smelting was brought to Southern Africa by farming peoples nearly 2 000 years ago. The earliest evidence we have comes from northern Zimbabwe where both iron and copper were being mined and smelted in about AD 200. Less than two centuries later iron was being smelted at Broederstroom in the Transvaal. Archaeologists have found, in the middle of a 5th century village, the remains of two iron-smelting furnaces, piles of ore (*bogale*) and a scattering of slag (*manyelo*).

The mineral most widely and continuously mined was iron. This could be made into tools, hoes, knives, razors, awls (for making holes in leather), axes and spears. Copper was mined from the same time but never on the same scale as iron. It was used mainly for making jewellery, bracelets, beads, pins, and chains. Tin was also mined from an early time, but was difficult to find and was never exploited like iron and copper. Gold mining probably did not start until about AD 900 in Zimbabwe. It soon spread to the north-east of Botswana. In Botswana the main mineral mined was iron, although evidence of copper mining has been found near Serowe dating back to about AD 650. Look at the map, Fig. 32 showing early mining areas in Southern Africa.

Even at places as remote as Tsodilo, iron smelting and working was taking place as early as AD 850 and possibly earlier.

The processing of ore

The processing of metal-bearing rock or ore into tools involves four major stages, each of which requires different skills.

Prospecting

Prospecting is the search for a place where the rock is so rich in mineral that it is worth mining.

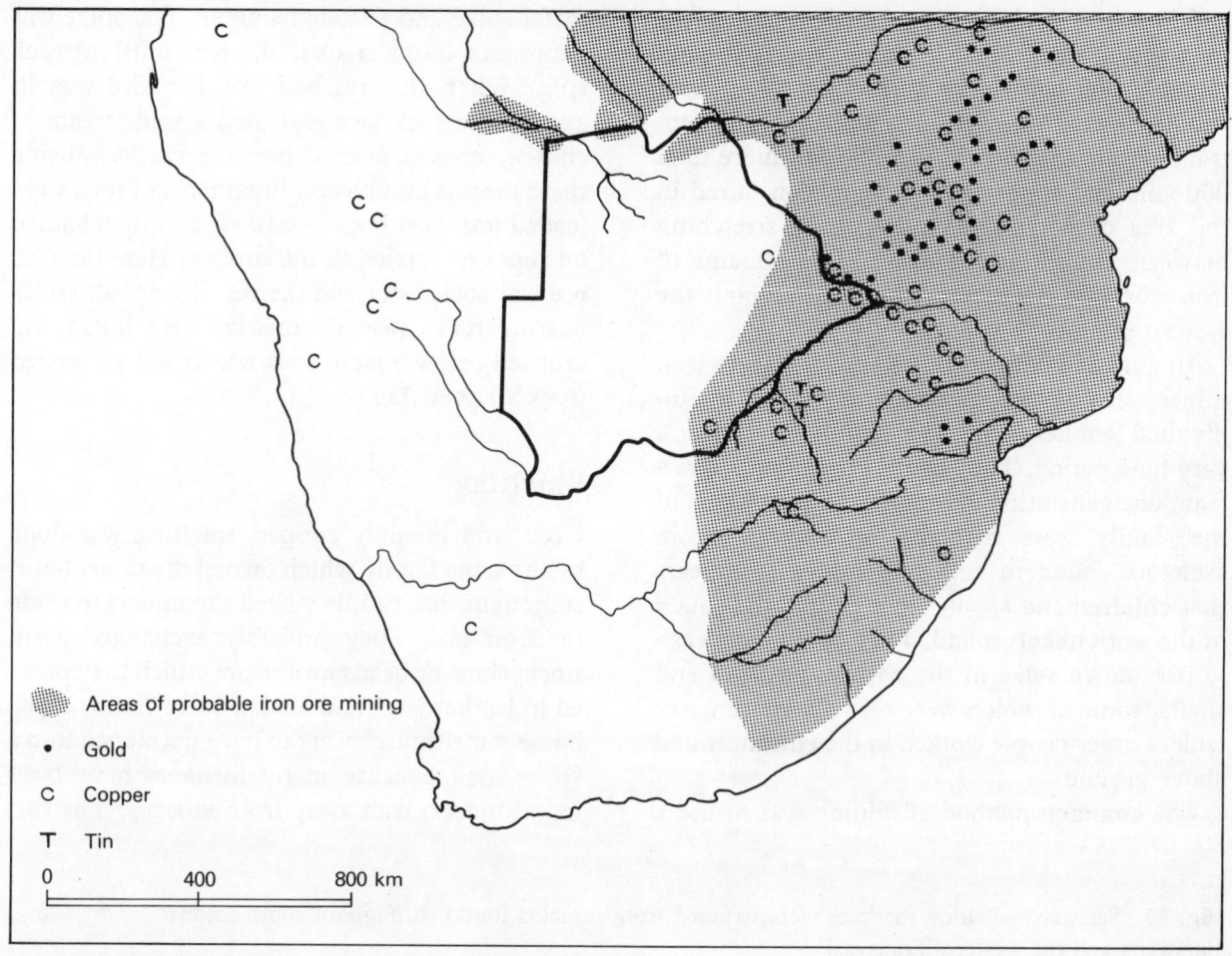

Fig. 32 Early mining sites and areas in Southern Africa

In the case of iron this is not too difficult since the rock is usually stained red and is heavy and fairly common. Gold is much more difficult to find. It says much for the skill of the early prospectors that when white prospectors came to Southern Africa, almost every deposit they found had already been worked by our ancestors.

Mining

Most early mines consisted of trenches or pits dug into the rock. These varied in size from a metre deep and two metres long to vast excavations several metres deep and nearly a kilometre long. Probably all early communities did some small-scale mining, taking ore from surface trenches and pits. But by AD 750, with increases in population and a greater demand for minerals, some communities specialised in mining. Some mines had small entrances and were dug deep into the ground. Shafts led down into the rock and from these passages led away following the areas where the ore was richest. The deepest known shaft in Botswana was sunk 26 metres below the surface. Sometimes a hole was dug into a hillside and then enlarged until a large cavern was formed. Near Thamaga a number of such caverns were dug close together until they became so large that they collapsed.

We may never know how many ancient mines there are in Botswana. Surface excavations have been eroded, the sides collapsing to fill in pits and trenches, leaving little evidence today except for a dip in the ground. Many of the early gold mines which had shafts were either filled with rubble when they were abandoned or the entrances were carefully hidden. So far, more than 200 gold and copper mines have been found in the area of north-eastern Botswana stretching between Dukwe and Tobane. The remains of iron workings have been found throughout the eastern side of the country.

All gold and copper mines and the larger iron mines were the property of, and worked by, individual families or lineages (family lines) over a very long period. They handed their skills down from one generation to the next. All members of the family were involved in mining. From skeletons found in collapsed mines it appears that children and small, older people did much of the work underground. They could most easily pass down some of the narrow passages and shafts, some of which were only 26 centimetres wide. Larger people worked in the entrances and above ground.

The common method of mining was to use a metal spike and a stone hammer. The spike was hammered into a crack in the rock until the rock split. When this method failed, a fire was lit against the rock face and then a thin stream of cold water was poured into the cracks causing them to split into pieces. Fragments of rock were loaded into skin bags or baskets and then hauled on ropes or carried to the surface. Here the rich ore was sorted out and the rest discarded. Gold-bearing rocks (usually quartz) were burnt and crushed below a large rock which was see-sawed (rocked) over them.

Smelting

Gold, and possibly copper, smelting was done by the same family which owned the mine, but it is thought that people visited the miners to trade for iron ore. They probably exchanged corn, stock, skins or beads for the ore which they packed in leather bags and loaded on to cattle to take home. Smelting appears to have developed into a secret skill because many furnaces have been found hidden well away from villages. The fur-

Fig. 33 Setswana smelting furnace, reconstructed from remains found throughout south-eastern Botswana and the western Transvaal

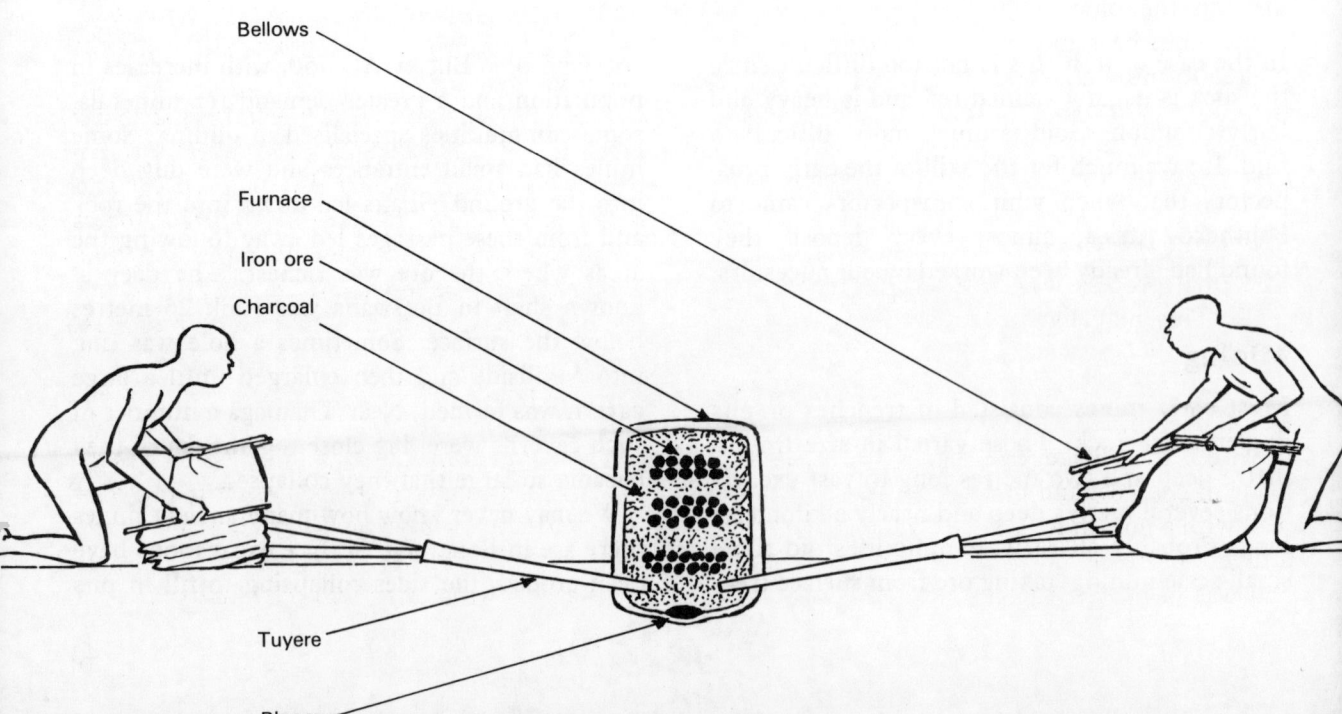

Fig. 34 A Motswana blacksmith operating bellows. Making iron tools requires very high temperatures

nace was built of clay and ant heap. It consisted of an oval wall about one metre high and 50 centimetres in diameter. Usually two clay pipes led into the bottom of the furnace from the outside. Inside the furnace a layer of charcoal was covered by a layer of crushed ore, then another layer of charcoal and another of ore until the furnace was full and the top closed. Air from bellows (*mouba*) was pumped into the furnace through the pipes. The charcoal developed a tremendous heat and the iron in the rock slowly melted forming a layer in the bottom of the furnace, known as 'bloom'. After cooling the bloom was removed and cleaned.

Working iron

The final process was to make the bloom into tools. This may have been done by the same people or by others who came to buy the bloom. The blacksmith (*mothudi*) was an extremely skilful person. He worked at an open fire, usually within the village. See Fig. 34. The fire was made of charcoal and had on one side a low clay wall with a hole in it. Through this hole was put a tuyere made of clay. This looked like a funnel and was to protect the end of the bellows. The blacksmith then fitted the nozzle of his bellows into the tuyere and pumped air into the fire. The bloom was laid in the charcoal and soon became hot. It was then taken from the fire and hammered on a stone anvil. By repeatedly hammering and heating, the blacksmith removed most of the impurities (charcoal, stone and dirt) leaving a piece of hardened iron which he could shape. He had a variety of tools which included metal tongs, chisels, spikes and stone hammers. With these he was able to make a great variety of tools and jewellery.

The smelting of the iron ore in particular required a great amount of skill. Recently scientists have been recreating the old furnaces and trying to smelt iron in them. The whole process has been found much more complicated than was originally believed. So far they have not succeeded in copying the skill of our forefathers.

Questions

1 List the main minerals mined in Southern Africa during the Iron Age. How many of them are mined today in Botswana?
2 Describe briefly in your own words the four stages of processing rock ore into tools.

9 The Beginning of the Kingdoms 1000-1250

Between about AD 900 and 950 sudden changes began to take place. New styles in pottery decoration, larger cattle herds and a greater interest in mining, particularly for precious minerals such as gold, began to appear. Some historians believe these changes were brought about by an immigration of new peoples. If this was so, we would expect to see more general changes in the lifestyle of the people, but these did not occur. The way of life of the newcomers, if they really existed, and that of the older inhabitants, was much the same. The main change appears to have been one in wealth, the new people were better able to make themselves rich.

On the other hand, it may have been that the cattle-owning people of the drier areas had produced their own strata (levels) of rich and poor and it was out of these societies that the new people came to dominate the area. If we look at the Toutswe people we do not see amongst them the same changes which were taking place among most of their neighbours. This suggests it may have been the rich Toutswe cattle owners who were spreading out to control surrounding areas.

Anyway, changes took place. Pottery styles changed. The new homes were much larger and were built on high ground, often on hills, huts were better constructed and communities began to own more stock. Mining activities increased, particularly for gold, copper and even for tin. Trade also seems to have increased as we find many more glass beads in village sites.

This was the end of the Early Iron Age, during which people had lived in small communities, and the beginning of the Late Iron Age, when communities grew both in size and wealth. Mining and trade increased and rich families began to control huge areas of land.

These changes took place on much of the inland plateau of Southern Africa, particularly in what is now western Zimbabwe and the Transvaal. They do not appear to have occurred in the areas of Botswana south and west of the Motloutse River, where rainfall is lower.

In the area of the upper Shashe River and stretching eastwards into Zimbabwe, pottery styles which began there have developed continuously until modern times. This suggests that the same people have lived there for at least a thousand years. Probably these people spoke ancient Chishona dialects. Tjikalanga, a dialect of Chishona, has probably been the major language of the area for all this time. Almost certainly some of the Bakalanga living there today are the descendants of these people.

Changes in settlement

During the Early Iron Age settlements were normally on the upper slopes of valley floors. Towards the end of this period settlements were positioned higher, many being situated on hilltops. The new people all lived on hills. Scientists are not sure why this was.

Early homes had been small, often less than two metres across. These were much bigger, sometimes with a width of more than three metres. We do not know if the earlier huts were

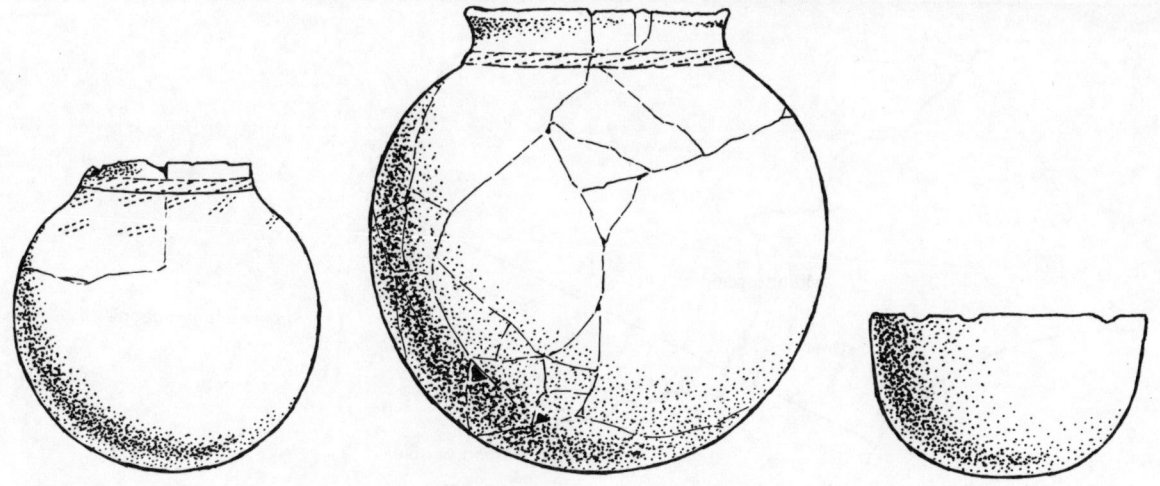

Fig. 35 Pottery from Toutswemogala, about AD 1100

thatched or not, but their floors were on the ground, not raised on rocks like those at Broederstroom. It is possible they were built of thin poles sunk into the ground with the tops bent inwards and tied together, the gaps stuffed with scrub and the whole building well-plastered with mud. On the other hand, they may have had a separate pole roof which was thatched. The new houses almost certainly did have a separate roof which was thatched, and walls made of thicker posts with a heavy coating of mud both inside and out. Stone terracing began to appear in some of the villages. Because these new settlements tended to be on hilltop slopes it may have been necessary to try and stabilise (keep still) the surface on which the villages were built. This was done by setting out rows of rocks which developed into low walls to stop earth eroding.

Pottery

While pottery cannot talk, we can guess that when one type of pottery is suddenly replaced by another, something important has occurred, almost certainly the arrival of a new people.

This is what happened over much of Southern Africa in about the 10th century. The type of and decorations on pottery suddenly changed. Compare the pottery in Fig. 35 with that in Fig. 28 on page 35. This supports the idea that a new group of people came to the area.

In different areas there were slight differences of design in the new pottery styles which leads us to believe they were not one people, but several closely related groups with a common lifestyle and probably speaking dialects of one language. Look at the map, Fig. 36 on page 48, and see where the people settled in the areas to the north and east of the Toutswe people. By their pottery styles they have been divided into three groups. Because we still do not know for certain what languages they spoke, they are called after the sites where they were first identified, Mambo, Bambandyanalo and Gumanye.

Mining and trade

During the Early Iron Age in Botswana, mining had been confined mainly to iron and specularite. Copper was mined, but in small quantities and the few copper ornaments found in excavations of this period may have been the results of trade. No gold had been mined here although it had been mined in the north for more than 300 years. Probably a steady trade had sprung up

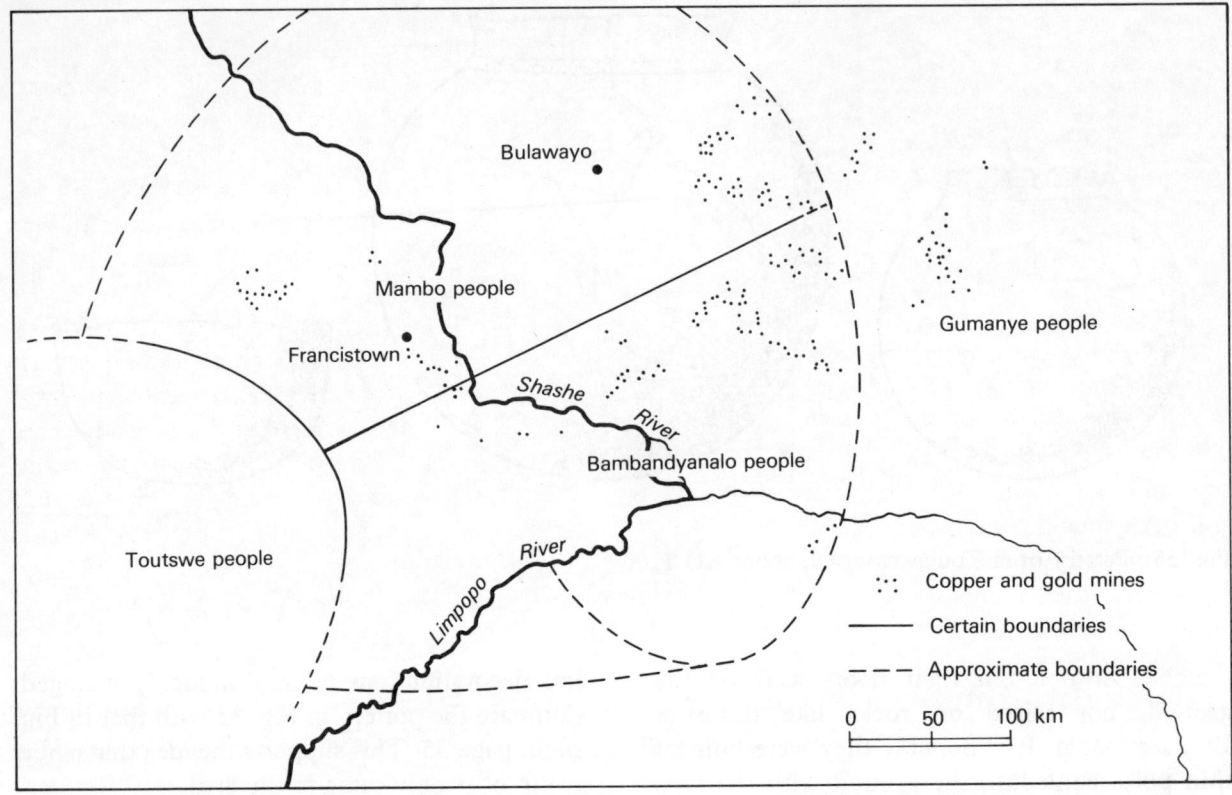

Fig. 36 The population in eastern Botswana about AD 1100

through the villages to the east coast. We find Indian beads appearing in western Zimbabwe by AD 300 and in many places in Botswana by AD 800.

Changes started to take place fairly rapidly. By AD 1000 the gold mines around where the Ramokgwebane River joins the Shashe had probably opened, and possibly also the copper mines near Matsitama. The probable trade route passed down the Shashe to its junction with the Limpopo and then eastwards to the Sabe and so to the coast. Cattle had provided the wealth to make some of the Bambandyanalo people richer and more powerful than others. Gold helped the largely crop-producing societies to the north and east. However, their wealth must have depended on cattle as most of the gold was traded eastwards. By AD 1050 these societies had also started to change. At one site, Bambandyanalo, a bigger and presumably more powerful society began to appear.

The Bambandyanalo people

These people were probably already involved in the fur, ivory and specularite trade to the east. They may also have traded salt from the rich deposits nearby. Excavations show the Bambandyanalo people lived in a series of villages on the same site each about 200 metres across. In the middle was a large cattle kraal which was surrounded by houses.

Their first village shows little evidence of ironware although bone tools were plentiful. There was a short break in occupation and then the same pottery occurs indicating the same people, but this time ironware is plentiful, together with beads and sea shells from the coast. They had obviously suddenly entered the major trade that was commencing in south-western Zimbabwe. Another item to appear at this stage was the spindle-whorl, a flat clay disc with a hole through the centre. A stick was fixed into the

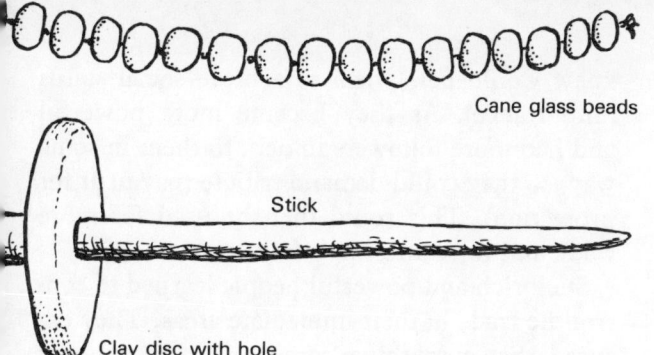

Fig. 37 Trade goods of the type found in south-western Zimbabwe AD 1200 to 1400: beads from Persia and India. Spindle-whorls indicate local cotton cloth production

hole and the 'whorl' was used to spin thread. It had been thought that coloured cloth from Asia made up a part of the trade goods from the east. However, the Bambandyanalo people soon learned to spin and weave their own cloth.

Considerable contact appears to have sprung up between the Bambandyanalo people, the Mambo people in the north and the Toutswe people in the west. We see this from the differing varieties of pottery which begin to be found mixed with those of the other areas. Possibly this contact involved both trade and intermarriage. This would account for the pottery finds provided women made the pots and went to live at their husbands' homes. Certainly it indicates a surplus of wealth.

Look at the map, Fig. 38, and follow the possible trade. From the Toutswe people came furs, cattle, and specularite which were exchanged for beads, salt, grain, and perhaps a little cloth. From the Mambo people came gold, copper and ivory in exchange for cattle, beads, salt and cloth. From the Bambandyanalo people gold, copper, furs, specularite and cattle came in from the west in exchange for beads, cloth and salt. They sent gold, copper, furs, specularite, salt and ivory east in exchange for beads and cloth. Some slaves were also being traded eastwards,

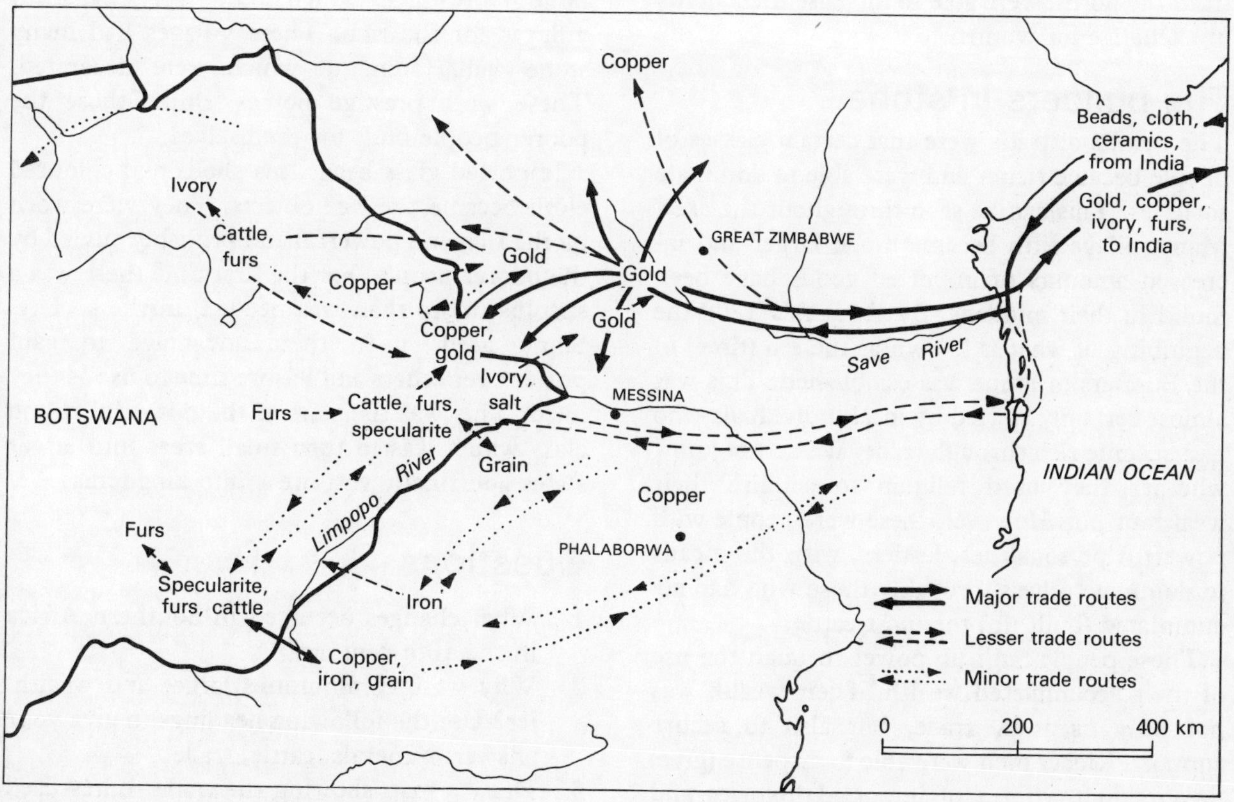

Fig. 38 Possible trade AD 1050 to 1350

probably from the poorer areas which had no cattle, minerals or salt to trade. Up to about AD 1200 trade was probably restricted by distance, people not travelling more than 60 kilometres or so. Once the value of goods to be traded was well established, it is possible that traders came to places like Bambandyanalo right from the coast. People from the interior may have gone the whole distance in the opposite direction.

In the south-east of Botswana, trade was also beginning to increase, although not to the same extent as in the north. The only signs we see are small beads, probably from the north, and a few copper ornaments which must have come in from the east. We assume that in exchange furs, specularite and possibly cattle went out. By about AD 1050 we begin to find some southern pottery appearing in the middens of the Toutswe people but never the other way around. Maybe the wealthier Toutswe people were attracting wives from the south, while the poorer southerners, unable to draw wives in their turn from the north, were able to increase their herds in exchange for women.

The builders in stone

The results of trade were that certain classes of people became richer and were able to dominate societies. This can be seen throughout the area. Many village sites became much larger and increased amounts of imported goods have been found in their middens. By about AD 1200 the beginning of what is known as the era (time) of the Builders in Stone was established. This was almost certainly started by local individuals who had become rich through trade. We do not know whether they used religion to acquire their wealth or not. However, these were people with powerful personalities, leaders, with the means to dominate others, probably those who had accumulated (built up) the most cattle.

These people built up power through the use of their accumulated wealth. Their wealth was not only used for trade, but also to secure support. Richer men were able to dispense (give) favours in the form of imported luxuries and local wealth, such as cattle, to those they knew would help them to achieve social status (importance). As they became more powerful and had more followers in debt to them in some way, so they could demand tribute (payment for protection). This could then be used for more trade and to secure more followers.

Such rich and powerful people learned to control the trade in their immediate areas. They ensured that everything coming in or going out passed through their hands. The average person was no longer free to act as he wished, he had to conform to the way society operated. As richer people gained more control they were able to insist that others should mine gold and copper, hunt for furs and ivory, pay tribute in corn, and provide labour. In exchange they could reward with wealth or power. As the influence of these rich people spread, so they needed others to watch over their interests in more distant places. This gave rise to different strata (levels) of rich and poor which spread throughout the land. These were the people who hired or controlled a large work-force which built very beautiful villages for the rich. These villages had many stone walls, some of which were decorated. These were prestige homes unlike those the poorer people built for themselves.

Imported glass beads, sea shells and coloured cloth became prestige objects. They were worn by the rich and powerful and probably envied by the poorer people. For the first time there was a surplus (more than was needed) in the society. Some used it to their advantage to gain power over others and leisure time to use as they liked. This was the start of the powerful ruling class which was to turn small areas into larger states and finally vast areas into kingdoms.

Questions

1. What changes occurred in Southern Africa in the 10th century?
2. Why were communities larger and wealthier? Use the following headings to give your answer: minerals, cattle, trade.
3. Draw a map showing the trade routes used in about AD 1200.

10 Botswana and the Great Zimbabwe Empire 1200-1350

In the last chapter we saw how a few people began to grow rich and powerful. They were able to impose levies (*sehuba*) on their subjects, to control trade and have leisure time to spend on matters not directly connected with food production. Amongst the Toutswe people this had been brought about through cattle, amongst the Mambo people through mining and amongst the earlier Bambandyanalo people probably through ivory, cattle and furs. The Zimbabwe Empire was created almost certainly as a result of the careful control of trade from the interior being funnelled through the town of Zimbabwe itself to the coast.

Before we look at the rise of the Great Zimbabwe Empire we should look briefly at the areas lying to the south and west. It was because of them that Great Zimbabwe became so powerful. By AD 1150 mining had become a considerable industry, particularly in western Zimbabwe. The important minerals were copper and gold. Copper was traded locally but most of the gold was sent to the east coast from where Muslim traders took it north to the great trading centre of Kilwa to be shipped across the ocean to India. Ivory also went to India and probably even to China.

Mining

Minerals tend to be concentrated in certain areas. In these areas the agriculturalists (farmers) became successful miners. Many of these mines were very close together and involved the whole community living around them. For instance, there are 46 separate known workings in an area of 50 km^2 around Matsitama, though probably only 8 or 10 of them were being mined at one time. Other major copper mining areas were at Messina (Musina) and Phalaborwa in the Transvaal, with some smaller areas not far from Gaborone and at Melita near Kanye. The miners did not give up agriculture as they still needed to produce their own food. Since women may have been the main underground miners and since the deeper mines flooded during the rains, mining probably took place only during the winter and spring, well before the rains and crop season started.

Typical villages in Botswana about AD 1200

Moritsane

Moritsane is a small hill near Gabane. On its summit was a cattle kraal about 20-30 metres across. To the south and west were a number of small huts and some granaries built on stones. Below on the plain were small fields where millet, sorghum and melons were grown. The people living here kept cattle, sheep and goats. They worked iron and even today we can see the remains of a small opencast mine on the hill just to the south of their village. They traded in all directions. To the west they traded iron to the San in exchange for furs. To the east they traded specularite and cattle in exchange for copper ornaments. To the north they traded furs in exchange for beads from Asia. In addition, some of their women married to the north bringing cattle back to Moritsane to increase their herds. The men hunted, mainly for meat but also for furs and ivory, to increase the supplies they bartered from the San.

Sung

Sung is a large hill west of Shoshong. There are the remains of a huge Toutswe-type settlement built at four different levels. At the top of the hill was a flat clearing with a large cattle kraal surrounded by many huts, some of them raised above the others on a terrace. Lower down the west side of the hill two separate levels each contained a number of homes and granaries. At the bottom of the hill and stretching for some distance were a large number of huts and granaries. In all there may have been more than a hundred huts, possibly the homes for as many as 500 people. Sung was an important central village, the home of the ruler of the whole area from the Mhalatswe River to the Kalahari. He controlled this area and the 500 or more other villages in it. Around the lower village were fields growing sorghum, millet and melons. The village people worked iron, but their main interest was their large herds of cattle, sheep and goats. These were distributed to all the smaller villages and some were kept in the Kalahari at places such as Lebung. The ruler and his relatives spent much of their time looking after their people, settling disputes (arguments) and organising trade. This was carried out mostly with the people to the north-east, although some was directed to the south.

These were Toutswe people with links far to the north and east. To the west they had many San working for them, looking after their stock in the Kalahari, hunting for fur and working in the homes in the smaller villages on the edge of the Kalahari. For their work they received iron arrowheads and spears, clay pots, milk, and protection from those who would not trade fairly with them.

Mambo village

Close to where the Ramokgwebane and the Shashe Rivers meet was another village occupied by some Mambo people. This village was situated on the top of a ridge looking westwards over the Shashe River. It was much smaller than Sung but larger than Moritsane. A stone wall was built to enclose about half a hectare of land on a slight rise in the ridge. Within the wall were eight well-built houses and some granaries placed on the smooth rock of the rise. Outside the wall were some slightly inferior houses, granaries and fields. About a kilometre to the north-east was a gold mine. Within the wall lived a district governor and his family. He was important because he ruled the area for a king at Great Zimbabwe and controlled all the trade and mining. The women produced more crops than they needed because they had to give a part of their harvest to the district governor who passed some of it on to the king.

During winter and spring everybody worked at the mine. The ore was brought to the surface and crushed. Each small piece which showed any sign of gold was ground in a hole in the rock. The fine powdered rock was taken to the river and washed until all the rock dust had been removed leaving only the gold. The gold powder was melted in small clay moulds and then handed to the district governor who rewarded the miners with a few beads or sheep. The district governor sent the gold to the king who sent back beads and cloth. The district governor kept most of these for himself and his family, but some of them were given to those who supported him and to the miners.

These people traded in other things as well as gold. They got salt from the east, some of which they sent south and west and in return received skins which they sent east. People living as far away as Mmadinare recognised this man as their leader and brought him corn and iron tools, such as hoes, as tribute. In return, he gave them protection against others living further away and conducted their trade for them with the king in the east.

Because the district governor received all the beads that came from the east, he was the only one to distribute them in this area. People wanted the beads because to wear them was a sign of prestige (importance), so they worked for the district governor. Part of their work had been to build the stone wall around his village. This wall was not for defence nor to keep cattle kraaled. It was to show that the owner was more important than other people.

Mmamagwe

Where the Motloutse and Limpopo Rivers meet is a hill and valley known as Mmamagwe on which was another large village. There were some rough stone walls on the hill and a few large houses with granaries built directly on to the bare rock. In the valley below was a large village of poorer homesteads with several stock kraals. Towards the river were numerous small fields planted with sorghum and millet. There were probably more than 200 people living in this village. The whole area was thickly populated with villages on almost every hill and in all the protected places in the valleys. It had become rich in cattle mainly because it was well positioned for trade with people coming from all directions. Just to the north-east on the other side of the Limpopo was Mapungubwe, The Place of the Jackal, a hill with a similar settlement on it where the king of the whole area lived.

There was little mining in the area except for iron. However, there was trade in gold and copper ore which was brought in by oxback. The ore was crushed in holes carefully bored in the rock slopes near the river. The women spent most of their time growing crops while the men herded cattle and hunted. The men hunted elephant with spears and axes, and by digging deep holes in the paths leading to the rivers and setting these with sharp stakes. There were still many San in the area, some of them living next to the large villages. These people were used for herding, hunting and as servants. Some men had taken San as wives. They lived in the large villages and continued to make eggshell beads and some stone tools.

Bateti villages

At Toromoja on the Boteti River lived the Bateti, a group of Khoe people. They lived in small villages, their round, mat-covered houses set in a circle and surrounded by a thorn fence. At night they kept their stock, long-horned cattle, sheep and goats, in the middle of the village. They lived mainly on fish and zebra and other animals which were caught in the pits they dug by the river, and plants, particularly water-lily rhizomes (*tswii*), which they dug from the river bed. They had a few San servants working for them, mostly hunting small furry animals and collecting wild food. Sometimes they took their skins and ivory and travelled north-west to trade with the people living at Maun, or south-eastwards to the villages of the Toutswe people. They exchanged their skins and ivory for iron tools, copper and tobacco. Sometimes they may also have received a few beads and perhaps some stock. Occasionally the Toutswe people may have travelled to the Boteti to trade with them.

Zu/oasi hunters

At the Tsodilo Hills lived the Zu/oasi. They did not stay in one place for long but moved around building new villages every few months although they always stayed near the hills. They lived by hunting and collecting. Occasionally they painted pictures of animals and people on the rocks of the hills. Up in the hills was a small village of Bantu-speaking people who kept cattle, sheep and goats, grew a few crops and forged iron tools. The Zu/oasi visited them to barter their skins for iron beads and arrowheads, spears, salt, copper ornaments, tobacco and pottery. The copper and beads may have come all the way from eastern Botswana or from Zambia or Namibia.

This then was the position in Botswana: agriculturalist-miners, pastoralists (stock farmers) and forager-hunters lived side by side. The population was widely scattered, but slowly organising itself. People were intermarrying and coming to depend more and more on each other for luxuries they could not produce in their own areas.

Botswana and the rise of the Zimbabwe Empire

It was, apparently, the steadily increasing trade with the east coast which gave rise to the Zimbabwe Empire, making even richer certain families which already owned large herds of cattle. This trade originated in the gold-rich areas to the north-east of the Shashe River. By AD 1150 a ruling class was forming, particularly in mining areas, building larger settlements which often included stone walls. It was probably about this time that the first real traders began to come to the area from the coast seeking gold, copper, ivory, furs and possibly slaves who would help to carry the goods.

While people were becoming rich in the west, a ruler in Zimbabwe built a village amongst the rocks on a hilltop overlooking a valley, close to the present-day town of Masvingo. The position of his village, on one of the main tributaries of the Sabe River, helped him to control some of the trade passing to the east coast. By about 1300 he, or his descendant, had gained considerable wealth and influence by controlling much of this trade. Probably it was both as a rich man and as a religious leader that he was able to gain the power and influence he eventually achieved. By 1350 he had gathered many people around him and moved his village into the valley. There a large and skilled labour force began to construct the town of Great Zimbabwe.

This town included a complex of large, carefully finished stone walls, terraces and covered passageways. It contained beautiful houses built of heavy clay. The ruler attracted other nobles who built their houses around his until the town finally contained 11 000 or more people living in

Fig. 39 Inside the enclosure of Great Zimbabwe. Girls were probably initiated here at one time

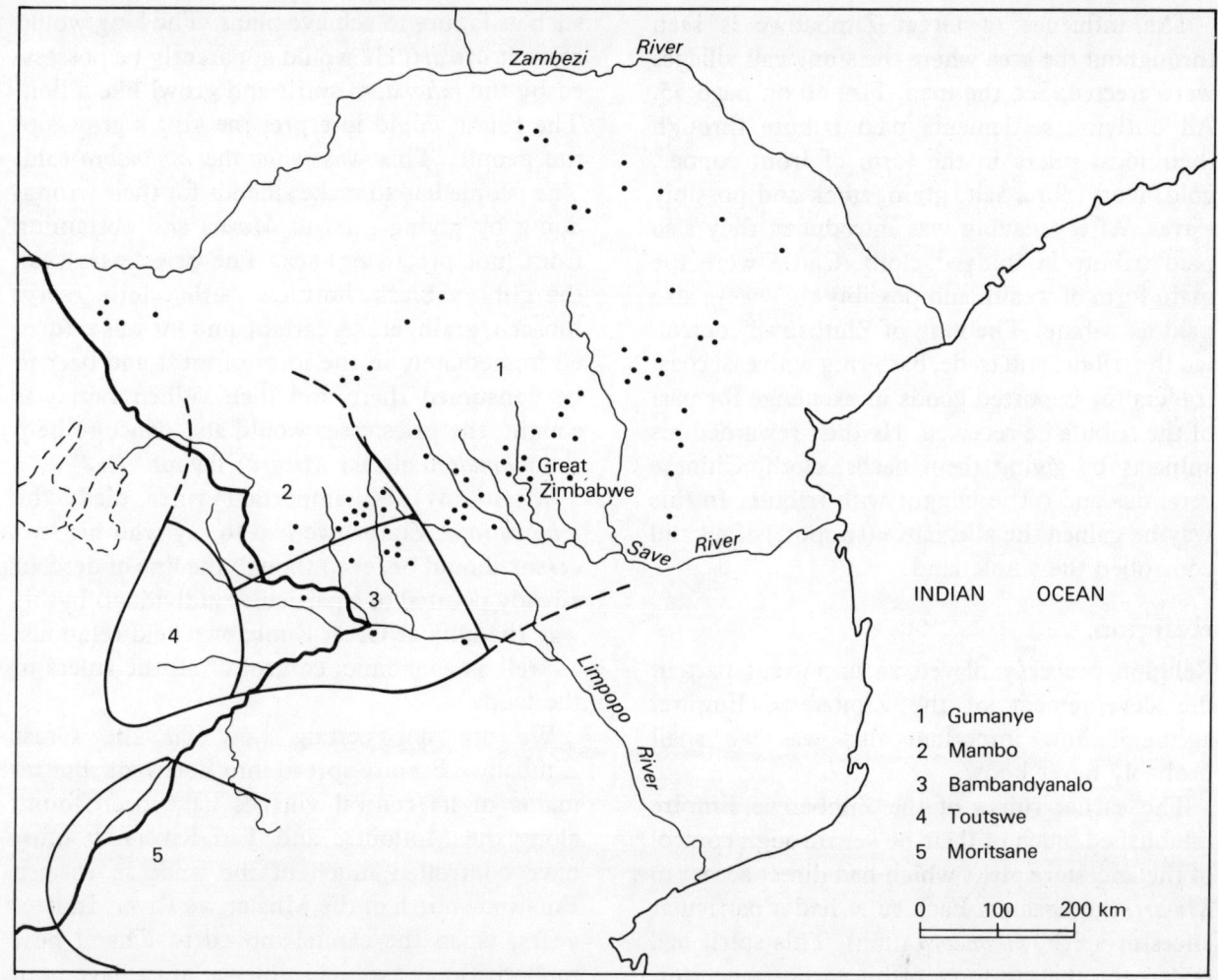

Fig. 40 Early stonewall sites built in Zimbabwe style

great wealth. During the period from AD 1250 to 1450 at least 150 much smaller, walled settlements were built. They stretched in a great crescent from the Tati River north-eastwards almost to the Zambezi. These settlements each contained about 16 adults living within the stone walls and a greater number of less important people living outside them. It is estimated that, during the 200-year lifetime of the Great Zimbabwe Empire, only about a third of these villages were occupied at any one time. The remains of these villages are all very similar suggesting they all belonged to people of the same culture. These were the rich who controlled the whole country. The town of Great Zimbabwe, with more than 11 000 inhabitants, was by far the most important centre. Its noble population probably numbered twice that of all the other scattered villages put together.

Archaeologists excavating Great Zimbabwe town found an enormous wealth of imported goods: ceramics (pottery) from China, glass from Persia, beads from many countries, as well as quantities of gold, copper, bronze and forged iron implements (tools). The town was the centre of all trade during this period. Cloth was introduced from India and almost certainly all the rich wore cloth clothes and jewellery made of copper, bronze or gold as well as glass beads and sea shells.

The influence of Great Zimbabwe is seen throughout the area where the stonewall villages were erected. See the map, Fig. 40 on page 55. All outlying settlements paid tribute through their local rulers in the form of iron, copper, gold, ivory, furs, salt, grain, stock and possibly slaves. After weaving was introduced they also paid tribute in undyed cloth. Cattle were the main form of wealth and possibly they were also paid as tribute. The king of Zimbabwe controlled the tribute and trade, bartering with east coast traders for imported goods in exchange for part of the tribute he received. He then rewarded his subjects by giving them beads, cloth, Chinese ceramics and cattle bought with tribute. In this way he gained the allegiance (support) of all and controlled the whole land.

Religion

Religion probably played an important part in the development of the Zimbabwe Empire, although how important this was we shall probably never know.

The earlier rulers of the Zimbabwe Empire established much of their power through control of the ancestor spirits which had direct access to *Mwari*, the Creator. Each ruler had a particular ancestor spirit, *mhondoro* (lion). This spirit had once been the life force of his earliest ancestor, but on his death had entered a lion. The spirit controlled the well-being of the ruler and all his people and had influence with *Mwari*, God, who sent the rain to bring life to the land. Apparently, as the king at Great Zimbabwe gained in economic power, so his *mhondoro* gained in religious power. By about 1350 the king at Great Zimbabwe (and his *mhondoro*) had become the most powerful in the land and controlled all other rulers (and their *mhondoro*). *Mwari* was served through the king's *mhondoro* by priests and priestesses who had important ritual functions to perform. The *mhondoro* spirit guarded the well-being of the people and punished them if they did not conform to good custom. The punishment usually took the form of sickness, defeat in battle, natural disasters such as hailstorms and drought, and personal disasters such as failure to achieve plans. The king would consult *Mwari*. He would apparently be possessed by the *mhondoro* spirit and growl like a lion. The priest would interpret the king's growls to the people. This was what the *mhondoro* said. The people had to make amends for their wrongdoing by giving gifts to *Mwari* and abstaining from (not practising) sex. The priestesses took the gifts of black, hornless cattle, cloth, ivory, tobacco, grain, etc. A certain amount was returned immediately in the form of meat and beer to be consumed there and then. When rain was sought, the priestesses would also dance to help the *mhondoro* attract *Mwari's* favour.

When any less important ruler died, the *mhondoro* at Zimbabwe had to say who his successor should be, even though the line of descent already pointed to a particular individual. In this way the king at Great Zimbabwe held religious, as well as economic, control of all the rulers in the land.

We are not certain how far the Great Zimbabwe Empire spread into Botswana, but remains of its central villages have been found along the Motloutse and Tati Rivers. It must have controlled much of the trade in eastern Botswana north of the Mhalatswe River. In later years, when the capital moved to Khami near modern Bulawayo, its influence must have been even greater.

Questions

1. Of which of the villages described in this chapter are the following statements true?
   (a) The settlement was on top of or around a hilltop.
   (b) The people kept cattle.
   (c) The people grew millet, sorghum and melons.
   (d) The people worked iron.
   (e) The people engaged in trade.
2. What was the most important reason for the rise of the Zimbabwe Empire?
3. Imagine you are a visitor to Great Zimbabwe. Write a letter to a friend describing what you have seen.

11 Origins of the Batswana and Bakgalagadi

This chapter describes how the two nations, the Bakgalagadi and the Batswana, formed. It shows how they came to have the various divisions they have today (see Fig. 41 on pages 58-9). It describes events spread over a very long period and ending about 1700. This date has been chosen because oral history becomes more accurate from then onwards. From about 1790 great changes began to occur in Southern Africa. This was mainly as a result of increases in population and pressure from European settlers around the South African coast. Chapter 12 gives a description of Batswana life before 1790.

Early origins

The communities which later grew into the Bakgalagadi, the Batswana and the Basotho began to form in the western Transvaal and Botswana in about AD 1200. Probably the Amanguni in south-east Africa and the Vashona, Bavenda and Batsonga to the north and east were also beginning to form distinct cultural groups at the same time.

Some history books say that these peoples entered Southern Africa in a series of invasions (waves) and were already divided into their distinct cultural groups, but this is incorrect. They grew out of the intermarriage between the first Bantu-speaking farmers and the San and Khoe.

The small groups of iron-age farmers entered a country inhabited by the Khoe and San. The farmers were very few in number compared with the Khoe and San. Today's Bantu-speaking peoples of Southern Africa are the descendants of mainly Khoesan peoples with some Negroid influence. In AD 1200 our ancestors probably had more Khoesan characteristics than we have today. Because of their advanced technology, their knowledge of agriculture, pottery and iron-working, the early Bantu-speakers were able to dominate the larger Khoesan population. However, the Khoesan influence can still be seen today. For instance the Batswana and Bakgalagadi are lighter in skin colour than the Bantu-speaking peoples further north. They also have Khoesan characteristics such as almond-shaped eyes, thin lips and high cheek-bones. Also the click sounds found in some Southern African languages come from Khoesan languages.

It is very difficult to show that settlements dated around 1200 belonged to the same peoples as exist now. No unique features of their culture (such as pottery decoration) were the same then as they are today.

However, modern Batswana pottery is similar to that found in the western Transvaal and south-eastern Botswana and dated to about 800 years ago. This suggests that, although we cannot say those early people were, for example, Bakwena, we can say they were some of the ancestors of the Batswana and Bakgalagadi. We can be certain the Batswana have lived in this area for 800 years. The archaeologist who excavated Broederstroom has shown similarities between the pottery found there belonging to

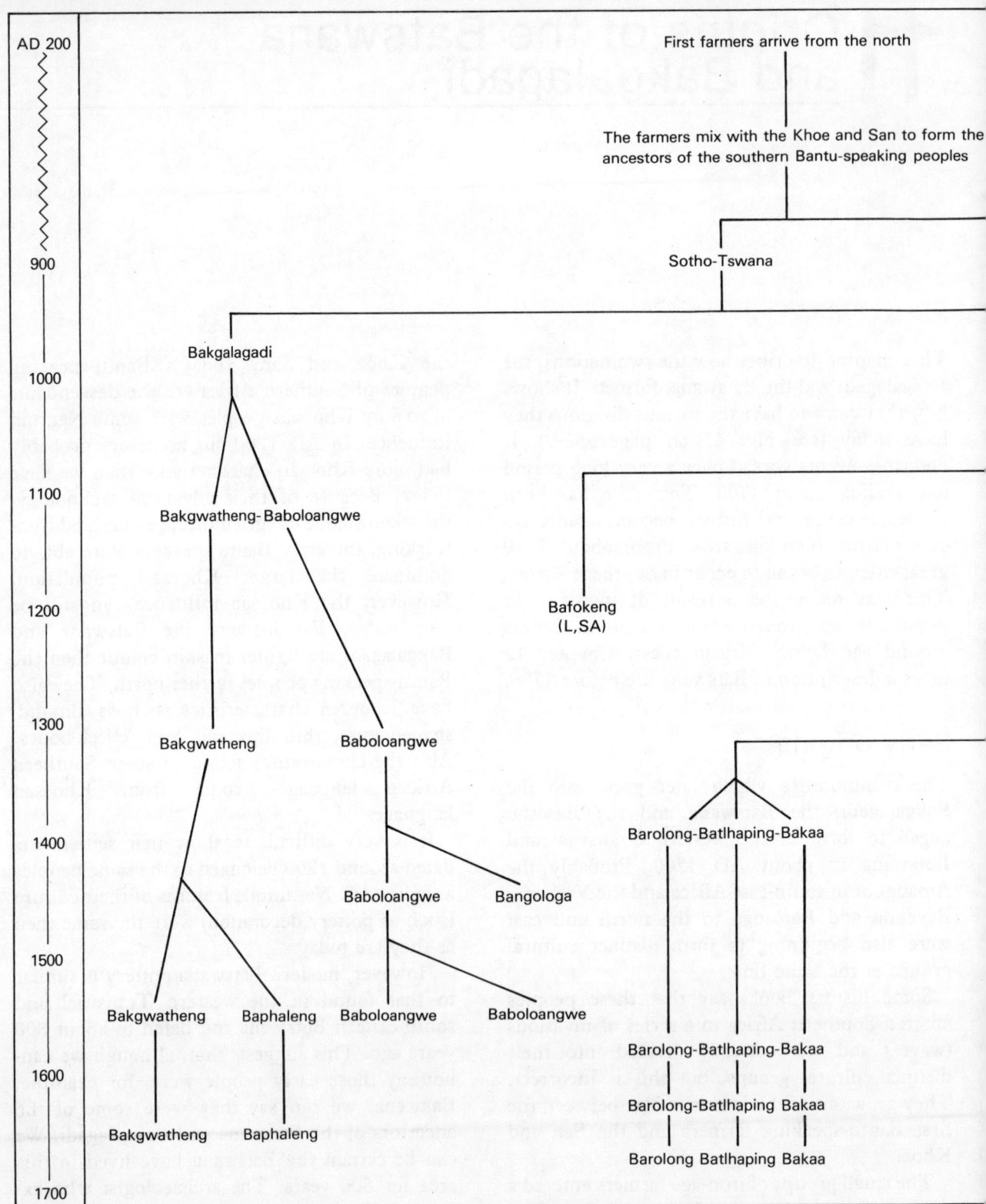

Fig. 41 Diagram showing the relationship between the Sotho-Tswana groups now living in Botswana

N.B. Where names separate it means the group concerned split apart and moved away from each other; the Bafokeng did not disappear in 1200, they still exist today.

(L) group in Lesotho

(SA) group in South Africa

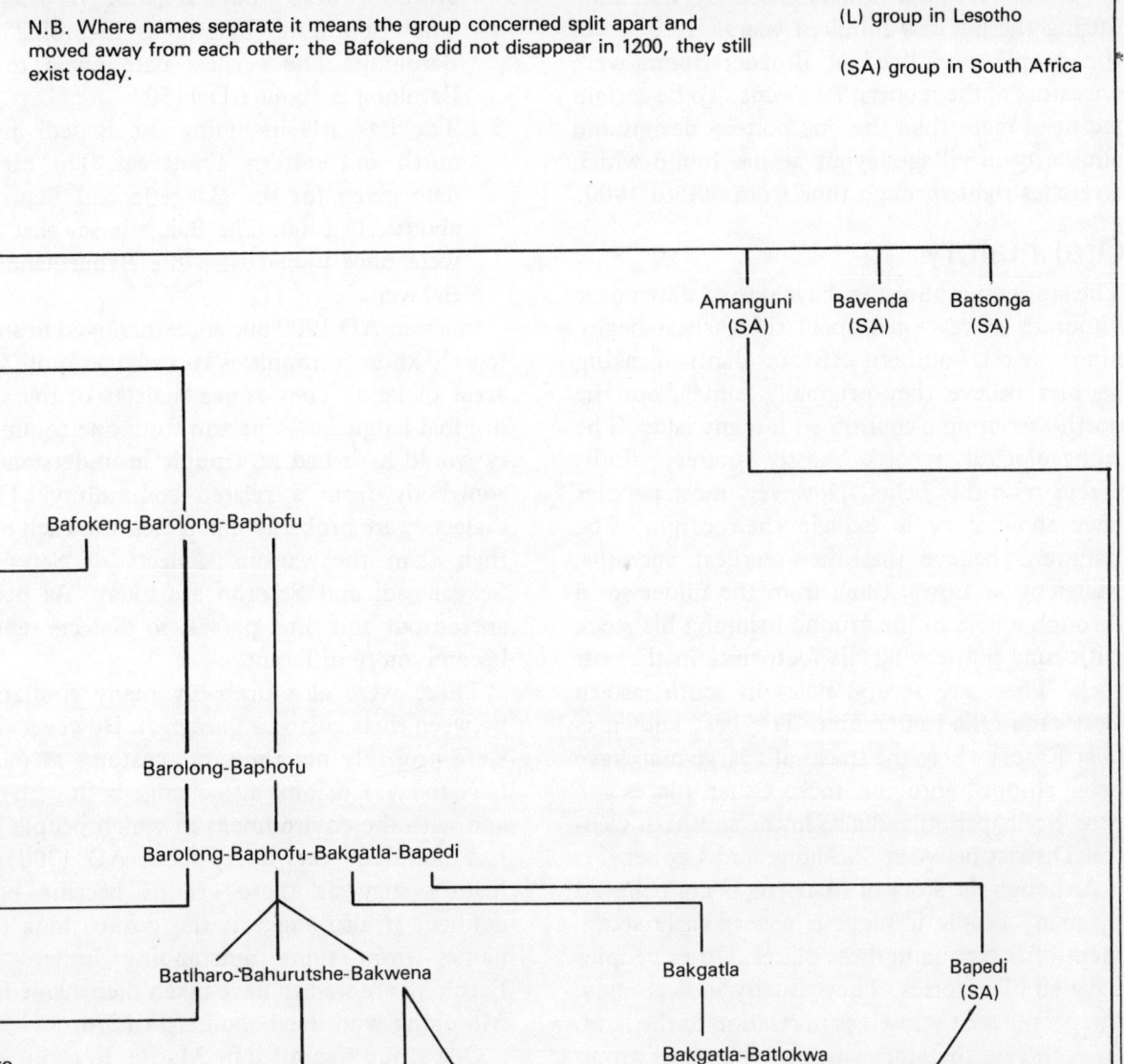

59

about AD 500 and pottery made by Batswana during the last few hundred years. He believes the people who lived at Broederstroom were ancestors of the modern Batswana. To be certain we need more than the one pottery design and similarity in village layout he has found which stretches right through time from 500 to 1900.

Oral history

The stories our ancestors have passed down over hundreds of years tell about the earliest beginnings. Most Southern African Bantu-speaking peoples believe they originally came from the north-east, from a country with many lakes. The archaeological record, mostly pottery finds, agrees with this belief. However, most peoples have some story to explain their origin. The Batswana believe that their earliest ancestor, Matsieng or Lowe, came from the underworld through a hole in the ground bringing his stock with him and leaving his footprints in the soft rock. There are several holes in south-eastern Botswana called after him. The best known is near Rasesa where the tracks of a large man have been chipped into the rock. Other places are near Botlhapatlou and also in the southern Central District between Shoshong and Lephepe.

Although the story of Matsieng is not believed by many people it suggests a very early settlement of Batswana in these places. Other peoples have similar stories. They usually indicate how the people see themselves in relation to the land. In each case the story suggests that each group has its own unique origin in an area and that no other people have a better claim to the land.

The Sotho-Tswana peoples trace their ancestry back to five major groups (see Fig. 41, pages 58-9).

1 The Bakgalagadi including the Bakgwatheng, Bangologa and Babolaongwe. The Bakgalagadi are believed to have been the first to occupy the edges of the Kalahari.
2 The Bafokeng including the Badighoya. The earliest date given to the Bafokeng is about AD 1150.
3 The Western Batswana including the Bahurutshe and Bakwena. The earliest date given for these groups is about AD 1220.
4 The Southern Batswana including the Barolong. The earliest date given to the Barolong is about AD 1150.
5 The Bakgatla including the Bapedi in the north and eastern Transvaal. The earliest date given for the Bakgatla and Bapedi is about AD 1400. The Bakgatla say that they were once joined with the Bahurutshe and Bakwena.

In about AD 1200 our ancestors lived in small, loosely-knit communities spread over quite wide areas of land. They spoke dialects of the same original language. A person from one community would have had no trouble in understanding somebody from a related community. These dialects were probably much closer to each other then than the various dialects of Setswana, Sekgalagadi and Sesotho are today. As people spread out and time passes, so dialects tend to become more different.

There were also probably many similarities between their customs (*mekgwa*). However, they were probably not the same customs as people have today. Customs also change both with time and with the environment in which people live.

A hundred years later, about AD 1300, oral history suggests these groups became better defined. It also suggests the groups took their names from some outstanding leader. The Barolong are said to have taken their name from Morolong who lived about AD 1270.

One group was ruled by Masilo. In about 1400 a group which came to be called the Batlharo broke away. Later, perhaps about 1500, it was ruled by Malope. One story relates that Malope had no male children in his first house, only a daughter called Mohurutshe, while in the second house he had a son called Kwena. There was argument because some people wanted the daughter to be the ruler while others said that only a man could rule. They split and those who followed Mohurutshe were called the Bahurutshe and those who followed Kwena were called the Bakwena. Later still the Bakwena split again and one section moved to the area of modern Lesotho and surrounding areas now in South Africa.

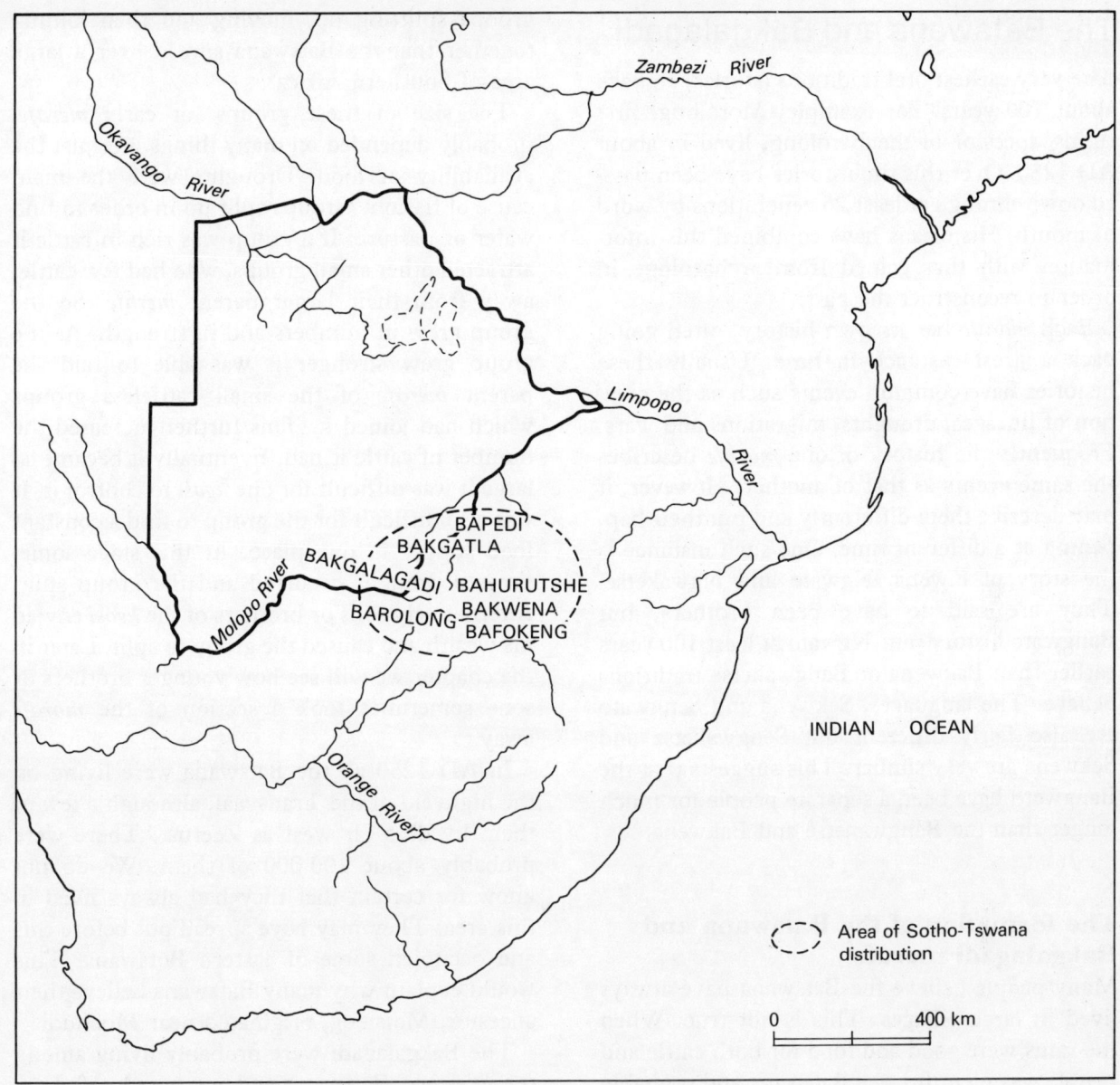

Fig. 42 Possible distribution of Sotho-Tswana peoples about 1400

These stories suggest that the groups were becoming too large to be ruled by one person and that they were dividing. Although each section was separated from the others, their rulers were related to each other by marriage or descent. Perhaps this was because people were not living in one community, but were spread out and the political organisation was not strong.

The diagram, Fig. 41 on pages 58 to 59 shows how the various *merafe* of today trace their ancestry back to one original people.

Look also at the map, Fig. 42 which shows how we think the various groups were distributed about 1400. We cannot be certain, but we can guess that the Bakgalagadi were living in the west, the Barolong in the south, the Bahurutshe, Bakwena and Bafokeng in the east, and the Bakgatla and Bapedi in the north.

61

The Batswana and Bakgalagadi

The very earliest oral traditions (stories) go back about 700 years. For example, Morolong, first ruling ancestor of the Barolong, lived in about AD 1280. Over this time stories have been passed down through at least 25 generations by word of mouth. Historians have combined this information with that gained from archaeology in order to reconstruct the past.

Each *morafe* has its own history, often going back a great distance in time. Usually these histories have common events such as the creation of lineages, droughts, migrations and wars. Frequently the history of one *morafe* describes the same events as that of another. However, it may describe them differently and put their happening at a different time. One such instance is the story of Kwena, Ngwato and Ngwaketse. They are said to have been brothers, but Bangwato history puts Ngwato at least 100 years earlier than Bakwena or Bangwaketse traditions believe. The languages, Sekwena and Sengwato are also fairly different but Sengwaketse and Sekwena are very similar. This suggests that the Bangwato have been a separate people for much longer than the Bangwaketse and Bakwena.

The formation of the Batswana and Bakgalagadi merafe

Many people believe the Batswana have always lived in large villages. This is not true. When the rains were good and food for both cattle and people was plentiful, the Batswana and probably the Bakgalagadi formed big groups. But when drought struck they divided up into much smaller groups. For instance, in about 1550, when Kgabo took some Bakwena to live near Dithejwane they numbered only about 60 people. But within 50 years they had grown in number to more than a thousand.

This is the history of the Batswana: groups of people splitting up and then other groups joining together. The splitting up of groups is called fission. The joining together of groups is called amalgamation. It is because of this process of groups splitting up, moving and then joining together that the Batswana spread over a large area of Southern Africa.

The size of these groups, or early *merafe*, probably depended on many things, not just the availability of food. Droughts were the main cause of fission. Groups split up in order to find water or pasture. If a group was rich in cattle it attracted other small groups, who had few cattle, away from their larger parent *merafe*. So the group grew in numbers and in strength. As the group grew stronger it was able to raid the parent *merafe* of the small cattleless groups which had joined it. This further increased the number of cattle it had. Eventually it became so large it was difficult for one *kgosi* to control it. It was also difficult for the group to find a constant food supply in one place. At this stage sometimes a drought occurred and the group split. Alternatively sons or brothers of the *kgosi* envied his wealth and caused the group to split. Later in the chapter we will see how younger brothers or sons sometimes took a section of the *morafe* away.

In AD 1250 all the Batswana were living on the highveld of the Transvaal, although a few of them lived as far west as Zeerust. There were probably about 100 000 of them. We do not know for certain that they had always lived in this area. They may have spread out before this and occupied some of eastern Botswana. This would explain why many Batswana believe their ancestor, Matsieng, originated near Mochudi.

The Bakgalagadi were probably living among the Western Batswana and westwards of them into the drier areas of Botswana. There is no doubt that the Batswana, Basotho and Bakgalagadi are closely related, springing from one original people. Although the dialects of Sekgalagadi form a language distinct from Setswana the many similarities in customs *(mekgwa)*, between the two peoples suggest that they have been closely related in the past.

AD 1200-1400

During the period AD 1200-1400 populations

increased rapidly and spaces between villages far from each other began to fill. It was more difficult to move when land became less fertile due to repeated planting and overgrazing by domestic stock. As these communities grew, so stronger political organisations were needed to control them.

People who lived in the same area and spoke the same dialect cooperated with each other rather than with people living over the mountains whose language was slightly different. In this way early communities formed. As some became more powerful than others through wealth in cattle, mining or trading, so less powerful groups tended to join them.

Three early groups, the Barolong, Bafokeng and Bakgalagadi, seem to have distinguished themselves in some way. The Barolong took their name from an early leader, Morolong, whose name may come from the ancient word *rola* (the action of forging iron). His son was called *Noto* meaning 'Hammer', and one of the

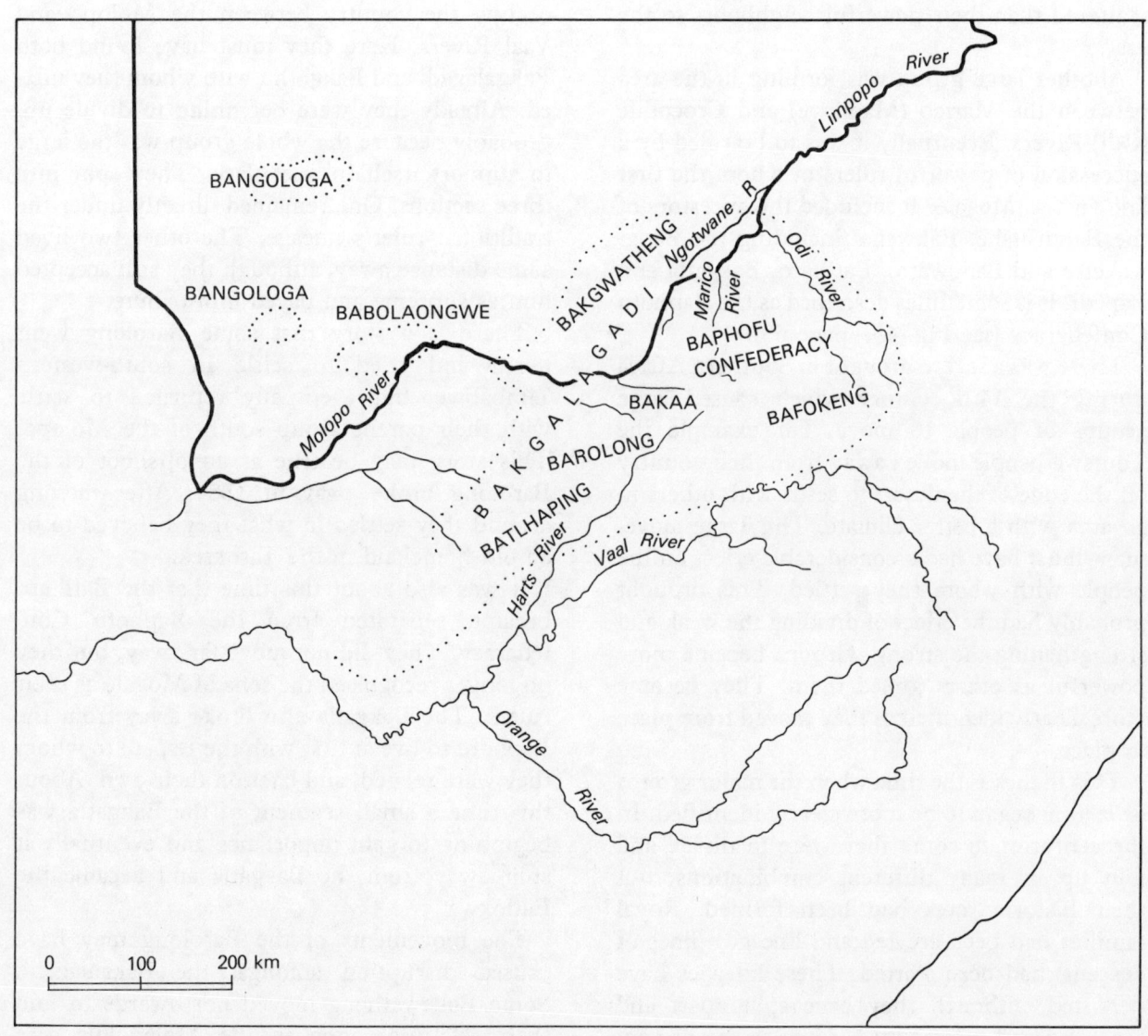

Fig. 43 Approximate distribution of Sotho-Tswana peoples about 1500

Barolong totems (emblems) is *Tshipi* meaning 'Iron' suggesting they gained importance through mining or working in iron.

Little is known about the Bafokeng. The dialect they spoke was probably different from that of the early Barolong. Many of them moved south-eastwards to form a part of the early population of modern Lesotho.

The Bakgalagadi peoples probably lived to the west of the other Sotho-Tswana along the fringes of the Kalahari Desert. They broke away early from the main population and their communities remained smaller, more mobile and scattered than their powerful neighbours to the east.

Another large group was forming in the area between the Marico (Madikwe) and Crocodile (Odi) Rivers. Eventually it was to be ruled by a succession of powerful rulers of whom the first known was Mogale. It included the ancestors of the Bahurutshe, Bakwena (including the Bangwaketse and Bangwato), Batlharo, Bakgatla and Bapedi. It is sometimes described as the Baphofu Confederacy (see Fig. 43, page 63).

There was a severe drought in Southern Africa during the 14th century which caused large groups of people to move. For example the Toutswe people moved away from their country on the edge of the desert to settle with others in an area with a better climate. This large movement must have had a considerable effect on the people with whom they settled. This drought probably had the effect of dividing the weak and strengthening the strong. Groups became more powerful as others joined them. They became more clearly identified as they moved from place to place.

This then was the time when the major groups or *merafe* began to be more clearly identified. In the centuries to come they were to divide and join up in many different combinations, but their historic roots had been formed. Royal families had been created and lineages (lines of descent) had been started. These lineages have persisted, although they have split apart and then rejoined many times, down to the present day.

AD 1400-1500

Between AD 1400 and 1500 some large movements of people took place. Also the whole of the Sotho-Tswana population spread itself from Pretoria in the east to the Kalahari in the west and from the junction of the Madikwe and Odi Rivers in the north to the Vaal River (Lekwa) in the south. (See Fig. 43, page 63.) Larger groups began to fragment, although each section still recognised one central power, or lineage of rulers.

The Barolong were probably the first to make a definite move. They travelled southwards to occupy the country between the Molopo and Vaal Rivers. Here they must have found both Bakgalagadi and Bakgothu with whom they mixed. Already they were beginning to divide up, probably because the whole group was too large to support itself in one place. They split into three sections. One remained directly under the traditional ruler's lineage. The other two lived some distance away, although they still accepted him as supreme and payed him tribute.

There is a story that some Barolong went north and tried to settle in south-western Zimbabwe, but eventually returned to settle with their parent group south of the Molopo. This story may be true as an offshoot of the Barolong broke away in 1884. After moving around they settled in what they believed to be an old homeland in the Tati area.

It was also about this time that the Batlharo became separated from the Baphofu Confederacy. They did not move far away, but they no longer recognised the sons of Mogale as their rulers. The Bakgatla also broke away from the Baphofu to live at first with the Bapedi to whom they were related, and later on their own. About this time a small segment of the Bakgatla was beginning to gain importance and eventually it split away from the Bakgatla and became the Batlokwa.

The movements of the Barolong may have caused disruption amongst the Bakgalagadi. Some Bakgwatheng moved northwards to join their relatives living in the Molepolole area while the Babolaongwe travelled westwards down the Molopo to settle near Werda. They soon split and a section under Mongologe travelled on to settle first at Mabuasehube. They later settled amidst the pans of Matsheng where they became known by their ruler's name, Bangologa.

Break up of the Baphofu Confederacy AD 1500-1600

It was during the 16th century that the Baphofu Confederacy broke up into a number of important groups. Many of these later moved westwards into Botswana. Steadily expanding populations, a steep decline in the productivity of the land, increases in wealth (domestic stock) and drought were probably the main reasons for the continuing break up or fragmentation. Oral history records arguments over succession, over the care of stock and over arable lands as the actual causes. But these latter reasons were probably only the spark which ignited discontent resulting in the division of large groups. When fragmentation occurred, powerful segments were often able to stand on their own. Weaker segments joined other groups possibly related to them in the distant past. Such unions often failed resulting in new fragmentation. Small segments sometimes returned to their parent group.

In about AD 1500 the Baphofu under Malope were living in the area of the upper Limpopo watershed. They must have been spread out along the river valleys in several distinct groups although they all paid tribute to the one ruler. One story says that Malope had heirs in two houses; a daughter, Mohurutshe, in the first, and a son, Kwena, in the second. On his death the Baphofu split up. One section under Mohurutshe moved southwards from Majwanamatshwaana (near Pretoria) where they had been living. Another section under Kwena moved eastwards towards modern Rustenburg. In about 1530 the Bakwena split again. Many of them moved southwards across the Vaal River to settle eventually in the Orange Free State and Lesotho.

Kwena is said to have had two younger brothers, Ngwaketse and Ngwato. Both were rulers in their own right with sections under them, although they still paid tribute to their elder brother. We now know that Ngwaketse and Ngwato did not live at the same time and that probably these two sections were ruled by their descendants, not by these men themselves.

At this time there was a terrible drought known to this day as *Tlala e e boitshegang*. Searching for a better place to live a group of Bakwena under their leader Mogopa moved up the Madikwe River. They established their home at a place called Rathantang not far from modern Buffelsdrift. This group included the Bangwaketse and Bangwato sections. In about 1540 Mogopa heard that the drought had ended and decided to return to the area near Pretoria. His younger brother, Kgabo, said he would remain with some of the Bakwena and follow later. Once Mogopa had left for Majwanamatshwaana, Kgabo and about ten families crossed into what is now Botswana and settled in the hilly country at Dithejwane, just west of Molepolole, where they found Bakgwatheng, Babolaongwe, Baphaleng and other Bakgalagadi peoples already living. Shortly afterwards Kgabo was joined by other Bakwena who had remained on the Madikwe River. These probably included the Bangwaketse and Bangwato.

Also about this time the Babolaongwe living near Werda broke up. Two groups moved eastwards up the Molopo, one later heading north to join its relatives in the Dithejwane Hills. The other travelled south-eastwards to the Orange Free State and possibly even into what is now Lesotho.

The same drought caused a break up of the Barolong who were living somewhere west of modern Zeerust. A younger son, Phuduhutswana, took a section of the *morafe* away from his father, Tshesebe, and settled at Dikgatlhong on the confluence (junction) of the Harts and Vaal Rivers. The famine was so severe that they were forced to catch and eat fish, from which time they have been known as the Batlhaping (people of the fish). Even though they had split away from their parent *morafe*, they still recognised Tshesebe as their *Kgosi* and paid tribute to him.

AD 1600-1700

More droughts occurred during the 17th century. The traditional lands of the Batswana, lying to the east of the Ngotwane River, became less fertile and populations increased. So, by 1700, the Batswana occupied a much greater area of land than they ever had in the past.

The middle of the century saw many break ups amongst the Batswana *merafe*. It was these splits and the resulting *merafe* which were to form the nuclei or parent groups of most of the

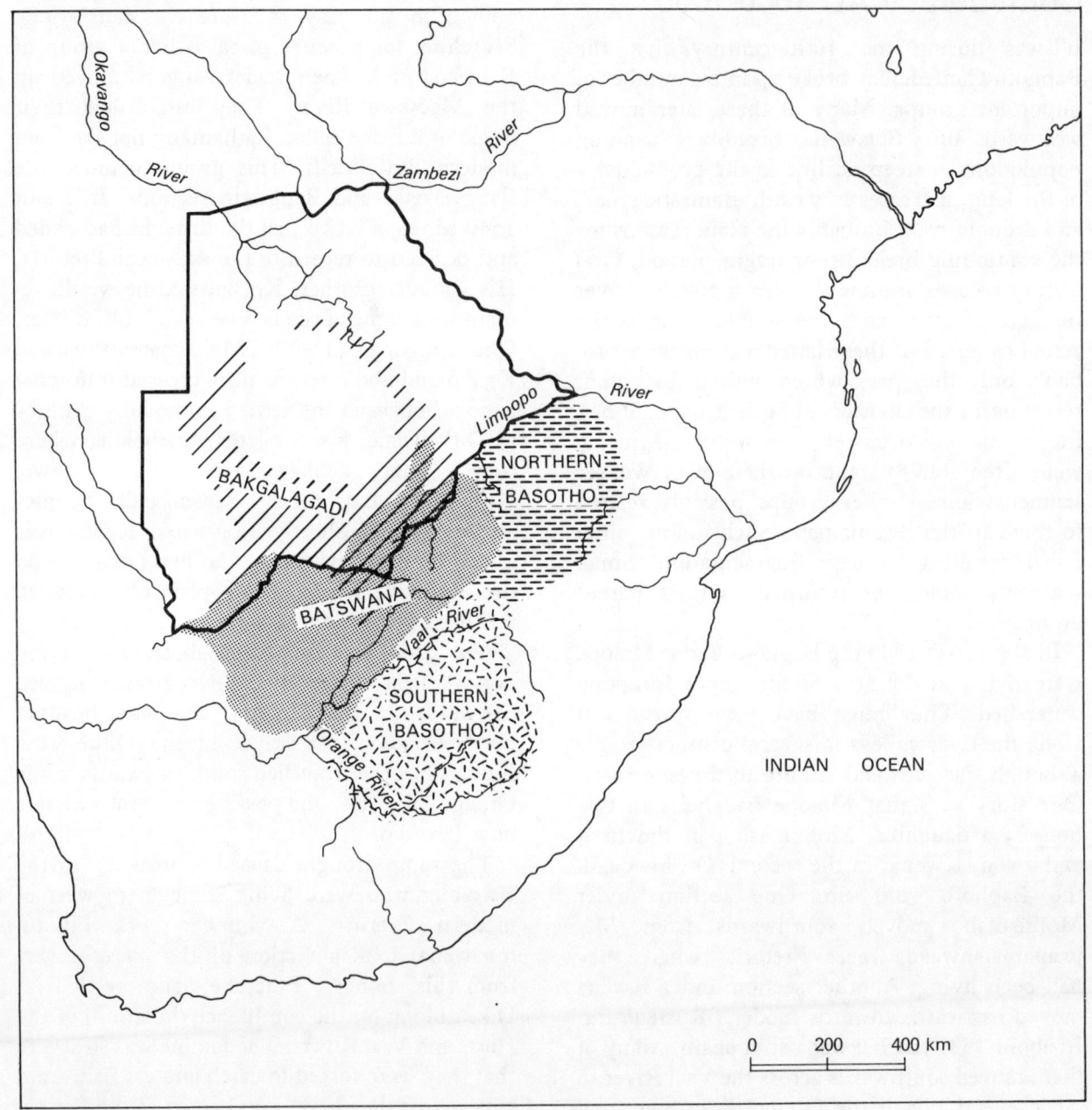

Fig. 44 Distribution of Sotho-Tswana peoples about 1750

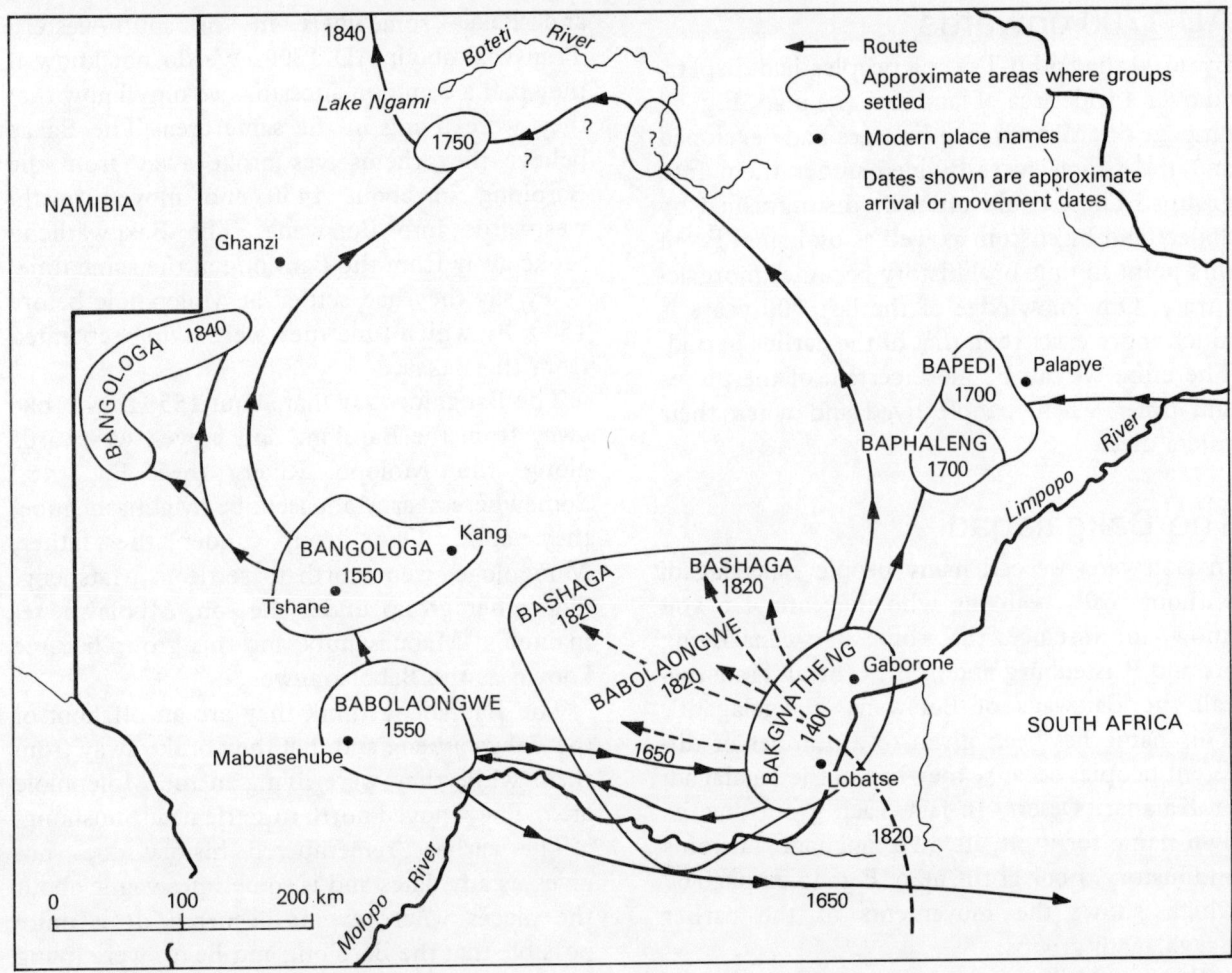

Fig. 45 Settlement of the Bakgalagadi groups

modern Batswana nations.

Early in the 17th century the Bakgatla who had been living near Rustenburg split up. First a large section under Thabane moved away to the north. Then the remainder, under his elder brother, Mogale, moved eastwards to a place north of Pretoria. Matshege, the son of Mogale, died about 1650 leaving a daughter in the first house and a son in the second. Some Bakgatla followed the daughter, Mosetlha, while others followed the son, Kgafela.

A little earlier a less important split had taken place south of the Molopo. A section of the Barolong living at Magogwe broke away and moved northwards. The Barolong said 'Ba ka ya' meaning 'They can depart', and from then they were known as the Bakaa.

The Bahurutshe also split up. A group moved north-eastwards to Shoshong and became known as the Bakhurutshe. Later they split again and moved northwards to the Shashe River.

During this same period both the Bangwaketse and the Bangwato broke away from the Bakwena. The Bangwaketse moved south-eastwards. The Bangwato moved first eastwards and then northwards.

Often these smaller groups joined together, but usually this did not last long. For a short period the Bakaa lived first with the Bakwena and then with the Bakhurutshe, but each small group sought its own independence and went its own way.

AD 1700 onwards

By 1700 the Sotho-Tswana peoples had dispersed over a wide area of land. See the map, Fig. 44 on page 66. Many strong lineages had developed and the people were divided under them into groups. These could often be distinguished by dialect and by custom as well as by name. From this point in time oral history becomes more accurate. Our knowledge of the last 300 years is much more exact than that of the earlier period. Therefore we can be more certain of the places and times where people lived and when their rulers died.

The Bakgalagadi

In Botswana we call many people Bakgalagadi without really realising who they are. Do you know, for instance, that some Batswana living around Rustenburg and in the central Transvaal call the Batswana of Botswana 'Bakgalagadi'? This name has been given to a number of different peoples because they live in the Kgalagadi or Kalahari Desert. In fact, each group has its own name for itself, its own language, customs and history. Look at the map, Fig. 45 on page 67 which shows the movements of the earlier Bakgalagadi groups.

Today there are five main groups of Bakgalagadi. These are the Bakgwatheng, Babolaongwe, Bangologa, Baphaleng and Bashaga. There is another group in the Central District, the Bapedi, but they probably have Bavenda origins and do not speak a dialect similar to those of the other groups.

The Bakgwatheng, Babolaongwe, Bangologa and Baphaleng trace their ancestry back to a common origin. The Bashaga originally lived with the Batlhaping, Batlharo and Barolong and fled into the Kalahari about the beginning of the 19th century. They joined with the Babolaongwe adopting their customs and dialect. It is possible that they were remnants of Babolaongwe groups which had been living with the southern Batswana.

The remembered history of the Bakgwatheng and Bangologa places them with the Barolong and Bakaa somewhere in the south-western Transvaal about AD 1300. We do not know if they had a common ancestor, we only know that they were living in the same area. The Bakaa believe they themselves broke away from the Barolong in about 1450 and moved north-westwards into Botswana. The Bakgwatheng broke away from the Barolong at the same time. They say they had settled at Molepolole before 1500, by which time they were living separated from the Bakaa.

The Bangologa say that about 1550 they broke away from the Barolong and moved westwards along the Molopo River. (See Fig. 46.) Somewhere near Mabuasehube (Mabuashegube) they split. One group under the father, Mongologe, went north to settle in Matsheng. The other group under the son, Mbolawe, remained at Mabuasehube and this group became known as the Babolaongwe.

The Baphaleng think they are an offshoot of the Bakgwatheng and that they broke away from them while they were living in the Molepolole area. They moved north to settle near Shoshong.

The earliest remembered history does not gives us any dates and is sometimes vague about the places where events occurred. It is quite possible that the Barolong and Bakaa were living in the south-western Transvaal long before AD 1300. Remembered history may have shortened the time which actually passed. To be more accurate we must compare remembered history with the information gained from archaeology.

The earliest pottery we have found in the south-east comes from a place near Dithejwane. It probably dates to between AD 500 and 600. Other pottery has been found in Seoke (near Lobatse), Moritsane, Broadhurst, and many other places. This pottery has many similarities, particularly a herring-bone decoration around the neck and thickened rim. We believe that it all belongs to the same tradition, that is, it was made by people who were descended from each other. Some of them may have moved away while others came to join them. But, essentially, the people living at Broadhurst in AD 1400 were descended from the same general people of

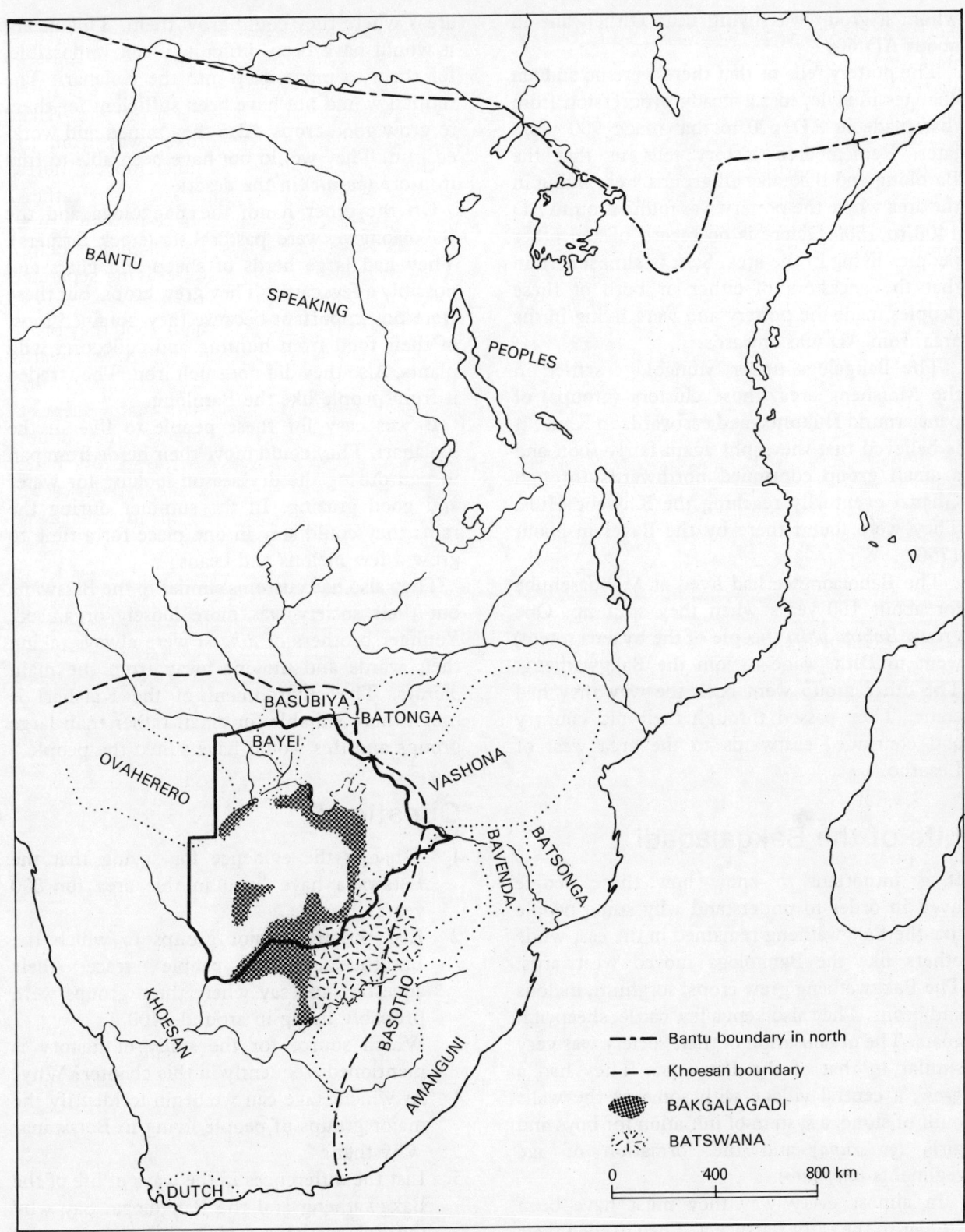

Fig. 46 Distribution of Southern African population about 1700

whom a group was living near Dithejwane in about AD 600.

The pottery tells us that there were no sudden changes in style, just a steady progression from that made in AD 600 to that made 900 years later. Remembered history tells us that the Barolong and Bakgalagadi groups were living in the area where the pottery was found around AD 1400 to 1500. There is no record of any other peoples living in the area. So it is almost certain that the ancestors of either or both of these peoples made the pottery and were living in the area from AD 600 onwards.

The Bangologa under Mongologe settled in the Matsheng area, those clusters (groups) of pans around Hukuntsi and eastwards to Kang. It is believed that they split again fairly soon and a small group continued northwards through Ghanzi eventually reaching the Khwebe Hills. They were found there by the Bayei in about 1750.

The Babolaongwe had lived at Mabuasehube for about 100 years when they split up. One group *Babina phiri* (people of the hyaena totem) went to Dithejwane to join the Bakgwatheng. The other group went back the way they had come. They passed through their old country and continued eastwards to the area west of Lesotho.

Life of the Bakgalagadi

It is important to know how these people lived in order to understand why some people like the Bakgwatheng remained in the east while others like the Bangologa moved westwards. The Bakgwatheng grew crops; sorghum, melons and beans. They also kept a few cattle, sheep and goats. The organisation of their society was very similar to that of the Batswana. They had a *kgosi*, a central village with some of the walls built of stone, a system of initiation for boys and girls (*go rupa*) and the formation of age regiments (*mephato*).

In almost every way they must have been similar to the early Batswana. They needed their crops to live and were unable to move out of areas where they could grow them. This meant it would have been difficult, if not impossible, for them to move deep into the Kalahari. The rainfall would not have been sufficient for them to grow good crops. Also they mined and worked iron. They would not have been able to find iron ore (*bogale*) in the desert.

On the other hand, the Bangologa and the Babolaongwe were pastoralists (stock farmers). They had large herds of sheep and goats and possibly a few cattle. They grew crops, but these were not important because they obtained most of their food from hunting and collecting wild plants. Also they did not smelt iron. They traded it from people like the Barolong.

It was easy for these people to live in the Kalahari. They could move their herds from pan to pan during the dry season looking for water and good grazing. In the summer during the rains they could stay in one place for a time to grow a few melons and beans.

They also had customs similar to the Batswana but their society was more loosely organised. Younger brothers of *dikgosi* were always taking their wards and moving away from the main *morafe*. The environment of the Kalahari is much more suitable for small rather than large groups and this would have suited the people.

Questions

1. What is the evidence for saying that the Batswana have lived in this area for 800 years?
2. List the five major groups to which the Basotho-Batswana people trace their ancestry, and say where these groups were probably living in around 1400.
3. Which source for the study of history is mentioned frequently in this chapter? Why?
4. At which stage can we begin to identify the major groups of people living in Botswana? Why then?
5. List the differences in the ways of life of the Bakgwatheng and the Bangologa. Say why the Bakgwatheng remained in the east, and the Bangologa moved westwards.

12 Life of the Batswana before the Difaqane

The lifestyle of different Batswana groups probably varied considerably. In wetter areas people were able to grow crops while in drier areas they depended more on hunting and collecting wild food. In drier areas they moved about following game and the ripening of plants. Such conditions favoured cattle-raising but were bad for crop production.

The Batswana living on the higher land in the east, the Bakgatla, Bahurutshe, Batlokwa, Bakwena ba ga Mogopa, grew good crops except when rains were very poor. They collected some wild plant foods and sent out hunting parties which were sometimes away for several months. They lived in larger settlements which, around AD 1500, began to include stone walls. The Batswana living in the south, the Barolong, Batlharo and Batlhaping, also relied on growing crops, but spent more time hunting than their brothers in the east. The Western Batswana, the Bakwena ba ga Kgabo, Bangwaketse, Bangwato and Batawana relied on hunting and grew a few quick crops such as beans and melons, and gathered wild plants. Their hunting grounds were very distant. The Bangwato, living near the Metsemotlhaba River, hunted in the hilly country around Serowe. By 1795, when the Batawana broke away from the Bangwato, the Bakwena hunted as far to the north-west as Lake Ngami.

Each group or *morafe* was independent of all other groups in every matter except ritual. The leader, *kgosi*, was the head of his group answerable to no other leader in terms of the law. It was only in matters of ritual, such as the

Fig. 47 A Mokwena warrior, the spear was used for throwing and the battle-axe for hand fighting

71

tasting of the first fruits at harvest time, that they recognised a superior. The son of the Hurutshe *kgosi* was the first to taste the fruits (*molomo*) showing the Bahurutshe were the senior *morafe*. Such a custom emphasised the historic relationship between the Batswana groups and the need to cooperate.

The royal family provided the rulers of the *morafe*, no commoner could take their place. If a ruler was bad, his people tended to follow and support one of his relatives until an open disagreement took place. Then the *morafe* often split with one group moving away to settle elsewhere.

The *kgosi* was to the *morafe* like the heart is to the body. He pumped the life-blood which kept the *morafe* alive. He was the leader in all things and nothing could be done without him. He brought the rain and health to the people, strengthened the army and defended the people. He administered the law and saw that every person received justice. He held much of the wealth of the *morafe* and saw that no one was in need. Although he was the leader, he was also the voice of the people. He led discussions in the *kgotla* and then summed up the general view.

The Batswana have always kept cattle. Probably, at one time nearly all the cattle were the property of royal families and common people owned few if any stock. The *kgosi* controlled the use of cattle by allowing his relatives to keep large herds. In their turn, they controlled the distribution of their stock amongst their relatives and the common people. The people knew that if they offended a royal person he might take their stock from them and give them to another. This system made sure that people obeyed their leaders. When a person allowed another the use of his stock he could expect much in return. People who received cattle herded for him, helped with agriculture, brought skins and meat, supported him in trouble, fought for him and even provided domestic service in his home. Cattle separated the rich from the poor. Those who

Fig. 48 Part of a village drawn by the traveller and artist Daniell. This type of *sefalana* (granary) is no longer made

owned cattle were rich. Those who did not own cattle had to cooperate with the rich to obtain the use of the cattle. It was impossible to live without cattle, they were needed to celebrate every important occasion, birth, initiation, marriage, health and death. The giving of cattle between members of a family or a *morafe* showed and strengthened the relationships which existed between them. The slaughtering of a beast and the communal eating of meat kept people living happily together.

The Batswana were very careful to make certain cattle never left the family. They might be lent by way of *mafisa*, but they were never given away. Even in marriage people made certain that the animals given in *bogadi* to the bride's parents never left the family. This was done by the custom of a man first marrying his mother's sister's daughter, and then his mother's brother's daughter. He knew that when his children married their cousins the cattle given for his wife would come back to him.

Social relations

Batswana *merafe* are divided by many social levels. At the centre and most important are those people who trace their ancestry back to founder (first) members. They are known by their ancestral *seboko* or praise name. Amongst the Bakwena and Bangwaketse this is 'Kwena' (crocodile). Amongst the Bangwato it is 'Phuti' (duiker). Amongst the Bakgatla ba ga Kgafela it is 'Kgabo' (monkey).

These people form the ruling class. Most important amongst them is the *kgosi* and his family. They can trace their ancestry back to the founder of the Batswana, Mogale, together with the rest of the members of their immediate group.

Next in importance come Batswana from other *merafe* who have broken away from their *kgosi* and now become members of the *morafe*. Their wards in the central village are usually placed close to those of the ruling people.

After them come people of non-Batswana *merafe*, people such as the Babirwa, Batswapong, Ovambanderu, Balozi, Amandebele, Bakalanga, etc. Historically, these peoples usually had their wards on the edge of the village, or lived in separate villages well away from the capital.

Among the Bakwena, for instance, the lowest peoples were usually the Bakgalagadi, although their position has changed from time to time depending on the circumstances of the *morafe*. During the 15th and 16th centuries, when the Bakwena were small and weak, they accepted Bakgalagadi into the *morafe* as citizens. The Batawana did the same in about 1805 when they were weak. At other times when the *morafe* has been strong the Bakgalagadi have been treated as very inferior.

Finally there were the San. These people were generally made to live away from the village and were never considered as members of the *morafe*. However they were sometimes attached to a family for whom they had to hunt, carry out domestic work, clear agricultural fields and occasionally herd cattle.

One way this class structure was maintained was through marriage. People normally married only within their own social class. In particular *dikgosi* tried to strengthen their ties with other *merafe* by marrying their daughters to their royalty. Normally a Motswana would only marry another Motswana, not someone he considered inferior to himself. However Khama III married his daughters to the royal families of the Bakaa and Batalaote to try and strengthen the *morafe*. No Motswana would marry a Mokgalagadi or a San but they might take a Mokgalagadi as a second wife when the *morafe* was weak. Normally the children of marriages and unions between Batswana and either Bakgalagadi or San were brought up as servants, (also serfs) *malata*. They never attained membership of the *morafe*. They could not inherit any of their fathers' property.

The *kgosi* was in final control of all the property in the *morafe*. The real wealth consisted of cattle and sheep which were kept in a number of common herds, usually some distance from the capital. The *kgosi* had the power to give these into the care of members of his *morafe*, both to

Fig. 49 Daniell's painting of Dithakong. Daniell was the first white man to bring pictures of Batswana to the outside world in about 1802

royalty and to common people. This system again showed clearly the different social levels since the *kgosi* had under his own control large numbers of stock. He distributed these mainly to his own relatives. They, in turn, could distribute them to their children and to members of their wards, *makgotla*. Any commoner who received cattle became important in the *morafe*.

When a ward was formed it normally consisted of the sons of a *kgosi* from one mother and families put with them to be their supporters and servants. These people were known as *batlhanka*. These *batlhanka* were ordinary members of the *morafe*, free to own cattle, keep their own homes and grow their own crops. At the same time they were expected to work for the senior families in their ward, to do domestic and agricultural labour and to support them in the affairs of the *morafe*.

All royal Batswana, many common Batswana and even some non-Batswana were entitled to the services of Bakgalagadi. Whole Bakgalagadi families were permanently attached to Batswana families and had to work for them whenever required. These people were treated extremely badly. They were not allowed to own property of their own, often not allowed to live in the same area as their masters and not allowed to marry without their consent. They were not even allowed to eat from the same food dishes after their masters had fed. They were forced to become serfs, *malata*, little better than slaves and to do anything their masters asked. They were not free to move away and could be sent to work for other Batswana. In this way Bakgalagadi families were divided and children were taken from their parents.

Traditionally, most of the Bakgalagadi lived on Bakwena land. The Bakgwatheng managed to retain some independence and grew their own crops. They moved from Molepolole to just south of Letlhakeng in the early 1800s. They wanted to win the favour of Moruakgomo, the Kwena *kgosi* who had stolen the *bogosi* from the rightful heir, Segokotlo. So in 1824 they sent some ivory to Moruakgomo. At the time he was desperate for goods to trade for guns. He wanted to arm himself for defence and to fight Segokotlo. He saw the opportunity to obtain ivory and furs and also to rid himself of the Bakgalagadi.

Moruakgomo took all the property of those Bakgalagadi who were not already serfs, *malata*, and drove them out into the Kalahari. He forced them to hunt for him. He appointed important Bakwena to keep a permanent watch on them in the desert and take from them anything they hunted. Many Bakgalagadi hid themselves deep in the desert. Eventually they learned to trade their ivory and skins with the Bateti to the north, from whom they got some stock and guns. But most of the Bakgalagadi were forced to live a desperate life in the desert, constantly being chased by Bakwena. This went on for 60 years, until they were freed by Sechele I.

Other *merafe* such as the Bangwaketse and Bangwato also treated the Bakgalagadi extremely badly, but they did not take all their property from them. Some people argue that the Bakgalagadi received many benefits from being servants of the Batswana. In fact their only benefit was protection by their masters from other Batswana who also wanted to exploit them.

A typical *morafe*

Let us look at a typical group (*morafe*) which may have existed some time during the 18th or 19th centuries. At the head was the *kgosi* with the members of his family, his brothers, uncles, cousins and children, all with their families. Attached to them were other Batswana families and numbers of people who acted as servants and were commonly known as *Batlhanka*. This was the central part of the *morafe* and was known as *kgosing*. They lived clustered together although each family and its servants occupied an area separate from other families.

A little away from this village, but still within sight, was another village very similar in layout. Here lived another group of Batswana which had left its parent group to join this one. It had its own leader and his family. However they all held a lower status than the *kgosi* and looked to him for government.

Some distance away, and possibly out of sight, was yet another village composed of Bakgalagadi, either Bakgwatheng or Babolaongwe, who worked for the Batswana. As time passed, so these villages grew larger. This was usually by the addition of other groups which joined them and then recognised their *kgosi* as their own ruler. Some of these villages grew very large with many sections or wards in them. As they grew bigger, so the *kgosi* put members of his own family into the junior sections to rule them on his behalf. By about 1800 some of these villages probably had about 10 000 inhabitants.

With the steady increase in size and wealth of these *merafe*, so the army became more and more important. The army was made up of age regiments. When the son of a *kgosi* reached about 16 years of age, the *kgosi* announced the holding of *bogwera*. This was an initiation school through which all the young men had to go. It was held every four or five years and lasted for about five months. The boys were taken into a remote place, circumcised and then taught how to behave as men. This involved learning the law, customs and history of the *morafe*, learning how to fight and cooperate with each other, learning respect for older people, and learning how to undergo great hardship. When *bogwera* finished the boys were brought to the *kgotla*, formed into a regiment (*mophato*), and given a regimental name. In future they remained in that regiment and must be available at all times

Fig. 50 *Bojale,* or female initiation. A photograph of Balete girls taken in the 1880s. The bundles of sticks were a form of test causing much discomfort and also identified the group as a whole: a kind of uniform

Fig. 51 *Bogwera* or male initiation

Fig. 52 A village painted by Burchell. Pack oxen were used for transport before sledges were introduced

for duty. Sometimes the *kgosi* called them to go hunting, to raid cattle, to clear lands, fetch reeds, build fences or even just to entertain. A little later the *kgosi* announced *bojale* and all the girls were formed into a similar regiment. They went through a similar period of training although it was neither long nor harsh. These important institutions (customs) have their origins many hundreds of years back.

In each instance it was the *kgosi's* son or daughter who became the leader of the regiment with which he or she was initiated. Thus, each regiment, was led by a son or close relative of the *kgosi*. This gave him great power over his army. For the first few years after the formation of a regiment it was kept very busy. But when a new regiment was formed, so the duties of senior regiments were relaxed and the men were allowed to marry.

Regiments spent a lot of time hunting, particularly during the winter The groups' hunting grounds could be a long way from their village. In the 18th century the Bangwato hunted in the hills around Serowe and north-westwards to the Boteti. The Bahurutshe hunted around the Nata River and the Bakwena hunted as far to the west as Lake Ngami. The Bangwaketse hunted in the Kalahari around Tshane and Kang, and the Batlharo and Barolong hunted down the Molopo westwards to Bokspits. They went equipped for a long journey, taking oxen with them to carry provisions and to bring back meat and skins. In those days there were no waggons, sledges or donkeys and everything was carried on the oxen's backs.

Hunting was generally a communal affair. Usually one or more regiments took part, although individuals and families sometimes hunted for themselves. The *kgosi* would order a hunt, *letsholo*, and say which regiments should take part in it. It was the duty of all called to take part. Anyone who did not do so might be

Fig. 53 A Motswana carrying meat. Note the sunshade

deep. This was covered with branches and earth to hide it. From it, two fences of bushes were built in the shape of a funnel. These were about a kilometre long and a kilometre wide at the mouth. The regiments surrounded or sometimes used grass fires to drive a herd or herds of game into the funnel and so into the pit (see Fig. 54, page 79). Other soldiers hid behind the fence. If any game jumped out of the pit they stabbed it with spears.

The animals killed belonged to the *kgosi* who kept or divided them as he considered best. These hunts were very important in Batswana life. The *kgosi* called them at special times, before raids and battles, during *bogwera*, and before an important meeting when he expected disagreement. Sometimes the *kgosi* called them when he and his secret advisers, the *khuduthamaga*, wished to kill someone without a public execution. The person was killed on the hunt and all knew that no questions could be asked.

The most important aspect of the *matsholo* was to unify the *morafe*, to make people cooperate with each other in a dangerous undertaking. This gave the *morafe* strength and helped the *kgosi* to make his own position as leader very clear. Such hunts were also carried out by the Bakgalagadi. Possibly amongst them they were even more important than they were to the Batswana. This was because they helped to hold together a people who did not have the same strong political organisation as the Batswana. They would stop individual families from straying far from the main group.

Boys, who had not been initiated into regiments, and servants looked after the cattle. The cattle were usually kept some distance from the village. Close to the village were the agricultural lands. The men looked for patches of loamy soil because they knew these were the most fertile. Here they cleared off brush which they burnt. When the rains came the *kgosi* gave the order to plant. Both men and women worked on the lands digging the soil and planting the seeds of sorghum, melons and beans. Often the tool they used consisted of a fairly heavy stick with a

severely punished or even killed.

Hunts were of two types. The *mephato* sometimes went out for long or short periods into areas where there were large herds of game. The soldiers slowly encircled a herd and closed in, stabbing the animals as they tried to break through the circle. This type of a hunt was often held just before a battle to make the soldiers ready for fighting. Sebego, *kgosi* of the Bangwaketse, held such a hunt just before he attacked the Bakololo at Dithubaruba (see page 106).

The other type of hunt involved a special trap called *hopo* in Sekgalagadi. Men, women and children went to a place where large herds often grazed or came to drink. Here they dug a deep hole about twelve metres wide and four metres

Fig. 54 The pit, a part of the *hopo* hunting trap drawn by Livingstone. Batswana hunted communally; many people were needed to drive the animals and dig the pit

pointed end. They did not all use metal hoes. The *kgosi* then gave the order to weed and later to harvest. Each family had to keep to this schedule, neither planting, nor weeding, nor harvesting before or after his command. In this way all people worked at the same pace and all reaped the same harvest. This was important in maintaining a happy society since no one could do better than another and no one could be idle and rely on another for help later.

For the Batswana who lived in the drier areas in the west the collection of wild food was more important than growing crops. Often they moved their villages as the soil became poor or wild food became more plentiful elsewhere. Because the men were the hunters and the herders, they were the main producers of food. They brought meat for food and skins which could be traded eastwards for grain. They also brought milk which formed an important part of their diet. The milk was soured in a skin container (*lekuka*) and called *madila*. This was brought in from the grazing areas to the central village. For much of the year they ate meat, *madila*, wild foods such as honey, fruit, roots, caterpillars, tortoises, hares, nuts, fungi and rodents, and what crops they could either grow or trade.

Because they moved often their homes were not constructed like those of the Batswana living in the east. Often their villages were built on high ground, even on the tops of hills. The houses they built when they first crossed the Ngotwane were called *mothibelafatshe*. They consisted of branches with the thick ends sunk in a circle into the ground and the thin ends bent inwards and tied together. Clumps of grass were laid over these branches and tied down with bark. Later, they built better houses known as *moraro* because of their three parts: roof, supports and walls. The roof was made of rafters, thatched and supported on poles. Under this an inner circular wall was made of bushes bound tightly together. These homes were easy to make and as easily abandoned (left) as the group moved.

Although the Western Batswana mined specularite (*sebilo*) it is not certain that they were iron miners as well. Many oral traditions say the

Bakwena and the Bangwato traded their iron from the Barolong, Balete and Batlokwa. Certainly they were great skin workers. They collected the skins of the animals they hunted and made all their dependants and *batlhanka* bring them the skins of fur-bearing animals such as jackal, fox, genet and caracal. Skins of lion, leopard and cheetah belonged to the *kgosi* who paid the man who brought them with a calf or sheep. An important part of a man's life was spent in sewing skins into blankets. This was something which he might do in the *kgotla*. These fur blankets were traded with the Bakgothu for sheep and with other Batswana for iron, and possibly grain.

The Western Batswana of 200 or more years ago had an ordered society. The *kgosi* ruled on behalf of the people. He brought the rain and health. He controlled all the property through a complicated system of politics and relationships, both of blood and servitude. He controlled the activities of the year; planting, weeding, harvesting and hunting. He organised the army and ordered its activities. Everybody knew their exact position in society, what they should do at any time and even who they should marry. Such a system ensured that the rich remained rich and the poor remained poor. It also meant that the political structure remained virtually the same, as nobody could fight to change it.

Questions

1 List the rights and duties of the *kgosi*, as described in this chapter.
2 Describe the main social levels found in a Batswana *morafe*.
3 Imagine you are writing to a friend in another country. Try to describe the main features of Batswana traditional life as it was 200 years ago.

13 Origins of the Bakalanga

The Torwa period

It is impossible today to sort out all the early history of the peoples who call themselves Bakalanga. There is little doubt the ancestors of some of them have lived in the area of the upper Shashe River for more than a thousand years. It is very probable that some of their ancestors come from the Toutswe and Mambo peoples who occupied a part of eastern Botswana as early as AD 800. During the 600 years between 1300 and 1900 so many changes took place and so many immigrants arrived, that it is now difficult to separate one group from another.

During the period from about AD 1100 to 1840 three separate states or kingdoms emerged in what is today called the Republic of Zimbabwe. Each of these states overlapped into Botswana. The first of these was Great Zimbabwe (see page 54). The second state was formed in about 1450 under a dynasty of rulers known as the Torwa and lasted until 1680. The third state was that of the Barozvi which was destroyed in 1840. These latter states probably had even more influence on north-eastern Botswana than the Zimbabwe State.

Soon after 1400 the Zimbabwe State began to lose its power. This was probably because the land was over-used and crops, grazing, wildlife and firewood were declining. Suddenly, Khami in the west, situated close to modern Bulawayo, began to increase in power. It became far more important than Great Zimbabwe in the east. Exactly what happened is unknown. Perhaps a district governor became so rich he was able to take the control away from Great Zimbabwe. Perhaps the king at Great Zimbabwe moved to Khami or some of his senior people went to establish an opposition state. Whatever happened, Khami became powerful because of its location (place). It is in the centre of some of the best grazing lands and richest gold reefs on the Southern African plateau.

In many ways Khami was a continuation of the Zimbabwe State. The whole country was ruled by the Torwa Kings from Khami. 'Torwa' means 'foreigner' in Chikaranga (a Chishona dialect spoken in south-eastern Zimbabwe and different from Tjikalanga spoken in the west). The name emphasises the way they ruled. The general population continued to support themselves as they had in the past, mainly by growing crops, hunting, collecting wild food and keeping some stock. The Torwa were like colonial rulers. They established their homes throughout the country, but held themselves above the general population.

They remained a close-knit society marrying only amongst themselves. Their magnificent homes were built mainly on hills and rocky outcrops. Like the Zimbabwe villages, their homes consisted of enclosures built of stones. The walls were highly decorated, the stones being laid in herring-bone, chevron-shaped (v-shaped) and check patterns. Within the enclosures were massive homes with elaborate courtyards sometimes mounted on artificial platforms. Clay *daga* was used for wall and courtyard

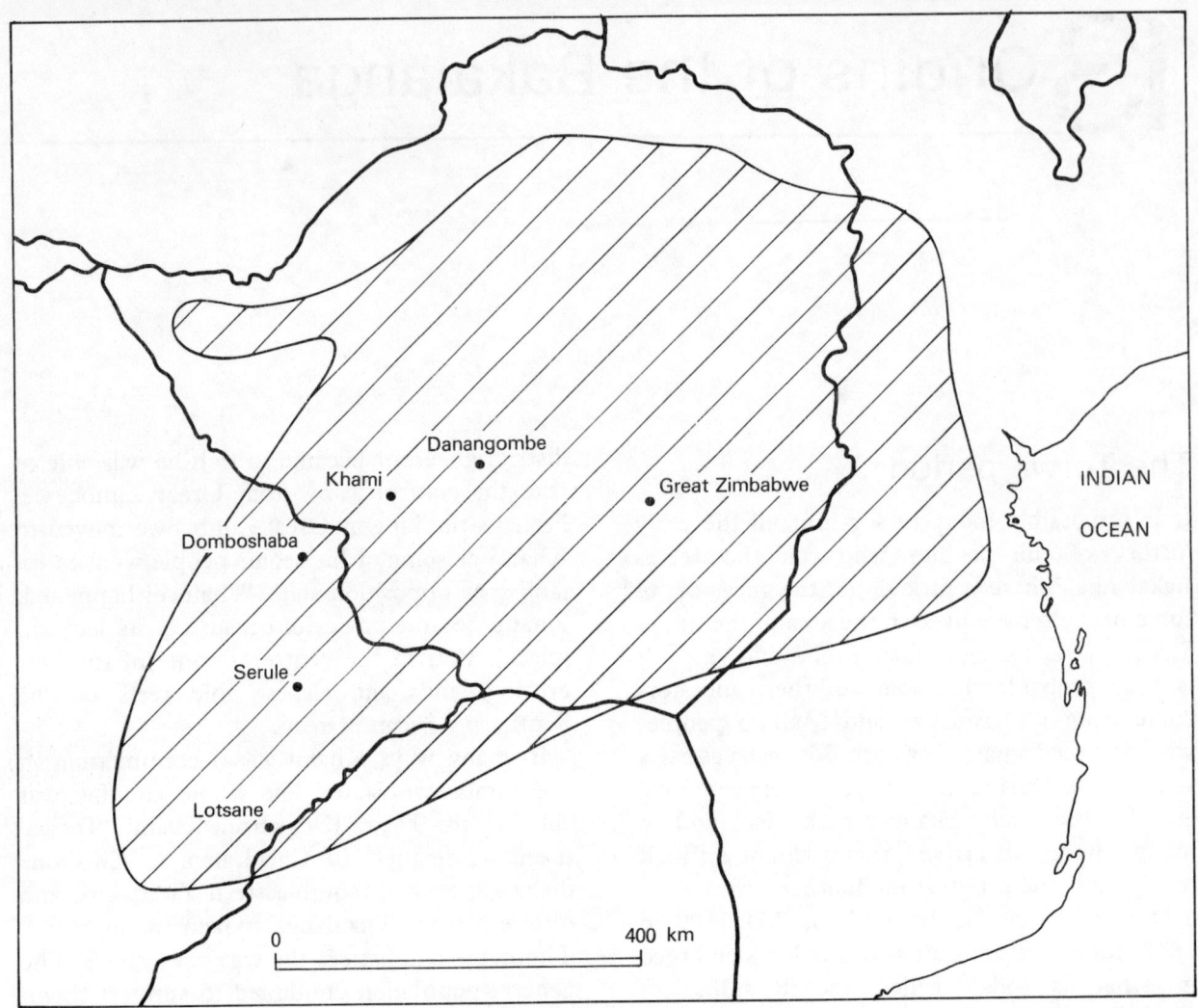

Fig. 55 The approximate limits of the Torwa State about 1550

construction. These interior walls were often very thick and beautifully moulded. The houses were round or oval with a diameter of up to eight or nine metres (see Fig. 56, page 83).

The Torwa rulers or district governors were each known as *mambo*. They wore woven robes made of spun cotton sometimes dyed blue, and jewellery made of gold, copper and ivory. Beads imported from the coast and coming from Europe and India as well, were common, so were sea shells. There were local dishes made of soapstone and beautiful decorated clay pots. Ceramic bowls from as far away as China and glass from Persia could also be found.

They lived in great splendour and had many servants. The men spent much of their time in special meeting places adjoining their homes. Their wives had similar buildings a little below and closely connected to the men's.

They controlled most of the cattle and all the trade in the area, and so had all the wealth. The local population was expected to work in the mines digging gold, copper and iron. They were also expected to forge tools and jewellery, spin cloth, bring in skins and ivory from their hunting and pay regular tribute in grain and stock. In addition, they had to build the beautiful homes of their masters and be ready to serve

Fig. 56 Naletale, a Khami-type settlement inhabited about 1500 to 1650. It is well known as the most highly decorated settlement: note the designs

them at any time.

Some of the produce of the area was sent by the *mambo* to the king at Khami where it was sorted. From here gold, ivory, copper, furs, precious woods and possibly slaves were sent to the coast in exchange for glass beads, sea shells, ceramics, glass and dyed cloth. These district governors controlled the Bakalanga although the latter had their own system of traditional leaders. The *mambo* probably took little interest in local affairs provided work was done and sufficient cattle, gold, grain and other goods were produced.

The remains of their homes have been found at many places in eastern Botswana. The best known are at Leswingo, Vukwe and Serule although many others exist stretching from the confluence of the Lotsane and Limpopo Rivers along the Shashe and Motloutse Rivers to west of the railway line. Their influence on the area must have been considerable. They controlled nearly all major trade to the area a little south of modern Mahalapye.

At first they had little to do with the local population. As time went by they became more and more involved with them and, in doing so, began to lose their rigid control. By the 1680s their language was Tjikalanga, the same as that spoken by the people they had ruled. By 1650 gold was becoming much more difficult to find and the population had grown. Probably the same droughts which had helped to split the Batswana in the south affected the lands of the Torwa. Much of their means for obtaining wealth had gone. So in 1683 they were easily conquered by the Varozvi.

The Varozvi

The Torwa were defeated without much fighting. The name 'Varozvi' means 'Destroyers'. They came from the north-east, from the headwaters of the Hunyani River. Like the Torwa, they were also descendants of the original rulers at Great Zimbabwe. Their king *(changamire)* moved the capital from Khami northwards to Danangombe (now known as Dlhodlho) some 120 kilometres away.

They occupied the old Torwa homes. Then, to make sure they kept their new power, they married into the Torwa families. They, in turn, began to speak Tjikalanga. The new rulers probably never managed to become as wealthy as the Torwa. They never established any new stonewall capitals although they may have extended the ones they took over. The move to Danangombe, about three days' journey further from the Botswana border, meant that they lost some of their power in Botswana. By 1696, the *changamire* had spread his control over much of modern Zimbabwe. But his army was drawn only from Varozvi families, common people were not recruited. As a result, the *changamire* had little strength. It was not long before his sons were fighting each other for parts of his huge kingdom. Realising they had little real power, the Varozvi used others to do their ruling for them. In the first place, they allowed the Torwa to continue to carry out the general administration of their areas. This probably involved making people work, keeping the peace and obtaining goods as tribute for trade. Like the Torwa, the Varozvi let the Bakalanga hereditary rulers, *vaishe*, govern their own people.

Fig. 57 Majojo, the Khami-type settlement is at Serule in Botswana. Note the blocked doorway and herring-bone designs

Although they allowed others to rule for them, the Varozvi insisted on three things in order to keep control.
1. They had to approve all new rulers. Sometimes they chose a ruler who was not the heir if they thought he would be more loyal to them.
2. They allocated (gave out) all land.
3. They collected all tribute from the original district governors' homes.

At first they were successful, but gradually they lost their control. This was because many Vakaranga started to move into the area from eastern Zimbabwe and there were big increases in population. Also the gold trade had declined and some of the traditional population moved away to look for more fertile land.

As control slackened, so more and more immigrants began to arrive. Babirwa crossed the Limpopo from Nareng in the northern Transvaal, settling on the lower Shashe and Motloutse. Bakhurutshe came northwards from Shoshong to settle first at Serowe and then on the upper Shashe. Groups of Bapedi, Balete and Batswapong crossed through the tsetse areas of the upper Limpopo and settled around the Tswapong Hills. Even Bavenda from the northern Transvaal began to work their way up the Limpopo and Shashe Rivers. At first the Varozvi tried to protect their Bakalanga subjects. But after a while they helped whichever group they thought would help them. Sometimes they helped Bakalanga against the immigrants and sometimes the reverse.

All these movements had a great effect on the Bakalanga. With loss of Varozvi power, so Batswana *merafe* like the Bakaa and Bakhurutshe, began to rule the Bakalanga. In some instances the Batswana absorbed the Bakalanga. In others the Bakalanga absorbed small groups of Babirwa, Bapedi and even Barolong.

By 1835 the Bakalanga consisted of many different peoples who had come to live with the original inhabitants and now spoke their language and practised their customs. There was no longer any single powerful leader although people such as Ndumba had many followers. A succession of invasions between 1830 and 1840 finally broke the Varozvi power.

The Varozvi were attacked first by two separate groups which had been chased from their homes during the wars of the Difaqane (see Chapter 15). First came Mpanga's Basotho (people from the area of modern Swaziland) and then Ngwamamaseko's Amanguni from the south. Both were defeated, but the Varozvi army was badly damaged.

Next came Zwangendaba with another Amanguni army. After the battle he moved northwards and settled near modern Harare. But he returned to attack again before he finally crossed the Zambezi in 1835.

Next the Varozvi were attacked by Nyamazana, Zwangendaba's cousin. Her first attack was beaten off, but she returned, this time attacking the capital at Danangombe. The *changamire* was driven from his home and killed. Nyamazana left the Varozvi State intact, but without a leader.

Finally the end came for the Varozvi in 1838-40 with the arrival of the Amandebele. Without a leader and their army broken they were unable to resist the Amandebele army. The first to arrive was a section under Gundwane who settled in the country of Ndumba, one of the stronger Bakalanga leaders. In 1840 Mzilikazi came from the north-west with the remainder of the army. He systematically drove the Bakalanga and the Bakhurutshe out of the country. They fled south to the lands of the Bangwato. This left the area of the headwaters of the Shashe River more or less unoccupied.

The Varozvi appointed a new *changamire* and made one last effort to regain power. In about 1850 they rose against the Amandebele but were totally defeated. The Bakalanga had no powerful leaders. They had lived under colonial rule for 600 years. On the defeat of the Varozvi they simply changed one master for another. The Amandebele allowed the Bakalanga rulers to continue to look after their own people.

Mzilikazi claimed all the land in the north stretching southwards to the Motloutse River. The Bangwato claimed all the southern lands stretching northwards to the Ramokgwebane. Neither Khama of the Bangwato nor Mzilikazi of the Amandebele was anxious to start a war over the land they both claimed. Slowly the Bakalanga began to return and re-establish themselves on the Shashe. They were forced to pay tribute to Mzilikazi and some of the young men were taken for his army. Khama also sent his tax collectors to the area and they paid tribute to him as well.

The Bakalanga have probably lived in the same area for a thousand years. For the last 600 years they were ruled by foreigners. Each set of rulers kept to themselves at first, but finally they married into the Bakalanga society and adopted their language. Although Bakalanga leadership has always been weak, the society must have been strong. Nearly all the immigrant groups who came to live with the Bakalanga slowly adopted their language and customs. The Bakalanga culturally conquered their conquerors.

Bakalanga life about 1700

The Bakalanga were agriculturalists growing many crops in their fertile lands. They also kept cattle, sheep and goats. They did not live in large villages but in small interrelated settlements around a particular landmark such as a hill, a valley, a small river or a clearing in the forest.

Bakalanga rulers were hereditary, the eldest son inheriting from his father, but they had little real power as they were all governed by the Varozvi. The Varozvi kept their power over the Bakalanga in two ways. Their God, Mwari or Mwali, was the creator of earth and life. He brought the rain to make crops grow. The Varozvi appointed the priests of Mwari and so controlled the rain that watered Bakalanga crops. They also approved a Mukalanga ruler by giving him black beads of symbolic power which came from Mwari. If they did not want the traditional successor as the new ruler, they gave the beads to someone else whom they thought would cooperate with them.

Amongst the Bakalanga it was not the nation which was important, but the community living together. Because they were ruled by the Varozvi, Bakalanga rulers had little power. They were unable to unite their people or even to form their own army. These communities consisted of interrelated families, which owned all the arable land, and foreigners who had joined them and been given rights to use some of the land. To gain control in a community a man and his family married only into families which owned land adjoining their own. Often a man would marry not just one wife from such a family but two or even three. As a family became powerful through ownership of land, so the community established a shrine to the family ancestor on the land. The whole community recognised the power of this shrine. They carried out ceremonies at the shrine to ensure health and happiness. In this way, it was the heads of land-owning families who held the real power amongst the Bakalanga, not the traditional rulers.

The Bakalanga used property and rights as means of gaining control in their own families and communities. When a man received the *loola* (bridewealth) for his daughter, he divided it amongst his relatives giving it to those whom he thought would give him the strongest support in return. The same happened when a man died. His heir divided the property and gave it to those from whom he needed help. The division of property was never final. There were always arguments which could result in property being redivided. However, communities were generally strengthened by these arguments rather than divided.

Powerful families had another way of securing support. If a man was too poor to give *loola* for his wife he went to live permanently at her parents' home. When his children were born they belonged to their grandfather. The grandfather sometimes gave the man one of his daughters so that when she married the man could take the bridewealth. He could use it to obtain another wife, but he could never use it for his first wife and so free himself.

Let us try to imagine how the Bakalanga lived about 200 years ago. At the centre was the Murozvi and his family, living in splendour in a village on a hill. It had stone walls and large homes built with thick *daga* walls. The Murozvi controlled the many small settlements of Bakalanga living around him, through the hereditary rulers. This control mainly consisted of collecting tribute. This was used to provide the Varozvi with many cattle, an easy life and goods to trade for imported articles such as dyed cloth, beads and ceramic dishes from Asia and Europe.

A Mukalanga ruler sometimes had many small communities under him, but his control of them was not strong. His power came from his right to collect tribute for the Varozvi and his right to settle disputes over property. He had no real rights over land, these were held by the communities themselves.

These communities were the centre of Bakalanga life. They consisted of up to 20 or 30 families all living within sight of each other. Each family owned a few livestock which were kraaled every night in the settlement and herded during the day. Wherever land for agriculture could be found it was cleared. Because iron for making tools was difficult to obtain these lands were often small. Both men and women worked on the lands growing sorghum, millet, several varieties of pumpkins and melons, cow-peas, beans, roots and sweet reed. The men spent much time hunting in the winter. They particularly hunted elephant since they had to provide their Varozvi masters with a yearly supply of ivory.

By this time most of the gold in the area had been mined. Only a few families worked in the mines during the winter to obtain gold for the Varozvi. Each community also had its blacksmith. There was no secret about iron-working. The furnaces, *zhamba* and *tjida*, were built in sheltered places but anybody including women and children could watch. Usually people dug their own ore, sometimes bringing it from a great distance on ox-back. The iron ore, *monkula*, was given to the smith who smelted it in

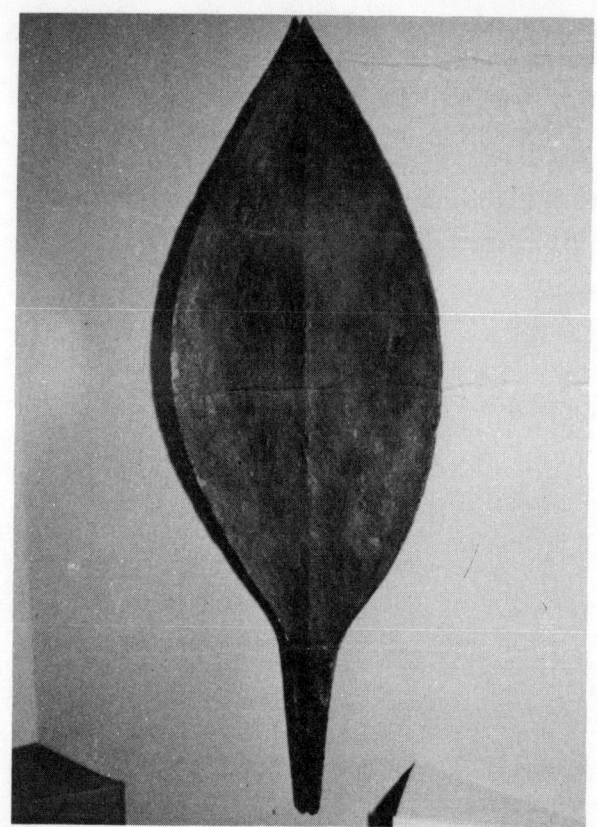

Fig. 58 A Tjikalanga marriage hoe (height 540 mm). These hoes were used as bridewealth and symbolically represented the agricultural potential of the bride

his *zhamba* using a goatskin bellows, *imvuto*, and then fashioned it in his *tjida*.

Marriage hoes were made by the blacksmith. They were huge iron hoes, made in two pieces and then fired together with ground slag, *zhaya*. Often a part of the *loola* consisted of a number of these big hoes. They were given to replace, to some extent, the agricultural work the bride would have performed in her own home.

When men were not working in the fields, or hunting, or mining, they spent much of their time sitting in the family or community meeting place discussing the distribution of property. If these arguments could not be settled locally, they were taken to the local ruler, *ishe*, who tried to settle them. He would often settle them to his own advantage.

The Bakalanga had no army and looked to the Varozvi, their masters, to defend them. Because they had no strength of their own they were unable to stop the large numbers of immigrants who entered their country. All they could do was to bind the immigrants to them so as to increase their own local power.

Questions

1 Describe briefly the home of a Torwa *mambo*.
2 List the various groups of foreigners who ruled the Bakalanga. What evidence is there that the Bakalanga society was strong?
3 Write briefly about the life lived by the Bakalanga using the following headings.
   (a) Leadership
   (b) Communities
   (c) Hunting
   (d) Mining

14 Northern Botswana 1600-1850

Northern and north-western Botswana have always been cut off from the eastern parts of the country by wide areas of waterless country and the forests which spread south from Zimbabwe and were once infested by tsetse fly. The history of eastern Botswana is closely linked with that of Zimbabwe and South Africa. The history of the north is linked to Zambia and the middle Zambezi area.

Although much of the north is covered by Kalahari sands, there are three great river systems which flow into it from the north. The

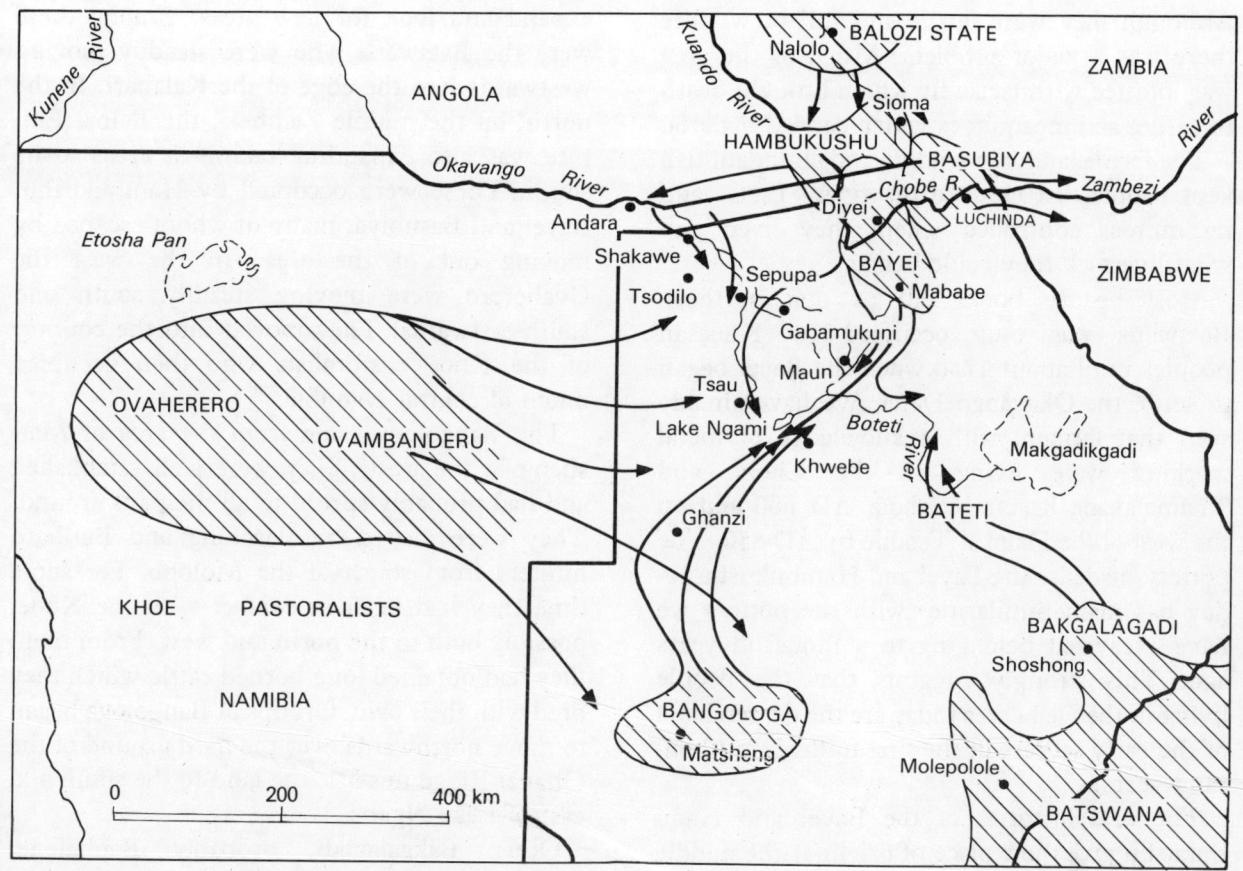

Fig. 59 Northern Botswana about 1750

most important of these for Botswana are the Okavango and Chobe. The Zambezi merely touches Botswana at Kazungula. Even so, before colonial powers drew lines on maps to divide Africa into many separate countries, the Zambezi system formed a part of the homeland of the peoples who now live in northern Botswana.

These large waterways, which spread out in places to form lakes, swamps, flood plains and the Okavango Delta, provided a very different type of country to that of eastern Botswana. These large areas of water rose and fell with the floods caused by the annual rains. They contained many areas of fertile land and carried huge populations of fish and water animals such as hippopotamus, lechwe (*letswee*), sitatunga (*naakong*) and crocodile. During times of the year when there was no rain many other animals such as elephant and buffalo came from the surrounding country to live on the river banks. Although they were fertile and full of wildlife there was a major problem. Much of the area was infested with tsetse fly which brought death to cattle, and mosquitoes which carried malaria.

The fertile land, the wildlife and abundant fish kept people tied close to the river. Tsetse and mosquitoes controlled where they lived and what livestock they could keep.

Most history books tell us that northern Botswana was only occupied by Khoesan peoples until about 1750 when the Bayei began to settle the Okavango Delta. We have already seen that farmers with a knowledge of metal working were living on the Chobe and Thamalakane Rivers by about AD 600 and on the west of the Delta at Tsodilo by AD 850. The pottery made by the Bayei and Hambukushu today has many similarities with the pottery we have excavated belonging to a thousand years ago. This strongly suggests that the people living in the Delta area today are the descendants of the early settlers of the first millenium (thousand years).

The oral histories of the Bayei and Hambukushu give their place of origin as the middle Zambezi and Chobe areas. This appears to contradict the archaeological evidence. However, it is possible that the ancestors of the Bayei and Hambukushu did live in northern Botswana in the remote past and then moved back into the Zambezi/Chobe area, perhaps during the 14th or 15th centuries. Later we will see there is some evidence for this.

In northern Botswana there were a number of unrelated groups of people. There were San foragers who lived in small camps throughout the area. There were Khoe pastoralists who kept cattle and sheep and lived on the Boteti, Nchabe and Okavango Rivers. The Hambukushu, Bayei and Basubiya lived in the Zambezi/Chobe area. The Ovaherero lived in what is now called Namibia. The Bangologa lived in the Matsheng area of the Kalahari and the Batswana lived in the south-east.

There was a great increase in population by about 1500 and then a series of droughts. Because of this many populations began to expand and look for new areas. Among these were the Batswana who were steadily moving westwards into the edge of the Kalahari. In the north, on the middle Zambezi, the Balozi Empire was also expanding taking in areas to its south. These were occupied by Hambukushu, Bayei and Basubiya, many of whom escaped by moving out of the area. In the west the Ovaherero were moving steadily south and south-eastwards. They moved into the country of the Khoe pastoralists who then occupied much of central Namibia.

The Bangologa came from the area of Matsheng in the west. They were well established and had probably spread to all the pans around. They were visited by Barolong and Batlharo hunters from south of the Molopo. For some time they had been in contact with the Khoe, possibly both to the north and west. From them they had obtained long-horned cattle which they bred with their own. Groups of Bangologa began to move northwards over the hard ground of the Ghanzi Ridge to settle the land to the south and east of Lake Ngami.

Other Bakgalagadi, probably Baphaleng, began to leave the country around Shoshong and to head north-westwards towards the Boteti

River. Here they found the cattle-owning Khoe, the Bateti, with whom they settled. Years later they were joined by Bashaga, another Bakgalagadi group, who had followed the edge of the desert northwards from the rocky country around Molepolole.

The Bakgalagadi probably learned from the Bateti how to build fences along the bank of a river leaving gaps in places where wild animals came to drink. Here they dug deep holes in which they put sharp sticks facing upwards. They covered the holes with branches, grass and earth so that animals coming to drink stepped on the covering. They fell through and were stabbed in the pit below.

Ovaherero and Ovambanderu

The Ovaherero and their cousins the Ovambanderu were true pastoralists. They kept large herds of cattle, sheep and goats, but did not grow any crops at all. Today most of them live in Namibia, but there are also many Ovaherero and particularly Ovambanderu living in Botswana.

Fig. 60 Omuherero woman in Botswana today making the staple food, *omaere,* a type of sour milk

They have two stories which explain their origin. The first tells how they once lived in a country, to the north-east of their present home, a country full of water and wide reedbeds. This country was called the Reed Land, *Ehi raruu*. Even then the Ovaherero owned large herds. For some reason connected with these, perhaps because of the spread of tsetse fly, some of them, under Huru, the son of Mangava, decided to leave their home and travel south-west. Eventually they reached the open plains of northern Namibia. The second story tells of an *omumboronbongo* tree which grew near the Etosha Pan. Out of this tree came Mukuru, the first man, bringing wild animals, cattle and sheep.

Historians believe the Ovaherero crossed the Okavango River and settled in Namibia about 1500. They were once closely associated with the Ovambo who live just to their north. However, the Ovambo are agriculturalists and the Ovaherero are pastoralists. Perhaps it was their different ways of life which caused the groups to separate. Soon after the arrival of the Ovaherero in Namibia they were followed by the Ovambanderu. They are also pastoralists with similar customs and language to the Ovaherero. The Ovaherero immediately fought the Ovambanderu, taking most of their cattle. Another party of Ovambanderu coming from the north joined the first group and they moved eastwards to settle near the present Botswana border.

During the 17th century these people increased their herds and started to spread southwards. They spread into the lands of the Nama, a Khoe people with large herds of sheep. Droughts and steady increases in population caused them to move eastwards and southeastwards trying to avoid the lands of the Nama. We do not know when they entered Botswana, but some of them were grazing their cattle on the western shores of Lake Ngami by the end of the 18th century. Others had crossed the Ghanzi Ridge and were living at Monnyelatsela when Sebego's Bangwaketse found them there in the 1830s. Others moved even further south and eventually settled in the Tshabong area at places such as Omaweneno.

Today most Ovaherero and Ovambanderu live a settled life, but this was not so in the past. Traditionally, the nation was divided into *oruzo* or religious clans. All men belonged to an *oruzo* of which there were about 20. Each *oruzo* was headed by a leader/priest who was the wealthiest man in the clan. All families belonging to one *oruzo* lived close together. Their homes were made of large branches with the thick ends buried in a circle in the ground and then the ends bent inwards and tied. Other branches were tied round these and then the whole structure was coated with a mixture of clay and cow dung. These huts were built by the women. The leader/priest was always very wealthy. He owned many cattle (sometimes more than a thousand) and sheep. He also managed a huge herd of cattle which belonged to the *oruzo*. This herd could only be used for the benefit of its members.

The Ovaherero were ancestor worshippers. They believed that all trouble was brought by their dead relatives. Only the leader/priest could sacrifice to the ancestors and this had to be done at the grave. Consequently, they knew the names of their ancestors and the position of their graves going back for more than 200 years.

The leader/priest was also the only person who could light the holy fire and his eldest daughter was the only person who could look after it. This holy fire was a gift of Mukuru, the first ancestor, and had to be kept lighted. All decisions were taken at the holy fire. If the decision was important, then a beast was killed and an offering to the ancestors made beside the fire. If a man wanted to set up a village of his own, he had to obtain living coals (coals which were alight) from the leader/priest's fire.

Everybody also belonged to another social group called an *eanda*. There were six *omaanda*. No man could marry a wife who belonged to the same *eanda* as himself. Also, when he died, all his livestock were inherited by his brothers from the same mother, not by his own children.

When the leader/priest died, between 50 and 100 cattle were killed over a period of a month or more and the skulls piled on his grave. Once the funeral was finished, the village was abandoned and the holy fire carried to a new pasture where a new village was built.

Men spent most of their time looking after the cattle and sheep. The village huts were placed in a circle inside which were kraals for the calves and lambs. The herds were bedded down next to the village at night. The men also went out hunting using heavy bows and arrows, spears and traps. They had no iron except what they could trade from the Batswana in the east, so their spears were made of wood.

The women went out collecting wild food, milked the cows and prepared *omaere*, a type of sour milk which was their main food (see Fig. 60, page 91). They lived on this milk, the game they could kill, cattle when they died or were sacrificed, and wild plants.

When the first European travellers met the Ovaherero and Ovambanderu they found that, as well as those who owned cattle and lived in large villages, there were many small groups who owned no livestock. They lived by hunting and collecting. The Europeans believed that these people had lost their livestock to the Nama who often raided them. Such small groups would live like the San for long periods until they could raid livestock and start to build their own small herds again.

The peoples of the river

Probably the most important farming peoples to live in northern Botswana during early times were the Bayei, Hambukushu, and Basubiya. These peoples came from Central Africa and at some time in the remote past made their way down the Zambezi River. They may have occupied parts of northern Botswana for a thousand years or more.

Little archaeological work has been done in northern Botswana so most of our information has come from oral history. This means that the time taken for events to occur may have been shortened.

Sometime before 1600, a group of people known as the Aluwi (later called Balozi) were pushed down the upper Zambezi. They settled on the wide flood plains north of Katima-mulilo in what is now western Zambia. They began to build a strong nation by gathering all the peoples they found already living there and developing their skills in agriculture, boat building, fishing, hunting and metalwork. By about 1700 they had become very powerful. They had also begun to expand southwards again looking for more people to take into their state.

Meanwhile, to the south of the Chobe River another movement had started to take place. About 1600 the Bayei and Basubiya (who call themselves the Bekuhane) were living together in the area of the Mababe. The Hambukushu were living just to their north. According to tradition an argument arose over the ownership of a lion skin. This skin belonged to the greatest leader and showed his importance. The Bayei fought the Basubiya and were conquered. They moved to the Linyanti River and settled the lands of Ngasa. They established a capital at Diyei. The Basubiya moved to the Chobe River and established their capital at Luchindo (which is near the modern bridge at Ngoma). They called this land Itenge. The Basubiya grew very powerful. Their state stretched westwards to the Okavango and included the Bayei. It stretched northwards to Siomo, eastwards to the country of the Batonga who lived to the east of the Victoria Falls, and southwards to Nunga where tsetse fly infested the forest.

By about 1680 the Balozi had spread their state southwards. They did this mainly by allowing royal relatives to take control of weaker peoples living on the borders of the state. One royal relative who did this was Mwanambinyi. He went south in about 1680 and conquered the Basubiya, Hambukushu and northern Bayei.

The Bayei, who now had two masters, the Basubiya and the Balozi, began to move southwards into Botswana. Small parties moved down the waterways following the Magqwegana River to the Okavango Delta. Then they moved south-eastwards towards the Boteti and Lake Ngami. Others drove their small herds of cattle overland, avoiding areas of tsetse fly, to meet at Toteng. One of the early migrants, Hankuzi, married the daughter of a Bakakhwe (Khoe) leader. This formed a friendship between the Bayei and the Bakakhwe who already kept cattle in the area.

In about 1720 the Balozi king or *litunga*, Ngalama, had managed to spread his power through the kingdom. He asked for much more tribute and wanted vassals (people who worked almost as slaves). They were needed to build the earth mounds on which the Balozi constructed their villages on the flood plain. By about 1750 Ngalama's successor, Ngombela, controlled the whole of the Zambezi/Chobe area and ruled it with a hand of iron. Soon most of the Bayei had fled southwards and were living in the Okavango Delta. Groups of Hambukushu began to move westwards to the Kuando River. Some Hambukushu, the Hamashi, stayed behind and became a part of the Balozi State, but most of them left. Even at Kuando they were not safe as the Balozi came after them, so they then travelled far to the west. Eventually they settled on the Okavango River near modern Andara. Even here they were not safe however. They were visited by Mambari or Ovimbundu traders from the northern Angolan coast. Many of these Mambari traders were the sons of Portuguese men and African women. They came to trade old guns for ivory and slaves. The Hambukushu leaders became greedy and tried to sell some of their own people to the Mambari. Soon the Hambukushu left their leaders and travelled down the Okavango River to settle the whole area as far south as Seronga, Gabamukuni and Sepopa.

The Basubiya had a fairly strong political organisation under a central leader. This kept the group united and helped them to conquer

Fig. 61 A *mokoro* in the Okavango Delta. This form of river transport opened up the region to black hunters and fishermen

other, less well-organised, peoples.

The Balozi state had reached a peak under its great ruler, Mulambwa, when he died in 1830. Arguments started as to who should succeed him. While these were in progress the Balozi were attacked by the Bakololo of Sebitoane (see page 106). The Bakololo easily defeated the Balozi (whom they called Barotse). Then they turned on the Basubiya defeating them also. Although the Basubiya were allowed to keep their leaders they became a part of the new Balozi Empire and remained so until the fall of the Bakololo in 1865.

The Basubiya, Bayei and Hambukushu had many customs in common showing they had lived together. The main one was the custom of a man inheriting both his position and wealth through his mother's brother. These were all river peoples although each had a different way of life to the others. This helped each of them to live in a slightly different type of country.

The Basubiya

The Basubiya were mainly agriculturalists although they kept a few cattle and some sheep and goats. The hoed the wide flood plains in autumn and then waited for the winter flood. After it had passed they planted their crops, mostly millet, sweet reed and melons, in the wet soil. By the time the rains came their crops were tall and it was rare for them to suffer from drought. They were also great fishermen and travelled through the shallow water in their *mekoro* (canoes, see Fig. 61, page 94). The men hunted, usually by chasing wildlife into the water and then driving their *mekoro* close to the swimming animals and stabbing them with spears.

The Bayei

The Bayei were also agriculturalists. They owned a few livestock and also hoed the flood plains like the Basubiya. Their political organisation was not nearly as strong as that of the Basubiya. This meant there was no central control to keep them in one place. They had many minor leaders

Fig. 62 A Seyei fish basket

each of whom had a number of villages under his control. These villages were often very temporary. Huts were made of a few poles dug into the ground, the spaces between them being filled with reeds. The roof consisted of a number of woven reed mats which were laid over bent sticks tied to the walls. Often large groups rolled up their mats, put all their property in their *mekoro* and moved through the waterways of the Okavango Delta to remote islands. There they spent several months hunting, catching fish and collecting wild food. They particularly liked the bulb of the water-lily, *tswii*, and the old stems of papyrus, *koma*.

The Bayei liked to live in areas of shallow water, particularly where there were narrow waterways and many flood plains. They stood up to push their *mekoro* along the channels and through the reeds using a long pole. They fished in shallow water using two main techniques. The first involved building a long fence, *nteta*, made of very thin sticks tied tightly together and reaching from the bottom to above the surface of the water. This stretched from one side of a water channel to the other. In several places in this fence they would fix a basket-trap, *mcwii*, with its mouth facing in the direction from which the water was flowing. Fish, unable to get through the fence, entered the basket-traps and were caught. The other method involved a basket shaped like a funnel with a hole in the side. See Fig. 61. This was carried in shallow water. When the carrier saw a fish, he thrust the basket over it and down to the bottom. The fish was then removed by hand through the hole in the side. They also used nets made from *mogotse* (*sansevieria*) which were either laid in the rivers parallel to reed beds, or dragged between two canoes.

The Bayei were great hippopotamus hunters. A man gained great prestige or honour by killing a hippopotamus, which was considered the lord of the river. Two general methods were used. The first could be carried out by one or two men. See Fig. 63. A path was selected down which hippopotamus (A) went to the water. A very large spear (B), usually weighted with rocks (C), was hung in a tree pointing downwards. Often the blade (D) was poisoned. A rope was stretched across the path (E). The rope went up the trunk of the tree to a small stick which stopped the spear from falling. When the hippopotamus walked into the rope the small stick was pulled out and the weighted spear dropped, stabbing the hippopotamus deep in its back.

The second method required the cooperation of a group of people and was very exciting. See Fig. 64 on page 97. A large raft, *huzhenje*, was made of papyrus reeds. *Mekoro* were placed on this and the hunters hid in the middle of the raft behind them. The raft was allowed to drift down the channel until it was amongst a group of hippopotamuses. Then the men stood up and drove harpoons (*diira*) into the animals. Immediately the *mekoro* were pushed into the water and the hunters tried to reach the bank while holding on to the ropes attached to the harpoons. If they reached the bank they tied the ropes to trees and later, when the hippopotamuses were exhausted, stabbed them with heavy spears. Often the hippopotamuses turned on the *mekoro* biting and upsetting them. Sometimes the hunters were killed. The harpoons had heavy wooden handles and these dragged behind the hippopotamus until they became stuck in the reeds. When the hippopotamus was weak the hunters would approach it in their *mekoro* and kill it with spears.

The Hambukushu

The Hambukushu were a river people and expert fishermen, but were more involved with agriculture than the Bayei. They cut the scrub

Fig. 63 A Seyei spear trap. An effective way of hunting large and dangerous animals. Can you see how it works?

Fig. 64 Bayei hunting hippopotamus

on the dry river banks, burnt it and planted a wide variety of millet, cane, pumpkins and roots. They liked the deep water areas where the floods rose but the water did not spread over their lands. They sat down in their *mekoro* to paddle them rather than standing as the Bayei did. They made nets out of *sansevieria* plants and stretched these in the river to catch the fish.

Like many other peoples, the Hambukushu have stories about their origin. Most of these suggest they come from the Zambezi River. But there is one which says that they always lived on the Okavango. It says that Nyambi, their first ancestor, who became God, climbed a spider's web to heaven because his people were always fighting. Another story says that Nyambi lowered the first Hambukushu on a rope on to the Female Hill at Tsodilo. After lowering the people on a rope he lowered their cattle. The Hambukushu still point to some grooves in the rock of the hills. They say these were made by the hooves of their cattle when the earth was still soft.

Like the Bayei, the Hambukushu learned to live, during times of drought, on what they gathered from the river and surrounding country. Fish was their staple diet during droughts. Whole families fished. The men used their canoes and the women and children worked in the shallows with large baskets. These were laid side by side in shallow water. Then the fishers walked down the water beating it with their hands or a stick and driving the fish into the baskets. They also made long journeys into the forest to gather three particular fruits. The *mungongo* has a kernel which does not rot and can be kept for more than a year, the *motsaudi* is a red, sweet fruit, and the *mabola* can be dried and made into porridge or beer.

The Hambukushu had a clever means of hunting elephant. They took the blade of a spear which had a barb in it and fixed this into a heavy piece of wood. They dug shallow holes on paths used by elephants and then set these spear blades facing upwards. The elephant stood on this, driving the blade deep into the bottom of its foot, after which it could not walk. When it was weak, men came with axes and slashed the tendons in its back legs so that it fell down and could be speared.

The Hambukushu, throughout northern Botswana and northwards into Angola and Zambia, are famous for their great rain-making powers. They say that one of their great leaders, Mashango, was the first rain-maker. The story goes that it was during the time when the Balozi ruled the Hambukushu. They were living at Mashi on the Kuando River. Mashango found a strange white object like a huge egg in a springhare hole. Each time he shook it the skies thundered and rain fell. He made rain for his masters, the Balozi, and they were so pleased that they gave the Hambukushu many gifts. Mashango's fame spread, but after a while, when rain fell every year, the Balozi stopped giving gifts. Then the Hambukushu left the Kuando and moved westwards to the Okavango River which they called the Ruare. Many people still believe in the power of the Hambukushu to make rain and think that if they are offended there will be no floods in the Okavango Delta. This is one reason why more powerful neighbours did not attack the Hambukushu.

The coming of the Batawana

Probably Batswana had been hunting in northern Botswana for 150 years or more before the first groups settled there permanently. Sometime early in the 18th century a group of Bakhurutshe moved north-westwards to the Boteti River and settled on an island near Xhumo.

About 1790 there was trouble amongst the Bangwato. Their *kgosi*, Mathiba, had married a Mokwena and had had a son by her called Tawana. This was before he married his chief wife (*mohumagadi*). At a *kgotla* he announced that Tawana would succeed him rather than Khama, the son of the *mohumagadi*. Immediately the *morafe* was split and it looked as if there would be a civil war. Mathiba took advice from the Bakwena who told him to send Tawana and his followers to Khwebe. Mathiba refused to do this. Khama attacked Tawana, and Tawana and his father took refuge with the Bakwena at Lephepe.

The Bakwena did not want them and soon persuaded them to leave. They were led by Thogo, a Mokwena, to the Boteti where they stayed for a short period near Kedia Hill. They did not like having the Bakhurutshe near them and so they moved westwards through the desert to Khwebe. Mathiba wanted to return home and after arguing with his son, left the group and returned to Lephepe. From that time they were called the Batawana.

At Khwebe they found scattered groups of Bangologa. They had already suffered malaria at Boteti and did not want to live near Lake Ngami where malaria was very common so they asked the Bangologa to join them. Some Bangologa did join them and the Batawana started taking Bangologa women as second and third wives. In this way the Batawana started to rebuild a *morafe*.

By 1824 the *morafe* had become well established and moved north to settle at the east end of Lake Ngami where they came into close contact with the Bayei. Because their customs were so different, they did not marry Bayei women, although they lived peacefully near them. At this time a few Bayei families who were very poor began to attach themselves to the Batawana more or less as servants. They worked for the Batawana and in return received some benefits from their masters. The Batawana had a strong army and political organisation which soon dominated the Bangologa, Bayei and the few San with whom they came into contact. They herded their cattle to the west of Lake Ngami where they found and fought with the Ovambanderu and drove them away.

In about 1830 they learned of the approach of Sebitoane and his Bakololo who had stayed at Kedia for a short time on their journey north. Moremi I, now *kgosi* of the Batawana, moved westwards along the south shore of Lake Ngami. His younger brother, Motswakhumo, took another group south to Ghanzi where they rounded up many of their cattle and fled northwards up the west bank of the Thaoge River. They stayed for a short period in the northern areas of the Delta but then moved on into Angola.

Moremi's army rounded the west end of the Lake and met the Bakololo on the Xautsa plain. The Batawana were defeated and lost many of their cattle. They followed Motswakhumo. Then, using the *mekoro* of the Bayei, they hid themselves on the islands around Gabamukuni.

Sebitoane went south-west towards Ghanzi where he attacked the Ovambanderu and some Khoe. He moved into waterless country and became lost. Then he lost most of his cattle and his ten-year-old son was killed. He decided to return to Lake Ngami. The Bakololo eventually reached Gabamukuni to find the Batawana had left for the north-east. They travelled first up the Magqwegana and then settled on the Linyanti.

The Bakololo surrounded the Batawana one night and, attacking at dawn, again defeated them. Moremi's wife, her son, Letsholathebe, and a few others, escaped and went to the Basubiya. But most of the Batawana were taken by the Bakololo to the Chobe River.

The Batawana remained with the Bakololo for some years even intermarrying with them. Sebitoane made some of the Batawana his councillors. After a while the Bakololo became jealous of this and told Sebitoane the Batawana planned to kill him. Sebitoane decided to kill the Batawana men, but they were warned and fled.

They were led by Mogalakwe southwards towards their old home. On the way they met Letsholathebe and his mother who accompanied them to Toteng. On their arrival they had no cattle and food. They invited the Bangologa and Bayei to become members of their *morafe* and help them to become re-established. When they ignored the Batawana, the Batawana turned on them. The Batawana took many of their cattle and their property and demanded food from them. The Bayei did not fight, believing the Batawana had a special medicine, *pheko*, which made them strong.

After this, the Batawana soon established themselves as the rulers of Ngamiland. Some of the Bangologa, who had similar customs to them, were brought into the Batawana capital and given a ward. Most of them became servants of the Batawana. But the Batawana continued to marry Bangologa women. The Batawana took all the Bayei's stock and forced them to give tribute in grain and furs. Apart from that they ignored the Bayei at first. Later, they placed Batawana *dikgosana* in charge of various areas to control the Bayei. Those Bangologa and Bayei who were not prepared to accept the Batawana rule were allowed to move away, either into the desert or into the Okavango Delta.

During the next ten years the Batawana slowly spread their power to cover much of Ngamiland and southwards to Ghanzi. They divided this wide country into areas. Members of the Royal Family were put into these areas to rule them directly. The Batawana no longer tried to administer them from Toteng. The Bayei were allowed to keep their leaders. They became directly responsible to the Batawana and had to provide tribute. Later they also had to supply children to act as servants in Batawana homes. Around Toteng and at the homes of district governors, Bayei families became attached to Batawana. Whole families would live with their masters, who treated them like children. They worked for their masters and were not allowed to own any property nor to represent themselves in the *kgotla*. Their children were sent to the Bayei initiation schools after which they were put into a Batawana regiment. In this way the Batawana made their army strong, but denied the Bayei any rights. They treated them as *batlhanka*.

By 1850 when the first European traders began to arrive in the area, Letsholathebe ruled the area from Maun to Tsau. Like other Batswana *dikgoši*, he tried to control all outside trade by making the Europeans establish their trading centres in his village. But, like elsewhere, the traders soon found it was much more profitable to trade direct, particularly with the Bayei. They would give much more for far less than the Batawana. As trade began to make local produce more valuable, so Letsholathebe

Fig. 65 Letsholathebe at Lake Ngami, selling ivory. *Dikgosi* retained personal trading rights in ivory (painting by Thomas Baines)

spread his state to cover much of the Okavango area. Even so, apart from the visits of tribute collectors about twice a year, many of the Bayei and Hambukushu escaped from the Batawana rule. It was many years later that Moremi II spread Batawana rule to Shakawe and Ghanzi. Later still Sekgoma Letsholathebe spread it even further southwards to the Okwa, eastwards to the Makgadikgadi, westwards into Namibia, and northwards into Andara.

Questions

1 Give an example from this chapter of a contradition between archaelogical evidence and oral history.
2 Name the different groups of people living in northern Botswana between 1600 and 1850.
3 Using one sentence for each, write down the six most important facts about the life of the Ovaherero.
4 What customs did the Basubiya, the Bayei and the Hambukushu have in common? What were the main differences between them?
5 How did the Batawana rule Ngamiland?

15 Difaqane, a Time of Troubles: the 1820s

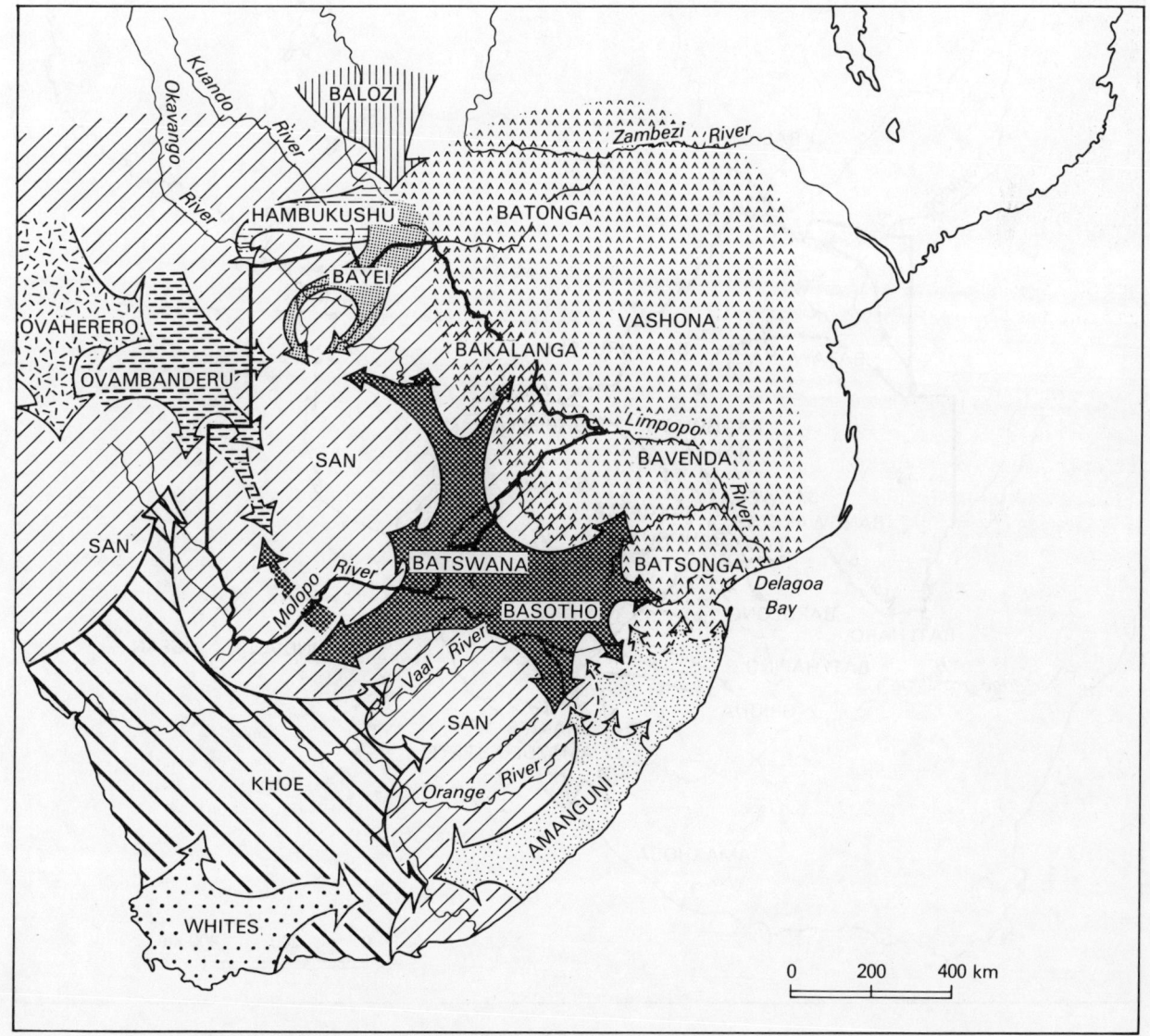

Fig. 66 About 1800, population explosion which led to the *Difaqane*

101

In the 18th century many small groups established themselves into *merafe*. They spread out and conquered weaker peoples. See Fig. 66 which shows the way in which populations expanded. Towards the end of the century much of the more fertile land throughout Southern Africa was populated by agriculturalists. Some of these farmers owned large herds of livestock.

In the south-east the Amanguni peoples had occupied the whole area between the Drakensberg and the coast. To their north the country was populated by Basotho and Batswana peoples. The whole of the inland eastern plateau provided a home for the Sotho-Tswana peoples. Their area stretched westwards into the drier country of the Kalahari. The Varozvi Empire extended in the north-west from the edges of the Kalahari almost to the Indian Ocean. In the north the Balozi Empire had expanded south and westwards to take in much of the Zambezi/Chobe area and westwards almost to the Okavango. In the west the Ovaherero were

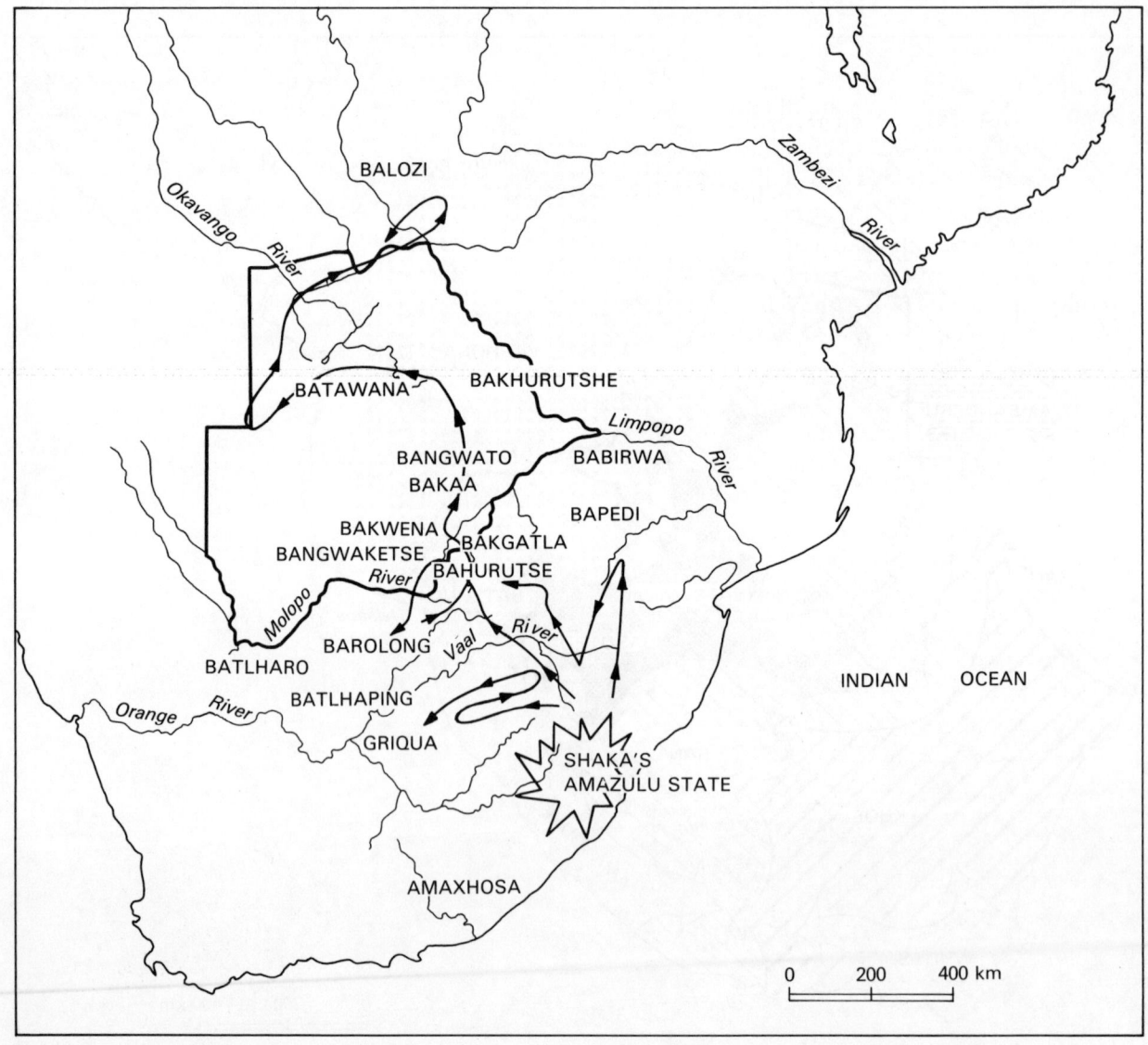

Fig. 67 The position of Batswana groups at the start of the Difaqane, about 1820, and the direction of the main invasions

steadily pushing the Ovambanderu south-eastwards into Botswana. The pastoral Khoe occupied the lands south of the Ovambanderu, far south of the Orange River.

Finally, there were Europeans who had settled in the Cape 150 years earlier. They were now rapidly spreading out, taking the Khoe's traditional grazing lands and pressing against the Amanguni in the east. There was no space left for expansion, yet populations continued to increase. More land was constantly needed. Small groups were already finding it difficult or impossible to maintain their independence. Often they lost their land and cattle to larger and stronger peoples. By 1800 Botswana was beginning to receive refugees from south of the Molopo River. These people were leaving the countries of the Barolong, Batlharo and Batlhaping. They were making for the area around Molepolole where they joined the Bakgwatheng and Babolaongwe. Although they said they were of Batswana stock, they were probably Bakgalagadi in origin. On their arrival in Botswana they were called Bashaga.

In the first years of the 19th century fighting began. This was to grow until the whole of Southern Africa was affected. Nations were destroyed or lost their food and cattle. They had to travel throughout the country, attacking whoever they met in an attempt to find food and a new home. The Basotho and the Batswana suffered the most as many groups were broken up and others fled across the Kalahari. Fig. 67 shows the position of the Batswana groups at the start of Difaqane.

Fighting amongst the Amanguni in 1818 was caused by the expansion of the Zulu state under Shaka. This resulted in the Amahlubi losing all their grain and cattle and being forced off their land. They turned on their neighbours, the Batlokwa, a large *morafe* ruled by a regent, Mmanthatisi. In turn, the Batlokwa moved west attacking the Bafokeng. They were followed by the Amahlubi who had already eaten the food they had taken from the Batlokwa. The Amahlubi also attacked the Bafokeng. The Baphuting and Bahlakoana were also attacked.

All these groups began to move north-westwards seeking a new home, more cattle, better food and peace.

Soon the whole country between the Drakensberg and the Vaal River was in chaos. Bands of armed soldiers accompanied by women and children searched the area for food. Soon these bands formed into three major hordes (large groups). Mmanthatisi led the Batlokwa, Mpangazita led the Amahlubi, and Matiwane led the Amangwane. These hordes moved back and forth across the land attacking all they met and driving them into the north and west.

Many of the peoples attacked by these hordes fled to the north-west. They crossed the Vaal River and in turn attacked the Batswana living there. They formed themselves into four major

Fig. 68 A Motswana warrior during the Difaqane. The shield was designed to protect the man from spears which were thrown

hordes: the Baphuting under Ratsebe, the Bahlakoana under Nkgaraganye, some Bafokeng under Mangwane (later to be called the Bakololo), and the Bataung under Moletsane.

In 1822 a further group set out for the area north of the Vaal River. Mzilikazi, *Inkosi* (King) of the Amakhumalo, defied (went against) his king, Shaka, over the ownership of some cattle. He fled northwards with 300 people and gathered others on the way. They first attacked the Bapedi and drove their *kgosi*, Sekwati, and his followers to the north. Still close to Shaka, they moved south-westwards and settled to the south of the Vaal. But a year later they had crossed the Vaal again and settled at Majwanamatshwaana, the old home of the Bakwena. Here they established a number of military towns. From these they attacked those people to the west and north who were left after the Basotho hordes had been through the area. Men were killed and women and children brought into the new state.

Chaos raged in the area between the Vaal and the Drakensberg for many years. However, three groups of people are important: Mzilikazi and his Amandebele, Ratsebe and Tshwane with their Baphuting, and Sebitoane (the younger brother of Mangwane who took over from him when he was killed by a lion) and his Bafokeng.

The Baphuting

Of the three groups the Baphuting are the least important, although for a short while they attacked one group of Batswana after another causing terrible damage. In January 1823 they crossed the Vaal and attacked the Barolong under Sefunelo. They then turned north-eastwards and drove the Bahurutshe from their walled town of Kaditshwene, destroying it. Moving westwards they attacked Makaba, the

Fig. 69 A Setswana homestead showing similar construction to that of today

Fig. 70 Batswana warriors being strengthened by medicine before battle

strongest *kgosi* in the area. Although Makaba and his Bangwaketse retreated from Kgwakgwe they managed to turn the Baphuting southwards. There the Baphuting conquered the Barolong at Khunwana and settled in their ripe fields of corn to feast and recover.

The Baphuting then moved southwards intending to strike at the Batlhaping, but the missionary, Robert Moffat, hurried to Griquatown. He persuaded the government agent to enlist the help of some armed Griqua on behalf of the Batlhaping. As the Baphuting approached Dithakong, the Batlhaping capital, they were joined by Nkgaraganye and his Bahlakoana. The Batlhaping fled from their town which was immediately occupied by the Baphuting and Bahlakoana. A European traveller called Melville who was present estimated the combined horde at about 50 000 people.

On 26 June 1823 about one hundred Griqua, carrying guns and mounted on horseback, attacked the Bahlakoana who were camped just outside the town, and drove them into it. The Griqua followed, shooting all they saw. Terrified by the noise, the Bahlakoana and Baphuting fled. They left about 500 women and children behind in the town and they were butchered by the Batlhaping who had followed the Griqua.

Also present in the area of Dithakong were Sebitoane with his Bafokeng and Moletsane with the Bataung. They probably did not take part in the battle though. The Bahlakoana lost their leader, Nkgaraganye, in the battle. They fled to the north-east where for some years they continued to fight the smaller Batswana *merafe*. Sebitoane and Moletsane moved northwards pushing their way through the Barolong, defeating the Bahurutshe and Bakgatla. Finally they were attacked and driven westwards by the Amandebele. At some point Moletsane split away and moved southwards again. In August 1824 he was attacked by a combined force of Barolong and Griqua at Pitsane. He then retreated southwards into the modern Orange Free State, although 17 Barolong *dikgosi* were killed.

Sebitoane attacked the Bakwena and drove them from their fortified town of Dithubaruba in the Dithejwane Hills. Here he settled while the Bakwena went south to join the Bangwaketse. Robert Moffat, standing on Kgwakgwe Hill, was able to count 14 separate divisions of Makaba's Bangwaketse capital and estimated the total population at about 70 000 people. Had the Batswana combined earlier, they would have lost their crops, but they might well have defeated all the hordes of the Difaqane and saved many of their cattle. They did not combine, probably because they lived in separate communities. They were accustomed to joining each other against another Batswana enemy, but were not used to fighting powerful foreigners.

From the last months of 1824 the situation in south-eastern Botswana changed. Two powerful leaders were both trying to establish new states. In the east Mzilikazi was establishing his Amandebele State with its capital at Majwanamatswaana. In the west Sebitoane had settled at Dithubaruba and was attempting to do the same. Mzilikazi had well-established regimental towns and used the Amazulu method of fighting at close quarters with a large shield and short stabbing spear. Consequently he was much more successful than Sebitoane.

Sebitoane and the Bakololo

Sebitoane now called his followers 'Bakololo' after the name of the clan, Kollo, of his favourite wife. He set out to conquer his Batswana neighbours (see Fig. 71). First he went north attacking the Bangwato and taking some of their cattle. The Bangwato moved to the Kutse Hills where they thought they could better defend themselves. But Sebitoane attacked again severely defeating them and taking most of their cattle.

The Bangwato moved to the north attacking the Bakalanga. Eventually they were defeated by the Bakalanga in the Matopo Hills and their *kgosi*, Kgari, was killed.

Sebitoane turned south and attacked the Bangwaketse and Bakwena at Kgwakgwe. The Bakwena stood aside during the battle, some of them even fighting on Sebitoane's side. Makaba was killed, betrayed by the Bakwena. The Bangwaketse were defeated. The next year Sebitoane attacked again, this time defeating Makaba's son, Sebego. The Bangwaketse moved away from Kgwakgwe and the Bakwena, now homeless, fled across the desert, many of them eventually settling for a short period near Lake Ngami.

Sebitoane now ruled the eastern Kalahari. However, he had only a small following and one town, so his position was not strong. In 1826 he attacked the Bangwaketse again, and again defeated them taking most of the cattle they had left. Sebego decided to revenge himself. He got the help of two European travellers, Bain and Biddulph, and some Griqua who were accompanying them, and set out for Dithubaruba. The two whites only reluctantly agreed to take part on the conditions that Sebego took only his own cattle and that they loaded their guns with powder and no shot. At dawn on 29 August 1826 they surrounded Dithubaruba, drove out the Bakololo, burnt the town and seized all the cattle. Sebitoane then settled in the hills just to the north of Molepolole, and remained there for the next two years.

In about 1829 Sebitoane again raided the Bangwato, splitting the *morafe*. Many of them fled to the Makgadikgadi while others hid in the surrounding hills. The Bakololo followed them to the Makgadikgadi and then moved westwards to the Boteti. They seized the long-horned cattle of the Bateti and then settled at Kedia.

About three years later they moved westwards again. This time they attacked the Batawana on the Xautsa plain. After travelling down to Ghanzi and being defeated by the Ovambanderu they moved northwards. Eventually they conquered the Batawana and settled in the Balozi Kingdom.

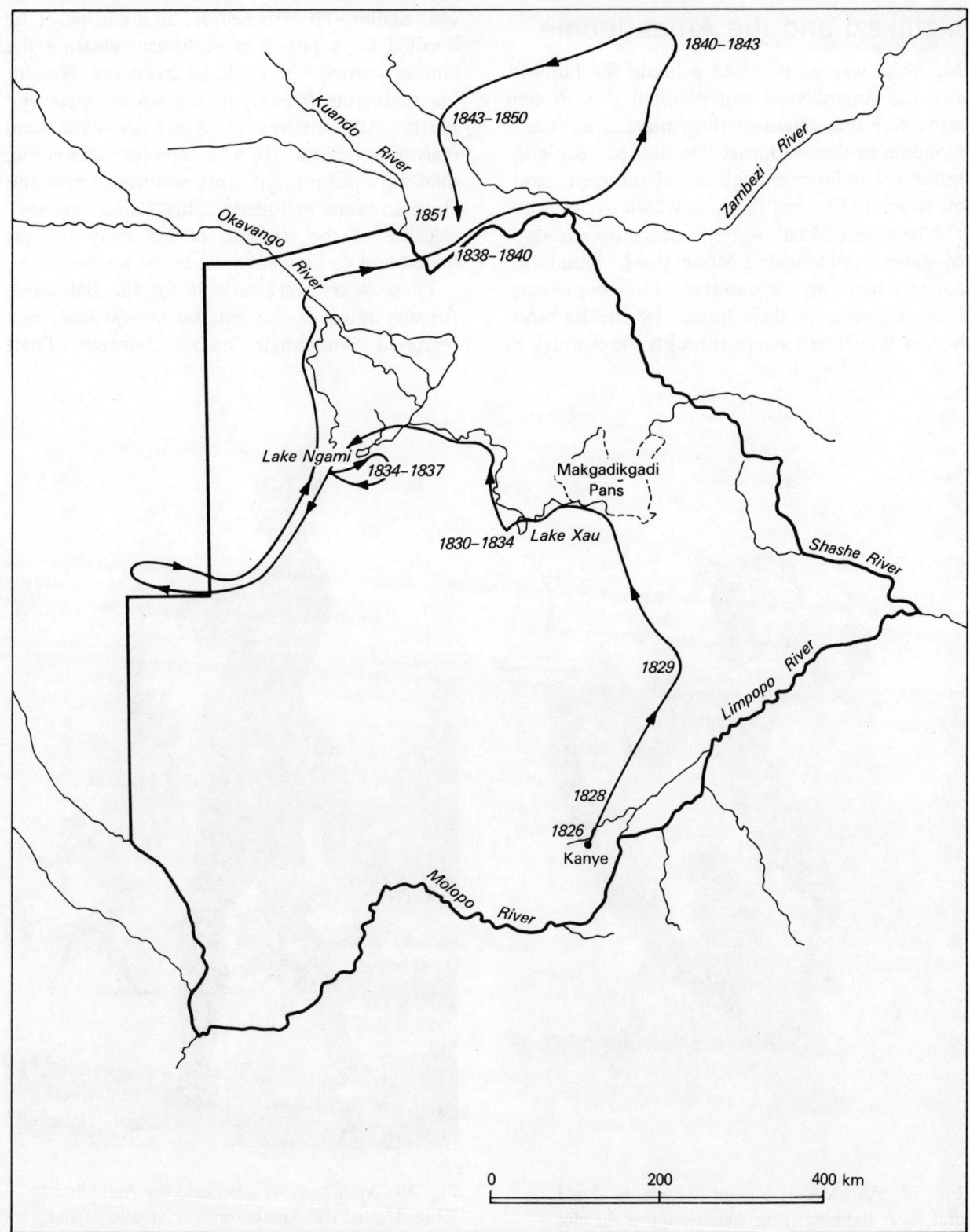

Fig. 71 The route taken by the Bakololo

Mzilikazi and the Amandebele

Mzilikazi wanted to make a home for himself and his Amandebele and planned this in the same way that Shaka of the Amazulu built his kingdom in the south-east. He needed people to build a state large enough to defend itself, land on which to live and peace in which to develop.

When Mzilikazi settled near present-day Magaliesberg (Mogale's Mountain) he found the country more or less deserted. The people had been driven from their homes by the Basotho hordes which had swept through the country a year earlier. To gain people, land and peace he decided on a policy of ruthlessly clearing the land of anyone who could be an enemy. He sent his regiments (*izimpi*) to the south, west and north. All settlements were destroyed and resistance broken. He took captives. The young men were put into his army and the women and children were included in his state (*isitshaba*). Because of the strength of his army he was feared and so he gained peace for his people.

Those years were terrible for the Batswana. Already most of the smaller *merafe* had been scattered and their homes burned. Their

Fig. 72 An Indebele warrior. The large shield and short stabbing spear were designed for close fighting. This method of fighting was invented by Shaka

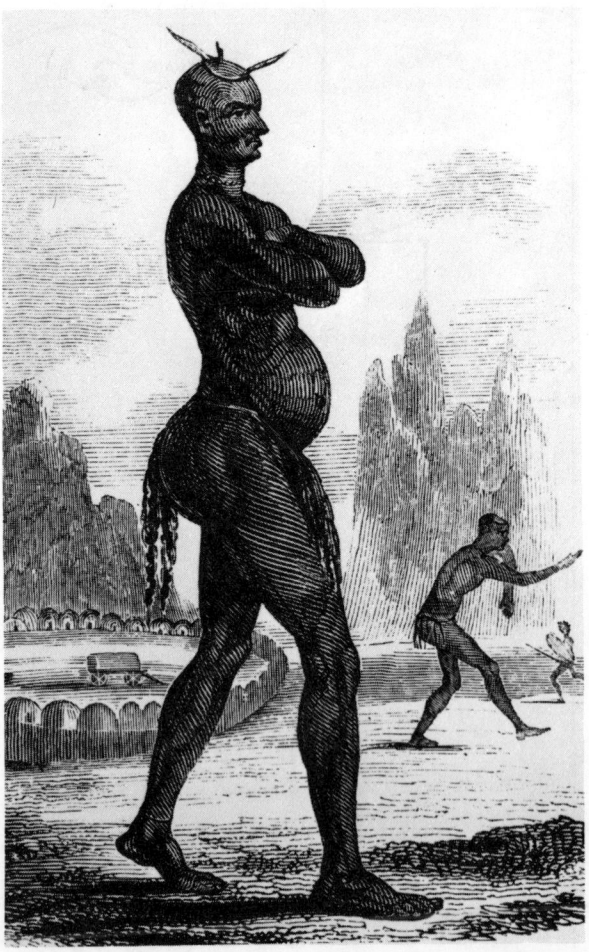

Fig. 73 Mzilikazi, who became the Amandebele King. He led the Amakhumalo clan away from Shaka's state and then ruled much of the Transvaal and south-east Botswana

Fig. 74 A hillside Batswana settlement, probably in north-east Botswana, a refuge from the Amandebele, about 1880

political and economic organisations were broken. The whole land was filled with small groups of people moving from place to place, hiding in the hills, unable to grow crops and left to live by collecting wild food or stealing from their more fortunate neighbours. Only Sebego, with his huge following, managed to keep his *morafe* intact, and even he lost most of his cattle.

When Mzilikazi heard how Sebego had defeated the Bakololo, he sent his *izimpi* to Sebego to demand tribute. Then he attacked the defeated Bakololo and took their remaining cattle. At first Sebego paid tribute to Mzilikazi, but later he became more confident and refused. The Amandebele attacked the Bangwaketse and drove them from their home. First they settled near Letlhakeng, but hearing the Amandebele were coming they moved westwards to Luze (Dutle). Mzilikazi sent an *impi* after them. But the Batswana guides who led the *impi* to Luze took them into country full of thorn trees where the Bangwaketse attacked and defeated them. Fearing revenge, Sebego took many of his Bangwaketse westwards into the Ghanzi District and finally southwards to Lehututu. There they remained, out of reach of the Amandebele.

The Amazulu attacked Mzilikazi at Magaliesberg. He decided to move westwards out of their reach. He moved his capital to Mosega near modern Zeerust and built his own home a little distance away at Egaba. He now came into close contact with the remnants of the Batswana who were living west of the Ngotwane River. They were in no position to defend themselves. By this time Sebitoane had realised he could not fight with Mzilikazi and had taken his Bakololo north. In 1830 Mzilikazi ruled the whole land from the Vaal River in the south to the junction of the Ngotwane and Odi Rivers in the north, and from the Ngotwane in the west to Magaliesberg in the east (see the map, Fig. 77).

The arrival of the Voortrekkers in 1836

The Cape was ruled by the British although most of its white inhabitants were Dutch, French or German. Apart from Cape Town in the south-west there were no other real towns. Most of the white population lived as pastoral farmers although they grew a few crops and some vegetables.

Many of these farmers did not establish permanent homes. They moved eastwards with their herds of cattle and flocks of sheep, staying for a few years in one place and then moving eastwards again. They took with them their servants, Khoe, Blacks from Malagasie and some Malays who had been imported as slaves. These farmers believed they had two rights. Any adult White might take and use as much land as he needed for his livestock, and no one had the right to interfere with his servants. Many of these servants were either slaves or treated as slaves.

The British Government in Cape Town tried to control the steady expansion of these farmers. They also tried to free the slaves and allow them to own property and receive wages. The Boers (the Dutch word for a farmer) were opposed to this so they moved steadily away from British control. There were two reasons for this: the land was becoming crowded and overgrazed, and they felt that the further they were from the centre of government in Cape Town, the freer they would be to live as they wished. This in-

Fig. 75 A Voortrekker camp. Constantly on the move, these people hunted for food during the winter, but settled for a short time during the summer to grow crops

cluded keeping slaves and continuing inequality between Whites and non-Whites. They did not expect to escape the Government forever, but they wanted freedom for as long as possible.

By 1830 many interrelated groups of these mobile Boers (Trekboers) had spread far to the north-east and were crossing the Orange River to settle amongst the Griqua. They were to have a considerable effect on the migration that was shortly to follow.

In 1834 and 1835 advance parties of Trekboers reported back to the Cape that the area on either side of the Vaal River was deserted of people and a suitable place for farming. They did not realise two things. Firstly, until recently the land had been inhabited by Batswana who, although chased out by the Amandebele, still considered it their home. Secondly, Mzilikazi was keeping it free of people so that he had no neighbours to interfere with his developing state.

In 1835 a few more prominent Boers began to

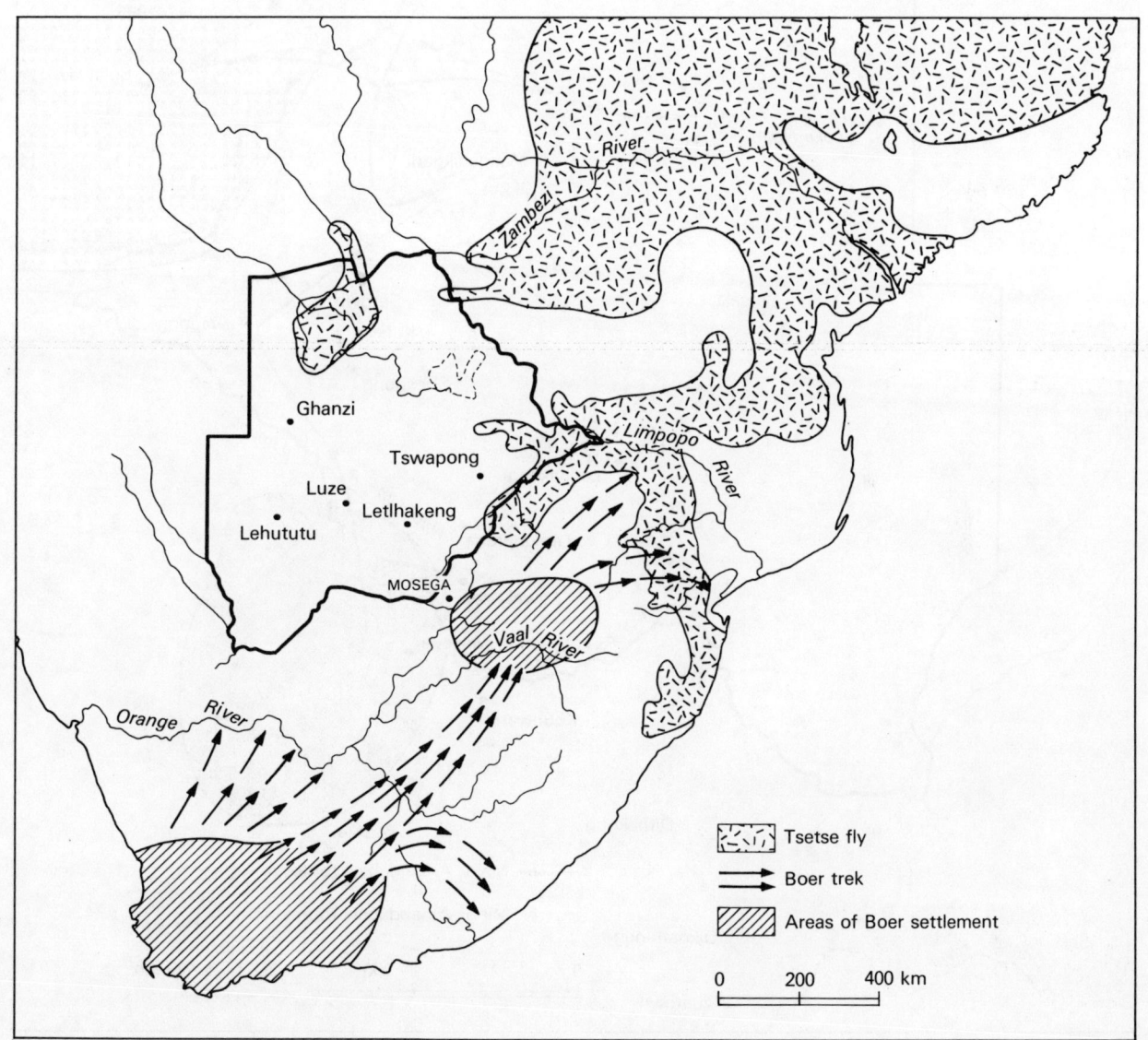

Fig. 76   The Boer Trek and the distribution of tsetse fly about 1836

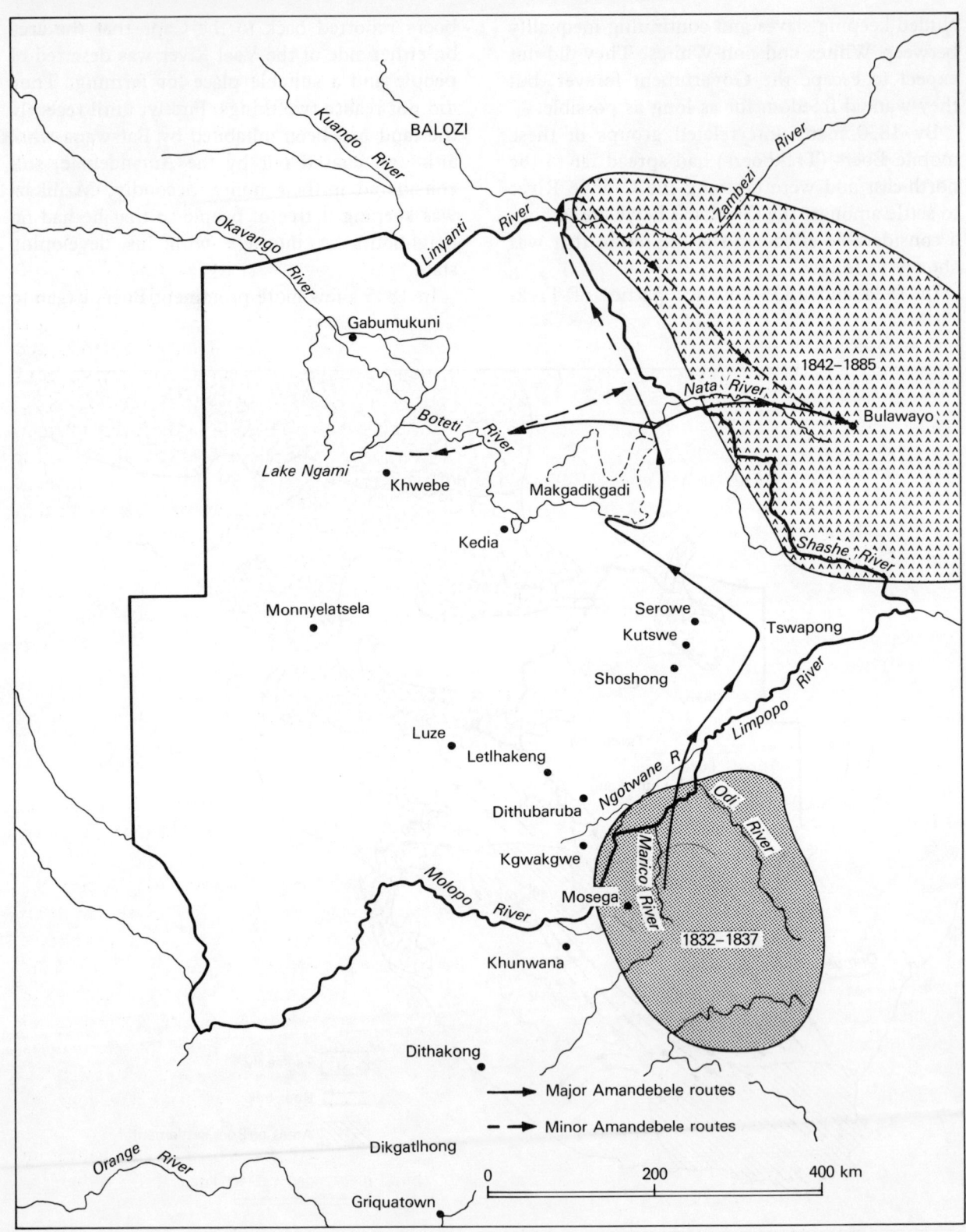

Fig. 77 Amandebele states from 1832 to 1837 and from 1842 to 1885

collect their relatives around them and move northwards in separate parties heading for the Orange and Vaal Rivers. This was the beginning of the Boer Trek or Afrikaner Difaqane. See Fig. 76. Once across the Orange River many of the smaller parties formed into larger ones and proceeded together towards the Vaal River.

One of the first of these parties led by Potgieter and Cilliers settled along the Vaal River early in 1836. They spread out and began to herd their cattle and sheep over a wide area. Mzilikazi heard of these farmers arriving on land he considered to be his and settling without permission. In August 1836 he sent two *izimpi* to investigate. They attacked two parties of Boers before returning. The Boers, realising they would be attacked again, came together at a place south of the Vaal River (later called Vegkop). They put their wagons in a circle and withdrew inside, waiting for the Amandebele who attacked in great force on 16 October. Although the Amandebele were unable to break through the ring of wagons they took nearly all the Boers' livestock.

Shortly afterwards a new party of Boers arrived under Maritz. Potgieter had been helped by Moroka, a Morolong *kgosi*, who had taken his party to Thaba Nchu and fed them. Now 107 Boers and about 40 well-armed servants set out to attack Mzilikazi. With them went a party of Barolong to herd any livestock captured. They attacked Mosega, killed over 400 people and recaptured all of Potgieter's livestock.

Later in the year Mzilikazi was again attacked by the Amazulu and then in November another party of Boers attacked him. A running fight continued for more than a week with the mounted Boers chasing the Amandebele and shooting from horseback. Mzilikazi crossed the Limpopo and moved northwards to settle in Tswapong. See Fig. 77. In an effort to obtain food and cattle he attacked the Bangwato driving them to the Makgadikgadi. In 1838 he moved again, this time to Nata. Here his *isitshaba* split. One party entered what is now Zimbabwe. Mzilikazi and the rest struck west and north looking for a new home. Two years later he joined the first party near the area of modern Bulawayo.

Having driven the Amandebele from the land, the Boers considered it to be theirs by right of conquest. Once more they spread out and started their pastoral farming. Tsetse fly in the north and malaria in the east kept them mainly to southern and western Transvaal.

Once Mzilikazi was gone the Batswana were free to return to their homes and re-establish their *merafe*. Soon numbers of Batswana were moving back into the area occupied by the Boers. The Bangwaketse and Bakwena returned to their old homes. Smaller groups who lived just outside Boer lands began to rebuild and re-establish themselves. As a united, armed force the Boers had been able to defeat the most powerful ruler on the Southern African plateau. Once they were scattered again they were unable to stop Batswana resettling in their lands. Also they could not control the stronger *merafe* on their borders. During the following years large numbers of Batswana returned and settled. The Boers could not stop them, but they allowed them to remain on the Boer farms only if they worked for them.

Conclusion

This period of conflict is known as the Difaqane. For almost twenty years the Batswana had lived under war or the threat of war. Most *merafe* had been split and many people driven into the desert. For long periods of time *dikgosi* had been forced to live together in exile. When the *merafe* began to re-establish themselves their old members did not always come together again. Sometimes they continued to live with people of a different *morafe*. This is one of the reasons why every *morafe* now has wards of foreigners.

The Difaqane gave rise to three new states or kingdoms.

1   The Amandebele established themselves in the western Transvaal and then moved to Zimbabwe.
2   The Bakololo first established themselves in eastern Botswana and then moved to

western Zambia.
3 The Boers replaced the Amandebele in the Transvaal and brought a new threat to the Batswana.

Questions

1 What were the chief causes of the fighting that occurred all over Southern Africa in the 19th century?
2 List the various groups of people attacked by Sebitoane and the Bakololo between 1824 and 1829.
3 What effect did Mzilikazi and the Amandebele have on Sebego and the Bangwaketse, and on Sebitoane and the Bakololo?
4 Why did the Voortrekkers want to settle around the Vaal River? What did they not realise?

16 The Batswana after the Difaqane

At the end of the Difaqane the Batswana *merafe* were scattered. Some groups had taken refuge in the Kalahari. Others, sometimes broken into very small sections, had remained in the general area of their homeland. The *dikgosi* had lost much of their control because they were unable to defend their people or even to feed them. Many royal relatives, younger brothers and uncles, were trying to seize power.

The Batswana had also lost much of their land in the western Transvaal where Mzilikazi had first established his new state and had then been replaced by the Voortrekkers. Apart from land, the *merafe* had also lost a large part of their cattle herds. These were traditional wealth upon which a *kgosi* had relied for keeping his people as a single unit.

The reconstruction started, not at *morafe* level, but at the level of minor groups or segments (parts). The Bakwena were split into two major groups under Sechele and Segokotlo and several minor groups. The Bangwato were also split into several groups living between the Mhalapswe River and the Makgadikgadi Pans. The Bangwaketse were split into three major groups under Sebego, Bome and Segotshane and several minor groups.

The importance of guns

One of the first steps the *dikgosi* took was to arm themselves with guns. They obtained these from Griqua and European traders who started to enter their country in the 1820s. They had seen how a few men mounted on horseback and armed with guns could put huge armies to flight. (This was shown by the battles at Dithakong and Dithubaruba.) They also recognised the use of guns in hunting for ivory and skins to trade for more guns.

As the traders arrived, so each *kgosi* tried to prevent them from going further north and to get them to trade with him only. At first this worked and the northern end of the trade route

Fig. 78 Horses and guns made hunting much easier, but led to great reductions in wildlife

Fig. 79 Kgosi Sechele and his wife, MmaKgari. Sechele was installed as Kgosi in 1829

was established first on the Orange River. (See Fig. 81, on page 119.) Then, as the elephants were finished, the northern end of the trade route was established successively at the capitals of the Barolong, Bangwaketse, Bakwena and Bangwato. In each instance *dikgosi* were able to control trading amongst their people so long as elephant were plentiful. Once they became scarce so individuals began to trade at night behind the *kgosi's* back. Then the traders moved north to the next *morafe*.

Guns gave the *dikgosi* even more power than they had previously had through the use of cattle. As the only people in the *merafe* with guns they were able to hand these out to trusted people and so gain their support. Horses were another important item of trade. A man mounted on a horse with a gun could kill several elephant in one day. Before it had taken many people a lot of work to kill one elephant.

Guns were to play a very important part in the future in establishing Batswana independence.

Kgosi Sechele refused to accept Boer control. In August 1852 Commandant P.E. Scholtz took 300 Boers to Dimawe to teach Sechele a lesson. There was a battle. The Bakwena lost, with 60 dead and 200 women and children captured, but with their guns they killed 36 Boers. This was the first time the Transvaal Boers had been fired upon by Batswana and the incident made them realise that if they wanted to take more Batswana land they would have to fight for it. Without guns the Bakwena could never have killed so many Boers. This incident more than any other up to this time helped the Batswana to save their land.

The *dikgosi* recognised the need to have many people in their *merafe*. Otherwise they would have no chance to defend themselves in the future. Land was short because the Boers had taken much of it. Therefore they needed to establish themselves firmly on the land they still owned. The possibility of moving to new land no longer existed.

One of the first moves was to consolidate the *morafe*, to bring the group firmly together and to reorganise the political system. This was started by Kgari amongst the Bangwato as early as 1824. The pattern of reorganisation among the Bangwato was the same as that for other *merafe*.

Before looking closely at the restructuring of the Batswana *merafe* it is important to understand how they were traditionally organised.

Traditional *merafe* organisation

Traditionally, the Batswana of the ruling *morafe* considered they had rights over the use of a large area of land and rights to tribute and respect from other groups on the same land. They lived in one village often set near hills for defence. This village consisted of a number of wards (*makgotla*). These wards were formed in two ways.
1 If a *kgosi* took three wives, then he created three new wards and put the sons of each wife into a separate ward to rule it. To them he also attached common families to act as supporters and servants.
2 Other wards usually consisted of groups of Batswana of different *merafe* who had split away and come to accept him as their *kgosi*. With each generation new wards were created.

Batswana of other groups might also live in the same area under their own ruler. While in the area they were expected to pay respect and tribute, but they could move away. There were also non-Batswana who were left very much to themselves. They had to pay tribute and respect, but did not have to live in the central village and were not considered members of the *morafe*.

Finally, there were some subservient groups, usually Bakgalagadi. They either lived in their own ward in the central villlage, or were attached to royal houses. They acted as servants, were not generally able to own property and had few rights. They were not considered to be members of the *morafe*.

A *kgosi* appointed trusted commoners to head wards in central villages which were not under his immediate relatives or traditional royalty. These ward heads were known as *basimane ba kgosi*.

The reconstruction of the Bangwato State

To reconstruct the Bangwato State, Kgari used various methods. First he instituted the *kgamelo* system. *Kgamelo* were cattle, usually the spoils of war, which belonged to the *kgosi*. They were given to a commoner to look after on behalf of the *kgosi*. The commoner was not allowed to eat or trade them without permission, and he had to send regular supplies of *madila* to the *kgosi*. Otherwise he could use *kgamelo* for himself. Kgari gained a lot of support from the common people through this system. *Kgamelo*-holders were careful not to offend him as the *kgamelo* and everything else they owned could be taken away from them.

Kgari gave *kgamelo* to his *basimane* which added greatly to their power. This gave Kgari a balance in his *kgotla*. Those royals who had had the support of all the common people before now found their strength in the *kgotla* weakened. This created much greater unity in the *morafe*.

Then began a systematic campaign to drive out of the area any peoples who might be a threat or who could not be brought into the *morafe*. In 1849 Sekgoma I, who was the *kgosi*, attacked the Bakaa near Shoshong and drove them from the area. He attacked the Babirwa and Balete living north and south of the Tswapong Hills and conquered all the Batswapong peoples except the Baseleka. They remained unconquered until the time of Khama III because they lived on a hill surrounded by tsetse fly near the Limpopo. The Bakalanga, trapped between the Amandebele in the north and the Bangwato in the south, submitted without fighting. In this way the Bangwato made all the weaker groups living on their land pay tribute and respect to them.

The next move was to make subject peoples more closely allied to the central *morafe*. *Basimane* were appointed to look after the subject

Fig. 80 Khama III, a major figure in 19th century politics

sections and eight districts, each of which fell under a *mosimane*. At first the *basimane* remained in their own wards in the capital, but eventually they moved to their districts and established their homes there. This provided the subject groups with a much closer association with the *morafe*.

Traditional subject leaders such as the rulers of the Baphaleng, Batalaote and Batswapong were allowed to look after their own people and to rule them by their own custom. They collected the tribute and were allowed to keep some of it. However, they were not allowed to hold their own initiation, *bogwera*, which was held only by the *kgosi*. Young men of subject groups were initiated in Bangwato regiments and so became much closer to becoming Bangwato.

What Kgari had started Khama III completed. He spread his control over all the country from the Limpopo to the Boteti and from Bukalanga in the north to Lephepe in the south. Other *merafe* were re-established in the same way. When the Batawana escaped from the Bakololo and returned to Toteng they tried to incorporate the Bangologa and Bayei into their nation. When the Bangologa and Bayei refused they took their cattle from them and made them serfs. However, with time they too were given wards although, for the Bayei, this was not until the 1940s.

Political, social and economic reconstruction followed a similar pattern amongst other *merafe*. This resulted in more consolidated (strengthened) states.

people and to represent them. They were known as *basimane ba mafatshe*. They had the duty of making regular visits to their people, allocating land, collecting tribute (some of which they could keep for themselves), settling disputes between minor groups and hearing appeals. The country of the Bangwato was divided into four

Questions

1 List four effects the Difaqane had on Batswana *merafe*.
2 Why were the *dikgosi* now anxious to obtain guns and horses?
3 Describe the ways in which Kgari built up the power of the Bangwato using the following headings.
   (a) The *kgamelo* system
   (b) Defeat of enemies
   (c) *Basimane ba mafatshe*
   (d) Treatment of subject rulers

17 Trade and Changes in the Economy

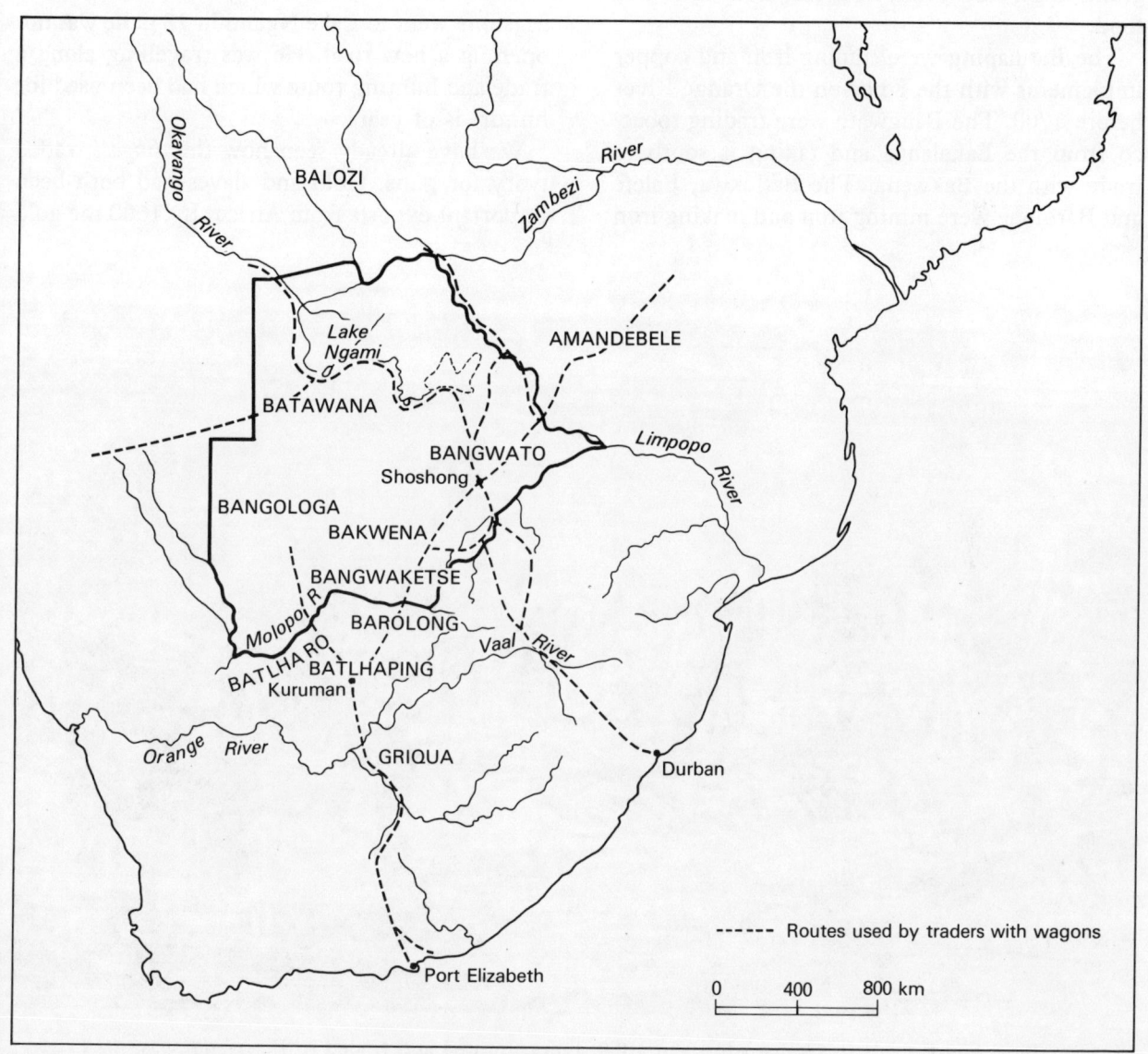

Fig. 81 Trade routes developed between 1800 and 1860

Before 1800

Even before the long-distance traders came with their wagons early in the 19th century, the Batswana were great traders. They traded both amongst themselves and with their neighbours. Occasionally they traded for goods made outside Africa which had come all the way from the coast, things such as beads, cloth and sea shells. Mainly they traded for things they produced themselves such as iron and copper tools and ornaments, specularite (*sebilo*), furs, tobacco, grain, dogs, stock, salt, iron ore, ivory and wild food.

The Batlhaping were trading iron and copper implements with the Khoe on the Orange River before 1700. The Bangwato were trading tobacco from the Bakalanga and taking it south to trade with the Bakwena. The Batlokwa, Balete and Barolong were mining iron and making iron tools which they traded to the Bakwena, possibly in exchange for specularite and furs.

Trading was very important as it kept communications alive over great distances. It gave people a chance to meet on friendly terms. It also meant that people could supply their own needs when they could not make or grow things for themselves.

Trade routes stretched all across Botswana and far into neighbouring areas. Long before the Griqua and European traders arrived people were travelling from Molepolole to Lake Ngami and southwards to the Orange River. When Livingstone went to Lake Ngami in 1849 he was not opening a new road. He was travelling along a trade and hunting route which had been used for hundreds of years.

We have already seen how the *dikgosi* traded ivory for guns. Gold and slaves had both been important exports from Africa. By 1600 the gold

Fig. 82 Ivory and fur sale in Grahamstown in 1850. Ivory, hunted and traded in Botswana, was transported by wagon to the coast where it was sold at much higher prices

Fig. 83 Griqua men riding oxen (from a drawing by Andrew Smith). The Griqua, a mixture of Khoe and White, spoke Dutch and were the first long-distance traders to enter Bostwana.

trade was beginning to die out and the ivory trade took its place. By 1800 ivory was probably the largest and by far the most important export from Africa. Much of it went to India where it was used for making Hindu marriage bracelets, jewellery and carved ornaments. Some of it also went to China and Europe. It was much more valuable than other produce such as furs and feathers because it could be easily transported. It did not rot or otherwise suffer through age. Ivory was the one item the wagon traders wanted and in exchange the *dikgosi* wanted guns.

The Griqua were the first wagon traders to reach Botswana. They lived on the Orange River where they had come from the south to escape the rule of the Dutch. Mostly they were Khoe people with some white ancestry. They had kept their links with the south. They traded with the Dutch for guns, ammunition, and manufactured goods such as woven clothing, ironware, trinkets and mirrors. Many of them spoke Dutch as their home language.

After 1800

Once elephant became scarce on the Orange River the Griqua started to come north to hunt and also to trade for ivory. By 1805 Bangwaketse were carrying ivory to the Orange River to trade with them. This was the start of the ivory trail into Botswana.

The Griqua, more than anybody else, opened Botswana to wagon travel. By 1847 they had crossed the edges of the Kalahari to Ngamiland. By 1850 they had reached the Chobe River. By 1852 they had travelled right up the west side of the Okavango Delta to reach Andara on the Angolan border. They were followed by a few Batlhaping and Barolong who also bought wagons and became hunter-traders like the Griqua, travelling throughout Botswana.

Travelling by wagon was very difficult and expensive. In the first place, a wagon in the Cape cost, in 1820, between £30 and £40 or, in today's money, about P65. But money was worth much

Fig. 84 Wagons often broke down on the rough roads. The wheels were rimmed with iron

more then than it is now. £30 was the amount a European soldier of that period earned in two years. The earliest European travellers to Botswana said that a journey lasting a year could cost about £600 or P1 000. This was what a common soldier of that time earned in 30 years in the army.

After crossing the Orange River there were no roads, only footpaths. Often wagon travellers had to use people to cut roads through thick thorn bush. Sometimes wagons had to be unloaded and taken to pieces and carried over rocky country or floated over rivers. Travelling was very slow and 20 kilometres was a good journey for one day.

There were long stretches of country, sometimes 50 kilometres or more, where there was no water. Water was carried on the wagons. Sometimes the wagons were left and the oxen driven to the nearest water and then brought back to pull the wagons a few kilometres. Then they were again taken to drink and brought back again to pull the wagons a bit further.

Wagons were made of wood and had iron tyres on the wheels. Often the wheels or the wooden axles broke and had to be repaired. Oxen died of thirst, from drinking bad water or from tsetse fly bites. Horses died of tick bite. It was not easy to travel by wagon in those days.

Wagons made long distance trade for ivory possible. A good wagon could carry 3 000 kilograms or about 200 elephant tusks. When this ivory was sold in the Cape it was worth about £1 200 or P2 000. This meant that a year's travel could show a good profit.

European traders

As we have already seen, the early traders were Griqua, Batlhaping and Barolong, not Europeans. The Europeans who started to come to Botswana after 1810 were mostly adventurers. They wanted to see new lands, new people and to hunt animals they had never seen before. Other Europeans who came at this time were missionaries who wanted to change Setswana life to make the Batswana believe in the Christian God and live according to the Bible.

Travel was very expensive so the Europeans came with goods to trade. By trading and hunting elephant they could take back enough ivory to pay for their whole journey. As these first European visitors to Botswana began to return to the Cape and tell stories of what they had seen and hunted, so the traders began to move into Botswana. They brought coloured cloth, strong trousers, salt, cotton blankets, cheap clothes, brass wire, snuff boxes, iron hoes and cooking pots, knives and axes, ox-drawn ploughs, metal spoons, mirrors, china plates and cups, patent medicines, coloured beads, guns, lead and bullet moulds, powder, tinder-boxes for making fire, wine and brandy. See Fig. 85.

Most of these trade goods were almost worthless. The type of gun sold to the Batswana cost about P1.20 at the Cape. This could be sold for a large tusk weighing 30 kilograms and which could be sold at the Cape for P35. Europeans were not the only people to make huge profits. The Griqua often brought sheep for sale as they had difficulty in buying trade goods on the Orange River. In those days one sheep, worth about 70t, was exchanged for a tusk worth about P16. When Barolong traders first went to Lehututu with their wagons they exchanged a tinder box worth 20t for a tusk worth P16.

With the traders came money. At first the Batswana did not want to sell for money as they did not know what it was. But later they saw European hunters and traders paying their

Fig. 85 Trade goods such as guns, beads and clothing were brought by Europeans

Fig. 86 A simple ox plough, similar to those used in the 1800s

Griqua, Barolong and Batlhaping servants with money and they began to understand how it could be used.

All Batswana wanted guns, but the *dikgosi* controlled the trade and other people had nothing they could use to buy them. Soon they learned that people from the south, mostly Griqua and Batlhaping, would work for a hunter or trader for a year and receive as payment a gun and ammunition. Some Batswana as early as 1840 walked to the Orange River to work on Boer farms for money so they could buy guns. This was the start of migrant labour.

Changes brought about by trade

The introduction of long-distance or wagon trade and the goods traded resulted in many changes in Botswana.

The power of the *dikgosi*

One of the most important changes affected the position of *dikgosi*. They tried to control trade by making the traders deal only with them. They insisted the traders camped, and later built their stores, in the capital village. They also insisted on receiving presents such as clothes and brandy before they would trade. At first trade gave them a new way of gaining power amongst their people. But soon the traders found ways to deal with commoners. Once commoners had guns they were able to hunt for themselves and become rich. This meant that the *dikgosi* started to lose their new power. Common people were able to make themselves rich through trade. Now *dikgosi* could no longer say who should be rich and who should be poor. The new class of rich commoners owed nothing to the *dikgosi*. They were therefore able to some extent to become independent of the traditional system.

Expansion of states

Guns helped the Batswana to keep the Boers out. Guns also helped the Batswana to unite their countries. Khama III had a small mounted and armed force, a cavalry, which he used when he attacked minor *merafe* which refused to obey him. It was this cavalry which enabled him to defeat the Amandebele in 1863.

The need to get ivory to trade made the *dikgosi* try to expand their countries. Although the Bangwato claimed the Boteti and other distant places as their hunting grounds, they took little interest in these areas. This changed when the value of ivory was realised. Soon they were sending not only their hunters, but also their tribute collectors to distant places such as Boteti, Motloutse and Limpopo to claim their *sehuba* in ivory. Because of ivory hunting the Batawana State increased in size until it reached right into the Caprivi.

Communications

Wagon travel opened permanent roads where only paths had been and provided a means of communication. Even in the Okavango where wagons could not go, the *mokoro* began to be used to transport trade goods into remote areas and to bring ivory out. It made the whole country seem much smaller because it was so much easier to reach distant places. People began to travel much more.

Shoshong: a trading centre

Trade and wagon travel helped Khama III to turn Shoshong from a small village into an important trading centre. Because of its position Khama managed to make it the trading centre of the north for more than 40 years. Most traders saw Shoshong as a place to stop before making the final journey. They would set off on the great distances to Lake Ngami, to Bulozi and to Matabeleland. First Sekgoma I, and later Khama III, did everything they could to prevent the traders going on. They did not want to lose their control over the trade.

In fact, the traders themselves found it convenient to settle in Shoshong. They could trade there with the elephant hunters, both European and Batswana, who came in from these distant places. Traders working in Ngamiland, Bulozi and Matabeleland found it convenient to buy their goods in Shoshong. They preferred to pay higher prices rather than make the journey to the Cape which could take six months. Shoshong soon had a small European community including missionaries, traders and a few hunters who made it their headquarters. Their square houses with tin roofs, wooden furniture, wagons and ploughs set a new pattern for living.

The import of manufactured goods

Before the import of manufactured goods (iron pots, axes, cloth, ready-made clothes), people made everything they needed themselves (clay pots, baskets, leather clothes, iron tools and copper jewellery). If they did not have something, they traded for it with their neighbour. The import of European goods had two direct effects on the traditional economy. People began to stop making things because it was easier to buy them. They stopped mining and smelting iron and copper because it was easier to buy a metal hoe or a length of brass wire to make a

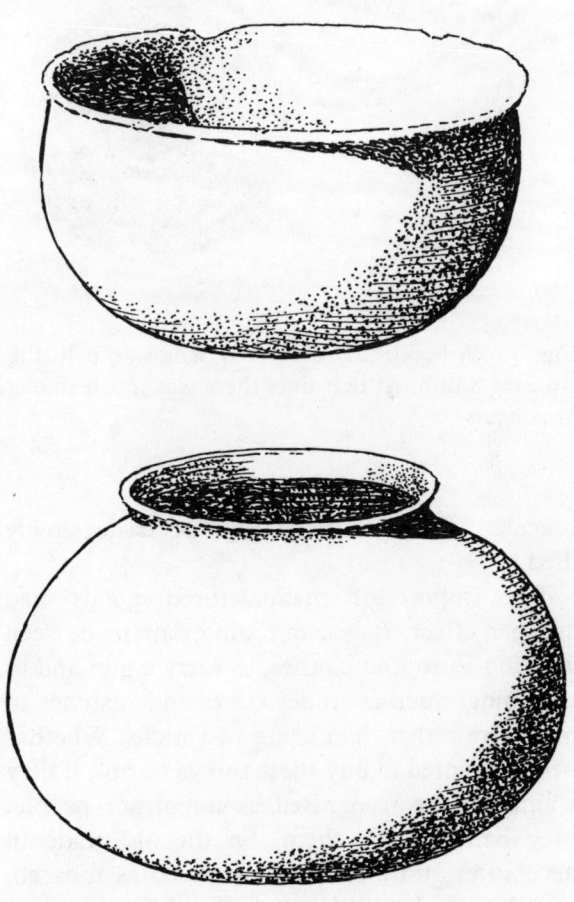

Fig. 87 Pottery from Manyelanong, made in about 1800

Fig. 88 A beautifully decorated Sengwato belt, the only item that still remains of all those collected by Andrew Smith. At that time there was much fine craftsmanship in clothes, jewellery, weapons and ornaments

bracelet. The traditional type of trade slowly died.

The import of manufactured goods had another effect. It became important to be seen wearing European clothes, to carry a gun and to use things such as tinder boxes and matches to make fire rather than using two sticks. Whether people wanted to buy these things or not, if they wanted to be recognised as important people, they had to have them. So the old trade in necessities and a few luxuries such as tobacco, jewellery and salt changed. People had to buy luxuries such as clothes, guns, and brandy. People did not want to sell their stock so they had to hunt to obtain goods for trade.

The destruction of wildlife

The last important change was the destruction of the wildlife. Before 1800 elephant, buffalo, rhinoceros and zebra could be found all over eastern Botswana and far into the Kalahari at places such as Letlhakeng, Kang, Lehututu, Bokspits and Ghanzi. Everybody hunted: the European adventurers, the *dikgosi*, the Griqua, Barolong and Batlhaping traders, the Batswana and the Bakgalagadi. Soon most of the wildlife had been killed in those areas where there was no tsetse fly, and therefore it became difficult or impossible to find ivory, skins and ostrich feathers to trade.

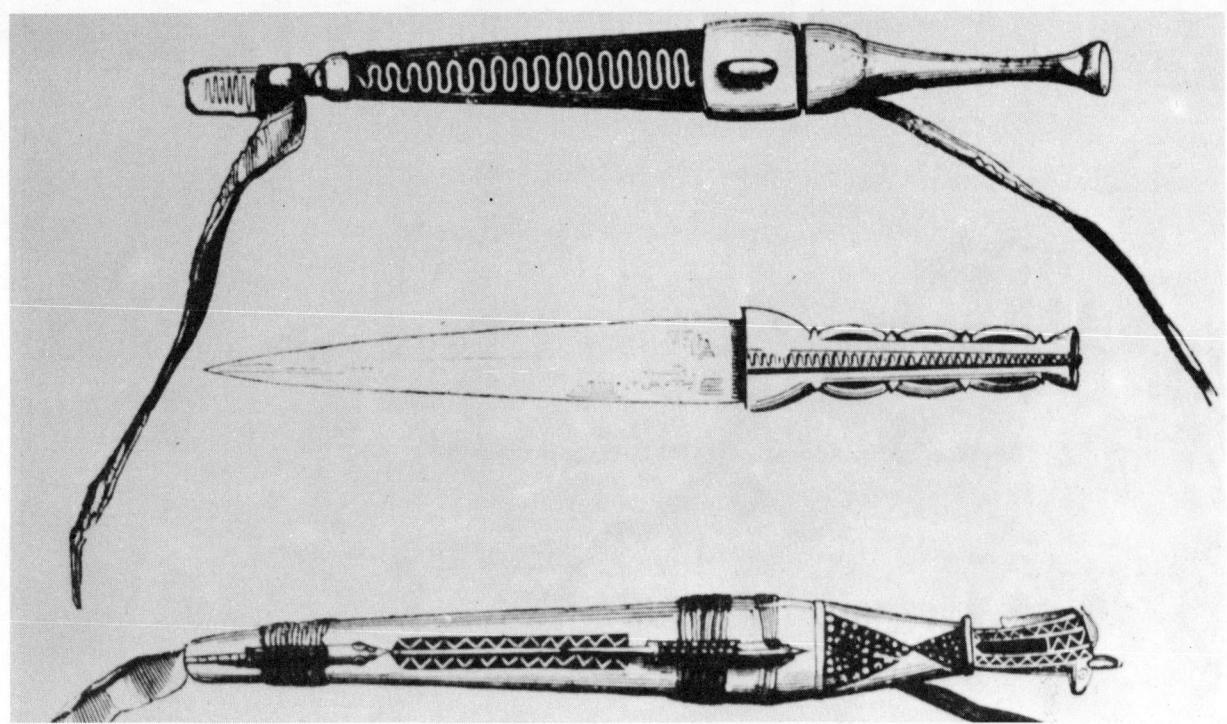

Fig. 89 Knives, exquisitely decorated

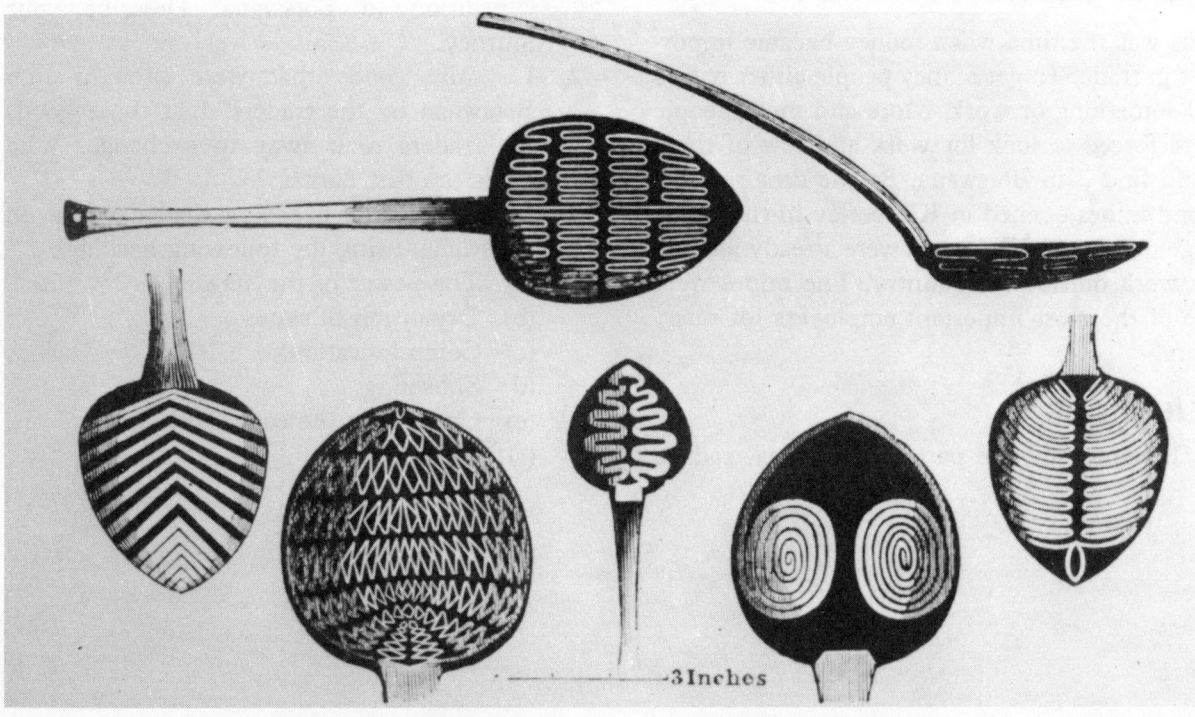

Fig. 90 Highly decorated spoons

127

Fig. 91 The mail coach north of Francistown in about 1897

Migrant labour

This was the time when money became important in trade. To get money people either had to sell something or work. More and more people were forced to look for work and few of them could find it in Botswana. By the time the diamond mines opened in Kimberley in the 1860s large numbers of Batswana were already looking for work outside the country. The mines were one of the most important employers for many years.

Questions

1. Imagine you are part of a Griqua trading expedition to Botswana. Describe your journey.
2. List the goods that were brought into Botswana by the traders. List those goods the traders took away in exchange. Who made the best bargain?
3. Explain the effects of long distance trade on Botswana, using the following headings.
   (a) The power of the *dikgosi*
   (b) Expansion of states
   (c) Communications
   (d) Shoshong
   (e) Changes in the economy
   (f) Wildlife

18 The Missionaries

During the 19th century missionaries were active in Southern Africa. Some of them extended their work to the land of the Batswana. Missionaries came to the Batswana because they had heard about the Batswana from travellers to the interior.

At that time missionaries went all over the world to preach the gospel. They believed that people would not be saved unless they were Christians. In order to convert people to Christianity, Christian churches in Europe and America formed Missionary Societies (groups) which sent missionaries throughout the world. One of these societies was the London Missionary Society (LMS), which was formed in 1795. Its first missionaries settled at the Cape Colony in 1799. By 1801 they had contacted the Griqua. In 1807, J.M. Kok and W. Edwards were preaching amongst the Batlhaping. Edwards reached Kanye, the Bangwaketse capital, in 1808, but he spent his time trading in ivory rather than preaching. He later left missionary work and became a slave-owning farmer in the Cape Colony.

In 1813 the LMS sent John Campbell to select sites for new mission stations in the interior. He reached Dithakong north of Kudumane (Kuruman), where he met Mothibi, king of the Batlhaping. In 1816, the Society sent two other missionaries to preach to the Batlhaping. Mothibi was not interested in Christianity but in trade. So the king did not show much interest in the missionaries. The Batswana were generally suspicious of missionaries in those early days because they spoke about bringing a new way of life. For this reason missionaries encouraged traders to trade with the Batswana. They hoped that this would indirectly help the spread of Christianity.

The importance of Kudumane

It soon became very clear to the LMS that they

Fig. 92 John Campbell, the first LMS missionary to reach the Batlhaping at Dithakong in 1813

Fig. 93 Kudumane (Kuruman) in about 1825, the first LMS mission station among the Batswana. From there Christianity spread to other parts of Batswana country

needed a station in the interior from which to spread the gospel. Robert Moffat was responsible for starting a station. He came to Southern Africa in 1817 and founded Kudumane where he settled with Hamilton in 1821. The importance of Kudumane was that it became the centre from which to spread Christianity to the interior. (See Fig. 93.) African evangelists (preachers) were trained there. These evangelists spread Christianity among the Batswana. They worked alone or together with the missionaries.

Moffat

Robert Moffat succeeded in spreading Christianity where others had failed. This was partly because he was a hard working man. The Batswana regarded him as an honest man who did not interfere in their politics. Because he was liked and respected, he made it possible for the other missionaries to be accepted by the Batswana. But the changes that had taken place in Southern Africa also enabled him to succeed. At that time traders had brought firearms to the interior and people who had guns often easily succeeded in battle. The coming of the difaqane caused destruction all over. An incident happened that made Moffat welcome among the Batswana. In 1823 difaqane groups attacked the Batlhaping. Moffat brought Griqua gunmen who defeated the difaqane groups. In 1824, the Griqua horsemen

Fig. 94 Robert Moffat, who started missionary work among the Batswana. It was he who brought Griqua gunmen to defend the Batlhaping against the Boers

accompanying Moffat drove some invaders from Pitsane and saved the Barolong. This assistance also helped Moffat to be readily accepted by the southern Batswana. Every ruler now wanted guns to protect and strengthen his state. Batswana rulers began to ask missionaries to settle among them. The main aim was to get guns through the presence of missionaries. This was because traders often went where missionaries worked. Another factor which made Batswana like Moffat was that he visited Mzilikazi, king of the Amandebele, at Mosega in 1829, and tried to persuade him not to attack the Batswana. He had little success but the Batswana appreciated (liked) his attempt.

Livingstone

In 1841 David Livingstone came to Kudumane. By 1842, he had visited the Bakwena, Bakgatla, Bangwato and Bakalanga. In 1845 he married Moffat's daughter, Mary, and settled among the Bakwena at Kolobeng. He taught Kgosi Sechele I how to read and write and converted him to Christianity. Sechele's seeming total conversion did not last long. He soon realised that Christianity went against Bakwena customs. He therefore accepted Christianity half-heartedly.

Livingstone's real interest was not in missionary work but in exploration. He wanted to open new areas of Africa to British trade and Christianity. He also wanted to record new scientific knowledge gained through exploration.

In 1849 he, together with the traders Oswell and Murray, reached Lake Ngami. They were guided by a Mokwena man and were the first white people to see this lake. Kgosi Letsholathebe I welcomed them and traded his ivory for guns. Thereafter Livingstone sent his family to England and went to explore Central Africa where he later died. The Batswana liked Livingstone because he cured illness. He was a medical doctor. They also liked him because he was the son-in-law of the much liked Robert Moffat. His wife, Mary, seems also to have won the love of the Bakwena because she worked

Fig. 95 David Livingstone, missionary, doctor and explorer. He taught Sechele I how to read and write

hard among them and spoke Setswana well. Although he remained a missionary all his life, Livingstone spent most of his time exploring rather than preaching.

In 1859 the missionaries of the Hermannsburg Society, a German Lutheran missionary society, brought Christianity to the Bangwato at Shoshong under Sekgoma I. The Hermannsburg missionaries had first settled among the Bakwena in 1857 after Livingstone's departure. They soon left because of some misunderstanding with Sechele I. Sekgoma I did not become a Christian but his son Khama Boikanyo Sekgoma (later Khama III), and his brother, Kgamane, did so. It was the Lutherans who baptised Khama in 1860 although he later joined the LMS. The Hermannsburg missionary, Heinrich Schulenburg, left for South Africa in 1862

Fig. 96 Heinrich Schulenburg (far left) a German Lutheran missionary, among the Balete. (Note the Molete teacher in front of the class.) It was he who baptised Khama in 1860

because of some quarrel with his Society in Natal. This ended the Lutheran Church's activities among the Bangwato. In 1862 the LMS sent its own missionaries led by John Mackenzie to work among the Bangwato. The Bangwato Lutherans such as Khama then became LMS followers.

The Bangwato church undertook to spread Christianity to the interior as far as Ngamiland. After Livingstone's visit to Ngamiland, Letsholathebe I continually asked for missionaries to come to his land. For a long time the LMS was unwilling to send missionaries because Ngamiland had malaria. Also it was distant and the sandy Kalahari made travelling there difficult. Moremi II, Letsholathebe's successor, asked Khama III to send missionaries. Finally the Bangwato church sent Reverend James Hepburn and some Bangwato Christians to start church work in Ngamiland in 1877. Hepburn

Fig. 97 Khukhu Mogodi, who with Hepburn and African evangelists, started missionary work among the Batawana

left and missionary work was done by African evangelists led by Khukhu Mogodi. Mogodi was later dismissed because he engaged in trade. He had to trade in order to earn a living because the LMS did not give him much financial support. After many years of service Mogodi retired and was awarded a certificate of merit by the LMS. He died in 1925 at the age of 96. He was replaced by evangelist Somolekae. Missionary work was done mainly by Africans with very little European help in the early days.

Other missionary bodies worked among other Batswana groups. The Dutch Reformed Church worked among the Bakgatla, the Lutheran Church among the Balete, and the Anglican Church mainly among the Bakhurutshe in the Tati District. By the 1880s every major village had a resident missionary. From the major villages in each *morafe*, church work spread to the outlying areas.

Missionaries and politics

Although missionaries stated that they were not interested in politics, they sometimes found themselves involved in Batswana politics. Missionaries generally supported Christian rulers against non-Christian ones. For example, the LMS missionaries secretly supported Khama III in his dispute with his father, Sekgoma I, in the 1870s. This was because Khama was a Christian and Sekgoma had rejected Christianity. They hoped to be able to work more freely and successfully under a Christian king.

The early missionaries were more careful, however, not to interfere in Batswana politics because there was no Colonial Government to protect them. They had to try to please African kings in order to be allowed to preach. But the missionaries who came later had the protection of the Colonial Government. So they were not always very careful in dealing with African rulers. They did not respect African rulers as much as the earlier missionaries had done. Quite often they appealed to the Colonial Government to remove kings who resisted Christianity. For example, in Ngamiland Reverend Wookey supported the removal of Sekgoma Letsholathebe from the kingship (*bogosi*). He did this because Sekgoma defended Setswana culture against the influence of Christianity.

Sometimes missionaries engaged in politics because the rulers requested them to do so. Those missionaries who were trusted by Batswana rulers were asked to act as interpreters, secretaries and advisers in relations between the Batswana and Europeans. But the missionaries had to be careful not to get too involved in domestic politics. If they did, they could be expelled. For example, Khama III expelled Hepburn from his country in 1892 for this reason and later he removed Lloyd from Shoshong in 1913.

Missionaries played an important part in bringing Bechuanaland under British rule. They encouraged Britain to colonise the land of the Batswana. This was true especially of Reverend John Mackenzie. They had the following reasons for wanting the Batswana to be under British rule.

1. The LMS missionaries were British citizens and so they wanted their own country to rule the lands of the Batswana.
2. They feared that if Britain did not rule the land of the Batswana, the Boers would colonise it. The LMS would then be replaced by the Dutch Reformed Church. So they wanted to use British power to protect their spiritual empire. They also knew that the Boers hated them.
3. They believed that under British rule the Batswana rulers would be powerless to resist Christianity.
4. They wanted Britain to change those African customs they considered 'heathen'. In this way, they believed that Africans would then accept Christianity readily.
5. The missionaries also wanted to prevent African lands from being taken away by the Boers, and to protect Africans from Boer attacks. Reverend Mackenzie, in particular, criticised the Boers for ill-treating the Batswana.

For these reasons the LMS missionaries advised Batswana to accept British protection. In fact, John Mackenzie urged Britain to take over the land of the Batswana. Mackenzie accompanied General Warren when he came to declare a protectorate over the Batswana. In short, the missionaries supported British rule as a way of spreading Christianity. This is an important difference between missionaries and traders. Traders supported British rule in order to make profit.

Missionaries and Setswana culture

Most missionaries despised and disliked Setswana customs, especially the most important ones such as *bogadi* (bridewealth), rain making, polygamy, *bogwera* and *bojale* (male and female initiation schools, see Fig. 50 and Fig. 51, on page 76) and beer drinking. They worked hard to destroy these customs. On the other hand the Batswana valued their customs and therefore wanted to protect and preserve them. This is what caused conflict between the Batswana and the missionaries.

But why did the missionaries dislike Setswana customs? Firstly the missionaries wrongly believed that European culture was superior to all cultures of the world. Therefore, they respected only those people who adopted (took) European culture (western culture). Many missionaries believed that a true Christian was someone who adopted western culture. To them Setswana culture was a sign of heathenism. This, of course, was incorrect. All customs or cultures are important to people who practise them. The other reason was that missionaries found out that the stronger the customs, the more difficult it was to convert the people. This is why they wanted to destroy the most important Setswana customs. They thought these prevented Batswana from becoming Christians. The people the missionaries disliked most were the *dingaka* (medicine men) because they were

Fig. 98 Khama III, about 1882. He had some success in ending some Sengwato customs which were disliked by the LMS. He was not entirely successful however because of the strong belief in Setswana culture

Fig. 99 An independent church baptism. This was done by completely submerging the person being baptised

the defenders of customs. They also worked closely with the rulers to make rain.

Did the missionaries succeed in the battle against customs? There were some minor successes. For example, such *dikgosi* as Khama III stopped *bogadi*, rain making, *bogwera*, *bojale*, and beer drinking. But in most *merafe* Setswana customs continued to exist. Even among the Bangwato, Khama did not manage completely to end all the customs which the LMS disliked. This is why today some Setswana customs continue to flourish. Customs only disappear entirely when the people themselves no longer find them useful or when they have found something to replace them. For example, in most Batswana states missionary education replaced the initiation schools.

Independent churches

One problem which faced the missionaries was the rise of independent churches. They were started and run by Batswana Christians who left missionary churches. The independent church movement was sometimes called Ethiopianism. The name Ethiopianism came from the Biblical name Ethiopia which meant Africa. So all Africans were referred to in the Bible as Ethiopians. The followers of independent churches were proud to be associated with Ethiopia or Abyssinia. This was because it had a very ancient Christian Coptic church which was run entirely by Africans. The Coptic church was older than European churches. Later, the name Ethiopia was associated with independence because that country was the only one in Africa not colonised by outsiders. It was ruled completely by Africans. Like Ethiopia, therefore, independent churches were controlled by Africans. Independent churches were most common in countries where Africans or black people were oppressed most by Europeans such as in South Africa and America. Because of white domination (rule) in church matters, black people started their own churches to get rid of this domination.

Mothoagae's Church

In Botswana, the independent church movement was small. It started because missionaries sometimes interfered in domestic politics. So some rulers were happy when Batswana started their own churches as this reduced missionary influence. The unhappiness with missionary education also made some Batswana start their own churches. Some African evangelists started their own churches because the European missionaries did not allow them to have important positions in the church. Europeans always supervised Africans and not the other way round. The Europeans despised the Africans. Sometimes missionaries practised racism. For all these reasons, Batswana started their own churches.

One example of an independent church among the Batswana was the church of Mothoagae, a Mongwaketse evangelist. He became unhappy with the LMS because it wanted to transfer him to Lehututu in the Kalahari. He refused to go because of his wife's ill health. He also disagreed with the local missionary about how the church was run. He was dismissed from the church. In 1902 he formed his own independent church. He had the support of Kgosi Bathoen I. The church grew and won some followers. The church ended its work in the Bangwaketse area when Mothoagae was banished. Kgosi Bathoen I did this because he believed that Mothoagae supported his rival, Kwenaitsile. Mothoagae died in banishment.

There were other independent churches in other areas. In general, independent churches did not become widespread because the Batswana rulers still preferred the LMS. But their existence caused the LMS to try to reform in order to stop Batswana from leaving the church.

Benefits brought by missionaries

The missionaries did some bad things. For example they tried to destroy Setswana culture. But they also did some good things. They brought education and printed books in Setswana.

The Bible and Setswana literature (books)

Before the missionaries came knowledge was passed on by the spoken word. There was no writing or reading. The missionaries wanted the Batswana to know how to read so that they could read the Bible. In this way Christianity would spread quickly. We do not know exactly who wrote down the first Setswana. But in 1819, the missionary, James Read, wrote a small spelling book which was printed at Griquatown. John Campbell wrote the Lord's Prayer in Setswana. It was poorly written Setswana but it was a useful start. The prayer, for example, began: *'Hara a Chuna'* (*Rara Wa Rona* — Our Father).

Robert Moffat, assisted by Hamilton, made the first serious effort to produce Setswana literature. He translated Saint Luke's gospel and had it printed in Cape Town in 1830. He then established a printing press in Kudumane in 1831 and began to translate and print the Bible. This was the beginning of the press which continues to produce Setswana books today. J. Archell followed with the first Setswana grammar in 1837. By 1838 Moffat, helped by the other missionaries, had completed translating the New Testament. In 1841, William Ashton joined Moffat and played a major part in translating the Old Testament. This work was completed in 1857. By 1850, the printing press had grown so much that it employed a full time printer. The LMS did not print religious books only. They also printed newspapers in Setswana. In 1857, Ashton started a newspaper which he called *Mokaedi oa Bechuana le Muleri ea Mahuku* (The Instructor of the Batswana and Announcer of the News). Although the paper did not last long, it was the beginning of non-religious Setswana literature. Other newspapers followed later and many Batswana wrote in them.

Other missionaries also published books in Setswana. This literature helped to spread education and Christianity. Each missionary body published in the Setswana dialect of the people among whom they worked. The LMS published in Setlhaping, the Methodists in Serolong, the Lutherans in Sekwena, and later the Dutch Reformed Church in Sekgatla. They each used different orthography (spelling). This is why a single Setswana orthography did not develop for a long time. Even today attempts are being made to have one Setswana orthography.

Missionary education

One of the most important contributions made by the missionaries to the life of the Batswana was education. The first schools were started by missionaries. The most important of the missionary groups in the field of education, especially in the early days, was the LMS. In order to understand the kind of education given by the missionaries, we must know what their aim was. Missionaries mainly aimed at saving

Fig. 100 An early LMS church and classroom at Thamaga

souls and not at improving the economic or social life of the Batswana. This was especially true of the early missionaries. They wanted to convert the Batswana to Christianity. One of the ways to do this was to enable the people to read the Bible. This was the reason why the missionaries translated the Bible into Setswana. From this aim it is clear that missionary education would not concentrate on practical worldly subjects such as building, carpentry, etc. They stressed instead reading, writing and scripture. This aim of the LMS missionaries lasted for a long time and caused misunderstanding between them and the Batswana. They wanted practical education like that given at the Presbyterian school at Lovedale in South Africa, and the Paris Evangelical Missionary Society school at Morija in Lesotho. This shows that there was some difference between church schools. Some of them gave very good education. Because of complaints by the Batswana the LMS missionaries later slowly tried to give a better education. In short then, education was seen as a means of spreading Christianity.

Early stages in education

The history of education among the Batswana begins with the founding of Kudumane. Kudumane trained evangelists. These were Batswana men whose main duty was to preach the word of God. In addition to preaching, they also taught in the schools. These men were sent from Kudumane to the interior. So the spread of Christianity and education among the Batswana was done mainly by these young Africans rather than by the missionaries themselves. One of the earliest evangelists was Mebalwe. He, together with David Livingstone and Edwards, started mission work at Mabotsa near Zeerust among the Bakgatla ba ga Mmanaana in the 1840s. This was the first school among the Batswana north of Kudumane. After this other schools were started among the Bakwena by Livingstone. Schools were also started among the other *merafe* in later years by the LMS.

The LMS was not the only denomination which started education among the Batswana in the early years. Heinrich Schulenburg, the Hermannsburg missionary, taught Bangwato children. Among his first pupils were Khama, his brother Kgamane and Elizabeth Godisang who later became Khama III's wife, Mma-Bessie. When the Lutherans left, the LMS took over the schools and built new ones.

By the 1860s most Batswana *merafe* had schools. Only the Batawana were left behind, mainly because Ngamiland was far away and had malaria. So, there, the work of the church was left to African evangelists. The first was Khukhu Mogodi from 1877 to 1905 and then Somolekae joined him in the 1890s. They taught the Batawana but their education was not very successful during that early period. Teaching materials such as books, paper and pencils could not easily be transported to Ngamiland. The LMS did not give Khukhu enough support in money and in other ways.

As time passed, it was felt that the evangelists educated at Kudumane were not properly trained as school teachers. So a new school to train teachers was started in 1871 at Shoshong by Reverend Mackenzie. The school was moved to Kudumane in 1876 and was called the Moffat Institution in memory of Robert Moffat. The main weakness of the school was that it did not place enough emphasis on the practical subjects which Batswana parents wanted. There was, though, an attempt to introduce agriculture. However this failed because Batswana students revolted against manual labour. In 1897 the school closed down mainly because of misunderstandings between the missionaries and the Batswana.

By 1880 every major Batswana village had some schools. All the schools were primary and most teachers were Batswana. Although the emphasis was on religious education, some other subjects were taught. Most schools taught reading, writing, arithmetic, Setswana, domestic science such as sewing, baking and ironing for girls, a bit of history, some geography and, of course, scripture. This was an improvement over the earlier years when reading, writing and scripture were usually the only subjects. Except for domestic science, education was largely not practical. Very little English was taught. All teaching was in Setswana.

Problems of early education

Education often conflicted with the Batswana way of life. Parents did not always want to send

Fig. 101   The Moffat Institution built by the LMS for training evangelists and school teachers

Fig. 102 An outside class at a mission school: in those days this was very common

their children to school when there was important work to be done at home. This was especially true for boys who had to go to the cattle post (*moraka*) to look after cattle rather than attend school. Missionaries even tried a system of cattle post schools. The boys would be allowed to take books to the cattle post and teach each other. This system was unworkable because there were no teachers there and the cattle posts were very scattered. This meant that there was no supervision. The girls also did not go to school during the ploughing and harvesting seasons because they had to work on the lands. But they were in the village most of the time. So there were more girls than boys in the schools.

In the beginning only children of royalty and other important people went to school. This was partly because the poor could not afford school fees. But the main reason was that until later, Batswana rulers did not want the children of the other *merafe* under their rule to be educated.

Batswana rulers felt that education would give subject people more or less the same social status as themselves. They also feared that Christian teaching about the equality of all men might cause the subject people to revolt against their rule.

For example, the Batawana did not want the Bayei to learn. This attitude changed later when, for example, Khama III sent Bangwato teachers to teach the Bakalanga of Nswazwi in 1899. It is interesting that the children of these *merafe* were more interested in education than those of the ruling groups. This was because they saw education as the only way to advancement. This was especially true in the later years of the Protectorate when they could join the civil service. Another reason why many Bakalanga were educated was that they attended school in Southern Rhodesia where education was much more developed than in the Protectorate.

Another problem was the shortage of funds.

Missionary societies were not generally rich. Whatever money they had, they spent on spreading Christianity rather than on good education. Until 1904, the Protectorate administration did not grant any money for education at all. So, because of poor pay, the mission schools could not attract good teachers. It was not possible to buy good teaching materials. So the standard of education was poor.

Misunderstanding develops

This poor education together with the lack of practical subjects led to misunderstanding between the missionaries and the Batswana. Part of the reason for lack of practical subjects was that most young Batswana preferred academic subjects. Young Batswana felt that manual work lowered the high social status which they believed education brought. The Batswana parents were opposed to what they called 'book learning' (not practical). They wanted their children to be builders and carpenters. They wanted their children to be taught English so that they could understand the secrets of the white man. They wanted education for real life. Some parents showed their opposition by sending their children to better schools in South Africa. But when these young people returned, the LMS refused to hire them in their schools because they were taught by different missionary bodies. They probably feared that they would not teach religion as the LMS liked. They also felt that these young people were too radical (not tame). Another reason for the opposition to mission schools was that the Batswana felt that missionaries gave better education and more attention to traders' children than to Batswana pupils. In spite of these complaints, Batswana continued to send their children to these schools which were jointly run by the *merafe* and the church.

This misunderstanding led the Batswana to call for more control of the schools by the *dikgosi* and the *merafe*. Some *merafe* actually started their own self-help (*ipelegeng*) schools. These were called *kgotla* or ward schools. These schools usually did not charge any fees because they were built

Fig. 103 Simon Ratshosa, seated, left, at his wedding, one of the first Batswana to start *merafe* schools. Later he became a nationalist, critical of the Protectorate administration and the *dikgosi*

with *merafe* money. The teachers were young Batswana volunteers or they were Batswana paid by the *merafe*. The schools were under the control of the *dikgosi*. These schools were popular and competed with LMS ones. One such school among the Bangwato was called Serowe Public School and the Principal was Simon Ratshosa. They were also found among the Bakwena and the Bangwaketse. Some *merafe* even introduced a special education tax to pay for the running of these schools. The Bangwaketse and the Bakwena were the first to introduce a tax of two shillings (about 20 thebe) in 1901. The other *merafe* did this later. Then the colonial government copied this idea. The tax was paid by every taxpayer. The establishment of independent non-church schools showed clearly that the LMS education system was not satisfactory. In spite of all these weaknesses, however, the missionaries had laid the foundation for education among the

Batswana. By 1900 there were about 20 primary schools with about a thousand pupils in the Protectorate. The credit for this goes to the different missionary bodies: the LMS, the Dutch Reformed Church, the Anglicans, the Lutherans, the Roman Catholics, and to the *dikgosi* and the *merafe*, but not to the Protectorate administration.

Education was not the only good thing brought by the missionaries. They brought useful tools such as the ox plough and the wagon. Roger Price introduced the plough among the Bakwena. They also taught Batswana new forms of vegetable gardening and how to irrigate crops. They brought new items of European clothing and food such as bread, tea, coffee and sugar. The wives of some of the missionaries did a lot of useful work such as teaching sewing, baking and nursing the sick. Quite often they made friends with royal women and so made it easier for their husbands to work smoothly with the rulers. Most missionaries would not have been successful without the very considerable assistance of their wives. For example, the Moffat daughters, brought up among the Batswana, and speaking fluent Setswana, did much to further their husbands' work.

Questions

1. Give three reasons why Robert Moffat was popular among the Southern Batswana.
2. Hold a class debate on the issue, 'The missionary could only succeed if he destroyed Setswana customs.'
3. Give three reasons for the development of independent churches in Botswana.
4. Make a list, numbering your points, of the criticisms made by Batswana of missionary education.

19 British Rule in Botswana: The Beginning

Background

During the 19th century, European countries such as Britain, France and Germany had become rich because of the industrial revolution which had begun in earlier years. The industrial revolution led to the building of many factories in European countries. Businessmen owned

Fig. 104 Cotton mills in Manchester, about 1870. Cotton (and other raw materials) was imported from colonies and processed into clothing

these factories which produced goods of different kinds such as clothing and iron articles. They wanted to export these goods to other countries so as to make a profit. These businessmen or manufacturers also wanted to import raw materials, products used to manufacture goods, such as cotton, rubber, tea, iron and other minerals from other countries. So in the 19th century many European traders and miners went to non-European countries such as Africa, to look for:

1 new markets for their goods,
2 raw materials for their factories.

This desire of Europeans to go to other lands to make a profit is called imperialism.

Soon there was great competition among Europeans for markets in foreign lands. In order to have safe markets, traders and mineral seekers, who were called concessionaires, actively supported their governments in colonising those countries in which they were interested.

It is important to note that most foreign lands were colonised because of their wealth in raw materials. But sometimes, even if there was no wealth which Europeans knew about at the time, a country was colonised because it might have wealth in the future. Other countries were colonised not because they had wealth but because they were in an area through which a European country wanted to expand to reach rich countries.

The activities of European businessmen abroad were so profitable to their countries that European governments supported them by colonising foreign lands. In Africa this colonisation took place in the last quarter of the 19th century, especially between 1880 and 1900. This period is called the scramble (rush) for Africa. The land of the Batswana, which was not called Botswana at that time, was colonised during this period.

The competition for African colonies was so great that European countries were ready to fight each other. To avoid war, they met at the Berlin Conference in Germany in 1884 to decide how to divide or partition Africa among themselves peacefully. It is important to note that the Africans did not know that their independent countries were being shared among Europeans. After the Berlin Conference, the expansion of European imperialism in Africa became very fast and soon all African countries except Ethiopia had lost their independence.

Europeans carried out colonisation by different methods.

1 The most important method was conquest. Because of the industrial revolution which began in Europe, Europeans made powerful guns before other people had them. So they easily defeated people who used old weapons such as spears or bows and arrows. Europeans also possessed steam ships which enabled them to travel to distant places and attack from the sea.

2 Europeans also sometimes tricked rulers of foreign lands into giving away their lands. The most common method was to get a ruler who could not read or write to sign, usually by putting a cross, an agreement called a treaty. This gave away his land. In most cases these rulers did not understand what the treaty meant.

3 Sometimes rulers placed themselves under the protection of a European power because they feared enemies who wanted to destroy their state. Although they believed that they would remain independent under such protection this did not happen. The protecting power gradually took away the powers of the protected rulers.

The Boers attack the Batswana

The fall of the Amandebele state with its capital at Mosega must have caused delight among the Batswana. They believed that they could now live in peace. But in fact the fall of Mzilikazi brought new troubles from the Boers. See the map, Fig. 105. They regarded themselves as the inheritors of Mzilikazi's kingdom. Trouble began when the Boers told the Batswana rulers that their lands were now under Boer control because they had defeated the Batswana's Amandebele enemy. The Batswana rejected this claim and the Boers made preparations to attack them.

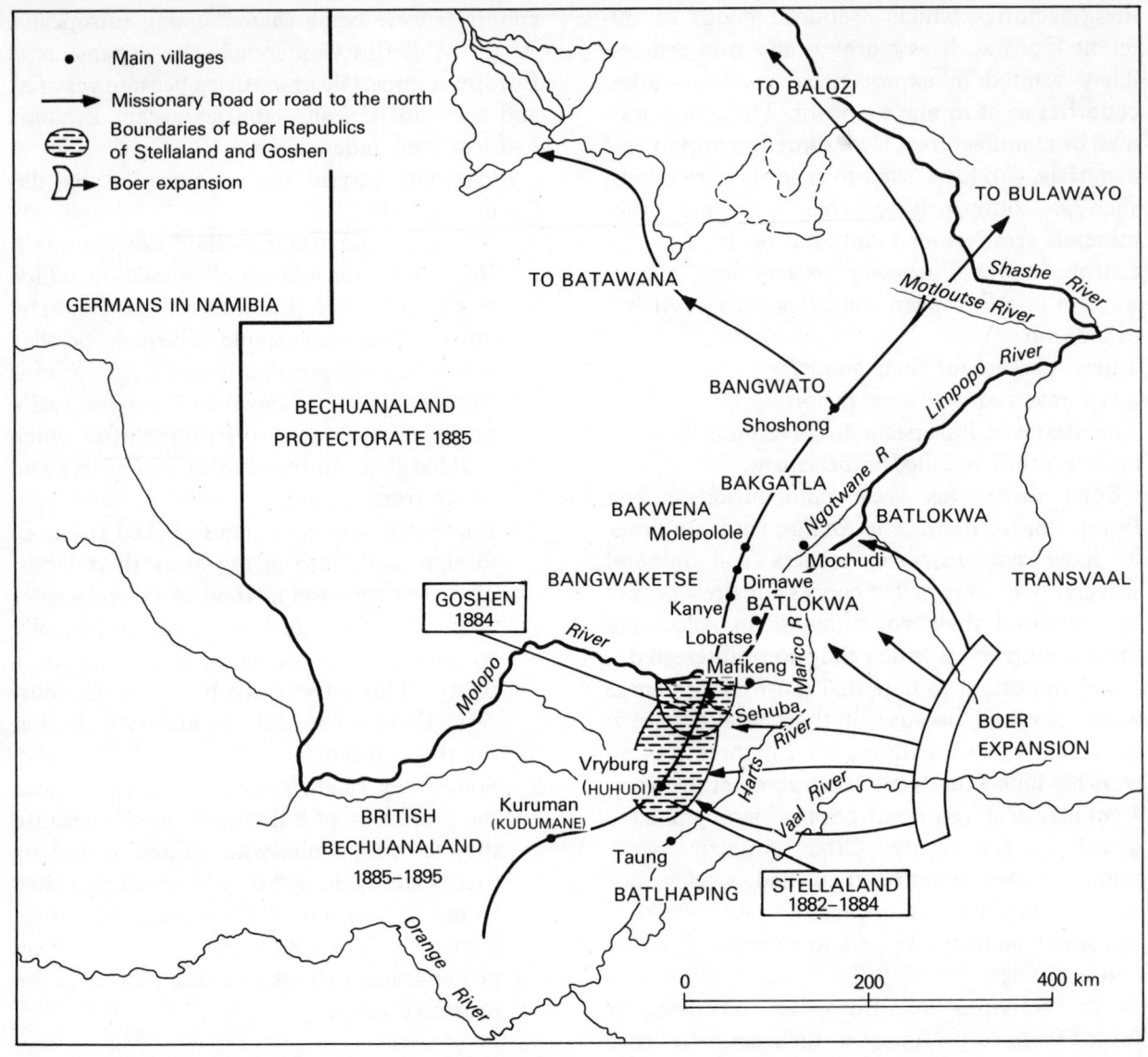

Fig. 105 Boer expansion and the route to the north

For some time the Boers had noticed that the Batswana were getting guns from traders. They feared that these guns would make the Batswana states difficult to defeat. The British Government still regarded the Boers as being under British control even after they had left the Cape. The Boers wanted to be free from British control so as to deal with the Africans as they liked.

In 1852 representatives of the Boers and the British met on the Sand River and signed an agreement called the Sand River Convention. They agreed as follows.
1 The Boers were allowed to rule the Transvaal, the young Boer State, according to their own laws and without British interference.
2 The British Government would not ally itself with Africans north of the Vaal River.
3 Britain would control the sale of arms and ammunition to Africans. But the Boers could buy as much ammunition as they wanted.

The Sand River Convention allowed the Boers to deal with the Africans as they wished. In fact Britain had allied herself with the Boers against the Africans.

By the time of the Convention some Batswana groups were already under Boer control, for example the Bakhurutshe and the Bakgatla ba ga Kgafela. But the Batlhaping, Barolong, Bakwena, Bangwaketse and Bangwato were independent. After signing the Convention the Boers called a meeting of the Batswana rulers to inform them that they were now under Boer rule. As we have seen rulers such as Sechele I rejected Boer rule. This resulted in the battle of Dimawe in 1852 (see page 116).

The Boers managed to capture about 200 women and children, destroy crops and burn down Dr Livingstone's house. After this the Boer commando (raiding party) then attacked the Bangwaketse and the Barolong of Montshiwa who had refused to help the Boers to fight Sechele. Sechele appealed to the British Government at the Cape Colony for protection. In those days 'protection' to the Batswana rulers did not mean placing themselves totally under colonial rule. It meant an alliance of independent states for the purpose of fighting a threat from outside (see page 151). Protection was refused because at that time Britain was not interested in colonising the lands of the Batswana. The scramble for this area had not yet begun. The Barolong, Bakwena, Bangwaketse and Bangwato formed an alliance to fight the Boers. The alliance was strengthened in the 1880s when the Bakgatla and the Batawana joined it.

The Bakgatla ba ga Kgafela had come under Boer domination after the fall of Mzilikazi's state. They lived on Boer farms and were forced to provide free labour. Kgosi Pilane and his son Kgamanyane tried to soften the burden of Boer rule by helping the Transvaal Boers in their wars against some African groups such as the Basotho in 1865. Boer oppression, however, did not end. In 1869 Kgamanyane told his people not to give free labour to the Boers. The Boers replied by having him flogged (beaten) publicly. Kgamanyane and some of his people left the Transvaal and settled at Mochudi in Bakwena country in 1871. In 1874 Kgamanyane died as a result, it is believed, of the beating.

The Batswana further north were also threatened by the Boers of the Transvaal. They considered all land north, east and west of them to belong to them. They wanted the country of the Bangwato. The discovery of gold in the Tati area in 1866 made the Boers claim this area. The Bangwato ruler, Macheng, refused to give them this area which the Amandebele also claimed as theirs.

In the 1870s some Boers who were unhappy with their government in the Transvaal wanted to travel across Bangwato country to create a new settlement somewhere in the Kalahari, Ngamiland or Angola. In 1876 King Khama III, ruler of the Bangwato, appealed to Sir Henry Barkly, the British Governor at the Cape Colony, for protection. However the Governor was unwilling to grant this protection.

In 1878 Khama warned that he would fight the Boers if they tried to take his country. In the end Khama allowed the Boers to pass through his country on their way to the west, but he did not allow them to settle in his country. Most of the Boers died of thirst in the Kalahari. This saved the Batawana because only a few of them reached Ngamiland and then passed on to Angola. A small number returned to South Africa.

Because of these constant attacks, threats, and expansion of the Boers, all the Batswana and indeed, all Africans in Southern Africa hated the Boers whom they called *maburu*. The Boers also took by force young African boys and girls to work for them as cheap labour on the farms. This was a form of slavery. Given a choice between the Boers and the British, the Batswana preferred the British. This is why Batswana rulers asked for British protection from the Boers.

Declaration of a British Protectorate over the Batswana

Although the Batswana *dikgosi* had asked for

Fig. 106 John Mackenzie in 1884: missionary and statesman who opposed Boer colonisation of Batswana territory

British protection from the Boers from the 1850s until the 1870s, it was not given.

Missionaries of the LMS such as the Reverend John Mackenzie, tried to get Britain to protect the Batswana, but did not succeed. Mackenzie wanted the land of the Batswana to be ruled by Britain for various reasons:

1. So that the Boers could not interfere with missionary work. He knew that the Boers hated missionaries because they taught Africans skills such as reading and writing. They also taught that all people were equal before God. The Boers believed that white people were superior to black people. They still believe this even today in South Africa. This is one of the reasons why there is *apartheid* there. *Apartheid* means sep-arateness or unequal treatment of people.
2. So that British traders could trade without Boer competition.
3. So that Britain could protect the Batswana from being attacked by the Boers and their land taken away by force. Mackenzie thought Britain would develop the land of the Batswana and spread European civilisation. Mackenzie is an example of a missionary who encouraged colonisation.

The British, however, did not want to spend money protecting the land of the Batswana. They did not consider this area important enough to them at that time. In fact, at that time the British Government did not want to spend too much money on colonies generally.

In 1885 Britain suddenly declared that it had put the lands of all the Batswana under its protection. See Fig. 109 on page 149. This announcement surprised the Batswana rulers because Britain had refused to protect them in earlier years. This time the Batswana had not asked for protection but it was given to them. In fact, the German Government was told about the Protectorate by Britain even before the Batswana were informed.

What made Britain change its mind and declare a Protectorate over the Batswana in 1885? The main reason why Britain declared a Protectorate in 1885 was not because they now wanted to protect the Batswana. The real reason was that the land of the Batswana had now become very important to Britain.

Why was Botswana now so important to Britain? In the 1880s, the trade in animal products such as ivory, ostrich feathers, skins and trophies still existed but it was not as important as in earlier years. There were some British traders in all large Batswana villages. But these economic activities alone did not cause Britain to declare a Protectorate.

In the 1880s, however, the land of the Batswana suddenly became important because of the competition among the British, the Germans and the Boers in Southern Africa. For many years British traders and missionaries had used the road from the Cape through Mafikeng,

Vryburg, Ga Ngwaketse, Kweneng to Shoshong where it branched to Bulawayo, Ngamiland and Bulozi or Barotseland (western Zambia). It was called the road to the north or the missionary road. It was used by the missionaries, hunters and traders. It was very important for British trade and expansion northwards. The economic importance of the road was increased by the discovery of diamonds at Kimberley in 1867. British capitalists owned the diamond mines and recruited labour from everywhere in Southern Africa. Already in the 1870s, Batswana sought work in Kimberley. Labour recruiters and the labourers used the missionary road. When gold was discovered at the Witwatersrand in 1884-85, the road became even more important for labour recruitment. Cecil John Rhodes, the wealthy Cape Colony politician, and one-time Prime Minister, also wanted to use the road to the north to expand to the lands of the Amandebele and the Mashona (Zimbabwe). The country was rumoured to be rich in gold and other minerals and so Rhodes and Britain wanted it.

In the meantime conflict between the Boers and the Batswana was continuing. The Transvaal was now a powerful state because of the wealth from gold mining. It was, therefore, able to expand forcefully. John Mackenzie went to England where he tried to get the British Government to agree to declare a Protectorate over the Batswana. He finally won the support of such important politicians as Joseph Chamberlain.

The anger of the British against the Boers was aroused by the murder of Christopher Bethell in 1884. Bethell belonged to an important British family. He was a relative of General Charles Warren who was later sent to declare a Protectorate over the lands of the Batswana. He was a friend of Montshiwa, was married to Tepo Boabile, a Morolong, and lived at Sehuba, the Barolong capital. In 1884, he was murdered by some Boers when they attacked the Barolong. Mackenzie used the murder of Bethell to show

Fig. 107 Diamond mining at Kimberley in the late 19th century. The area was divided into hundreds of small claims. Lines of claims were separated by roads as shown in the picture

why it was necessary for Britain to take over the area before the Boers grabbed it all. This incident caused the British public to call upon their Government to stop Boer filibustering (grabbing land).

It became quite clear to the British Government that the road to the north was in danger of being cut off. See Fig. 105, page 144. This would endanger British interests in the interior. There was a scramble for this area. The Boers threatened the road from the east. Some of them seized the Batlhaping land ruled by Mankurwane and created the independent Republic of Stellaland around Vryburg. They also took Barolong land near Mafikeng ruled by Montshiwa and called it the Republic of Goshen. In 1884 Paul Kruger, ruler of the Transvaal, tried to make Goshen part of the Transvaal. These two republics threatened to cut the road because it passed through their territory.

In 1884 the German Government declared a Protectorate over the southern part of Namibia (German South West Africa). They had already colonised Tanganyika. The British feared that the Germans and the Boers would unite against her and form a colony which would join the German colonies in Namibia and Tanganyika and the Boer republic of the Transvaal. This would cut the road permanently. The British Government had to act to protect the road.

In April 1884 the British Government declared a Protectorate south of the Molopo River over the lands of the Barolong and the Batlhaping. John Mackenzie was appointed Deputy Commissioner to rule the area and drive the Goshen Boers back to the Transvaal. He was also to settle the land question in Stellaland. Soon the High Commissioner, Hercules Robinson, thought that Mackenzie favoured the Africans. He replaced him with Cecil Rhodes. Rhodes gave the Stellalanders the land they claimed but he failed to expel the Goshenites who continued to attack Montshiwa and defeated him. The British Government decided to send a military force to expel the Boers.

Fig. 108 Montshiwa, hero of the Barolong. Despite his strong resistance to Boer colonisation his country near Mafikeng was seized by Boers and made into the Republic of Goshen

General Warren advances

In January 1885 General Charles Warren reached Bechuanaland with a force of about 4 000 soldiers. He was to clear the area of the filibusters. He met Kruger at Fourteen Streams and they agreed to fix the western border of the Transvaal. The Boer filibusters fled to the Transvaal. They feared to fight the strong British force. This ended the Republics of Goshen and Stellaland. In March 1885, the British informed Germany that they were extending their Protectorate to the area north of the

Molopo River up to 22 degrees of latitude south. This included the states of the Bakwena, Bangwaketse and the Bangwato. The whole area was to be called the Bechuanaland Protectorate. General Warren was sent to inform the Batswana rulers that they were now under British protection. Ngamiland was not included in the Protectorate until 1894. Britain had succeeded in protecting the road to the north. Later Warren quarrelled with the High Commissioner, Robinson, who favoured white settlers. Warren was dismissed and his soldiers withdrawn in August 1885.

Britain wanted to transfer the Protectorate to the Cape Colony. The Cape politicians did not want to take over Bechuanaland at that time. On 30 September 1885, the British divided the Protectorate into two parts. The part south of the Molopo known as British Bechuanaland became a Crown Colony with its capital at Vryburg. In November 1895, this colony was annexed to the Cape Colony. The area north of the Molopo remained a Protectorate also administered from Vryburg until 1895 when the capital was moved to Mafikeng.

Response of Batswana rulers to protectorate

Sir Charles Warren did not know how the Batswana *dikgosi* would react to the declaration of the Protectorate over their lands without their knowledge. He therefore decided to treat this matter carefully by visiting Khama III first and then the other rulers. He knew that Kgosi Khama was more friendly to the British than the other *dikgosi*. He also thought that if Khama accepted protection the others would follow his example. The British believed that Khama was respected by other Batswana rulers.

Warren and his party arrived at Shoshong, the Bangwato capital, and addressed a large crowd of about 2 000 at the *kgotla*. He informed the Bangwato that the Queen of England had decided to protect them from the Boers, the Amandebele and the Germans. The Bangwato must have been surprised because they had

Fig. 109 General (later Sir) Charles Warren in about 1890. It was he who declared the Protectorate in 1885

Khama's statement to General Charles Warren at the *kgotla* on 13 May 1885 regarding the Protectorate:

> 'I have to say that there are certain laws of my country which the Queen of England finds in operation and which are advantageous to my people and I wish that these laws should be established and not taken away by the Government of England. I refer to the law concerning intoxicating drinks, that they should not enter the country of the Bangwato whether among black or white people. I refer further to our law which declares that the lands of the Bangwato are not saleable. I say this law also is good. Let it be upheld and continue to be law.'

never had trouble from the Germans. As for the Amandebele, Khama had defeated them in 1863. The Boers were the only real threat and even they were not as threatening in 1885 as in the earlier years. But Khama feared that the Boers might cause trouble in the future. He remembered that he had always wanted British protection. So he, together with his counsellors and brothers, accepted British protection on 13 May 1885. The King told Warren that his country stretched northwards up to the Chobe and Zambezi Rivers. Eastwards it stretched to the area between Motloutse and Shashe Rivers. This area was also claimed by Lobengula, ruler of the Amandebele. These opposing claims later caused a dispute. Westwards, Khama claimed parts of Batawana territory. This later caused a quarrel with Sekgoma Letsholathebe, the Batawana ruler. To the south Khama claimed the Lephepe Wells which the Bakwena regarded as part of their country. This again later resulted in a dispute between him and Sechele I of the Bakwena. It is quite clear that the clever *kgosi* wanted to use British protection to his own advantage. Warren, however, refused to extend the Protectorate to all of Khama's country. Only the area south of the 22 degrees latitude south was protected. 22 degrees latitude is a straight line which runs from west to east passing north of Serowe and just south of Serule and Bobonong. It cut Khama's country in half. The Protectorate was extended to the rest of Khama's country in 1890.

In accepting protection, Khama offered the British parts of his country not much used by his people, especially for grazing and ploughing. He knew that white people would continue to come to his country. He wanted them to live in an area away from his people to avoid any problems. He emphasised that he would accept only good Englishmen and not Boers. The settlers would be carefully selected by an officer of the British Queen. Khama's intention was to use British settlers to protect his state. For example, along the Limpopo River they would prevent Boer penetration from the Transvaal. In the area between the Shashe and Motloutse Rivers, they would prevent Amandebele raids. Warren straight away sent an officer to tell Lobengula of the protection over Bangwato country to avoid future raids.

Although Khama readily accepted protection, he did not want the British to interfere with his government. He wanted to rule his people according to Bangwato law and custom. So he told Warren that he would work smoothly with the British but he did not want the British to take away the laws of the Bangwato. Some examples of the laws he wanted unchanged are:
1   he did not want any part of Bangwato land to be sold,
2   he wanted his law banning beer drinking to remain in force.

He was willing to let the British make laws to govern the Whites in his country and to settle cases between Africans and Europeans. It is clear that Kgosi Khama did not accept protection blindly. He wanted to benefit from protection without losing all his sovereignty and independence.

After getting Khama's support, Warren went to the southern rulers. Kgosi Gaseitsiwe of the Bangwaketse had some doubts about the Protectorate because he was not sure what the aim of Britain was in wanting to protect his country. In the end, however, he accepted protection. Like Khama he gave the British some land to the west and east of his country.

Warren met his first real opposition at the Bakwena capital. At an all day *kgotla* meeting Kgosi Sechele and his son Sebele opposed protection. They were surprised that Britain wanted to protect them at a time when there was no longer any threat, and yet such protection had been refused when they badly needed it. They were also unhappy that Britain had declared a Protectorate without first consulting them. They suspected that Britain wanted more than just to protect them. They thought that perhaps Britain wanted to take their land and end their independence. They wanted Britain to prove her honesty by recovering the Bangwaketse cattle stolen by the Boers. This would prove the usefulness of protection. This was not done.

Fig. 110 Sechele I and his wife. The first Christian ruler of the Bakwena; he was strongly opposed to the Protectorate declaration

Conversation between Sechele I's eldest son Sebele and Warren at the *Kgotla* in 1885. The conversation shows clearly that some Batswana rulers questioned protection because they had not been consulted when it was declared and did not understand what protection meant.

'*Sir C. Warren* I have been desired by the Queen's Government to give you the following notification. The Queen's Government has established a Protectorate over the part of Bechuanaland and the Kalahari west of the Transvaal, north of the Cape Colony, and westward towards Namaqualand.
Sechele Has the Chief nothing more to tell us?
Sir C. Warren No.
Sebele What in us has brought this on, that the country should be taken from us?
Sir C. Warren Does Sebele know what it means by the country being taken?
Sebele Seeing what I now know, the boundary line running northwards about Tati and round west in the Kalahari takes us all in, therefore it is that I ask, what in us has brought this on?
Sir C. Warren But does Sebele know what being taken means?
Sebele I have been told, and I have seen it in the papers, that our country is taken, and we the Bakwena were never consulted; therefore I ask why it has been taken.
Sir C. Warren I said that a Protectorate had been established, I did not say the country had been taken from them.
Sebele What is the Protectorate for?
Sir C. Warren Does Sebele consider his tribe requires no protection?
Sebele What is meant by protection?
Sir C. Warren The protection may mean protection from the inside or protection from the outside.
Sebele When a man takes a shield and holds it up, he holds it against something; what is it that we are to be protected against?
Sir C. Warren Is there nothing you want protection against?
Sebele You may see it, but we the Bakwena do not see it yet.
Sir C. Warren Does Sebele know what has just taken place down to the south at Montsioa's? [Montshiwa]
Sebele We, the Bakwena, are not Barolong.
Sir C. Warren What does Sebele mean?
Sebele A stem-buck cannot protect itself, but God protects it and lets it live.
Sir C. Warren Was it the same with you when you came here as refugees fleeing from the Boers?
Sebele A stem-buck gets into difficulties, but when it does so it must get out of them, and God helps it to do so.
Sir C. Warren Then does Sebele wish me to tell the Queen that the Bakwena are strong enough to protect themselves?
Sebele I have spoken of myself. There are others — Bakwena — who will now speak, but for myself I want no protection.'
Source: Public Records Office.

In the end Kgosidintsi, Sechele's brother and a man of great influence in Bakwena politics, pursuaded the King and Sebele to accept protection. He argued that the Bakwena had always wanted this protection as for example in 1852 after a Boer attack. So in the end the Bakwena unwillingly accepted protection. But Sechele stressed that in accepting protection he was not surrendering his kingship to the British. After the three kings whom the British considered to be the most important rulers in the Protectorate had agreed to protection, the British assumed that everyone else had accepted their protection. In 1894 when a British officer was sent to Ngamiland to extend the Protectorate over the Batawana, Kgosi Sekgoma Letsholathebe expressed opposition. In the end he too accepted protection.

It is clear that in 1885 no one clearly understood what protection actually meant. To the Batswana it meant protection from external threat, especially that of the Boers. The Batswana thought that once this danger had passed protection could be ended. They would continue to govern their people as before and remain independent without any British interference. To the British Government protectorate meant the protection of the road to the north. They did not want to govern the territory because it would be too expensive. Only Warren wanted protection to mean some form of government established in the Protectorate, but Britain rejected his suggestion. So from the very beginning Britain decided to neglect the Protectorate.

Resistance to British interference

The differing views about what protection meant soon caused some misunderstanding between the Batswana rulers and British officials. This is how the trouble began. After the declaration of the Protectorate, the British Government appointed Sir Sidney Shippard to be Resident Commissioner for the Protectorate on 1 October 1885. Shippard was a judge of the High Court of the Cape Colony and a friend of Cecil Rhodes. By 1888, it was becoming clear that the rulers in the southern part of the Protectorate were questioning the usefulness of the Protectorate. They saw the Batswana in British Bechuanaland, the area south of the Molopo River, being treated badly by the Boers. Some Boer raids still took place. So, except for Kgosi Khama, the other rulers began to express mistrust of the British and wanted to know what protection really meant.

The Kopong Conference

In order to end the unhappiness of the *dikgosi*, Sidney Shippard called a meeting at Kopong in 1889. Shippard's aim was to introduce some form of administration in the Protectorate. Among the topics to be discussed were the following.
1. The Batswana to pay hut tax in order to pay for the administration of the Protectorate.
2. Settlement of disputes among the *merafe* by the British.
3. Defence matters.
4. Digging of wells.
5. Communications such as the telegraph line, the railway and roads.

The Kopong meeting was attended by about 1 500 people. These topics raised much suspicion among the Batswana because they meant that the British Government wanted to interfere in their internal affairs. Talk of taxation meant that the Resident Commissioner would replace the *dikgosi* as the supreme ruler of the Batswana. This was not what protection meant to the Batswana. They were very unhappy and Sechele expressed their unhappiness to Shippard in the following words.

'When I gave my country to Her Majesty, I did not give over to her the Chieftainship. What is meant by the protection of the British Government? What is my position in my own town and country in relation to the Government?'

Sechele went on to tell Shippard that he did not want to be ruled by anybody and he would not pay tax to anyone. He wanted no roads to be built in his country.

The other *dikgosi*, Linchwe of the Bakgatla and Bathoen of the Bangwaketse, strongly supported the old Sechele and his son Sebele. They all argued that they did not need protection because the Boer threat had passed. The only item for discussion they accepted was the digging of wells because they needed them. Only Kgosi Khama expressed his support for the Protectorate.

Shippard tried but failed to win the support of the *dikgosi*. The Kopong meeting ended without any success. The Batswana were strongly against interference in their domestic affairs. It was clear at Kopong that the Batswana rulers regarded the Protectorate as protection from outside enemies such as the Boers and non-interference by the British in their domestic affairs. For many years to come this was how the Batswana understood the meaning of the Protectorate.

Questions

1. What name is given to the period of African colonisation between 1880 and 1900? Why was competition for African colonies among European countries so fierce?
2. Explain briefly why the Batswana wanted protection from the British against the Boers.
3. List the reasons why the British Government suddenly changed its mind and declared a Protectorate over the lands of the Batswana. The following headings may help you.
   (a) The missionary
   (b) John Mackenzie road
   (c) Christopher Bethell
   (d) Boer expansion
   (e) German expansion
4. What action was taken by the British on 30 September 1885?
5. What did 'protection' mean to
   (a) the Batswana,
   (b) the British Government,
   (c) Sir Charles Warren?

20 New Threat to the Protectorate

An important immediate result of the establishment of the Protectate was that the country now called Botswana was saved from Boer attacks or even outright incorporation (inclusion) into the South African Republic (Transvaal). The Batswana were now reasonably secure. But soon a new, far greater threat emerged. The new threat came from Cecil John Rhodes, a prominent politician in the Cape Colony, and from the Union of South Africa which was formed in 1910. Both these forces wanted to take over Bechuanaland and rule it. They had the support of powerful politicians in Great Britain. These plans failed, however, because the Batswana rulers, assisted by their sympathisers, vigorously opposed them. How did all this happen?

Cecil John Rhodes was an ambitious and very rich businessman and coloniser. He was rich because he owned a large share of the Kimberley diamond mine. This mine was the biggest diamond producer in the world. He wanted to get more and more wealth by colonising as many countries as possible north of the Cape Colony. In fact, he often talked of establishing a British empire from Cape to Cairo in Egypt. In order to colonise areas to the north of the Cape Colony successfully, he created a commercial company called the British South Africa Company (BSAC) in 1889. In the 1880s, concessionaires were everywhere in Southern Africa seeking mineral wealth. They operated as individuals or as companies. Rhodes and his BSAC were among them. Rhodes knew that the best way to beat his competitors and win the support of the British Government was to operate through a powerful, rich company. He succeeded in this and Britain looked upon him as its empire builder.

It was not difficult for Rhodes or any other strong British coloniser to win the support of the

Fig. 111 Cecil John Rhodes (1853-1902), businessman, politician and coloniser, on the left of the picture

Fig. 112 King Lobengula of the Amandebele and a concessionaire. Many such concessionaires caused African rulers to lose their lands by deceit

British Government in those days. The reason was that the British Government did not want to spend money on colonisation. It wanted to colonise as cheaply as possible by using commercial companies like the BSAC. In this way many other companies extended British power throughout the world. In order to support a company's colonisation efforts, the British Government normally expected that:

1. the company should obtain an authentic (true) concession or treaty from the ruler of the land,
2. the concession or treaty should be signed by the ruler who should grant it willingly,
3. the treaty should not be obtained by false means,
4. the ruler should fully understand the contents of the treaty.

In most cases concessionaires obtained treaties by false pretences and the rulers certainly did not fully understand the true meaning of these treaties. But still they were used to colonise various countries.

The immediate reason for forming the BSAC was to colonise the land of the Amandebele and the Mashona, the country which is called Zimbabwe today. There was great competition for that country because of its wealth. The Portuguese operating from Mozambique and the Transvaal Boers wanted it. In fact, it was believed that the Boers had signed a treaty of friendship with Lobengula, King of the Amandebele, in 1887. Rhodes hastily made a number of treaties with King Lobengula aimed at colonising the country. The most important of these was the Rudd Concession. This treaty was obtained in 1888 by Rhodes' men, Rudd, Maguire and Thompson who deceived the king into signing it. These men did not follow the guidelines above when they negotiated the treaty. The concession gave Rhodes the right to all minerals in the land of the Amandebele. On the basis of this concession which Lobengula later rejected, the British Government gave the BSAC a royal charter (permit) to colonise the country. It became known as Rhodesia, named after Rhodes. Between 1890 and 1893 the BSAC colonised Rhodesia after a bloody war with the Amandebele. How does Bechuanaland fit into all this?

When the British granted the royal charter to the BSAC, they intended that in the future the Protectorate would be transferred to that company. The area where the company was allowed to operate included Bechuanaland.

The only condition for the transfer was that the BSAC should get the consent of the Batswana rulers in order to avoid a possible conflict. Britain, through its High Commissioner at the Cape Colony, would assist the company as much as she possibly could. Thus already in 1889, just about four years after the declaration of the Protectorate, Britain had already decided to hand over Bechuanaland to a commercial company.

Rhodes plans to take over Bechuanaland

In the 1890s Rhodes wanted to build a railway line from the Cape Colony to his new colony of Rhodesia. But the railway would pass through the Protectorate where African rulers still exercised a lot of power. Rhodes feared that the Batswana would oppose the construction of the line through their land. They had already expressed their opposition at the Kopong meeting. So the only way he could build the line without opposition was to have the Protectorate transferred to his company. He also believed that the Protectorate might yield some mineral wealth in the future. Already gold mining was going on at Tati and the Batswana rulers were granting mineral concessions to several concessionaires. Rhodes wanted all the mineral rights in Bechuanaland to belong to the BSAC. Furthermore, Rhodes wanted to settle Europeans in parts of the Protectorate to take part in agriculture, especially ranching.

Rhodes took his first step to annex (take over) the Protectorate in 1891. He asked for permission to build a railway from the Cape Colony to Rhodesia via the Tati gold fields. He successfully argued that the building of the railway would help develop the Protectorate and therefore save the British Government some money since the BSAC would pay for these developments. So the British Government approved the railway scheme in 1892. The railway would, more importantly, be useful in developing the mineral wealth in Rhodesia for the benefit of Britain and the BSAC. Britain, through its High Commissioner, would persuade Batswana rulers to give the land needed for the railway. The agreement was reached secretly without the knowledge of the Batswana.

Soon Rhodes shifted from talking about building a railway through Bechuanaland to annexing the entire Protectorate. He wanted to make it part of Rhodesia. This was because of events which were taking place in the Transvaal. Rhodes now wanted to rule the Protectorate so that he could use it to attack the Transvaal and take it over from the Boers. Gold at the Witwatersrand (Johannesburg) had made the Boer Republic of the Transvaal very rich. The gold mines belonged to British businessmen including Rhodes. Rhodes did not like the idea of the Boers having all the political power in such a wealthy state. He wanted the Transvaal to be ruled by the British. Then they would be able to get all the profits from the gold mines without interference. He had to find a good reason to justify his attack. He found a pretext (false reason) in the complaints of the non-Boer white population of the Transvaal. They were called *Uitlanders* (outsiders) by the Boers. They complained of unequal treatment by the Boers. They complained, for example, that they did not have equal voting rights with the Boers. The real reason for the attack was that Rhodes wanted the gold mines. The railway would be very important too for carrying war supplies and soldiers.

Problem of the concessions

Before the BSAC could carry out its annexation (take over) plan, Rhodes and the British Government had to deal with the many concessions which the Batswana had already granted. These concessions gave away land in the area through which the railway would pass. This was also the area from which Rhodes planned to attack the South African Republic.

Following the declaration of the Protectorate, and especially after the discovery of gold at the Witwatersrand, concessionaires were everywhere in Bechuanaland. They were in search of concessions to prospect for minerals, and to trade, settle, farm or build communications. Some Batswana rulers granted these concessions. In nearly all cases the *dikgosi* did not understand that in signing these concessions they were giving away parts of their lands to European companies. This was because concessionaires never fully explained the full meaning of the concessions. Quite often when the full meaning of the concessions was explained, the rulers were surprised. They denied that they had ever given away their land.

In Setswana law and custom land could not be sold or be given away to an individual permanently. Land belonged to the *morafe* and the king controlled it on its behalf. This is why the Batswana were surprised when they were told that the concessions they had signed made them lose their land. Some of the reasons why the rulers granted concessions were:

1 they believed that they were leasing (lending) the land only for a while,
2 the concessionaires paid the rulers some money for the concessions,
3 the missionaries who were usually trusted by the *dikgosi* encouraged them to sign treaties. Often the missionaries acted as interpreters as well, and translated concessions into the Setswana language. But it must be said too that some missionaries advised rulers not to sign bad concessions.

In summary, we can say that Batswana kings granted concessions because they did not believe that they were losing anything by doing so. In their custom the *kgosi* could never lose control of the land.

An important factor which made concessionaires flock to Bechuanaland was that the Colonial Administration encouraged concessionaires to prospect there. The reason for this was that the Administration would get revenue (income) by taxing mining companies if minerals were discovered. They also got revenue from trading licences.

The following are examples of concessions.

Charles Riley, a trader at Mochudi, the Bakgatla capital, obtained a trading and manufacturing concession for a period of 99 years in Bangwaketse country. He also got another concession granting him a 99 year lease for 200 square miles (51 800 ha) of land. In asking for these concessions, Riley had emphasised only the building of stores which would sell cheap goods. The king liked this for it would help his people.

Another interesting case was that of a Barolong ruler, Letlogile, who in 1891 leased to Wilkinson 200 000 morgen (171 000 ha) of land. Wilkinson could buy the land at the end of 1894 for five shillings per thousand morgen (856 ha) and a royalty (a kind of tax) of £10 per year.

There were many other concessions granted in other *merafe*.

By 1892 the competition among concessionaires was fierce. It was clear that the Batswana were fast losing their lands to the concessionaires without realising it. The Colonial Government was worried about the very large number of concessions. It was worried not so much because concessions threatened Batswana land, but because they could make it difficult for the BSAC to build the railway and to take over Bechuanaland.

The Concessions Commission

In order, therefore, to make things easy for Rhodes and the BSAC, the High Commissioner set up a Concessions Commission in 1893. The British Government's aim was to cancel as many concessions as possible so as to remove competition against the BSAC. The Commission was given power to cancel all concessions which were signed after 1889, when the BSAC was created. Those which were not honestly obtained were also to be cancelled. During the meeting of the Commission some rulers realised how much they had been cheated by some of the concessionaires. Other rulers such as Sebele of the Bakwena regarded the setting up of the Commission as interference in their domestic affairs. He wanted to do what he liked with his land since he alone was King of the Bakwena.

The Commission succeeded in cancelling many of the concessions. This cleared the way

Fig. 113 Sir Henry Loch (1827-1900), who was replaced as High Commissioner because he opposed Rhodes' plans to take over Bechuanaland

Fig. 114 Sir Hercules Robinson (1824-1897), who was a friend of Rhodes, replaced Loch as High Commissioner. He wanted to hand over Bechuanaland to Rhodes' BSAC

for the BSAC to take over Bechuanaland. The only real problem left to deal with was that of the Batswana rulers. They complained that they had lost the royalties they received from the concessionaires. The BSAC agreed to pay the affected rulers, namely Sebele, Linchwe, Bathoen and Ikaneng, ruler of the Balete, some annual allowances. Having crushed his competitors with British help, Rhodes could now turn his attention to the transfer question.

Before 1894 Rhodes was busy fighting the Amandebele in Rhodesia so he did not pay much attention to Bechuanaland. After conquering the Amandebele, he turned his energies to Bechuanaland. At the end of 1894 he formally asked for an assurance that Britain would transfer the Protectorate to the BSAC. The British Secretary of State for Colonies, Lord Ripon, replied that this would be done when the time came. Rhodes was to submit proposals to the Colonial Secretary for his consideration. It is quite clear, therefore, that by 1894 the British Government was ready to hand over Bechuanaland to Rhodes. To make the transfer easy, Britain removed Sir Henry Loch, the High Commissioner, because he was opposed to the transfer. It replaced him with Sir Hercules Robinson who was Rhodes' friend and had some shares (a partnership) in the BSAC.

The Batswana meanwhile learned from missionaries and newspaper reports about the secret negotiations and virtual agreement to transfer their country to the BSAC. In July 1895 Kings Khama, Bathoen, Sebele and Linchwe sent petitions to the new Colonial Secretary, Joseph Chamberlain. They requested that their countries should not be given to the Company. They wanted to remain under the Queen's protection as agreed in 1885. The Batswana disliked the Company immensely (strongly) because they saw how harshly it ruled Rhodesia. They feared that they would lose their political power, land and property to the Company just like the Amandebele. They, especially Khama, also feared that the Company would allow liquor into Bechuanaland. Khama in particular considered the Company an enemy because of a recent encounter with it. In 1893 after conquering the Amandebele, Rhodes wanted to annex the disputed territory (the area between the Shashe and Motloutse Rivers including the Tati area) and was supported by the High Commissioner. Khama protested strongly and threatened to go to Britain to put his case before the British Government. The scheme was dropped.

Khama also disliked Rhodes because they had disagreed on how to fight the Amandebele in 1893. Khama had been asked by Britain to help the Company. He had agreed because the Amandebele were his old enemy. The disagreement led to Khama's withdrawal from the war and Rhodes said bad things about the king.

In general, at this time the Batswana rulers did not trust the British officials in the Protectorate from the High Commissioner downwards. This was because these officials tended to side with the BSAC. Because of this mistrust the *dikgosi* decided to travel to England to plead directly with the Colonial Office. When news of this journey became known, Rhodes sent his trusted man Dr S. Jameson, the Administrator of Rhodesia, to negotiate a treaty of annexation with Khama. To get Khama to agree, Jameson promised to settle the king's dissident (quarrelsome) brothers, Raditladi and Mphoeng, in Rhodesia. Khama refused. If he had agreed, Rhodes would have used the treaty to get the British Government to transfer the Protectorate to the BSAC.

The *dikgosi* go to England to protest

The three kings, Khama, Bathoen and Sebele went to England. They took with them their African advisers and the missionary W.C. Willoughby who was their interpreter. In Cape Town Rhodes interviewed the kings in an attempt to stop them from going to England. He feared they might succeed in persuading the British Government not to transfer the Protectorate. The High Commissioner, Rhodes' friend, also tried without success to stop the journey. The *dikgosi* rejected all those attempts and went to England.

In London, the kings made the following requests.
1. That they should remain a Protectorate as at present directly under the Queen.
2. That their autonomy (independence) be preserved.
3. That their lands should not be sold.
4. That liquor drinking be prohibited in their areas.

They criticised the Company for bad government in Rhodesia and praised the Queen's rule over the Protectorate. Joseph Chamberlain, the Colonial Secretary, told them that there was no danger in being transferred to the BSAC because the Company would obey the Queen's orders. So to be ruled by the Company was the same as being under the Queen. He then advised them to negotiate (discuss) details of the transfer with Rhodes' representatives. He also told them that the British Government could not break its promise to transfer Bechuanaland to the Company. Rhodes had sent his trusted man, Harris, to London to ensure that the Batswana rulers would not succeed. Having told the kings to reach an agreement with the BSAC, Chamberlain went on holiday.

Confrontation and settlement

Instead of negotiating with the BSAC, the kings toured England. They sought the support of the British people against the Company. The London Missionary Society organised the campaign. LMS respected and loved Khama because he was a staunch (strong) Christian ruler. The *dikgosi*, especially Khama, addressed several well attended meetings. Everywhere the kings emphasised that they wished to remain under the Queen and that they disliked Rhodes' Company because it would bring liquor and bad influence to their lands. They emphasised the protectorate agreement of 1885.

At that time in England there were many people who belonged to the temperance movement (a group which was against liquor drinking). They included the LMS and its supporters. They disliked the Company because it brought liquor to Rhodesia. There were the humanitarians and the anti-slavery groups which wanted the British Government to protect African rights. They disliked the Company for the terrible war in Rhodesia and for its harsh rule in that colony. Then there were those who wanted the British Empire to be ruled by Britain and not by a commercial company. All these groups supported the Batswana kings against the Company. They felt also that it would be unfair to break the protection agreement of 1885. They feared that this would make the Batswana mistrust the British Crown. There was also fear that a costly war like that against the Amandebele might break out if the Company were forced upon the Batswana.

When he returned from holiday, Chamberlain found several letters from the British people, mainly from church and business groups, protesting against the proposed hand over of the Protectorate. Fearing that the Government might be unpopular and lose votes at the next election over the transfer issue, Chamberlain changed his

Fig. 115 The three kings, Bathoen, Khama and Sebele with their adviser W.C. Willoughby. Pictured here in England, their protest saved the land of the Batswana from colonisation by Rhodes

mind. He announced the following settlement on 7 November 1895.
1. The railway was to be built on a narrow strip of land on the eastern side of the Protectorate. A fence would be built on both sides of the line to protect livestock.
2. Each king would cede (give) the land needed for the railway so as not to interfere with people's villages or ploughing lands.
3. The Protectorate status was to remain as agreed in 1885, and a Queen's Officer would be stationed at each king's capital.
4. The *dikgosi* were each given a reserve. This was an area set aside for use by Africans, in which the king would rule his people much as before with little interference from the British Government. These reserves roughly followed the old boundaries of the old states. The areas offered to Warren in 1885 and refused by Britain were now declared Crown land (the Queen's land).
5. The laws against liquor were to remain unchanged.
6. Taxation was to be introduced in order to pay for the administration of the Protectorate.

The Africans had in fact won against the powerful Rhodes and his Company. Rhodes did not get the Protectorate but he did get land for his railway.

It is quite clear that the Batswana rulers got what they wanted. They stopped Bechuanaland from becoming part of Rhodesia. Rhodes on the other hand lost. All he got was the strip of land for the railway and a vague (not straightforward) promise that the BSAC might be given the land outside the reserves in the future. This promise was not fulfilled as we shall see later. Rhodes rebuked (told off) his man Harris for being defeated by black men. He did not believe that Africans could be such clever politicians and statesmen. He was so angry that he told Khama to receive back the dissidents under Raditladi or else surrender the Bakalanga area to the BSAC. Rhodes had settled them in Rhodesia because he thought that Bechuanaland would be transferred to him. Khama refused.

Rhodes nearly wins

While the three kings were busy in England protesting against Rhodes' plan to take over Bechuanaland, Rhodes was trying to get land from some other Protectorate rulers. He was supported by the High Commissioner, Sir Hercules Robinson, in this plan. Shippard and Rhodes' brother Frank, the representative of the BSAC, visited Ikaneng, ruler of the Balete, to ask for a land concession. After much persuasion, Ikaneng granted a piece of land. Ikaneng thought that the Company needed the land only for a short time during the building of the railway.

Encouraged by this success, Shippard travelled to see Montshiwa of the Barolong. He persuaded Montshiwa to grant a piece of land at Pitsanaphotlokwe close to the Transvaal border. The High Commissioner recommended that these lands and areas of the Protectorate near the Transvaal border, through which the railway would pass, be transferred to the BSAC. The Colonial Office agreed to give the lands ceded by Ikaneng and Montshiwa to the BSAC. But it rejected the transfer of other areas. The Colonial Office was already suspicious that its officials in the Protectorate did not seem to be dealing fairly with the Batswana rulers. The BSAC quickly appointed Dr S. Jameson to be Resident Commissioner of the transferred areas of the Protectorate.

Ngamiland threatened

In the 1890s Rhodes wanted to take over Ngamiland and turn it into a colony for European settlement like Rhodesia. This European settler community could produce crops using the plentiful water from the Okavango Swamps. He also believed that Ngamiland was rich in diamonds. The British Government was not interested in including Ngamiland in the Protectorate. It regarded Ngamiland as a useless swamp.

But Ngamiland was near the German Colony of South West Africa. The British feared that

Germany might take over Ngamiland. It could expand from there eastwards towards the areas Britain considered important. Britain still had the fear that Germany might want to link up with the Transvaal. There were also frequent raids into Ngamiland by the Khoe from South West Africa. Britain was anxious to stop them. For these reasons Britain was ready to give Ngamiland to the BSAC. The British hoped that a European settlement in Ngamiland would stop all these problems and protect British interests. The only problem was that the Company had no concessions there. Also there were already concessionaires in the area who were opposed to Rhodes' plan to seize Ngamiland.

In 1888 the Batawana king, Moremi II, had granted a trader called Strombom and his friend Nicholls a prospecting concession over an area of about 600 square kilometres. In 1889 the king gave Strombom, Nicholls and Hicks another prospecting concession throughout Ngamiland. Strombom died and Nicholls and Hicks sold the concession to the British Westland Chartered Company (BWCC). It sent out a team led by Frederick Lugard to look for gold and diamonds in 1896-97. But they were not successful.

We have already seen how Britain favoured Rhodes and the BSAC above other concessionaires. Britain, therefore, wanted to push the other concessionaires out of Ngamiland. But the

Fig. 116 Moremi II. He granted the first concessions in Ngamiland

BWCC appeared before the Concessions Commission of 1893 to defend the Nicholls-Hicks concession. Sekgoma Letsholathebe, the new Batawana king, learned that the BWCC was claiming ownership of land in Ngamiland. He rejected their claim and cancelled the concession. The British Government accepted Sekgoma's rejection because it suited their plan to help Rhodes to get Ngamiland.

Rhodes learned of Sekgoma's rejection of the Nicholls-Hicks concession. So he sent his man, John Bosman, to seek a land concession from Sekgoma at the end of 1893. The High Commissioner also sent Captain Fuller to Ngamiland to persuade the Batawana ruler to grant a concession to the Company. It so happened that in 1893 some Boer trekkers from the Boer republics in South Africa wanted to establish a new republic in the north. Bosman was one of their leaders. Rhodes wanted to use them to colonise Ngamiland. He had used Whites from South Africa to colonise Mashonaland in the same way in 1890. He promised to settle the Boers in Ngamiland.

Bosman was not an honest man. Knowing that Sekgoma would not grant a land concession easily, he pretended that he was Queen Victoria's officer. He told Sekgoma that he came to seek a treaty of friendship between Sekgoma and Queen Victoria. The LMS missionary in Ngamiland, the Reverend James Wookey, supported Rhodes' plan. Sekgoma granted what he believed to be a treaty of friendship between two rulers and a prospecting concession in return for £50 per year. What he had signed were in fact a land concession and a mineral concession. The BSAC quickly brought the concessions before the Concessions Commission. They hoped to get permission to colonise Ngamiland. In 1894 the Colonial Office informed the Company that Britain was ready to approve the BSAC claim on Ngamiland.

Just at that time Sekgoma learned of the Boer trek supported by Rhodes. He also learned that the BSAC claimed that he had granted them land to settle the Boers. Sekgoma protested very vigorously against the BSAC. He stated that the concessions were obtained by false means.

Sekgoma's affidavit

> I, Sekgoma, do hereby certify the following statement to be true:
>
> I have neither given away the Country or sold any rights to it. These words of Bosman are new to me.
>
> When he came up he made himself out as a representative of the Imperial Government. I believed him, and he went on to tell me that he had come up to make a treaty of friendship. When I signed the documents I signed them in the full belief that I was signing a treaty of friendship and nothing whatever to do with giving away of my Country or selling it. He offered me a wagon and guns which I first refused, but on his pressing me I accepted five guns, as he said by my refusing his presents the Chief at the Cape would be very displeased.
>
> Bosman urged him to put his name to the paper as his (Sekgoma) name would appear together with the White Chief's name and they would see how he spelt his name.
>
> (Sd) Sekgoma.
>
> Witness of signature.
> (Sd) A.J. Wookey.
> C.P. Chesnaye, Sergt. B.B. Police

Bosman had never mentioned to him that he represented the Company. In addition, the Setswana and the English texts (words) of the concessions were different. He made it clear that he disliked both the Boers and the BSAC. He won the support of many individuals. One of these was an LMS African evangelist, Khukhu Mogodi. John S. Moffat, a British official stationed at Palapye, was also opposed to Company rule in Ngamiland. He believed the Boers whom the Company proposed to settle there would cause trouble. Moffat told the Colonial Office that he suspected that the Company had used false methods to get the concessions.

When the Bangwaketse and Bakwena rulers heard of the trek they protested that they did not want Boers to pass through their territories. Britain was now afraid that the Boer trek could cause an uprising in the Protectorate. The

British Government sent A.E. Walshe to investigate the concessions. He reported that they were obtained by false means. So Sekgoma was right after all. The British Government rejected the Bosman Concessions in December 1894. Rhodes decided to force the British Government to settle the Boers in the Ghanzi district. He encouraged them to go there without any concession. The British Government warned against this and told Rhodes to try to get a new concession from Sekgoma. But Sekgoma refused to grant one. At this time he had learned from the Bangwato that Rhodes wanted to take the lands of all the Batswana. The BWCC had obtained another concession from Sekgoma who wanted to use it against the BSAC. So the BWCC supported the *kgosi*. The High Commissioner told the angry Rhodes that the Batawana king could not grant a new concession.

But Britain wanted to settle the Boers in Ghanzi with or without Rhodes' help. Sekgoma was given a choice either to surrender Ghanzi or lose the whole of Ngamiland. Sekgoma reluctantly (unwillingly) gave away Ghanzi. It became a Crown Colony. It was planned that it would be transferred to the BSAC later.

The Jameson Raid causes Rhodes to fail

Events in the Transvaal soon destroyed Rhodes' hope of ever getting the Protectorate. On the night of 29-30 December 1895, the Jameson Raid took place. Dr S. Jameson invaded the Transvaal from Pitsanaphotlokwe within Bechuanaland. Rhodes had got this place from Montshiwa in order to use it for the raid. Jameson's raiders quickly surrendered to the Boers and the expected *Uitlanders* uprising did not take place.

The whole world criticised Britain for allowing its Protectorate to be used for attacking another country. Britain did not want its name spoilt. The British angrily told Rhodes that the Protectorate would not be transferred to him. The lands ceded to him by Ikaneng and Montshiwa in 1895 were taken away. The vague 1895 promise that the BSAC would be given land outside the reserves also failed. Ghanzi would not be given to the Company but would remain Crown Land. The Boer trekkers were settled there in 1898 by the High Commissioner and given farms. Their descendants are still there to-

Fig. 117 Jameson's surrender, 2 January 1896, to the Boers

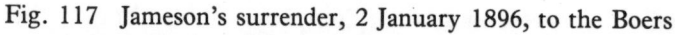

Fig. 118 The Amazulu of Cetshwayo badly defeated British troops at the battle of Isandlhwana

day. So an important result of the raid is that it saved the Batswana from the BSAC.

As time passed, the Jameson Raid was slowly forgotten. In 1904 the British Government transferred the land for the railway strip to the BSAC. The Company also got some blocks of land in Crown Land. These were the Gaborone, Lobatse and Tuli Blocks. The Tuli Block was actually the area Khama had ceded to the BSAC for the railway in 1895. It was later decided not to build the railway line through the Tuli Block. The area, however, remained the property of the Company. These together with the Tati District and Ghanzi became the only European areas in Bechuanaland. This arrangement ended Rhodes' attempts to take over Bechuanaland.

The Batswana rulers, especially Bathoen, Khama, Sebele and Sekgoma Letsholathebe, had fought hard to save the lands of the Batswana. They are, therefore, heroes in the history of Botswana.

The Union of South Africa threat: early attempts at unity and Boer resistance

The hostility the Boers felt towards the British at the Cape Colony continued after they had established their own states of the South African Republic (Transvaal) and the Orange Free State. This was because from time to time the British attempted to annex the Boer republics. This was especially so after diamonds were discovered at Kimberley and gold at the Witwatersrand. Britain now wanted a larger South Africa consisting of its two colonies of Natal and the Cape, and the two Boer Republics. Such a large colony would be wealthy and more economically beneficial to England. British businessmen, supported by the British Government, did not like the idea of letting the Boers continue to rule the mineral rich Boer Republics. Another reason for wanting a union was that Britain did not want to spend money on its colonies in South Africa. If the four territories united, they would be economically strong enough to pay for running their own affairs. A further reason for wanting a union was that a united South Africa would be strong enough to defend itself against any threat. Britain was worried about the continued resistance of Africans against white domination. For example, the British fought a bloody war against the Amazulu in 1880 after the Amazulu (of Cetshwayo ka Mpande) had badly defeated them at the battle of Isandlhwana in 1879. There were also memories of other resistance such as that by the Griqua, the Barolong and Batlhaping in 1878-79, and the Boer defeat by the Bapedi in 1877.

Britain wanted the Boers to unite with Natal and the Cape Colony into a British confederation (a loose union). As early as 1870-78, Britain's Colonial Secretaries, Lord Kimberley and Lord Carnarvon had tried without success to persuade them peacefully. The Boers under the leadership of Paul Kruger, President of the South African Republic, defiantly refused. So Carnarvon decided to use force. However, Kruger was a very stubborn leader and he was quite prepared to fight rather than surrender to the British.

In 1877 the South African Republic was badly defeated in an uprising of the Bapedi. The Republic was very weak. So Carnarvon sent Theophilus Shepstone, Secretary for Native Affairs in Natal, to take it over and rule it. The Boers were militarily weak and they used peaceful negotiations to try to regain their independence. They sent their leaders to London to do this. When this failed, Kruger prepared to fight and in 1881 Boer commandos defeated the British at the battle of Majuba Hill. The British gave the Boers limited (not full) independence in 1881. The Boers were unhappy because they wanted full independence. They continued to oppose British rule.

The new Colonial Secretary, Joseph Chamberlain, and the new High Commissioner, Sir Alfred Milner, were imperialists. They believed in British supremacy over all Southern Africa. They believed that the only method left to achieve a union of the four white states was war. Diplomatic efforts had failed. They made the British public support war against the Boers by exaggerating Boer ill-treatment of the *Uitlanders*. Using the *Uitlanders* as a pretext, they prepared for war. The Boers too feared that the British would destroy their independence. So on 11 October 1899 they went to war against the British. This was what Chamberlain and Milner wanted. The bloody war dragged on from 1899 to 1902.

Africans in the war

Although the Anglo-Boer War is often described as the white man's war, Africans were involved in it. Both white groups did not want Africans to join their armies. Whites were afraid that Africans would learn to use firearms. Later they might turn these guns against all Whites in South Africa. The Africans throughout Southern Africa hated the Boers more than they disliked the British because the Boers were more oppressive. The Africans in South Africa hoped that if Britain won, they would get some political and economic rights like Africans in the Cape Colony. They also knew that Africans in the Bechuanaland Protectorate enjoyed some freedom under Britain. So some Africans such as the Amazulu attacked the Boers. The Africans in the Transvaal were hostile to the Boers. The Boers were faced with British superior power and the hostility of the Africans. So they finally agreed to sign a peace treaty with the British in 1902 at Vereeniging.

Fig. 119 An armed African Scout directs British troops on their way through Bechuanaland to relieve Mafikeng

Bechuanaland and the war

The Protectorate was affected by the Anglo-Boer War. Some Batswana played a part in the war even though Britain had told them not to. However, only some parts of Bechuanaland, mainly in the south, were affected.

In 1899, the Boers besieged (surrounded) Mafikeng, the capital of Bechuanaland. Gould-Adams, the Resident Commissioner (1897-1901) and his staff could not leave the town. The Assistant Commissioner, Surmon, acted as Resident Commissioner until Gould-Adams was free. The Boers hoped to destroy the Government of the Protectorate. This did not happen because, in early 1900, British forces defeated the Boers at Crocodile Pools north of Mafikeng. In May 1900, they freed Mafikeng.

In the Protectorate itself there were rumours that the Boers wanted to attack the country because it was used during the Jameson Raid. The Boers feared that it would be used again in the Anglo-Boer War. It was also stated that the Boers wanted to attack Khama's country because Africans who refused to pay tax to the Transvaal fled there. Some Babirwa of Maunatlala and some Bagaseleka had done this. Boer movements were reported on the eastern border of the Bangwato country. Khama was prepared to fight them.

On the day the Anglo-Boer War started, the Boers went into Khama's country and cut the telegraph line near Palapye. They also cut the railway between Gaborone and Mafikeng. They wanted to stop communication between the British army in South Africa, Rhodesia and the Protectorate. They thought that this would stop Rhodesian soldiers and Protectorate police from entering the war. They also wanted to stop food supplies and war materials from reaching the British army. The British sent soldiers to expel (turn out) the Boers from Bechuanaland. They were helped by the Rhodesians. British soldiers guarded important places and bridges. Their

Fig. 120 Metsimaswana Bridge near Gaborone was destroyed by Boers. The picture shows British troops guarding the bridge after it had been repaired

Fig. 121 A Bakgatla regiment

main camps were at Gaborone and Lobatse. The Boers attacked both camps and the British abandoned (left) Gaborone for a while. Khama sent the Maalola regiment to guard the Mahalapye railway bridge. He had heard that the Boers were gathering on the eastern border. He sent some soldiers and scouts to guard the eastern border and watch Boer movements. The Maalola were given £1 728 at the end of the war for helping the British.

The Bakgatla of Linchwe I also participated in the war. In fact, the Bakgatla were more involved in the war than the other Batswana groups in the Protectorate. The Bakgatla joined the war when they helped the British and Rhodesian forces to defeat the Boers near Mochudi. In November 1899, the British asked the Bakgatla to fight a Boer force at Derdepoort along the Madikwe River (Marico). The Bakgatla expected British soldiers to help them, but in the end they fought alone. The British abandoned them. At first they defeated the Boers, but in the end the Boers succeeded. They attacked the Bakgatla troops at Sikwane village and burned down Bakgatla villages along the Madikwe. The Boers stole many cattle. However, they did not succeed in capturing Mochudi or holding on to Bakgatla territory.

The Boers took revenge on the Bakgatla living in the Transvaal. Linchwe replied by further attacks on the Boers as far as Pretoria. He took some cattle back to his country, Kgatleng. As the war went on, some Boers left their farms and Bakgatla occupied them, especially in the Saulspoort area. Until the end of the war, Bakgatla captured many Boer cattle some of which had been stolen from the Bakgatla before. Immediately after the war, Linchwe succeeded in getting British help to instal his brother, Ramono, as *kgosi* of the Bakgatla of the Transvaal. He bought some land in the Transvaal for the settlement of the Bakgatla. Some of the cattle raided from the Boers were shared among Linchwe's regiments as a reward for fighting so bravely.

The Batswana benefited economically from the war. They sold a lot of cattle for meat to the

Fig. 122 Linchwe I who led the Bakgatla in resistance against the Boers. (Photograph by Isaac Schapera)

British soldiers. Reverend Williams estimated that by 1900 they had earned £65 000. Some Batswana earned money by working at the British army camps.

Even though the Boers were defeated on the battlefield they won politically. Immediately after the war, the Republics were placed under Milner. He was appointed Governor. But in order to win Boer support for the idea of a union, Britain granted the Boer republics self-government or responsible government between 1906 and 1907. This pleased the Boers. But what pleased them even more was that Britain did not force them to give any political rights to Africans in the two Republics. The Boers at that time, just as today, did not want the Africans to vote. So even though the Africans had sup-

Fig. 123 Potchefstroom Camp: a concentration camp for Boer prisoners during the Anglo-Boer War

ported the British during the war, they did not get any benefit at all. Instead, the Boers got better treatment than they did. Throughout the history of South Africa, although the Boers and the British often quarrelled, they always united against Africans.

The Union of South Africa

After the war old Boer leaders such as Kruger were replaced by younger men such as Louis Botha and Jan Smuts who wanted a union of the four white states. They decided that it was better to win Boer domination of South Africa by political means rather than through war. Between 1910 and 1948, the Boers worked hard to control politics in South Africa. Boer nationalism succeeded when the Boer National Party won the election of 1948. In that year, the National Party Government made *apartheid* the law of South Africa.

Fear of Africans also made the two white groups want to unite. There were African revolts in the region. For example in the Bambata revolt in 1906, the Amazulu, under their ruler, Bambata, revolted against paying taxes. The Mashona and Amandebele rebelled against the BSAC in 1896-97. The Ovaherero and the Nama revolted against the Germans in Namibia from 1904 to 1908.

The leaders of the Boers and the English met from 1908 until 1909 to discuss the formation of a new united state. In 1910 the Union of South Africa was formed as a British Colony. The Boers agreed to the Union only after Britain had assured them that Africans' voting rights in the Cape Province would not be extended to the other provinces of the Union. In fact it was agreed that if the white Parliament so wished even the voting rights of non-Whites in the Cape would be taken away. The Africans in the Cape lost their voting rights in 1936. So the result of the Union for the Africans was that it ended all their political rights.

The Union of South Africa and Bechuanaland

The formation of the Union of South Africa was opposed by Africans inside and outside South Africa. The South African Blacks formed a political movement called the Native National Congress in 1912 to oppose the loss of political and economic rights. This movement was renamed the African National Congress (ANC).

In the High Commission Territories of Bechuanaland, Basutoland and Swaziland there was also fierce opposition to the Union. The reason for this was that the *South Africa Act* (Law) establishing the Union provided for the future incorporation (inclusion) of the three territories and Rhodesia. But the Act also stated that Britain would transfer the three territories after consulting their inhabitants.

Britain partly looked upon the High Commission Territories as sources of labour for the mines of South Africa. She had no other economic use for them and considered them to be a burden to her. So she wanted to hand them over to the Union which would use their own manpower and develop them economically. Britain did not believe that these territories could fully develop economically on their own. Britain, however, would only agree to the incorporation of Bechuanaland if Southern Rhodesia also joined the Union.

At the beginning South Africa wanted the Protectorates because they would provide more land for white farmers. Another reason was that the Whites of South Africa disliked British policy in these territories because it was different from the 'native policy' of the Union. In the Protectorates Africans enjoyed some political and civic rights and participated in running their own affairs to some extent. There were no pass laws in the Protectorates and segregation was mild. The white South Africans feared that this gave a 'bad' example to the Africans in South Africa. They wanted Africans in the whole region to have no rights at all. This could be done only by taking over the three territories. Another reason for wanting transfer was that South Africa wanted to secure and control cheap labour for its mines and farms. The migrant labour system was not good enough because South Africa could not make laws to recruit and control such labour in the Protectorates.

In the 1950s a further reason for wanting the Protectorates to join the Union was the introduction of the Bantustan policy. This policy divided the land in South Africa into Bantu (African) areas, which the Boers called Bantustans, and European areas. The Africans had only 13 per cent of the land and yet their number was much larger than that of the Whites. So the Government wanted the Protectorates in order to add more land to the Bantustans. They feared that land shortage would lead to revolts. South Africa also saw the Protectorates as markets for its manufactured goods.

Protest in Bechuanaland

The Batswana knew about the intention to transfer their land to the Union of South Africa. At that time some Batswana youth were educated enough to read about the transfer in the newspapers. The Batswana who studied or worked in the Union also learned about the transfer. The Batswana rulers learned that the Basotho had sent a delegation to London to protest. In 1906-7 the Protectorate *dikgosi* expressed their unhappiness. So in 1910 Lord Selborne, the High Commissioner, informed the *dikgosi* at Mafikeng that although Bechuanaland would be transferred some day, the transfer would be done after consultation with them. All the *dikgosi* united as they had done in 1895 to protest against transfer. King Khama even sent a petition to King George V, but without much success.

The Batswana stressed that they wished to remain a Protectorate as agreed in 1885 and 1895. They disliked the Union because of its oppressive 'native policy'. They had seen the Africans in the Union lose their land and did not want to suffer in the same way. Batswana who had studied or worked in the Union told of the oppression of black people.

Fig. 124 King Khama III sent a petition to the English King, George V, protesting against plans to incorporate Bechuanaland in the Union of South Africa

Fig. 125 General Hertzog (centre), Prime Minister of the Union of South Africa. He wanted to extend his racist 'native policy' to include the High Commission territories

In the 1920s General Hertzog, a Boer leader and ardent racist (person who believes strongly that his race is superior) was Prime Minister of the Union. In 1924 he put pressure on the British Government to transfer the High Commission Territories immediately. He wanted to extend his racist 'native policy' to these areas. In 1922 Southern Rhodesia had voted not to join the Union and so Britain was now free to let Bechuanaland join the Union without Southern Rhodesia. The Secretary of State for Colonies had, however, recently visited the three territories. He had wanted to find out how the Africans felt about transfer. In Bechuanaland Tshekedi Khama and Bathoen II put a strong case against transfer and threatened to take their case to London and fight it in the British law courts. The Secretary was afraid that the *dikgosi* were so strongly opposed to the transfer that they might revolt if forced to join the Union.

Britain was also becoming more and more unwilling to transfer the three territories. This was because of the race laws Hertzog was introducing in the Union. The British Government and the British voters did not like such strong racial laws. They thought such laws could only create problems.

Hertzog had the support of white farmers in the Protectorate. They asked Britain to transfer the Protectorate to South Africa. When Britain hesitated to transfer the Protectorate, Hertzog used economic pressure against the Protectorate. He banned the export to South Africa of cattle below a certain weight. This ban badly affected the Protectorate's economy which depended on cattle sales. The British Government and the Batswana did not surrender. Instead the Protectorate Administration found new beef markets in Northern Rhodesia (Zambia) and overseas. The cattle ban failed to work so Hertzog threatened to stop migrant labour from Bechuanaland and to reduce imports further. Britain and the Batswana resisted all these pressures.

The Boers continued for a long time to press for the transfer. The Batswana resisted, first through their *dikgosi* and later through the African Advisory Council. (See page 183.) In 1961 the Union of South Africa became a Republic and left the Commonwealth. This was the end of any serious attempt to transfer the High Commission Territories to South Africa.

It is quite clear that throughout most of the colonial period Bechuanaland was not quite safe because of external threats. It was mainly because of the statesmanship and resistance of the Batswana *dikgosi* that the land of the Batswana was preserved as separate from Rhodesia

Figs 126 and 127   Tshekedi Khama (left) and Bathoen II (right) who led the opposition to incorporation of Bechuanaland into South Africa

and South Africa. The *dikgosi* were assisted by various sympathisers in their brilliant resistance. This resistance enabled the Batswana to achieve independence in 1966 with their own country called the Republic of Botswana.

Questions

1. Provide the dates for the following events, and arrange them in the correct order.
    (a) The British Government approve the building of a railway through the Protectorate.
    (b) The Rudd Concession is signed.
    (c) Rhodes requests the transfer of the Protectorate to the BSAC.
    (d) The Chamberlain settlement is issued.
    (e) The BSAC is founded.
    (f) A Concessions Commission is set up.
    (g) Petitions are sent to Joseph Chamberlain.

2. Explain why the British Government wanted to hand over the High Commission Territories to the Union of South Africa, and why South Africa wanted them.

21 Administrative and Political Developments in the Protectorate

In order to understand fully the administrative, political and economic developments in the Protectorate we should remember the following. In general, Britain did not want to spend much money in ruling or developing its colonies. Colonies had to pay for themselves. In colonies which had many white people (settler colonies), such as Rhodesia, the Whites administered the colony for Britain. In colonies such as Bechuanaland there were very few Whites. So Britain ruled mainly through the indigenous (local) people under the supervision of white officials. This system was called Indirect Rule.

Britain did not use Indirect Rule because of any real respect for Setswana laws and customs. It did so mainly because this system of administration was cheap. Britain also feared that if it interfered too much with Setswana ways of doing things, the Batswana might revolt. Britain would then have to spend a lot of money putting down the uprising. We should also remember that Britain did not want the poor Protectorate. This is why she wanted to give it away. Britain did not wish to spend money on a country she was going to give away. This is also one reason why the capital town was outside the Protectorate until 1965 when Gaborone was built. For all these reasons, the Protectorate was neglected.

Protectorate administration 1885-91

After the declaration of the Protectorate in 1885, Britain felt that her main aim of protecting the road to the north was fulfilled. She therefore saw no need to set up a proper big administration. Warren wanted to establish some kind of administration, but the British Government stopped him. There was, however, a very small administration based outside the Protectorate.

Bechuanaland, like Basutoland and Swaziland, was placed under the High Commissioner who was also Governor of the Cape Colony. This is why the three countries were called the High Commission Territories. The High Commissioner lived in Cape Town. Later, his office was moved to Pretoria. When the Union of South Africa was formed, the High Commissioner also became Governor General of the Union. The first High Commissioner was Sir Hercules Robinson. Many people, including the *dikgosi* and the missionaries, complained about the High Commissioner having two jobs. Because of this he tended to favour the white people of South Africa. They also complained that he did not pay enough attention to Bechuanaland. So in 1931 he ceased to be the Governor General of the Union. The High Commissioner was under the supervision of the Colonial Office in London. The Government minister in charge of the Colonial Office was called the Colonial Secretary.

The Bechuanaland Protectorate was placed under the administration of Sir Sidney Shippard, Resident Commissioner living at Vryburg (Huhudi). In 1895, the headquarters of the Protectorate was moved to Mafikeng. Shippard was assisted by three Assistant Commissioners at

Fig. 128 Basotho were recruited into the Bechuanaland Border Police. Seen here a group with a white officer

Vryburg, Taung and Mafikeng. None of these officials lived in the Protectorate itself. Their duties were not clearly stated. They were generally to see to it that there was law and order. But they were not to interfere in the internal affairs of the Batswana.

The British Government was still concerned that the Amandebele, and especially the Boers, might invade Bechuanaland. So they created the Bechuanaland Border Police (BBP). These mounted (on horses) police patrolled the Transvaal border to protect Bechuanaland and the road to the north. This was the most important group in the Protectorate Administration. They were the only link between the Resident Commissioner and the various *dikgosi*. Later other links were provided with the creation of such offices as Assistant Commissioner in 1887, Resident Magistrate and Assistant Resident Magistrate in 1923, District Commissioner and Assistant District Commissioner in 1936. The BBP were sometimes sent to settle disputes. The BBP consisted of white men. In 1888-89 they recruited Basotho but they were dismissed because of racism by white officials it seems. Later the Basotho were brought back and they did well.

Although the British Government did not want to get involved in the internal affairs of the Protectorate, certain incidents pulled them in. Here are some examples from the Bangwato state.

Clever rulers such as Khama, who was also very much liked and trusted by the Administration, made use of the British Government to extend their power and territory. Khama wanted to impose tighter control over the smaller *merafe*. In the 1880s the Bagaseleka who lived near Ngwapa Hill, east of Shoshong near the Transvaal border, were ruled by Kobe. Kobe did not consider his people to be under Khama. But Khama claimed Kobe to be under him. Kobe allowed some Boers to live and hunt in his area against Khama's wishes.

In 1887, Khama sent a *mophato* (regiment) to attack Kobe for allowing the hated Boers to enter Bangwato country. The Administration did not want a big, costly war. They sent Bates of the BBP to settle the dispute and to find out whether the area indeed belonged to Khama. Shippard ruled that the area belonged to Khama but Kobe refused to accept this decision. He also refused to be ruled by Khama. Khama ordered an army of 4 000 men to attack Kobe. Kobe, his son Seleka, and their people fled to the Transvaal. This incident shows how rulers of major *merafe* could use colonialism to extend their rule over smaller groups.

Another incident was that involving a Boer called Grobler. In the 1880s Khama had problems with untrustworthy Whites who illegally entered his country from the Transvaal. They came to hunt, sell liquor or look for minerals. He, therefore, sent a *mophato* to guard the eastern border. It so happened that on his way from Lobengula's country Grobler passed through this area. Khama's men shot and badly hurt him and his men. He later died. The Transvaal Government protested to the British Government. Khama was asked to pay 1 350 cattle for use by Grobler's widow. He refused because Grobler had illegally entered his country and had resisted arrest. The British Government agreed to pay Grobler's widow £450 per year from Bechuanaland revenues (taxes) for the next fifty years.

It is quite clear that at the beginning there was very little British administration in the Protectorate. Britain was concerned mainly with external threats to Bechuanaland. The internal administration was left to the *dikgosi*. They ruled as they had always done in the past, and they liked it that way.

Setting up a new administration

The British men on the spot, from the High Commissioner downwards, were unhappy about the lack of a strong adminsitration for Bechuanaland. Shippard had tried to introduce it at Kopong in 1889, but the *dikgosi* had resisted.

A new High Commissioner, Sir Henry Loch was appointed. He believed in a strong administration. Until 1890 the northern boundary of the Protectorate was the 22 degrees south latitude. Loch persuaded the British Government to extend the border to include all of Khama's country. The *Order-in-Council* (British law) of 30 June 1890, extended the Protectorate to the Chobe and Zambezi Rivers.

Sir Henry Loch wanted a strong administration in order to stop the BSAC from taking over the Protectorate. He also argued that such an administration was needed to control the Europeans in Bechuanaland. Cases among Whites and between Whites and Blacks needed new courts of law. He believed that the *kgotla* could not deal with such cases. He also wanted to control trading, hunting and the increasing number of concession seekers. He argued that discipline in the police force and law and order in the country could be maintained only through a new, stronger administration.

The British Government was worried that the administration Loch wanted would cost a lot of money. Loch stated that the money would come from the Protectorate itself. Taxes of different kinds would raise the needed money. With this assurance (promise), the British Government authorised Loch by the *Order-in-Council* of 9 May 1891 to set up a proper Administration. He was empowered (given the power) to appoint the required officers and to do all other things necessary. The new Administration was to be a parallel or dual (double) one. There was to be a white man's administration based on British law. This would work side by side with an African administration based on Setswana law and custom. There was no Parliament so the High Commissioner would make laws for Bechuanaland by proclamation (announcement of new laws). In doing all this, the High Commissioner was to respect those African customs which did not conflict with (go against) British laws. This meant that the High Commissioner could do away with certain Setswana customs. The respect of Setswana customs was meant to prevent African opposition to the new Administration.

On 10 June 1891 Loch issued (gave) a proclamation establishing the new Administration. Sir Sidney Shippard was the Resident Commissioner for Bechuanaland. He was given Assistant Commissioners and a police inspector to assist him in his duties. One Assistant Commissioner was in charge of the southern parts of the Protectorate. The other was in charge of the northern parts. All these officers, except the Resident

Commissioner, lived in the Protectorate. Laws were made to control trading, guns and ammunition by issuing licences. Law courts were set up to try cases among Whites and between Whites and Blacks. The *dikgosi* continued to try cases between Africans at *kgotla*.

The new powers given to the Administration soon met with opposition from some *dikgosi*. The new powers of the High Commissioner enabled him to punish or even depose (remove) some *dikgosi*. Here are some examples.

The great Sechele I died in 1892 and was succeeded by his son Sebele I. The young new ruler wanted to rule the Bakwena without the interference of the Administration. He wanted to allow whoever he wished to trade and hunt in his area. He disregarded trading licences issued by the Administration. For example he allowed a Boer trader called Gideon Fourie to trade without a licence. Sebele also told some Indian traders that he would evict (chase away) them if they obtained trading licences. The young ruler ignored warnings from the Government. The administration fined him ten head of cattle for disobeying its orders. Sebele had many other quarrels with the Administration because he wanted to remain independent. One of these was caused by a dispute among the Bakwena. Some wanted Sebele to be the *kgosi*, and the others wanted his stepbrother Kgari. The Administration did not depose Sebele because he had more supporters. Kgari was told to leave Molepolole with his followers. He died at Kolobeng soon afterwards and his followers went to Bangwato country. They returned to Kweneng in 1920 during Sebele II's time.

In the 1890s the Batawana in Ngamiland were divided. Some wanted Sekgoma Letsholathebe as ruler. Others chose Mathiba Moremi. Sekgoma was a very strong ruler who wanted no interference by the Administration in Batawana affairs. He had displeased the Administration by refusing to give the BSAC a concession to settle the Boers at Ghanzi. He was disliked by missionaries because he defended Batawana customs against Christianity. He had also quarrelled with Khama about the boundary between the two states in the Boteti River area. For these reasons, the Administration wanted to depose him. The dispute with Mathiba gave the Administration the pretext (excuse). Sir Ralph Williams was the Resident Commissioner from 1902 to 1906. The High Commissioner sent him to depose Sekgoma. Sekgoma went to live at Kavimba with his followers and died there in 1912. His people later returned to Ngamiland.

The way in which the Administration dealt with Sebele and Sekgoma shows clearly that it was now far more powerful. It could interfere as it liked in Batswana affairs. The *dikgosi* were now not as independent as before.

Boundaries

The *Order-in-Council* of 1891 empowered the

Fig. 129 Sebele I who succeeded Sechele I as Kgosi of the Bakwena. Sebele particularly opposed the Protectorate administration interfering in the affairs of his *morafe*

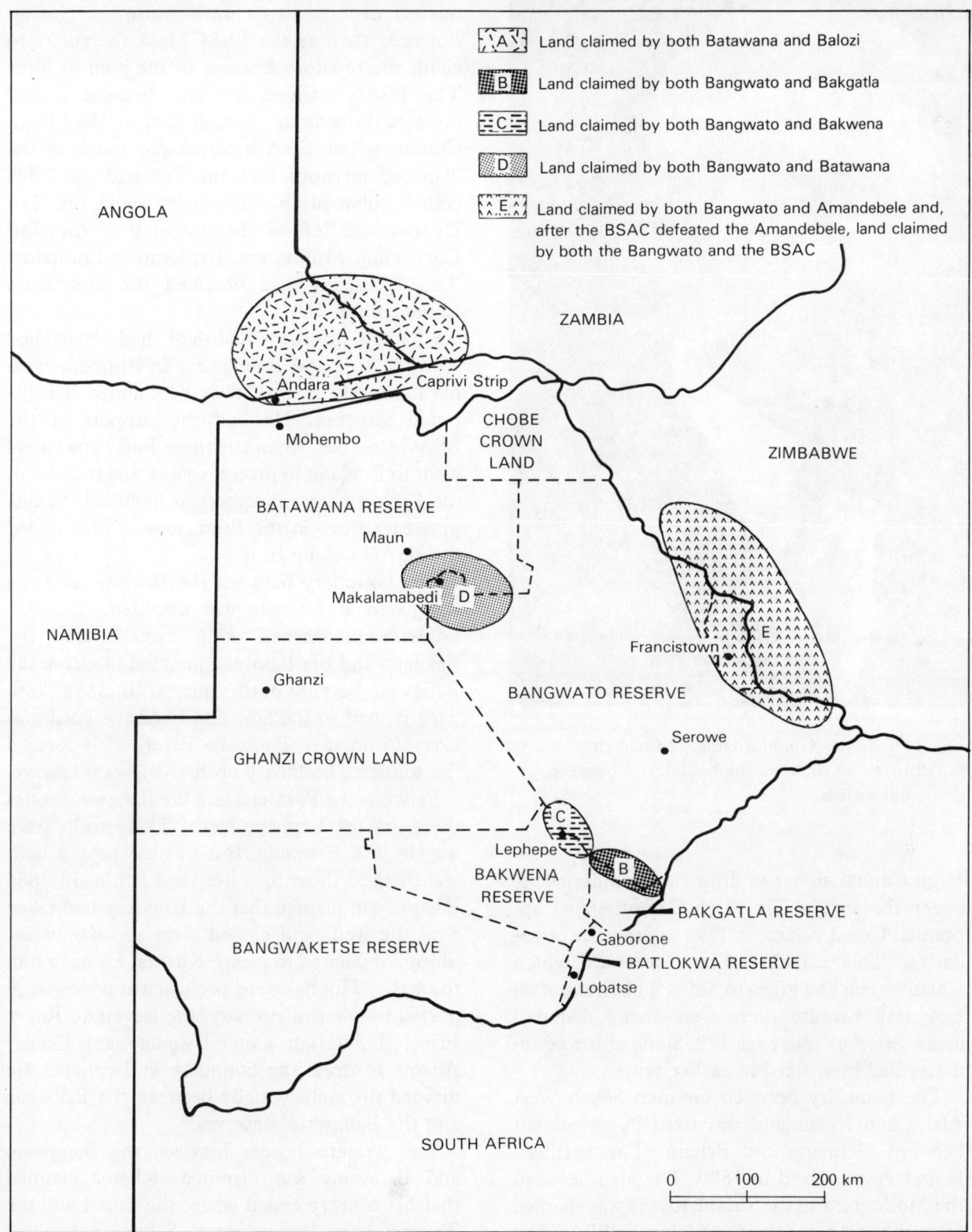

Fig. 130 Main border disputes after the Protectorate had been declared

Fig. 131 Major Gould-Adams who had the difficult task of drawing the boundaries between the major *merafe*

High Commissioner to draw the boundaries between the *merafe*. The High Commissioner appointed Gould-Adams in 1899 to draw the boundaries. This established the reserves which Chamberlain had given in 1895. This was not an easy task because there were many disputed areas. See Fig. 130, page 179. Some of the boundaries had been fixed in earlier years.

The boundary between German South West Africa and Ngamiland was fixed by agreement between Germany and Britain. The northern boundary was fixed in 1890. The area between the Motloutse and the Shashe Rivers was claimed by both the Amandebele and later the BSAC and the Bangwato. But the African rulers did not quarrel over the area until European concessionaires such as the BSAC used the rulers to claim the territory because of the gold at Tati. The BSAC claimed the area because it had replaced Lobengula. But, in fact, in 1892 High Commissioner Loch incorporated much of the disputed territory into the Protectorate. This ended Lobengula's claim to it. Only the Tati District was left as the property of the Tati Concession Mining and Exploration Company. This Company had obtained the area from Lobengula in 1887.

Khama's brother Raditladi had quarrelled with the king and gone to live in Rhodesia with his followers. In the 1890s he claimed the disputed territory. He had the support of the BSAC. In 1895 when the three Batswana rulers went to England to protest against the transfer of the Protectorate, Chamberlain included the disputed territory in the Protectorate. This ended the BSAC's claim to it.

The boundary between the Bakgatla and the Bangwato at Lokgalo was disputed. The Administration learned of a rumour that the Bakgatla and the Bakwena planned to attack the Bangwato because of this quarrel. In 1894 Shippard rushed to the area and fixed the border at Lokgalo on the Ngotwane River. This formed the southern boundary of the Bangwato reserve.

Between the Bakwena and the Bangwato states there are the Lephepe wells. These wells were dug by the Bakwena. But as time passed both *merafe* used them to water their cattle. In 1886 Khama complained that the Bakwena had taken over the wells and chased away the Bangwato. Shippard wanted to please Khama. He gave him the wells. The Bakwena protested and were supported by their missionary, the Reverend Roger Price. The High Commissioner sent Gould-Adams to draw the boundary at Lephepe. He divided the wells equally between the Bakwena and the Bangwato Reserves.

The western border between the Bangwato and Batawana was disputed. Khama claimed that his country ended where the Boteti and the Thamalakane Rivers meet. Sekgoma rejected this claim. Shippard, however, gave Khama the area. Sekgoma continued to protest. He was supported by the British Westland Chartered Company because it had mineral concessions in that part of Sekgoma's country. The High Commissioner sent Colonel Panzera in 1898 to draw the boundary. He fixed the boundary between the two reserves at Makalamabedi.

The boundary between the Batawana state and Bulozi (Barotseland in Zambia) was disputed. Kings Lewanika and Sekgoma quarrelled over the border. Both rulers claimed the area now called the Caprivi Strip. Sekgoma wanted the area because it was rich in ivory. Also he wanted the Hambukushu to be under his rule. Lewanika claimed the area because he wanted to continue to rule the Hambukushu. They had been under Balozi rule when they lived in Bulozi. The European colonial powers, Britain, Germany and Portugal ignored these claims. They gave the Caprivi Strip to Germany in 1890. But the dispute continued and in 1897 Gould-Adams was sent to fix the border. He favoured Sekgoma and gave him part of Bulozi. Lewanika protested strongly. In 1905 the western boundary between Angola and Bulozi was fixed. In the same year the High Commissioner fixed the northern boundary of the Batawana reserve at Mohembo. The Caprivi Strip became part of Namibia (South West Africa). After World War I it was ruled by the Protectorate from 1922 to 1929. It was then handed back to Namibia.

By 1899, most of the reserve boundaries were drawn. The Balete boundary was drawn in 1909 and the Batlokwa one in 1933. Bechuanaland was now clearly divided into reserves for occupation by Batswana only, and Crown Land and freehold land in the Tati district and the Gaborone, Ghanzi, Lobatse and Tuli blocks. Crown Land was unallocated land which could be used for future European settlement or for game reserves.

Taxation

In general, taxation in the colonies was mainly aimed at forcing the colonised people to work for Europeans. This was particularly true in settler colonies where European capitalists were short of labourers. Tax revenue was also used to pay for administration.

In the Protectorate the main reason for taxing Batswana was to raise money to pay for administration. The High Commissioner had promised that Bechuanaland would pay for its own administration. The *dikgosi* had already agreed to taxation in 1895. The High Commissioner introduced hut tax in 1899. Hut tax meant that every hut occupied by an adult male or males was taxed. If more than two males lived in one hut, each one paid. This tax was later changed to head or poll tax. Those who failed to pay tax were fined five pounds or sentenced to up to three months in jail.

The *dikgosi* were made tax collectors. They were paid ten per cent of the total tax collected in their area. This encouraged the *dikgosi* to make sure every tax payer paid tax. By 1911 administration was paid for from tax revenue. Britain gave only a small sum of money to add to the tax income.

In 1919 an additional new tax of three shillings per hut, called the native tax, was introduced. This money was put into the 'Native Fund'. This money was used for African education, to fight cattle diseases and for other projects which benefited Africans. In 1938 the hut tax and the native tax were combined to form the African tax. Every male of the age of eighteen years or more paid this tax. Between 1899 and 1965, these were the main taxes paid by Africans in Bechuanaland.

Results of taxation

Many African men were forced to seek work as migrant workers at the South African mines and farms. There were only a few jobs in Bechuanaland. As more men left, the burden of family work such as ploughing fell on the women. In some cases agricultural production fell. Some homes were broken because husbands were absent for long periods.

The introduction of taxation also led to the impoverishment (making poor) of those who had

Fig. 132 Receipts for hut taxes paid. These were small metal plaques. Note the dates and the spelling of Gaborone

few cattle. Those who did not find work had to sell cattle to pay the tax. Because the price of cattle was low, they sold many cattle in order to raise money for the tax and family needs. As time passed fewer and fewer Batswana owned cattle. Cattle were owned only by a few big cattle owners. There were, therefore, some Batswana who became very rich and some who became very poor.

The *digkosi*, of course, got richer from the ten per cent they received. Some used it for themselves. Others used it for the *morafe*. So taxation, like the old tribute (*sehuba*), was beneficial to the *dikgosi*. They strongly supported taxation.

It is clear that taxation was very hard on the Batswana. There were no jobs in the Protectorate and yet they were expected to find money for taxes. Bechuanaland was one of the poorest colonies, but it had to pay for its own administration.

New forms of administration
The African Advisory Council

As time passed the tasks of the Administration increased. There was a need to broaden the Administration to include various interested groups. It was no longer enough to rule by proclamation alone. In the 1920s there was a growing number of young educated Batswana, such as Simon Ratshosa, who wanted to take part in governing their country. Some of these educated men felt that the *dikgosi* no longer represented them properly. They also argued that they should take part in making the laws because they paid tax. For instance Kgosi Isang Pilane was an educated ruler. He wanted a strong Council which would give the Batswana unity, political education, and protect their interests.

The High Commissioner agreed to allow African participation in government. He did this mainly in order to stop discontent (unhappiness) among the young people. He also wanted to use the Council to get to know what Africans thought. In 1919 the Native Advisory Council was formed. It was later renamed the African Advisory Council because the Africans did not like the word 'native'. The High Commissioner was afraid of a powerful Council like the one Kgosi Pilane wanted. So he decided that the Council could only give advice. The Administration could ignore such advice if it wished.

The Council was composed of two representatives from each *morafe*, nominated by the people. In practice the *dikgosi* nominated the members who were usually headmen. The *dikgosi* were members. At first most *dikgosi* did not like the Council because they saw the educated Batswana as a threat. The Bangwato did not join the Council until 1940. But they attended the meetings of the Council. They did not want to join because they saw the Council as the first step in ending the powers the *dikgosi* were given in 1895.

The Resident Commissioner was the Council chairman. At the beginning the Resident Commissioner used the Council to hear what it thought of his proclamations. He also used it to make any other announcements. As time passed, the Council could debate any matters the members wanted to discuss. This allowed Africans to criticise the administration. They criticised many things, such as:
1 lack of Batswana in the Administration,
2 racial discrimination in government service,
3 low African salaries in government service,
4 lack of economic development in Bechuanaland,
5 poor education and health facilities.

An issue which the Council debated for many years was the transfer of Bechuanaland to the Union of South Africa. The Council strongly rejected this plan.

Some improvements happened because of the work of the Council. Tshekedi Khama, Bathoen Gaseitsiwe II and others used the Council to prevent the transfer of the Protectorate. The Council taught the Batswana that they could unite to get what they wanted. It also educated them politically. The Council also got the Resident Commissioner to report to it annually on the work of the Administration.

The European Advisory Council

In 1920 the European Advisory Council was formed to discuss matters affecting Europeans. The formation of two separate councils in one country shows that the Administration was prejudiced against racial integration. The members of the European Council were elected by constituencies like the members of the Botswana National Assembly are today. The Resident Commissioner was the chairman.

The Joint Advisory Council

The African Council did not like separate councils. They were unhappy because the Administration tended to favour the Whites. They were also unhappy because the European Council wanted to transfer Bechuanaland to the Union. In 1951 a Joint Advisory Council was formed. It consisted of an equal number of representatives from the two councils. It debated matters of concern to both Whites and Blacks. The other Councils continued to exist.

Reduction of the powers of the *dikgosi*

The 1891 proclamation had placed the *dikgosi* under the control of the Colonial Administration. But most rulers were still powerful and ran their own affairs. The Administration felt that the *dikgosi* were too powerful. They sometimes acted independently of the Administration. The Resident Commissioner, from 1929 to 1937 was

Fig. 133 The Joint Advisory Council (1953), which consisted of equal numbers of Africans and Europeans. Left to right standing: 1 G.J. McLaggan, 2 Tsheko Tsheko, 3 Pelaelo Ramokate, 4 Stephen Phetlhu, 5 A.D. Finchman, 6 M.L.A. Kgasa, 7 M.V.C. Royle, 8 C.R. Latimer. Left to right seated: 1 Tshekedi Khama, 2 L.S. Glover, 3 Kgosi Mokgosi Mokgosi, 4 C.H. Riley, 5 His Honour W.F. MacKenzie, 6 Kgosi Bathoen II, 7 R. England, 8 Thari Pilane.

Charles Rey. He wanted to reduce their powers. The Administration felt that the strong *dikgosi* violated British laws. They felt this was shown by the following incidents.

Khama III died in 1923 and was succeeded by Sekgoma Khama. He died in 1925 leaving a four-year-old son, Seretse Khama (first President of Botswana). Tshekedi was called back from Fort Hare University College in South Africa to be regent of the Bangwato. Tshekedi was a brave, clever, educated man who defended the rights of the Bangwato. He was also a strong ruler who did not like opposition.

In 1926, after a quarrel, Simon and Obeditse Ratshosa tried to shoot Tshekedi at the *kgotla*. They missed him and wounded two headmen. Tshekedi burned their houses and expelled them from Serowe. This case was taken right up to the Privy Council (the highest court) in England.

Another incident occurred in Serowe in 1933. A young white man called McIntosh misbehaved with Bangwato women. He fathered their children without marrying them. The usual punishment for such behaviour was flogging (beating) at the *kgotla*. Tshekedi rightly tried McIntosh at the *kgotla*. But when he ordered him to be beaten, McIntosh ran towards the regent. It seems he wanted to ask for mercy but the Bangwato thought he was going to attack Tshekedi. They caught and beat him. So Tshekedi did not actually flog McIntosh at all.

The Administration was very angry that a black man had tried and punished a white man. The Whites in South Africa and some in the Protectorate demanded that Tshekedi be punished. The Acting High Commissioner, Admiral Evans, came to Serowe from South Africa with some soldiers to try Tshekedi. Although the Bangwato supported Tshekedi, he was deposed and banished to Francistown in 1933. Humanitarians in England and some Europeans living in Serowe protested to the Colonial Office about

Tshekedi's banishment. The Bangwato too protested to the Administration. Tshekedi asked his lawyer, Buchanan, to sue (take to court) the Administration. When the Administration learned of this, they ended the ban. Tshekedi returned to Serowe after two weeks' banishment. Phineas McIntosh continued to live in Serowe even after Independence.

The Administration also complained that throughout Bechuanaland *botlhanka* still existed. The San especially were still badly treated. The British Government wanted to end *botlhanka* because:

1. the anti-slavery movement criticised colonial powers for not ending slavery, and *botlhanka* was a form of slavery,
2. the League of Nations also put pressure on colonial governments to end slavery,
3. the British Government wanted the *batlhanka* freed so that they could work in the British-owned mines in South Africa,
4. this, in turn, would earn money for the Protectorate through taxation.

In the 1930s Pim was sent to the Protectorate to advise on how the country could be developed. In his 1933 report he stated that as long as the *dikgosi* remained so powerful it would be difficult to develop the country. The *dikgosi* would resist laws which encouraged development. Pim was not absolutely correct. Some Batswana rulers were anxious to develop their reserves. Seepapitso and Bathoen II of the Bangwaketse, Isang, regent of the Bakgatla, and Tshekedi of the Bangwato, were such men.

The proclamations and resistance

In 1934, the High Commissioner issued two proclamations to reduce the powers of the *dikgosi*. The *Native Administration Proclamation* established a Tribal Council which would take

Fig. 134 Bathoen II in his office in Kanye, 1955

away most of the duties of the *kgosi* and the *kgotla*. The *kgosi* would rule with the agreement of the Council. The Council was to consist of the *kgosi* and Councillors approved by the *kgotla*. The *kgosi* was obliged (forced) to obey the Resident Commissioner. He was not allowed to collect taxes or tribute unless he was given permission by the Resident Commissioner. Above all, no one could be a *kgosi* without the approval of the British Government. The Administration could depose, suspend or banish a *kgosi*. All this was against Setswana custom. A *kgosi* was born a *kgosi*. He could not be removed except by the *morafe*.

The *Native Tribunals Proclamation* set up new law courts. The *kgosi* and some members of the Tribal Council belonged to a tribunal (court). This replaced the *kgotla* as a place where cases were tried. The *kgosi* was prohibited from trying major cases such as murder, rape, treason, etc. These were to be tried in European courts. This proclamation too was against Setswana custom because it took away the supreme power of the *kgotla*. The *kgosi* was no longer chief judge of his people.

Tshekedi and Bathoen II, supported by the other rulers, challenged these proclamations in 1936. They argued that the new laws violated the agreements of 1885 and 1895 between Batswana kings and the British. The British had promised not to interfere in the internal affairs of the Batswana. They argued that the proclamations violated Setswana customs and reduced *dikgosi* to a low status (position). They argued that according to the 1891 *Order-in-Council*, the Administration should 'respect' African custom. The *dikgosi* also saw the reduction of their power as a step towards incorporation into the Union of South Africa. This was another reason for their opposing the proclamations.

The two brave young rulers Tshekedi and Bathoen II took the Administration to court. Judge Watermeyer gave judgement against them. The *dikgosi* continued with their opposition. They wrote to the Colonial Office and put their case in the newspapers. There was much hostility between the *dikgosi* and the Administration. Carrying out development work became impossible. The Administration feared that there might even be an uprising.

The Protectorate Administration softens

Even though Tshekedi and Bathoen II had lost the case in court, the Administration realised that it must try to please the *dikgosi*. Charles Rey was replaced by a new Resident Commissioner (1937 to 1942), Charles Arden-Clarke. Arden-Clarke realised that the 1934 proclamations were too strong. He promised the *dikgosi* that he would make them weaker. He would leave the rulers some of their powers. He also told the Batswana that the question of the transfer to the Union would be dropped for some time. In 1938 he allowed the *dikgosi* to start African Treasuries to develop their reserves. The new Resident Commissioner also consulted and listened to the African Council. He carried out some of its recommendations. For example he built more schools and created the Board of Education to advise on African education. All these actions pleased the Batswana.

The most important thing Arden-Clarke did was to set up a committee to draft new proclamations. These were to replace the disliked 1934 ones. Tshekedi Khama, M. Seboni, Bogatsu Pilane, Sebopiwa Molema, Dr Silas Molema and some government officers were members. The Africans on the committee were members of the African Council.

In 1941 the High Commissioner, Sir Edward Harlech, visited Bechuanaland. He told the Batswana that new proclamations based on the recommendations of the committee would soon be announced. He felt that Rey had caused unhappiness among the Batswana. In 1943 the new proclamations were announced.

The new proclamations restored (brought back) some of the powers the *dikgosi* and the *kgotla* had lost in 1934. The Batswana rulers were empowered to carry out development projects in their areas. The High Commissioner could still appoint or depose a *kgosi*, but he must consult the *kgotla* before doing so. The *kgotla* was given back its importance in the *morafe*. The *kgosi* had to consult it and not the Tribal Council in all *morafe* matters. The *kgotla* would continue to work according to custom. The Tribal Councils were therefore ignored. It was decided also to have a High Court at Lobatse.

The Batswana accepted the new proclamations. There was peace again in the Protectorate.

Questions

1 Why did Britain rule the Protectorate through the system of 'Indirect Rule'?
2 What new powers were given to the High Commissioner by the proclamation of 10 June 1891?
3 List the taxes introduced between 1899 and 1965 in Bechuanaland. How were they collected?
4 Write brief notes on:
   (a) the African Council,
   (b) the European Council,
   (c) the Joint Advisory Council.
5 Why were the *Native Administration Proclamation* and the *Native Tribunals Proclamation* so unpopular? Why did the new proclamations of 1943 restore peace in the Protectorate?

22 Economic and Social Developments

The economy

In general, colonial economies never truly benefited the colonised people. The aim of the colonisers was usually to develop only those parts of the economy which benefited them. In the rich colonies, the wealth was largely taken away to be used in the mother country of the colonisers, such as Britain, France, etc. So the wealth of the colonies was used to develop the countries of the colonisers. This left the colony and its people poor. In the poor colonies, the colonisers did not bring in much money to develop the country. They usually simply neglected such a colony. This was true of Bechuanaland.

The following are some of the characteristics (signs) of a colonial economy.
1. The colonial power develops only those parts of the economy which largely benefit the colonisers. These are mainly exports to the coloniser's own country. So one of the characteristics of a colonial economy is that it aims to develop products for export. But the money got from the exports is not used fully to benefit the colonised.
2. The colonial power puts little money into the colony to develop it. The colonial power gets the colony to pay for its own administration. It does this by getting the colonised to provide the money in different ways e.g. taxes, labour, etc.
3. The transport system (roads, railways, etc.) is used for exports needed by the colonisers.
4. Few developments which directly benefit the colonised take place. Education and health facilities are usually poor.

Lack of development funds

An example of British neglect of the development of Bechuanaland is its failure to provide development funds (money). Until after World War II Britain provided very little money for development. The period 1885 to 1933 was the time of the greatest neglect. The little money Britain gave to Bechuanaland, beginning in 1899, was mainly to assist the railways as they carried Bechuanaland mail free of charge. But in 1909 this assistance was stopped, so Britain gave even less money to the Protectorate. Most of the tax revenue was used for paying administrative costs and not for development.

There were some small changes in the period between 1933 and 1955. In 1933, a commission led by Pim was sent to examine the economic situation in Bechuanaland. Complaints by the African Advisory Council and others had caused the British Government to take this action. The Pim Commission criticised the British Government for neglecting Bechuanaland so badly.

The growing nationalism in Africa during the 1940s caused Britain to pay more attention to its African colonies. In 1945, Britain set up the Colonial Development and Welfare Fund to develop the colonies. Bechuanaland obtained grants from the Fund to start the Department of Geological Surveys in 1948, for example. This aid increased from 1955 onwards. The British

Fig. 135 Jacob Matebele and family. A Mongwaketse master farmer picking cotton (1963). Given the opportunity, Africans grew cash crops

Government gave grants for administration and development projects.

It is clear from this that until a few years before Independence, Britain did not give much money to develop Bechuanaland. This resulted in extreme underdevelopment. A brief look at a few areas of the economy will show that indeed little development took place.

Agriculture

Subsistence farming remained the main agricultural activity during the colonial period. The only substantial commercial farming was in the European areas. This was mainly because the European farmers were given government loans to develop their farms. They could also sell their produce to South Africa at good prices. So they were able to buy better farming equipment, fertiliser and better seed. They also knew better farming methods. The Government also built roads connecting European farms to the railway to enable farmers to export their crops. Because they were not on communal (*merafe*) lands, European farmers could fence their farms and so protect their crops. These farmers grew cash crops, such as sunflowers and groundnuts.

Not very much was done to develop African agriculture. There was a need to teach subsistence farmers new methods of farming. There was also a need to introduce cash crop farming. The small improvements that took place were the work of the *dikgosi* and *merafe*. For example the Batswana adopted the use of ox ploughs. The Barolong introduced large-scale farming and used large machines such as tractors. They competed with white farmers, and got some government aid to promote maize growing.

In general, the Colonial Government paid more attention to the cattle industry than to arable (crop) farming. The Batswana were also interested more in cattle than in crop farming because cattle thrived and brought good revenues. The main reason for lack of development in crop farming was the poor rainfall.

In 1935, following the Pim Commission, a small Department of Agriculture was created. But it could not function properly because it did not get enough funds until the 1950s. It could not employ enough people or buy the necessary materials and equipment. Mahalapye was the headquarters of the new department because it was central. Mr Russell England was the chief Agricultural Officer. He was assisted by only four white officers and about twelve African demonstrators (*balemisi*). Centres of the department were established at Francistown, Lobatse and Seleme in Kgatleng. The main work of the department was to run experimental (trial) plots using modern methods. It also tried to develop good kinds of seed suitable for the Botswana climate. Batswana were expected to learn good farming methods by visiting these plots. So the aim was to teach by example. This method was not successful because the stations were far away from most Batswana. Transport was not good. Another problem was that most Batswana had no money to buy equipment. The Government did not give any assistance. A further reason for the failure was that there were no demonstrators living among the people to teach them in their own areas. However, the Government gave a free supply of good seed to farmers who came to the seed development station at Lobatse.

The outbreak of the war disturbed the experimental work of the department. Batswana were now required to produce food for the war by working in the 'War Lands'. There was little time and money left for experimental work.

In 1947 a new attempt was made to improve farming. The aim this time was to teach some Batswana to be master farmers. These would then give an example of good farming in their own areas. A person started training as a pupil farmer and passed through different stages until he became a master farmer (*selemi*). Agricultural demonstrators were placed in different areas to teach agriculture. Very few Batswana became master farmers mainly because they had not enough money to carry out the necessary improvements. Government help was not sufficient. The few who became master farmers were given certificates showing that they were good farmers. In 1960 the Government encouraged the building of a grinding mill at Lobatse so that farmers could sell their crops. This made some farmers, especially in the Barolong farms, increase their crop production. On the whole arable farming was not successful in the colonial period. One of the problems, of course, was that of poor and uncertain rainfall throughout Botswana. To provide water for crops, small irrigation schemes were started at Mogobane in 1937 and Kanye in 1943. There were also some irrigation works in the Tuli Block.

Cattle farming

Livestock farming was the only major agricultural activity in which the Government was interested. Beef sold well in world markets and Britain too needed beef. Beef sales brought revenue to the Government. Many Batswana were also keenly interested in cattle farming. It was their main economic activity. Indeed Batswana *merafe* did not always wait for the Colonial Government to introduce improvements in livestock farming. Some of them, such as the Bakgatla, the Bangwaketse, the Bakwena and the Bangwato (Tshekedi especially) bred good bulls for their *merafe* without Government help.

The Government took an early interest in cattle production, and put money into this indus-

Fig. 136 The traditional method of watering cattle, using a hollowed out tree trunk

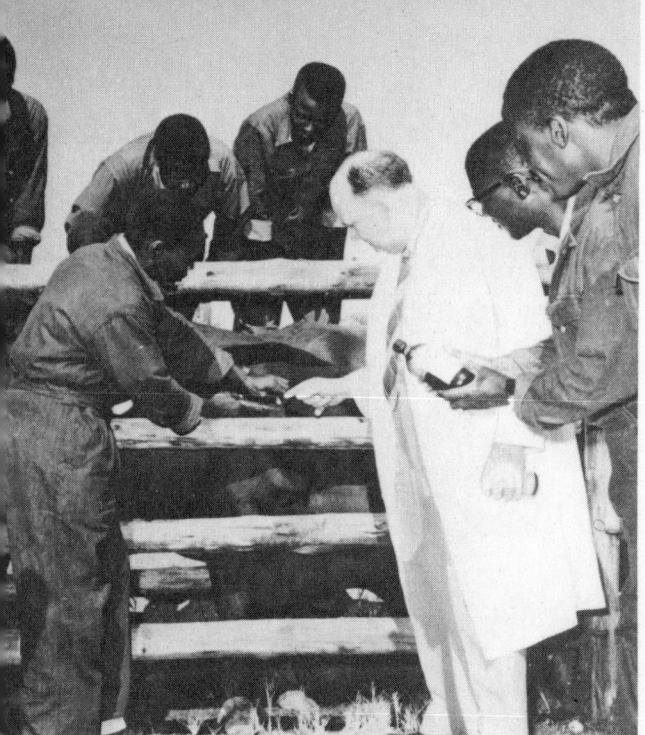

Fig. 137 A class of students at Ramatlabama Veterinary School (1963), learning how to innoculate cattle

try. In 1896-97, a cattle disease called rinderpest (*bololwane*) killed thousands of cattle. Another 10 000 infected cattle were shot in order to stop the spread of the disease. To prevent the occurrence (happening) of this disease and any others, the Government established the Veterinary Department in 1905. From the very beginning the department was given more employees and more money than the department concerned with crops. So it was more successful. As a result of its work, cattle diseases were either totally eradicated (wiped out), such as east coast fever, or were kept under control, such as foot-and-mouth disease. Although these diseases broke out from time to time vaccinating and quarantining cattle and cordon fencing controlled their spread. Because of these measures, cattle increased in numbers.

The Government also took measures to improve cattle breeds from the 1930s amd 1940s onwards. Bull camps were established to breed good bulls. The bulls were then sold to interested Batswana at subsidsed (low) prices. Artifical insemination of cows was also provided. Some Batswana gradually improved the quality of their cattle which then fetched higher prices.

The Lobatse abattoir

In order to promote beef exports, the Imperial Cold Storage Commission built an abattoir in Lobatse in 1934, but closed it two years later. It reopened in 1940 and closed again in 1941. It was then rented to Mafeking Creamery for a while. In 1954 the abattoir reopened with funds from the Commonwealth Development Corporation (CDC). From 1965 the Botswana Meat Commission (BMC) started to manage the abattoir, which controlled all beef exports.

The Colonial Government leased to the CDC large farms in the Molopo area (Molopo Farms). They were to be used for fattening cattle for its Lobatse abattoir. One of the most serious problems faced by the beef industry occurred in the 1920s. The Union of South Africa refused to accept Bechuanaland cattle. (See page 173.) Beef exports mainly benefited the Government, the CDC, a few rich Batswana cattle owners, European farmers and the European traders who bought and sold cattle. Because of transport difficulties most Batswana could not take their cattle to the abattoir. They sold them to traders at low prices.

Fig. 138 A beef canning factory at work in Lobatse (1963)

Dairying

Another aspect of the cattle industry was dairying. The Government did not pay as much attention to the dairy industry as it did to the beef industry. The dairy industry was started in 1926 in order to raise revenue when South Africa refused to take Bechuanaland beef cattle. The dairy section of the Agriculture Department was very small, however, and could not do a good job. The European farmers benefited more than Africans from dairying. This was mainly because they produced more and better quality cream from better breeds. They also got financial assistance from banks to buy better equipment. They had better markets, especially in South Africa, and they had better transport to the railway. Africans lacked the money to buy good milk cows and equipment. They had poor transport and were usually far from the railway. So their milk and cream sold at low prices. This was because it spoilt while being taken over long distances to the railway for export. Another reason for the lack of success of dairying was poor rainfall. Dairy cattle require more water and better pasture than beef cattle. These were not always available because of the arid conditions. In general the Bechuanaland dairy industry could not compete in quality, quantity and prices with the more developed ones in Rhodesia and South Africa.

Water development

The only part of Botswana with plenty of water is Ngamiland where the Okavango Delta is. The rest of the country has a shortage of water. The cattle industry required a lot of water. So boreholes had to be drilled. Boreholes provided water not only for cattle, but for people as well.

Drilling for water began in the early days of the Protectorate. This was not only done by the Colonial Government. The *dikgosi* drilled wells in the large villages. Water fees were charged among the Bakgatla and the Bangwaketse. By 1940 all major villages had boreholes. Individuals were also encouraged to drill boreholes or dig wells. The *dikgosi* changed water rights laws

Fig. 139 Members of the Geological Surveys Department drilling a borehole near Kanye (1963)

to allow a person with his own borehole to use it only for himself. This was not so with open water which belonged to everyone. They also made laws prohibiting boreholes from being too close to each other. This was to protect grazing land. The Bakgatla under Kgosi Isang formed syndicates (groups) in 1933 to drill or buy boreholes for use by the group only. No other *morafe* had this system. A syndicate is a group of people who jointly own property. They share the costs and profits.

The Geological Survey's major task was to survey for water. More boreholes were sunk throughout the country with funds from the Colonial Development and Welfare Fund. It soon proved that borehole water was not sufficient for large villages and towns. So in the 1960s dams such as the Gaborone Dam were built to provide water. Water drilling is an area where the Colonial Government did some fairly good work. This was because cattle were very important to the colonial economy.

Mining

Until after Independence little mining took place in Bechuanaland. This was because the Colonial Government did not have a strong mineral exploration programme. So few mineral deposits were discovered. Looking back, this was politically good for Botswana. If minerals had been found before Independence, Europeans would have come to Botswana in larger numbers. This happened in Rhodesia and South

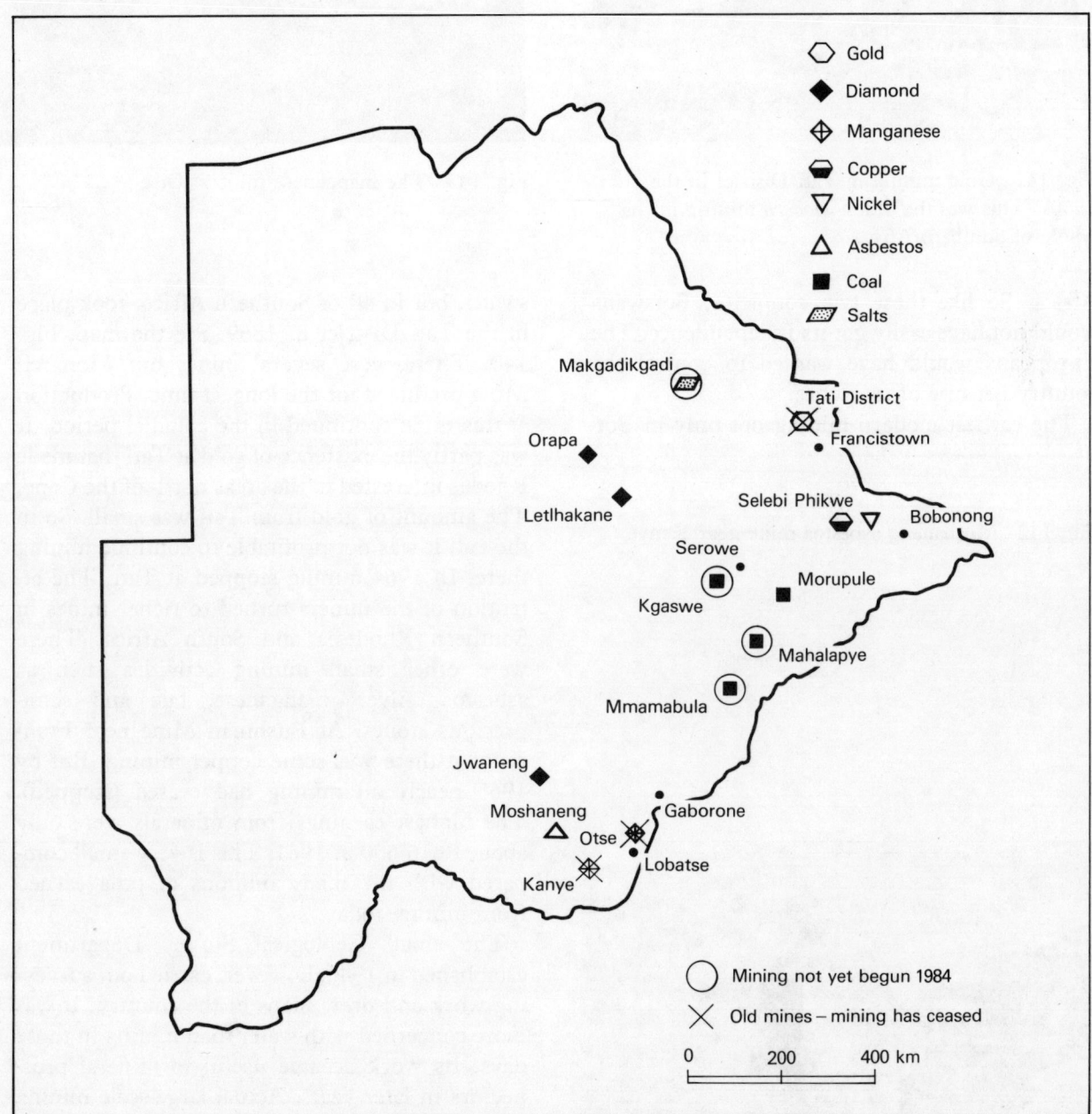

Fig. 140 Botswana mining past and present — some of the minerals

Fig. 141 Gold mining in Tati District in the 1860s. This was the oldest *modern* mining in the whole of Southern Africa

Fig. 143 The manganese mine at Otse

Africa. So like these two countries, Botswana would not have easily got its Independence. The Europeans would have wanted to control the country because of its riches.

The earliest modern mining not only in Bot-

Fig. 142 Moshaneng asbestos mine near Kanye

swana, but in all of Southern Africa, took place in the Tati District in 1869. See the map, Fig. 140. There were several mines but Monarch Mine produced for the longest time. Production at this mine continued in the colonial period. It was partly the existence of gold at Tati that made Rhodes interested in the areas north of the Cape. The amount of gold from Tati was small. So in the end it was not profitable to continue mining there. In 1964 mining stopped at Tati. The attention of the miners turned to richer mines in Southern Rhodesia and South Africa. There were other small mining activities such as asbestos, silver, manganese, talc and semi-precious stones. At Bushman Mine near Francistown there was some copper mining. But by 1966 nearly all mining had ceased (stopped). The highest earnings from minerals were only about P616 600 in 1961. This is very small compared with the many millions of pula earned from mining today.

The small Geological Survey Department established in 1948, however, carried out surveying work and drew maps of the country. It was more concerned with water than mining in those days. Its work became useful to mineral prospectors in later years. Actual large-scale mining did not take place until after Independence but prospecting went on, especially towards the end of the colonial period. For example, the Bamangwato Concessions Limited (BCL), a branch of the Roan Selection Trust Company of Rhodesia (RST) signed a prospecting agreement with Tshekedi Khama in 1959. In 1965 they discovered copper and nickel at Selebi Phikwe. Drilling for coal started in 1897, but by 1900 interest in coal had died down. This was because there was enough coal in Southern Rhodesia and South Africa. Coal was first discovered in the Morupule area near Palapye in 1939. In the 1950s the Geological Survey Department seriously undertook coal exploration in the Morupule area. Large deposits were later discovered there and at Mmamabula. Other explorations were carried out such as that by De Beers for diamonds. They found small amounts on the Motloutse riverbed. In 1967 they discovered major deposits at Orapa.

Transport

The underdevelopment of a country is usually shown by a poor transport system. This was the case with Bechuanaland. There were not enough goods produced to make the building of transport necessary. The main means of transport was the single track (line) railway owned by the Rhodesia Railways. The main reason for building the railway was not to develop Botswana but Southern Rhodesia. Bechuanaland, however, used the railway for its imports and few exports, mainly beef. The railway mainly benefited white farmers and the Colonial Administration. Most Batswana lived far away from the railway, so they did not use it much for travelling or carrying goods. There were no good roads linking Batswana areas to the railway. A railway system is useful to the people if it reaches the places where most of them live, or if they can reach it by other means. This was not the case in Bechuanaland. So the railway was of no direct benefit to the ordinary Batswana. They benefited indirectly, for example, by being able to buy goods in the shops. These goods came by rail.

There was an attempt in the 1930s to introduce railway lorries to link the main villages to

Fig. 144 A Rhodesia Railways train at Gaborone station. In the early days the train was used mainly for transporting goods

Fig. 145 Ox wagons are the oldest form of wheeled transport. Here shown is Sekgoma Khama's trek to the Nata River

the railway. The aim was to carry the traders' goods from the railway stations to the villages. People could also ride on these lorries. The *dikgosi* opposed this system. They feared that wagon transport would die out. Wagon transport was owned by Batswana. So if the lorries which were owned by the railway company were allowed, Batswana would lose money. Wagon transport was also much cheaper even though it was slower. It was also considered safer than lorries in those days. Gradually, however, traders introduced lorries and people used them. So wagons were eventually replaced, but smaller donkey carts continued to carry goods and people.

There were attempts to build another railway. This was to run from Rhodesia, through northern Botswana to Walvis Bay in South West Africa. This railway would have provided a transport system for the Kgalagadi and northern Botswana. Southern Rhodesia was mainly interested in the building of this railway for the export of its goods, especially Wankie coal. South Africa feared that such a railway would compete with its own railway system. So South Africa opposed it. The Protectorate Administration in the end also decided not to build the line. So the plan died.

The road system was largely neglected. At Independence there were only 7 200 kilometres of road. Nearly all of this was untarred. Most of the roads were wagon tracks. In fact, the wagon was the main means of ordinary transport until the 1930s. The better maintained gravel roads were the ones linking Botswana to Rhodesia and South Africa. The Government also built gravel roads to link European farming areas to the

Fig. 146 A trading store in Gaborone. Most trading stores belonged to non-Africans

railways. In 1930, for example, the Tuli Block white farmers put pressure on the Government to build the Tuli Block to Dibete Road. Bakgatla regiments and prisoners were used to build the road. Until Independence all roads were gravel roads. There were only five kilometres of tarred road from the Lobatse station to the High Court and about one kilometre of tarred street in Francistown. The Lobatse stretch was built for the visit of King George VI in 1947.

There were no other major economic activities than the ones described above. There were no manufacturing industries, except traditional beer brewing and craft industries. The only other economic activity worth mentioning in passing was trading. There were general dealers' shops in every major village. These sold goods imported mainly from South Africa or Southern Rhodesia. The shops were nearly all owned by European traders. The Batswana *dikgosi* had lost the control they had had over traders in the pre-colonial days. Trading licences were now issued by the Colonial Government. It is clear that there were no job opportunities in Bechuanaland. So Batswana went to South Africa as migrant workers.

Migrant labour

Batswana men went to South Africa to seek work mainly in order to earn money to pay tax. As time passed Batswana wanted more and more European goods. So they sought work in the South African mines and farms to earn money to buy goods.

The Colonial Administration encouraged migrant labour in order to get tax revenues. But it also wanted the South African mines to have labour. These mines were owned by British capitalists and the Protectorate Administration was also British. In 1899 the Administration began to make laws to control the recruitment of labour. Recruiting licences were sold to the mine labour recruiting organisations. In 1912 the fee was £25 (P40) per licence. This fee brought revenue to the Government.

As more mines opened, competition for labour became high. To avoid competition and in order to fix salaries at low levels, mining companies formed a Chamber of Mines in 1889. The Chamber formed the Native Labour Supply Association in 1896 to recruit labour. This organisation was not very successful. In 1900 the Witwatersrand Native Labour Association (WNLA) replaced it. Another organisation, the Native Recruiting Corporation (NRC) was formed in 1912. These two organisations did not compete but assisted each other. WNLA recruited in the north and NRC in the south of

Fig. 147 Men being recruited by an agent to work in the South African mines. One can only guess what promises the white agent is making

Fig. 148 Mine workers coming off work in the New State Areas about 1930. Note that they are being searched

Bechuanaland. As a result, many Batswana went to work in the South African mines.

The migrant labour system had some disadvantages.
1. The workers were paid low wages because they could not sell their labour wherever they liked.
2. Able-bodied men left Bechuanaland and so agricultural work was left to old people and women. Production of food crops probably went down.
3. The Batswana developed South Africa, instead of developing their own country.
4. Families sometimes broke up because husbands left their wives alone for long periods.
5. Miners returned with new diseases which badly affected the *merafe*.

There were some advantages, mainly to *dikgosi*, the Administration and the mines.
1. The *dikgosi* got part of the tax money. So the more Batswana went to the mines, the more money they got.
2. The Administration got revenue through taxation and licence fees.
3. Another gain was that social unrest due to unemployment was prevented.
4. The mines got cheap labour. This resulted in high profits for them.
5. The migrants themselves got some money to buy things for their families, and were able to pay taxes without having to sell cattle.

On the whole, the migrant labour system was bad because it exploited the Batswana. Even the African rulers sometimes stopped their people from going to work in South Africa. This was because of the high death rate, racial discrimination and ill-treatment. Another reason was that migrant labour disrupted the economic and social life of the *merafe*. Khama III and Linchwe I are examples of *dikgosi* who banned migrant labour for some time.

Landlessness in colonial times

In colonies with many European settlers such as Southern Rhodesia, Africans lost most of their land. European settlers used African land for large farms. The Africans were either forced to leave or work for the white farmers if they wished to stay. The farmers paid low wages or no wages at all. The Africans sometimes paid to stay on the farm through giving free labour. This resulted in extreme poverty and suffering.

In Botswana this situation was not common because there were few Europeans. So the African Reserves were quite large. However, landlessness and suffering occurred in some European areas such as Tuli Block, Ghanzi and Tati District. See the map, Fig. 130, page 179. We shall discuss only the Babirwa of Tuli Block as an example of how the Batswana in European areas lost their land.

Tuli Block

It has already been stated that Tuli Block was given to the BSAC in 1895. But the Babirwa under Kgosi Malema continued to live on their land in that area. They had not been consulted about their land being given away. Trouble began when the BSAC began to sell the land to white farmers after 1904. In 1910 the Babirwa were told that they were now landless. Such a landless person is called a tenant. They were to be tenants of the white farmers. Those who did not want to be tenants were ordered to leave Tuli Block. Malema and his people refused to move from the land. He considered it to be his by right from historic times.

In 1920 the BSAC asked the Administration to force the Babirwa to move. The Administration told Khama to remove them because they were in his reserve. Khama sent Modisaotsile, who was the Mongwato headman of Bobonong, to remove the brave, stubborn, independent-minded Malema. When the Babirwa heard of the approach of Modisaotsile and his regiment, many of them fled. Some went to Rhodesia and others, including Malema, went to South Africa. There they lived among the Babirwa in those countries. Some never returned to Botswana. Others returned later and settled outside the Tuli Block.

The remaining Babirwa were driven to Bobonong were they where forced to live under close guard. In 1921 some Babirwa returned from South Africa to Tuli Block where they had left their corn hidden. They were removed to Bobonong. The regiments treated people badly when they removed them. A few either died or were hurt. Their granaries and houses were burned down.

In 1922 Malema got his lawyer, Gluckman, to challenge his removal from Tuli Block. An inquiry was held and Khama admitted that his regiment had ill-treated the Babirwa. He agreed to pay Malema some cattle for his losses. Malema rejected the offer. He refused to live under Khama and wanted his land back. He was unsuccessful in this. He later dropped the case against Khama when he realised that he could not win in court. He asked the Government to settle him in the Gwanda District of Southern Rhodesia where other Babirwa lived. This request was not successful. Instead, the Administration wanted to settle Malema and his people on Crown Land at Boteti or Nekate, outside Khama's control. Malema rejected these areas as they were a long way from the other Babirwa areas.

After Khama's death his successor, Sekgoma, tried to solve the problem. British public opinion was sympathetic to the Babirwa. Gluckman had publicised the Babirwa case. So the Administration was anxious to solve this problem to avoid criticism. In 1925 the Malema group which had refused to live under Modisaotsile at Bobonong, was settled at Molalatau, not very far from Bobonong.

Malema himself refused to live in an area under Bangwato control. He was banished from the Protectorate. He and a few followers lived in different places such as Rhodesia, Transvaal and on McNeill's farm in the Tuli Block. The ban was ended in 1944. Malema returned to Bechuanaland. He died an old man, in 1960 at Molalatau where his descendants and followers still live today.

The Babirwa were not alone in losing their land. The Bakalanga in the Tati District also lost much of their land and became tenants of the Tati Company. The people of the Ghanzi district were similarly affected. The creation of Molopo Farms similarly took away the land of the Barolong and the Bangwaketse. The Bangwaketse under Bathoen II protested, but they did not succeed.

Changes in Khoe and San communities

By 1850 few areas remained unoccupied by either Batswana or some other farming group. In almost every area where water could be found by digging shallow wells people were keeping stock. During the rainy season, they would take their stock to waterless areas where rain formed pools in pans for a few days or weeks.

By this time the San and Khoe had lived for generations in contact with the pastoralists. In areas like those along the Nata and Boteti Rivers the Khoe had permanent homes and grew crops. They lived lives very similar to their Bantu-speaking neighbours. Many San were absorbed into farming groups and, in heavily populated areas, they began to disappear as a separate and distinct people.

It was only in remote areas which pastoralists did not reach, such as the Central Kalahari, that their traditional lifestyle continued without much change. In other areas of the Kalahari they formed loose associations with the Bakgalagadi. They traded skins with the Bakgalagadi for salt, iron, tobacco, and dogs. During the 19th century the Bakgalagadi began to treat the San as badly as they themselves had been treated by the Batswana. The Bakgalagadi took control of whole groups of San forcing them to hunt on their behalf as *batlhanka*. Their children became servants. San men were used to herd whatever stock the Bakgalagadi owned.

Some Bakgalagadi left their own communities and settled permanently with San groups introducing some of their customs. The men married San women and their children inherited whatever property they had. These Bakgalagadi gave up speaking their own dialects and adopted those of the San. Today they are generally known as *Balala*.

By 1900 most of the San had close contact with pastoral peoples. Many of them lived close to cattle posts and, while the women collected wild food, the men herded cattle and took occasional opportunities to go and hunt.

When the Ghanzi Farms were settled at the beginning of this century by Boers the area was already occupied by three different groups of San: the Nharo, //aufei and G/wi. They still lived mainly by hunting and collecting. As fences were erected first game, and then wild food, began to become scarce. The San could not understand what had happened. They were forced to work for the farmers or starve. The history of the Ghanzi San is well known because the settlement of their land has taken place during living memory.

What happened at Ghanzi is probably the same as what happened in many other parts of Botswana long ago. Farming people settled in areas occupied by San, hunted the game and allowed their stock to eat the wild food. The major difference is that elsewhere the San were slowly absorbed by the dominant farmer population. In Ghanzi the dominant white population did not make any attempt to mix with the San.

Today there are between 50 000 and 60 000 San living in Angola, Namibia and Zimbabwe, but mostly in Botswana. A few, a very few, still cling to their traditional lifestyle in the more remote areas of the central Kalahari. But the great majority live as servants around the boreholes of cattle owners. They live on the meagre wages they receive, on milk at boreholes and what food they can gather. When they can, they still hunt, but today this often involves borrowing a horse or donkey and a gun from someone else and sharing the kill with him. Some are permanently settled in villages such as Letlhakane where they make a living by acting as domestic servants, brewing beer or collecting wild food and firewood for sale. A few have become farmers and grow crops like other Batswana.

The Government has made efforts to integrate them into the population. Schools have been built at Cade, Dekar, Takatswane and in other places and many San children now go to school. Some men come to the towns to find work and are recruited for the South African mines.

The Government would like to see them brought into large villages and living as the rest of the population. This would solve the difficult problem of the large numbers who still live throughout the Kalahari and are occupying land which is rapidly being developed for the cattle industry. However, most San have no skills other than those they have inherited. They still need wide areas of land to live in. They have little hope of surviving in large villages at this stage. In time it is hoped that they will, however, live in permanent settlements.

Education under the Protectorate

At Independence, Botswana had very few educated people. This is why for many years after Independence was won, nearly all the most important and senior jobs were held by expatriates (*batswakwa* or foreigners). Britain had done very little to develop education in Bechuanaland. Bechuanaland had the worst educational system of all the British colonies in Africa. Until quite late, education was left almost entirely to the missionaries and the *merafe*.

We have already seen how Batswana were critical of missionary education. Because of this, the LMS decided to establish a new industrial college which would compete with South African schools. The school would teach both practical subjects such as building and carpentry and academic subjects. The Bangwato wanted the school to be at Palapye. They offered the old church building there as a school house. The LMS, however, wanted such a school to be on freehold land, not *morafe* land. They preferred a freehold area because they feared that they would not have full control of the school in an African reserve. Another possible reason for building the school outside Bechuanaland was that it was believed that the Protectorate would one day become part of South Africa.

Because of the Anglo-Boer War the opening of the new school was delayed. In 1904 Tiger Kloof was finally opened near Vryburg in South

Fig. 149 Tiger Kloof College near Vryburg in South Africa where many Batswana studied

Africa. This angered Khama III who had wanted the school to be in his reserve. The Bangwato also complained because Tiger Kloof was outside Bechuanaland and it was far from their country. So Khama boycotted the school by not sending Bangwato there. The boycott ended in 1905, and in 1906 Khama gave the school £120 to buy the school clock on the tower. Tiger Kloof aimed to teach practical subjects and to give the best education generally. In the early years there were problems. The Batswana students complained that the school rules were rather harsh. In fact, Simon Ratshosa, a Mongwato student, was expelled for complaining against these rules. In the end, however, Tiger Kloof became popular and educated many Batswana. Some of them hold important positions in education, politics, commerce and industry in Botswana today. In 1953 South Africa introduced Bantu education which was meant only for Africans and was inferior to European education. So Tiger Kloof was moved to Moeding in Bechuanaland.

Government aids education

Until 1904 the Protectorate Administration did not give any money to education at all. But some government officials began to advise the Administration to assist mission schools by giving grants-in-aid (money). The Batswana also criticised the Administration for neglecting education. So in 1904 the Administration appointed Sargant to look into the education system in the Protectorate. He was to make some recommendations to improve it. Sargant was Educational Adviser to the High Commissioner. He found out that missionary schools were not popular among the Batswana because they gave poor education. He noted that too much emphasis on religious education displeased the Batswana. On the other hand, he found that national schools were popular. The Africans also told Sargant that they wanted some control of the schools by Batswana. The Bakwena and the Bangwaketse had already introduced school committees to help run schools in their areas. The aim was to reduce missionary influence and so allow them to decide on the type of education they wanted for their children. The school committee system was later copied by the Administration for the whole Protectorate. Nowhere else in Africa south of the Zambezi River was there such a system at that time. This was a Batswana contribution to education administration. The system gave Batswana the opportunity to develop their own leaders in education. On the other hand it gave the Protectorate Administration the excuse not to care about developing education.

Results of Sargant's recommendations

One of the important recommendations Sargant made was that the Government should aid schools by giving annual grants. The first grant of £500 was made to the LMS in 1904. The LMS also got an annual grant for Tiger Kloof. Other missionary bodies also received grants soon after 1904 but these were insufficient. The grants were for buying teaching equipment and materials only. Most of the education expenses continued to be paid by the churches and the *merafe*.

Some improvements resulted from the Sargant recommendations. More practical subjects were taught. School administration improved when school committees were formed. These were similar to the earlier Bakwena and Bangwaketse ones. These committees enabled the Government, the *merafe* and the missionaries to control education jointly. Each committee consisted of the Assistant Resident Commissioner as chairman, the resident missionary as secretary, and the *Kgosi* and a local citizen as members. The main duty of the committees was to advise the Government on educational matters. The committees also worked out yearly financial estimates for the running of the schools. The committees took away from the missionaries the power to manage schools. They also planned the building of new schools.

Better school supervision also resulted from Sargant's work. The missionaries had failed to supervise schools properly. Because of their failure the Bangwaketse were the earliest *morafe* to introduce their own school supervision in 1920. They appointed a 'Tribal Representative' to supervise schools and report to the school committee. The Bakwena later followed this example. The Government also adopted (copied) this system and called these officers Sub-inspectors. This is the origin of today's education officers.

Other improvements in education administration followed the Sargant period. In 1928 Dumbrell was appointed Inspector of Schools for the whole of Bechuanaland. His first report showed that there was not very much improvement in the running of the education system. The Batswana were also critical of the Government's failure to run schools properly. The African Advisory Council and the Bechuanaland Protectorate African Teachers Association called for improvements. There were also government officials such as Dumbrell who felt that improvements must be made. As a result, in 1931, the Board of Advice on Education was formed. It consisted of representatives from Government, from missionary bodies and from the *merafe*. This was a Protectorate-wide body whose chairman was the Resident Commissioner. This was a further improvement on the school committee system. The Board took charge of all important matters relating to education. This was a move towards Government control of education. Control by the missionaries was further reduced. Batswana participation in educational matters was greatly increased by their representation on the Board.

The final stage in the development of Government control of education was the formation of the Education Department in 1935. Dumbrell was appointed Director of Education and was assisted in his duties by a number of education officers. The old school committees were enlarged. They were now chaired by the District Commissioners. The Department was responsible for formulating all educational policy and for supervising the schools. By 1938 Government control of primary schools was fully accomplished.

Financing education

With increased control of schools, the Government had to find ways to pay for education in addition to the grants which started in 1904. Britain was not willing to spend any more money. So the Batswana had to be made to pay for their own education. For many years the Batswana had raised money on their own to pay for education. In 1919 the Administration adopted the education tax of the Bakwena and the Bangwaketse. This system was extended to the whole country. Each African taxpayer paid three shillings a year in addition to his tax. The money was put into what was called the Native Fund. This was the main means of paying for education. In 1938 Tribal Treasuries were established for paying teachers, buying school books, equipment and building schools. Twenty per cent of each man's tax was put in each *morafe*'s treasury. By that time the education levy was made part of the normal tax paid by all African adult males. Later the percentage of the tax which went to the treasuries was increased to fifty. This remained the main source of education money until Independence. It is clear from this that the Batswana bore the burden of financing education. By 1938 there were 131 African primary schools with over 15 000 pupils.

The Mochudi National School

It is important to mention the Bakgatla National School or *Sekolo sa Phuthadikobo*. The building of the school in 1920 shows clearly that the Batswana were trying to be self-reliant in providing education for their children. The example of the Bakgatla probably encouraged such men as K.T. Motsete and Tshekedi Khama to start post-primary schools for Batswana in later years.

The Bakgatla built their own school because they were unhappy with the poor education given by the Dutch Reformed Church. There was only one English language school, the Linchwe Primary School, which went up to Standard Six. But it was still a mission school which did not want to teach such subjects as arithmetic because they were considered worldly.

In 1920 the Regent Kgosi Isang Pilane decided to build the Bakgatla National School which would teach subjects the Bakgatla wanted such as English, arithmetic, etc. up to Standard Six. The Bakgatla relied entirely on themselves to build the school. Men and women built the school together. Each man belonging to the Machechele *mophato* paid £5 towards the school. Those who did not have the money went to earn it in the mines in South Africa. The other *mephato* made bricks and did other kinds of work. The school was built on a hill, and so men and women carried bricks up the hill. Some of the women carried water to the builders. Bakgatla builders built the school houses. The school was completed in 1923 and was opened by the Duke of Athol. It educated both boys and girls. The first headmaster was Moruti Steesma. The house built for him later became the school for the blind. Today Bakgatla National School is the Phuthadikobo Museum.

Post primary education

Until the 1940s only primary education up to

Fig. 150 Isang Pilane, regent of the Bakgatla. His vision inspired the *morafe* to practise modern methods of agriculture and improve their education

Fig. 151 The Bakgatla National School in Mochudi, built through the inspiration of Isang Pilane and the efforts of the Bakgatla, it represents a triumph of *mephato* self-help

Standard Six was provided in Bechuanaland. The Government did not have any schools. Yet there was a great need for higher education as shown by the numbers of Batswana who went to South Africa and sometimes Southern Rhodesia for education. This led to some early attempts to provide post-(after) primary education.

K.T. Motsete's attempt

In 1931 the Bakalanga in Southern Rhodesia and Bechuanaland asked a fellow Mokalanga, K.T. Motsete, to start an industrial school. They wanted a school similar to Tiger Kloof in Bechuanaland. Motsete was not only a politician (see page 222) but he was also a great educator. He was educated in South Africa and Britain where he got a London University degree. He taught in South Africa and Nyasaland (Malawi). He was also a great musician.

In 1932 Motsete started the first secondary school at Nyewele in the Tshesebe area. It was later moved to Francistown in the Tati District in 1938. Motsete called his school the Tati Training Institution. The aims of the school were:
1 to train teachers for bush schools,
2 to offer commercial training such as book-keeping, typing, etc.,
3 to give secondary education subjects for the Junior Certificate of South Africa.

Motsete wanted to give Batswana both practical and sound academic training.

The school was started with funds from the Bakalanga, especially the people of Nswazwi, who were keen to educate their children. Some funds came from organisations in Britain and from the Phelps Stokes Foundation in the United States of America.

The school met with many political and financial problems. Tshekedi was opposed to the school. This was probably because he wanted all independent schools to be under his control as *kgosi*. But the more important reason seems to have been his dislike for Motsete. The two men had had several quarrels. In addition, the school was financed by the Nswazwi people with whom Tshekedi had also quarrelled. Tshekedi seems to have thought that the school had political aims because its founder and his supporters were his enemies. In actual fact, it seems that Motsete was truly interested in uplifting his people through good education.

The Colonial Government supported Tshekedi and opposed the school. The Government did not give aid to the school. So the Tati Institute had financial difficulties. In 1938 the Director of Education down-graded the school and recommended its closure. Because of the war, funds became scarce and in 1942 the school closed down. The establishment of the school was another example of how the Batswana relied on their own resources to provide education for their children, despite many setbacks.

Early Roman Catholic attempts

The Roman Catholic Church made an early attempt to start a secondary school. It also failed. In 1934 the Catholics started an Agricultural School at Forest Hill Farm near Kgale Hill. The school had Government support because it would improve the livestock industry from which the Government got revenue. The school aimed to produce self-reliant Batswana farmers. They would be taught farming including irrigation and animal husbandry. There would also be academic courses. Surprisingly, the school had no support from the *merafe* and so it had very few students. It is likely that the *merafe* did not support the Catholics because each one already had its own preferred church such as the LMS. The school closed in 1940.

Progress in secondary education in colonial times

Successful attempts to provide secondary education in colonial times were made by the Roman Catholic Church and Kgosi Tshekedi Khama.

The Catholic Church did not want its members' children to attend schools of other churches or secular (non-church) schools. This was because it did not want its followers to be influenced by other religions. For this reason, the Catholic Church throughout the world has always built its own educational institutions.

Fig. 152 An early practical typing lesson at St. Joseph's College, Kgale, the first successful secondary school in Botswana

In 1944 the Catholic Church opened St Joseph's Mission or Kgale near Kgale Hill. The school provided secondary education and later commercial training. This was the first successful secondary school in Bechuanaland. It was popular because it gave good academic and practical education.

Moeng College

One of the greatest examples of the spirit of self-help among the Batswana was the building of Moeng College. The school was built entirely through the efforts of the Bangwato led by Tshekedi. Tshekedi proposed a secondary industrial school at Serowe in 1934. But the outbreak of World War II prevented work on such a school. Tshekedi, like Motsete before him, wanted a school that would provide manpower for the development of Bechuanaland. He felt that South African schools did not give Africans all the necessary skills because of racism. He wanted a school that would enable Africans to compete equally with Whites.

After the war, the Government agreed to Tshekedi's scheme to build Moeng. Tshekedi chose Moeng valley as the site of the school. It is said he did this in memory of his father, Khama III, who liked the valley and visited it often. An important reason for choosing the area is that it had plenty of water. Work started in 1948. Through a special levy the Bangwato raised £100 000. Some people contributed cattle and labour through the regiments. Work was interrupted by the dispute which followed Seretse's marriage. But in 1951, Moeng opened its doors only to Bangwato students. It was a *morafe* college. In fact it was called Bamangwato College and was under Bangwato control. In 1956 the Government took over its control and opened it to all Batswana. In the 1950s the Bakgatla, Bakwena and Bangwaketse started their own *merafe* secondary schools. All these schools suffered from the shortage of trained teachers and money to buy equipment.

Until 1955, all post-primary schools were junior secondary schools. Fourth and fifth year studies were introduced in that year. By 1964 only four of the eight secondary schools offered a five-year course to only 39 students. This explains why there was such a shortage of trained manpower at Independence.

Government post-primary schools

The Colonial Government did not provide any secondary education until Gaborone Secondary School was opened in 1965. This was the only secondary school built before Independence by the Government. The Government ran the Teachers' Training Colleges at Serowe and Kanye opened in 1940. This was one way in which the Department of Education hoped to improve the standard of primary education. Vocational (practical) training was provided for nurses and male orderlies (nurses). This was at the Government hospitals in Serowe, Maun, Lobatse and Francistown from 1945 onwards. In 1964, the Government started the Botswana Training Centre to train craftsmen, secretaries and administrators for the public service.

University education

For many years Batswana had to go abroad, mostly to Fort Hare in South Africa, for degree studies. The Protectorate Administration gave grants to Fort Hare because it admitted Batswana. In 1952 the South African government began to prevent Batswana from going to Fort Hare. The High Commission Territories decided to start their own University. The introduction of Bantu education and the growth of *apartheid* also meant that Africans did not want to study in South Africa.

In 1946 the Roman Catholic Church started Pius XII College at Roma in Lesotho. The College gave degrees of the University of South Africa. In 1964 the Catholic Church and the British Government agreed to turn Pius XII into the University of Basutoland, Bechuanaland and Swaziland (UBBS). In 1966, UBBS became the University of Botswana, Lesotho and Swaziland (UBLS). In 1967, UBLS began granting its own degrees. The governments of the three independent countries shared equally the cost of running the University. Botswana now has its own university at Gaborone.

Health

One of the ways in which a government makes sure that its citizens will work hard and develop their country is to give them health care. Health care ensures that people are happy and fit to work. Yet in the colonial days health care was one of the most neglected areas. Nearly all health care was done by the missionaries. The first hospitals, such as those at Molepolole, Mochudi, Kanye and Maun, were started by missionaries. The Seventh Day Adventist Missionaries built the first Nurses' Training Centre. As in education, the Government provided better facilities only for Europeans. Yet the health of the Africans was poorer than that of the Whites. In 1960 there were only sixteen doctors in the

Fig. 153 People queueing outside a rural clinic. Health facilities were generally neglected by the Protectorate Administration

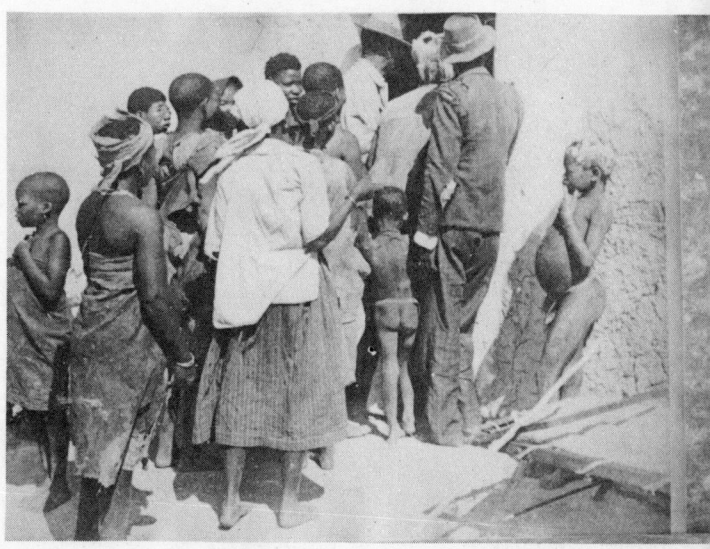

whole country. There were no hospitals, health centres or clinics outside the big villages.

One reason why there were no good health facilities for Africans was that there was no industry in Bechuanaland. In the colonial world the government or companies usually built clinics and hospitals for the workers. The reason was that healthy workers produced more goods. More goods brought more profit. Many Batswana had to go to South Africa or Rhodesia for medical care.

Questions

1 What are the two reasons why there was increased British aid to Botswana after 1955?
2 In which two of the following activities did the British Government show most interest?
   (a) Arable farming
   (b) Cattle farming
   (c) Dairy farming
   (d) Water development
3 Hold a class debate on the issue: 'The migrant labour system was bad for Botswana.'
4 List three improvements in education introduced by Sargant.
5 The following dates mark stages in the progress of education in Botswana. What events occurred?
   (a) 1928   (b) 1931   (c) 1935   (d) 1938
6 Give one example of Batswana self-reliance in education.

23 Two Important Events

Perhaps the two most important events that affected the Protectorate in the 1940s and 1950s were the Second World War, and Seretse Khama's marriage.

The First World War

Between 1914 and 1918 a major war was fought between Germany and the other European countries, mainly Britain, France and the United States of America. Some of these countries brought their colonies into the war. The Africans in Southern Africa, especially in the Union, supported Britain in the war. They hoped that Britain would in turn support them against white settler oppression. The Native (African) National Congress recruited Africans for the war. These Africans served in East Africa and France with the South African forces.

Some *dikgosi* in Bechuanaland, especially Khama III, also supported Britain in the war, but they sent money rather than men to help in the war. A few *dikgosi* in southern Bechuanaland sent men to serve as part of the South African Native Labour Contingent in France. The Contingent was withdrawn when the Africans revolted against racial discrimination by the white South African soldiers.

Some Boers in South Africa joined the Germans to fight Britain, their old enemy. Some of these rebels entered the Protectorate, but many were arrested with the help of Batswana rulers. The real threat to Bechuanaland came from the Germans in South West Africa. In 1915, however, South African forces defeated the Germans in Namibia and so Bechuanaland was made safe.

Germany was defeated and the League of Nations took over her colonies and gave them to different countries. They ruled them on its behalf. South West Africa was given to the Union of South Africa in 1920. The Caprivi Strip of South West Africa was ruled by the Bechuanaland Administration from 1922 to 1927, and then given back to South Africa.

After the war an influenza epidemic spread throughout the world and killed many people. It reached Bechuanaland in 1919.

The Second World War

The Second World War was fought between 1939 and 1945. All of Europe and the United States of America fought Germany. Italy was on Germany's side. Germany was ruled by Adolf Hitler. He wanted to conquer all of Europe and other parts of the world. This is why there was unity against him. The European countries brought their colonies into the war to fight and to provide food, money and other materials. In many cases the colonised people were forced to join the war. They considered it a white man's war. Many of the colonised resisted. This is one reason why the colonial powers began to make conditions better in the colonies. They wanted to avoid revolts.

The Batswana took part in the Second World War. From the very start of the war the *dikgosi* offered to help when the High Commissioner

Fig. 154 Hitler reviewing heavily armed troops in Warsaw, Poland, October 1939

asked them to do so. Why did they do this? Some historians say they did so because of loyalty to Britain. But why did they express loyalty to Britain? The reason was that the *dikgosi* believed that if they helped Britain, Bechuanaland would not be transferred to the Union of South Africa. It would be recognised as a separate country and remain so for ever.

In 1941 Tshekedi Khama proposed to set up what he called the Bechuanaland Protectorate Military Labour Corps. The other *merafe* supported this proposal. The Administration rejected the proposal and asked the Batswana to join the South African Union Defence Force to do some minor duties for the white South African soldiers. The Batswana refused to join the South Africans. They wanted to join the war as a separate country. They were not part of and did not want to be part of South Africa.

But soon Britain needed more soldiers. The Protectorate Administration asked the African Council and the *dikgosi* to provide soldiers. The *dikgosi* repeated Tshekedi's earlier offer and refused to join the South African Defence Force. The Administration agreed that the Batswana would fight as a separate group. The *dikgosi* began to recruit their people for the war. The Batswana war unit (group) was called the African Auxiliary Pioneer Corps (AAPC). They were trained at a camp in Lobatse.

Although all the *dikgosi* and many Batswana supported the war some Batswana did not. This was because many recruits did not understand why they should fight in a white people's war far away. They did not want to die in such a war. Many fled to the mines and farms in South

Africa. Some hid in the mountains. This resistance to the war was common among the small subject *merafe* such as the Bakalanga. Some of them did not always feel loyal to the *dikgosi*. But such resistance was also common in all the *merafe*. At Gabane, for example, recruits threw stones at Sebele II's recruiting messenger. So quite often people were forced by the Administration and the *dikgosi* to join the AAPC. Some were even flogged. Some of those who fled to South Africa wrote about how the Batswana were forced to join the war in a newspaper called *Inkululeko* (Freedom).

On the whole many Batswana joined the AAPC without being forced. By 1943 about 10 000 Batswana had joined the AAPC and fought very bravely in the Middle East, Europe and North Africa. Some did skilled jobs such as using anti-aircraft guns. Out of the 10 000 about 216 died in the war. In 1946 15 Batswana took part in the parade in England marking the defeat of Hitler. A memorial (remembrance) was built in Gaborone to honour the Batswana who died in the war.

Effects of the war on the Batswana

The Batswana did not only contribute soldiers to the war. They provided food and money. The Administration and the *dikgosi* got people to work on the *masotla* (*kgosi*'s lands) to produce food. These fields were now called 'war lands'. Every *morafe* was to provide food in this way and people were sometimes forced to work on these lands. Those refusing to work on the war lands had grain taken from their own lands. Grain stores were built in every major village. Some of the grain was sold to provide money for the war. Because of working on the war lands and also because many men either went to war or fled to South Africa, food production in the family lands fell. Many families suffered.

Fig. 155 Batswana soldiers in the British Army using anti-aircraft guns. The official caption to this photograph describes Batswana soldiers as 'excellent workers, conscientious, and unusually strong'

A war levy (tax) was introduced in 1941. Batswana tax payers, property owners, cattle owners and others were forced to pay this special tax. Many paid in cattle. A total of £89 000 was collected during the war. This levy impoverished many Batswana, especially small cattle owners. Many other contributions such as the Voluntary War Fund were introduced to pay for the administration of Bechuanaland and for the war. During the war Britain did not grant the Protectorate any more funds for its administration. The Batswana had to pay.

The Batswana also gave gifts of money to Britain. Altogether they gave £13 500 of which £5 200 was from the Bangwato alone. This money assisted Britain in buying two fighter aeroplanes. The aeroplanes were called *Bechuanaland* and *Kalahari* in honour of the Batswana. Some of the money collected was put into the Bechuanaland Soldiers Benefit Fund to care for the soldiers after the war.

The Bechuanaland Protectorate contributed to the war more men and money than most British African colonies. For example all the East African countries which together had 14 million people, contributed 28 companies (groups of soldiers). Bechuanaland alone, which had about 400 000 people, provided 59 companies.

The Nswazwi problem

After the 1943 proclamations were introduced (see page 186), Tshekedi settled down to develop his reserve. There was general peace in the Bangwato country. Only one incident before Seretse's marriage caused some disturbances. In the north-eastern part of the Bangwato Reserve there lived a group of Bakalanga called Bakanswazwi. They were ruled by John Madawo Nswazwi. He was born around 1875 and became ruler in 1910. He had worked at the mines in South Africa before becoming a ruler. Earlier this group had lived at Jetjeni in the Bukalanga area of Southern Rhodesia. They fled from the Amandebele and to the Bangwato area and asked for the protection of Sekgoma I, the Bangwato king. They were allowed to live fairly freely and

Fig. 156 John Nswazwi

happily in the Bukalanga area of Bangwato country. They were ruled indirectly through their own headman, and not by a Mongwato governor. Khama III regarded Nswazwi as his most trusted Mukalanga ruler even though he was not the most senior. Before Tshekedi's rule there was almost no trouble between them and the Bangwato.

The Bakanswazwi group had always regarded itself as fairly independent of the Bangwato. This feeling grew during the colonial period when the authority of the Government was felt more and more everywhere. In 1930 they unsuccessfully asked the High Commissioner to make them free from Bangwato authority, by giving them a separate reserve. But Tshekedi regarded every group in his reserve as being under his own direct rule. They had to obey his orders. He decided to appoint Bangwato governors to rule over the Bakalanga to ensure firm control of the area. The change from indirect to direct rule caused trouble.

Hut tax collection increased misunderstanding between Tshekedi and John Nswazwi. This shows how colonialism sometimes brought conflict between groups which had lived fairly peacefully before. The Nswazwi group tried to show its independence by refusing to pay tax to Tshekedi. John Nswazwi was arrested, tried and banished with some of his followers to Mafikeng. He had appealed successfully against banishment to Ghanzi.

His people continued to support him by refusing to pay tax. So in 1947 Tshekedi sent a *mophato*, led by Oteng Mphoeng, to collect taxes. Mphoeng prevented the Bakanswazwi from using their wells. They were put in an enclosure where, unfortunately, a pregnant woman, Levuna Mpapho, died. This caused a lot of unhappiness. The Bakalanga finally paid the tax. But the feelings were so high that a scuffle (fighting) broke out. After this, Nswazwi's people fled to Jetjeni, their old home. Their property was seized and sold. When John Nswazwi was freed, he joined them there. Some of them later returned to Bechuanaland and settled at Marapong.

Seretse Khama's marriage

Seretse Khama's marriage to an Englishwoman, Ruth Williams, on 29 September 1948, seriously affected the Bangwato and the whole Protectorate. The peace and cooperation between the Batswana and the Administration brought about by the 1943 proclamations was disturbed. The main cause of the disturbance was not the marriage itself, but the way the British Government handled the matter.

After the Nswazwi affair, Tshekedi settled down to build Moeng College. His nephew, Seretse, whom Tshekedi had brought up, was studying law in London. He had also studied at Fort Hare and Oxford. Tshekedi wanted Seretse to return as soon as possible to rule the Bangwato. Suddenly, in 1948, Tshekedi received a letter from Seretse informing him that he wanted to marry Miss Ruth Williams.

Now, Tshekedi was a strong defender of

Fig. 157 Seretse Khama and his wife, Ruth (1948)

Fig. 158 Seretse Khama explaining his marriage at a *kgotla* meeting in Serowe

Bangwato law and custom. According to custom, the *mohumagadi* (the *kgosi*'s great wife or queen) must be selected by the *morafe*. Normally, the *mohumagadi* should be from a royal family and should be a Motswana. It was uncommon for a ruler to marry outside the Batswana group. Even Africans who did not belong to the Batswana group were not usually acceptable. Tshekedi felt that Seretse's marriage was not in accordance with this custom and practice. He therefore opposed it very strongly for fear that it might badly affect the *morafe* and the *bogosi* (kingship). These were the main reasons for his opposition. The race of Ruth Williams seems to have played some part even though, later in 1951, Tshekedi accepted her as the *mohumagadi*.

Seretse got married although Tshekedi opposed the marriage. Tshekedi used all possible methods to end the marriage. If this failed, he would try to prevent Seretse's children by Ruth from being the heirs to the Bangwato *bogosi*. He explained that he still accepted Seretse as the *kgosi*. So it is clear that Tshekedi did not reject the marriage because he wanted the *bogosi* for himself and his children.

At first the *morafe* supported Tshekedi in rejecting the marriage at a *kgotla* meeting which lasted four days. Seretse requested another *kgotla* meeting. There some Bangwato supported him after he had apologised for not marrying according to custom. He told his people that if they rejected his wife, they would lose him. The Bangwato did not want to lose their proper *kgosi*.

After receiving the support of the *kgotla* Tshekedi asked the Administration to take action against the marriage but there was no action. He, therefore, called another *kgotla* meeting in June 1949 to show the Administration that the Bangwato wanted action. At this meeting the majority supported Seretse because they feared to lose their future *kgosi*. Some probably wrongly suspected that Tshekedi wanted the *bogosi*. According to Bangwato custom the matter should have ended there. The majority of the *morafe* had now accepted Ruth Williams as the *mohumagadi*. This did not happen, however, because Tshekedi continued his opposition.

After his defeat at the June *kgotla* meeting, Tshekedi and his followers left the Bangwato reserve and settled in the Bakwena area. Bathoen II supported Tshekedi because he believed that Seretse's marriage would destroy the Bangwato's *bogosi*. He too was a strong defender of Setswana customs. Even far off rulers such as those of Lesotho and Swaziland supported Tshekedi in what they considered his defence of African tradition (custom). Tshekedi had the strong support of the British Government. They did not support Tshekedi because they respected Bangwato customs. They did so because of racism in Southern Africa.

The white people of Southern Rhodesia and South Africa strongly opposed the marriage. They were incorrectly afraid that the marriage would make Africans in their countries want to marry Whites. These countries practised a terrible form of racial discrimination. Some Protectorate Whites also disliked the marriage. The British did not want to offend Southern Rhodesia, and in particular, South Africa. Britain did a lot of business with rich South Africa and did not want to anger the white Government there. There was a strong unity of Whites against Seretse.

The British said they opposed the marriage because they feared it would divide the Bangwato and disturb the peace. They did not state openly that they really opposed the marriage because they wanted to please South Africa. As we have seen, most Bangwato accepted the marriage and yet Britain continued to reject it. It was continued British opposition that disturbed the peace.

Seretse is banished

The British Government appointed a Commission chaired by Sir Walter Harragin, Chief Justice of the High Commission Territories. The commission was to inquire into the legality (lawfulness) of the marriage of Seretse. The report of the commission was never published. It is suspected that it was not published because it showed how Britain and South Africa agreed to act against Seretse. Or perhaps it said some things the Government did not like. Meanwhile Seretse had returned to live with his wife at Serowe and his people accepted them both.

Fig. 159 On hearing of his ban Seretse told reporters on the telephone, 'I am going to fight to get back to Bechuanaland'

Seretse, through his lawyers, Fraenkel and Gericke, asked the Administration to install him as a *kgosi*. Instead of doing this, the British Government invited Seretse and his wife to England for talks in 1950. They promised that they would be allowed to return to Bechuanaland. The Government, however, refused to give this assurance in writing. Ruth remained behind because Seretse feared that the British would not let her return. In London the British Government offered Seretse £1 100 per year if he relinquished (left) the *bogosi* and lived in England for ever. Seretse rejected the offer. Later he was offered a job in Jamaica but he also rejected this. The British Government prevented him from returning to Bechuanaland for at least five years.

Seretse was forced to live in England and his wife joined him there. He got an allowance from Britain. Seretse had been tricked. The Bangwato would have no *kgosi*. Tshekedi was also forbidden to enter the Bangwato reserve without permission. The British would rule the Bangwato through a 'Native Authority'. The District Commissioner was made the 'Native Authority' while the Administration tried to find a suitable African. The District Commissioner was assisted by Keaboka Kgamane as 'Senior Tribal Representative'.

Opposition to the ban

The Bangwato were asked to elect a new *kgosi*. They refused because Seretse was the *kgosi*. They argued that a *kgosi* is born and not elected. The Bangwato showed their opposition to Seretse's ban in many ways. They attacked Tshekedi's followers. They boycotted *kgotla* meetings and refused to obey the Administration. They refused to pay taxes and put up protest demonstrations. Sometimes they attacked police camps and the police who tried to stop the protests. Administration officials were also harassed. In Mahalapye for example a group of women attacked a police station.

The Bangwato sent a delegation of six people led by Peto Sekgoma and the Senior Tribal Representative, Keaboka, to ask for Seretse's return. When the British rejected this request Keaboka resigned. A big protest resulted. The District Commissioner sent police to stop the protest. The crowd attacked them. Many Bangwato were injured by the police. Three policemen died and several were hurt. Many administration officials were also hurt. The Administration brought in police from Southern Rhodesia and Basutoland to help the Bechuanaland police.

Fig. 160 The Bangwato delegation with Seretse Khama in England. Left to right: Keaboka Kgamane, Kgosi Mathangwane, M. Mpotokwane, Seretse Khama, ? , Kgosi Kobe of the Baseleka, ? , P. Sekgoma

Several Bangwato were arrested, put in prison and had to do hard labour. Keaboka and Peto Sekgoma were among those arrested. Soon after, another riot occurred in Palapye and police were called in. Among the supporters of Seretse were royals, young people and women who played a very important part. Some of the young people formed an opposition group some called the Bamangwato National Congress but it did not last for long.

Seretse asked to be allowed to go to Bechuanaland to end the disturbances, but Britain refused. They feared his popularity. Seretse appealed to his people from London to be calm. The riots stopped and they paid taxes but they continued not to cooperate fully with the Administration.

The protests and the arrest of the Bangwato worried the other rulers in Bechuanaland. Such *dikgosi* as Bathoen II, Kgari Sechele, Montshiwa, Molefi Pilane, accused Britain of causing trouble deliberately (purposely) in order to take over the powers of *dikgosi* in the whole Protectorate. But Britain did not listen to them. Kgosi Mokgosi of the Balete encouraged the Bangwato to refuse to elect a new *kgosi*. He was Seretse's strong supporter. The Administration warned Mokgosi. The Administration tried to silence Seretse's supporters.

The LMS usually played an important part in putting the case of the Batswana to the British Government. But it was quiet this time. They neither supported Tshekedi nor Seretse. The reason was probably that the *morafe* was split. They did not want to get into trouble by supporting one side or the other. They were probably afraid that if they did that even their church work would suffer.

Protests in Britain

In 1953, the Bangwato refused again to appoint a *kgosi*. The British nominated Rasebolai Kgamane to be 'Native Authority'. He was a quiet man who had served in World War II and was Tshekedi's supporter. The Bangwato refused to obey his orders because he was not their choice. A number of people were flogged at the *kgotla* for this. These included women. Rasebolai, however, tried his best to rule the *morafe* under these difficult circumstances.

In Britain Seretse had a lot of support from some Members of Parliament, especially those of the Labour Party. Fenner Brockway was their leader. Brockway organised a group called the Council for Defence of Seretse. There were other groups such as the Oxford University Socialist Club, the West Indian Society and the Council of Churches. All these groups supported Seretse and put pressure on the British Government to let him return to Bechuanaland. They educated the British public about the unfair treatment of Seretse and Ruth. The British Government refused to let Seretse return and be *kgosi*. The only time Seretse returned to Bechuanaland after his ban was when Tebogo, their first child, was born. His wife had not yet joined him in London. He was allowed to be there for only a very short time. He was greeted by several thousand people, some of them weeping, in Serowe. Seretse was very popular with his people.

Seretse is freed

When all these protests were taking place Seretse kept in touch with his people. In England he did not speak much. But he refused to be bribed (*go rekwa*) by the British Government. On one occasion in 1956 he spoke very strongly against the British Government. He accused it of acting childishly by continuing to ban him when his people wanted him. He refused to relinquish the *bogosi*.

Tshekedi now turned against the British. He recognised Ruth Williams as the *mohumagadi* and called for Seretse's return immediately. He now believed that the British wanted to destroy his *morafe*. He and the other *dikgosi* even believed that Britain wanted to use the Seretse affair in order to hand over Bechuanaland to South Africa. In 1952, Tshekedi was allowed to return to his people. He settled at Pilikwe with his followers. He criticised Rasebolai for doing little for the Bangwato. All the development projects had

Fig. 161 Crowds welcoming Seretse Khama on his triumphant return from banishment

stopped. In July 1956, Tshekedi went to England and saw Seretse secretly to settle their differences. They succeeded and presented an agreement to the British Government. The agreement would enable Seretse to return.

The agreement was that Seretse would renounce (give up) *bogosi*. His children would not claim the *bogosi*. He would, therefore, return as a private citizen. Tshekedi too would not claim the *bogosi* for himself or his children. Britain agreed to this arrangement because of the resistance of the Bangwato and Seretse's supporters in England. The Seretse affair had also made progress in Bechuanaland impossible. The Bangwato were ungovernable. The Administration spent a lot of money in trying to stop the protests. The Bangwato had also refused to negotiate a mining agreement with the Anglo-American Company without Seretse.

On 28 September 1956, Britain ended Seretse's ban. Seretse was free to return with his family and take part in Bangwato affairs as a private citizen. He was freed because of the support by his people who suffered a great deal for him, the support of groups in England and in the end the opposition of Tshekedi to the British. The British also feared further trouble if Seretse was not freed. Seretse's strong will and Ruth's determination also played an important part.

Seretse returned home and was welcomed by thousands of Bangwato who wanted him to be *kgosi*. Although this was not possible, the Bangwato never accepted 'made chiefs' like African (Native) Authorities. They continued to ask for their proper *kgosi*. In 1979 the eldest son of Seretse, Brigadier Ian Seretse Khama, was installed as *kgosi*.

Seretse became Vice-Chairman of the Bangwato 'Tribal Council' with Rasebolai as Chairman. Tshekedi was made Secretary two years later. The two great men served in the African Advisory Council. The courageous Tshekedi died in 1959. Seretse later became a member of the Legislative Council and later still the first President of independent Botswana. Happily nephew and uncle were friends again and the Bangwato enjoyed peace. Development work was carried out. The British Government's desire to please South Africa, rather than Seretse's marriage as such, had caused the problems for the Bangwato.

Questions

1. Explain why the *dikgosi* offered to help Britain in the Second World War.
2. Give two examples of how the Protectorate contributed financially to the British war effort. How did this affect the people?
3. Explain why Seretse Khama's marriage was opposed by
   (a) Tshekedi,
   (b) the British Government.
4. Imagine you are a journalist writing at the time when the Bangwato were asked to elected a new *kgosi*. Write an article covering the disturbances.

24 Nationalism and Independence

The coming of colonialism ended the independence of most African states. During the colonial period Africans were treated unequally by the Europeans.

The colonised protested against social, economic and political discrimination. There were usually two stages of protest. Firstly, the colonised wanted the colonisers to improve their situation by making reforms. This did not happen. During this stage there were no nationalist movements (political parties). In some cases there were some small groups or associations which fought to improve the welfare of their members.

Secondly, the colonised formed political parties which demanded political independence as the only way to improve their situation. This is called the stage of the new or decolonising nationalism. This new nationalism was different from the old nationalism. It wanted to decolonise, or in other words, to take away power from the colonisers. The old nationalism, or the reform stage, only wanted to change things within the same colonial system.

The reform stage

During this stage the Batswana were attempting only to make things better within the colonial system of government. They were not as yet demanding complete independence. There are some examples of associations which attempted to improve the welfare of their members.

The African Civil Service Association and the African Teachers' Association

The Protectorate's Civil Service was divided into the District Administration and the Tribal Administration. The Tribal Administration consisted only of Africans under the *kgosi*. They had poor conditions of work and low pay. The District Administration consisted of Africans and Europeans. The top and better paying jobs were held by Europeans. The Africans occupied lower posts and worked under the supervision of Europeans. Well qualified Africans with a lot of experience were not promoted to better jobs. So there was discrimination between Whites and Blacks. The African Advisory Council asked the Administration to promote qualified Africans. When nothing was done, the African civil servants formed the African Civil Service Association in 1949. They did this to protect their rights by getting the Administration to promote qualified Africans rapidly and by demanding better pay for all ranks. The Association worked closely with the African Advisory Council. For example in 1958 Tshekedi and Seretse urged the Administration to remove inequality between Blacks and Whites in the Civil Service.

As a result of pressure from the Association some changes took place in the civil service. Several Africans were promoted to higher posts in the 1960s. The Association taught its members that unity can produce results. Today the Association is called the Botswana Civil Service Association. Sir Peter Fawcus, the resident Commissioner, was also cooperative in promoting suitably qualified Batswana.

The teachers also formed the Bechuanaland Protectorate African Teachers' Association in 1931. They wanted to improve their conditions of service and African education in the Protectorate. Today the Association is called the Botswana Teachers' Union.

The Legislative Council (LEGCO)

In the 1950s Africans throughout British African colonies participated in government through Legislative Councils. The Batswana knew about this and they too wanted a LEGCO. They were no longer satisfied with the African Council or the Joint Council which they felt were powerless. The independence of Ghana in 1957 made Africans everywhere want independence soon. LEGCO was seen as a step towards independence. In 1958 M.L. Kgasa, Tshekedi Khama, Seretse Khama and Bathoen II spoke strongly in the African Council in favour of the formation of LEGCO. In that year Russell England, a member of the European Council who supported the Africans, introduced a motion in the Joint Council calling for the speedy introduction of LEGCO. Tshekedi Khama and Seretse Khama led the debate. They argued that Bechuanaland was behind all the other colonies because it had no LEGCO.

A committee consisting of Seretse Khama, Bathoen II, Dr S.M. Molema and J.G. Haskins was set up to draft a constitution (set of rules) for LEGCO. In 1960 LEGCO was formed and its first meeting was held in June 1961. LEGCO consisted of an equal number of Africans and Europeans although there were more Africans than Europeans in the country. The Europeans were elected by constituencies (electoral districts). The African members were elected by the African Council. There was one Asian representative elected by the Asian community. The Asians had complained that they had no Council where they could express their views. The African Council supported Asian inclusion in LEGCO. All along the Administration had refused to allow Asians to participate in the affairs of Bechuanaland. LEGCO replaced the European Council and the Joint Council. The African Council remained only for the purpose of electing Africans to LEGCO.

There was also an Executive Council which acted like the Cabinet (inner council) of LEGCO. Both administration officials and elected members were on it. The Resident Commissioner was its President (chairman). The Africans used LEGCO to criticise the Administration for its failure to develop Bechuanaland. They used it to make suggestions for improvements. LEGCO was formed at a time when a new form of nationalism was developing in Bechuanaland. The Africans, therefore, used LEGCO to demand independence. The days of the old nationalism which wanted only reforms were past.

The Road to Independence

The new nationalism which everywhere in Africa resulted in independence, developed in the 1960s in Bechuanaland. Before that, however, there were some beginnings of nationalist feeling. We have already seen how the Africans pressed for the establishment of LEGCO.

One of the people who expressed some kind of early nationalism was Simon Ratshosa of Serowe. This was before the creation of nationalist movements or political parties. Ratshosa was educated at Lovedale in South Africa, and was principal of Serowe Public School between 1905 and 1921. In the 1920s and 1930s he spoke and wrote about the need to reduce the powers of the *dikgosi*. He felt that the time had come for the Batswana to be ruled by a country-wide National Council. There would be a 'Native Progressive Party' within the Council. It would consist of the educated youth of Bechuanaland. This Council would stop what he described as the harsh rule of the *dikgosi*. He was also a critic of the Administration. He was one of the earliest Batswana to talk about a country-wide movement or organisation that would include all

Batswana whether they were royals or commoners. This is what made him an early nationalist.

In some African colonies the soldiers who returned from World War II played an important part in the nationalist movements. In Bechuanaland this did not happen. This was probably because there were no major towns or industrial centres in Bechuanaland. Nationalist movements normally developed in urban areas because of the bad living conditions there and the presence of a working class. Most Batswana soldiers returned to their villages where there was not much political activity. Some of those who went to South Africa like P.G. Matante joined the nationalist movements there.

Fig. 162 L.D. Raditladi, founder of Bechuanaland's first political party. It did not however have mass support

The Federal Party

The first political party in Bechuanaland was the Bechuanaland Protectorate Federal Party. It was formed in Serowe by Leetile D. Raditladi in 1959. In 1961 the party changed its name to the Liberal Party. Some Whites such as J. Openshaw joined the party. He became its Secretary-General.

The Federal Party did not oppose *bogosi*, but wanted this institution to be reformed. They opposed the racially balanced membership of LEGCO because it encouraged racism in Bechuanaland. They opposed the nomination of African members of LEGCO by the African Council because they felt that the *dikgosi* would nominate only the persons they favoured. This was not democratic they said. They wanted open elections by all adult Batswana. The party remained very small, however, and in 1962 it disappeared. It had not been able to spread throughout Bechuanaland.

The Bechuanaland (later Botswana) People's Party (BPP)

Strong nationalism came to Bechuanaland from South Africa. After the Sharpville shootings in 1960 and the ban of African political parties, about 1 400 people fled to Bechuanaland. Many of them were members of the African National Congress (ANC) and the Pan Africanist Congress (PAC). Some of them were Batswana, such as Motsamai Mpho who belonged to the ANC and Philip G. Matante of the PAC. These men formed political parties in Bechuanaland.

The first of these new parties whose activities covered the whole country was the Bechuanaland People's Party. It was formed in 1960. It was formed by K.T. Motsete who was its President, and was a well educated man. He had helped to start the Nyasaland African Congress in Nyasaland (Malawi) in 1944. He was a critic of the *dikgosi* who he thought were too harsh. He had had many quarrels with Tshekedi in the past. P.G. Matante, a Francistown businessman and former Johannesburg preacher, was the

Fig. 163 K.T. Motsete, founder and leader of the Bechuanaland People's Party (BPP)

Fig. 164 P.G. Matante, deputy leader, and later leader of the BPP. It was through him and Mpho that the party grew to have much popular support

Vice-President. Motsamai Mpho was the Secretary-General. Both Matante and Mpho were political organisers. They had learned this in South Africa. Many young people who had returned from South Africa joined the BPP.

The BPP was formed at the time when Britain was introducing constitutional changes through the Legislative Council. The party took advantage of this to demand Independence immediately. It attacked British colonialism for not developing Bechuanaland. It attacked racism as shown in the racial representation in LEGCO. Racism was also openly practised, especially in Francistown. Matante went to the United Nations in 1962 and 1963 to protest against British colonialism. Eventually LEGCO set up a Committee to examine all racially discriminatory laws. The Resident Commissioner (1959-64) was Peter Fawcus. He announced that the revision of the LEGCO constitution would take place sooner, in 1963 rather than in 1968.

The BPP wanted the LEGCO constitution to be abolished and an Independence constitution introduced immediately. The party organised protest demonstrations. During one of these protests Motsete led a group of over 800 people to the High Court in Lobatse. In Francistown there were clashes between the police and demonstrators. About 4 000 people took part. Police used tear gas to disperse (scatter) the crowds which Matante had addressed. People were arrested and for a while meetings of more than 12 people were banned.

The BPP's criticism of the Colonial Administration won it many followers, especially in the towns. But the party had some weaknesses. It did not win much support in the rural areas where the majority of the Batswana lived. However, the party was generally popular in Bakalanga rural areas. Probably the Bakalanga thought the BPP would enable them to participate (take part) in running the country. In historical times, they were generally excluded from positions of power. It was popular in the towns because of the poor living and working conditions and the presence of a politically aware working class. The rural people were generally not yet very politically aware. The call of the BPP for the abolition of the *bogosi* did not please the rural people who respected *bogosi*. So most of them did not join the BPP. The white people in Bechuanaland did not support the BPP because it expressed what they considered strong nationalism. It openly attacked those of them who practised racism.

The BPP splits

The BPP was soon weakened by feuds (quarrels) among its top leaders, Motsete, Matante and Mpho. Because of these feuds, Mpho was expelled from the party in 1962. He formed his own party called BPP Number Two. In 1964, he renamed it the Botswana Independence Party (BIP). The political beliefs of the BIP were not very different from those of the BPP. But the split enabled Mpho to speak more freely. There followed another split when Matante replaced Motsete as BPP leader. Nevertheless, Motsete formed what he called BPP Number One which ran for the 1965 election. Motsete's wing of the BPP eventually disappeared and Motsete ceased to be active in politics. His last major contribution to independent Botswana was the writing of the National Anthem: *Fatshe La Rona* (Our Land).

Why did the BPP split? Some say that the split was caused by accusations against Matante of abuse of party money. Others say Mpho wanted to take over power from Motsete. These may not have been the real causes. What seems to have been the main cause was the political differences between Matante and Mpho. These differences were the same as those which split the ANC and the PAC in South Africa. Matante was a PAC member whereas Mpho was an ANC follower. So the split was caused by political differences between the ANC and the PAC. The split be-

Fig. 165 Motsamai Mpho, founder and leader of the Botswana Independence Party (BIP)

tween Motsete and Matante seems to have been caused by Matante's feeling that the old man, Motsete, was not tough enough with the British. It was largely these weaknesses which caused the BPP's defeat in the elections of 1965. But it is also doubtful whether a party led by non-royals could have won elections at that time.

The Bechuanaland (later Botswana) Democratic Party (BDP)

In November 1961, Seretse Khama told the other African members of the Advisory Council of the need to form a new political party called the BDP. A committee was formed consisting of Seretse Khama, Quett Masire, A.M. Tsoebebe, Moutlakgola Nwako, Tsheko Tsheko, Goareng Mosinyi and Dabadaba Sedie. It met in Mahalapye to write the BDP constitution. In 1962 the BDP was formally formed at a meeting held under a *morula* tree in Gaborone, near Orapa House. The founders had been refused permi-

Fig. 166 A BIP official with a political poster

ssion by Kgosi Mmusi Pilame to hold a meeting in Mochudi. Seretse Khama became President of the party. A.M. Tsoebebe became Vice-President; Quett Masire, Secretary-General; Amos Dambe, Vice-Secretary; B. Steinberg, Treasurer; and A. Maribe, Vice-Treasurer. Most of the founders were men of some experience because they were members of the African Advisory Council and later of the Legislative Council. None of the leaders were followers of the South African nationalist movements. This saved the BDP from the splits that weakened the BPP. One can say that the BDP originated on Bechuanaland soil.

Why was the BDP founded? Like all African nationalist movements at that time, it was founded to strive for Independence. But the immediate reason for starting the party was to oppose the BPP. The founders of the BDP did not believe

Fig. 167 Seretse Khama, founder and leader of the Bechuanaland Democratic Party

that the BPP could successfully lead the country to peaceful independence. This is why they did not join the BPP, but chose instead to start a new party. The splits in the BPP and the radical (strong) nationalism of the BPP made the BDP founders believe that the BPP could not lead the country properly. They also disliked the influence of the ANC and the PAC in the BPP. They felt that a party with outside influence could not serve the country well. These seem to have been the main reasons why the BDP was formed. But some say that the Colonial Government, especially Peter Fawcus, urged the formation of the BDP. Certainly the Colonial Administration preferred the BDP to the BPP because the BDP was less radical. But both parties wanted Independence equally strongly.

The BDP stressed the need for multiracialism (races living together). It too demand Independence as soon as possible. It called for constitutional advancement. The party called for elections based on one man, one vote.

The BDP soon became a strong party. Its strongest support was in the rural areas. The leadership of Seretse, a member of the royal family, no doubt gave the party an advantage. Seretse was also popular because he had suffered under the British on account of his marriage. He had also shown his political ability in the Tribal Council, the African Council and LEGCO. The strongest support was from the Bangwato area. It had the largest population and number of electoral districts (constituencies). The BDP did not strongly attack *bogosi* as the BPP did. This was one reason for its strong rural support. The party was strong because it was well organised and united. It also had money to pay for running its affairs.

The Europeans also supported the BDP and some even joined it. This was because they saw it as being milder (softer) than the BPP. It also talked about multiracism whereas the BPP was regarded as pan-Africanist (Africa for Africans). The Whites wrongly took this to mean that the BPP would expel all of them. Indeed the BDP was so strong that it easily won the 1965 elections.

Constitutional advance

Because of the pressure of nationalism, constitutional talks were held in 1963. But at the last moment Motsete acted against the wishes of the BPP executive. He called for the delay of Independence by four years. He probably felt that his party needed more time to organise itself. He was attacked for this and he withdrew the suggestion. But his name was damaged by this to some extent.

The Lobatse Conference

Preliminary discussions on constitutional changes were held in Lobatse in July 1963. It was agreed to give Bechuanaland some measure of self-government. But this would be under the overall advice of the Resident Commissioner, Peter Fawcus. In 1964 the title 'Resident Commissioner' was changed to 'Queen's Commissioner' in preparation for Independence. The Lobatse agreement made the following provisions.

1. A National Assembly to which members would be elected through adult suffrage (votes). There would also be some nominated members and some British officials. The elected members would be in the majority.
2. Britain to be in charge of external affairs, defence, and the Public Service until Independence.
3. A cabinet with a Prime Minister and five ministers. But its chairman would be the Queen's Commissioner. He did his work with the advice of the Cabinet. The High Commissioner's Office was abolished in 1964. The National Assembly would seek the advice of the House of Chiefs on matters relating to *merafe* and the *bogosi*.

Europeans oppose Independence

Although some Europeans supported these changes, others opposed them because they did not want an African government. This was true especially of the farmers in the Tati District. They were led by Louis Mynhardt. They wanted the Tati District to be an independent state or to join Southern Rhodesia or South Africa. They appealed to South Africa for help but that failed. One of their leaders even tried to go to the United Nations to ask for help. This too failed.

Europeans also showed their opposition by opposing the integration (joining together) of schools so that white and black children could learn together. In Ghanzi white parents withdrew their children from a school because it was going to admit African children.

These provocative actions angered the Africans. Some Batswana demanded that all European farms be taken away without any payment. This demand was made by Mpho, leader of the BIP. This did not happen. Seretse Khama strongly warned the Europeans against any attempt to break up the country. Bechuanaland would become independent as one country. The attempts of the whites to secede (break away) from Bechuanaland failed. When the country became independent, some of them left for South Africa or Southern Rhodesia. The rest of them, however, remained and became Botswana citizens.

Independence

Elections were held in March 1965 on the basis of the Constitution of 1963. The BDP which had become a very strong, well-organised party won the election with a big majority. They took 28 of the 31 seats in the National Assembly. The BPP got the three remaining seats. The leader of the BDP, Seretse Khama, became the Prime Minister of the country's first African Government.

The new Government immediately asked the British Government to grant the country full Independence. A constitutional conference was held in London in February 1966. Matante walked out of the conference protesting that the BDP Government could not negotiate for Independence on behalf of the Batswana. He argued that the Government had not consulted the peo-

Fig. 168 Large numbers of people turned out to vote in the 1965 elections

ple properly about Independence. His protest, however, was unsuccessful. A new constitution similar to the 1963 one was agreed. The country became independent on 30 September 1966, as the new Republic of Botswana. This date has become a national holiday during which Batswana all over the country celebrate the achievement of Independence. Thanks to the long resistance of our forefathers, Botswana became independent as a separate, united country. Seretse Khama became the first President of Botswana. He was knighted (given the title 'Sir') by the British to honour him. From that time on he was called Sir Seretse Khama.

Botswana made its own flag to replace the

British one. The thick black band in the centre represents the African majority of the population and the thin white stripes stand for the Whites. The whole thing together stands for the non-racialism or the inter-racial policy of Botswana. The blue stands for the sky and rainwater which is the source of all life. The motto on the coat of arms is *Pula* (rain), which means 'blessings'. British rule had ended. *God Save the Queen*, the British national anthem, was replaced by *Fatshe la Rona*. There was joy everywhere.

When it became clear that Botswana would become independent, preparations were made to move the capital from Mafikeng to Gaborone. Gaborone was the name of the *kgosi* of the Batlokwa who died in 1932 at the age of about 106 years. The building of Gaborone started in 1963. The move from Mafikeng to Gaborone began in 1965.

Questions

1. What is meant by a 'Legislative Council'? Why did the Batswana want one? When was it set up? Who sat on it and how were they selected?
2. Write down two major weaknesses of the Bechuanaland Peoples' Party.
3. How many reasons can you give for the strength of the Bechuanaland Democratic Party? List them in what you think is their order of importance.

25 The Independence Period: Government and Politics

Introduction

Up to this point, we have looked at historical developments. Strictly speaking, sections of this part are not historical, because history deals only with past events. Some of the developments described here began in the past and have continued to the time of writing this book. This explains why we use both past and present tenses.

The happiness brought about by Independence was soon spoilt by a serve drought which lasted for more than five years. There had always been periodic droughts, but this one came at a critical time when the young Government was just establishing itself. Over 400 000 cattle died and there were no crops. Over 100 000 people had to be fed by the new Government. This took a lot of Government money. So the new Government was faced with a difficult task. Even without the drought, the new Government had inherited one of the poorest countries in colonial history, which it had to develop.

The new Government set up a governmental structure based on the constitution negotiated

Fig. 169 Cattle dying during a drought. Note the vultures

Fig. 170 Food aid, imported from abroad, was used to feed many thousands of people affected by the severe drought at Independence

with Britain in 1966. This constitution has operated with few changes until today. The governmental structure has two main levels, the Central Government and Local Government. On the political side, elections have continued to be held every five years since the first election in 1965. The foreign policy of Botswana has continued to develop since Independence.

At Independence, there was little hope that any real development would take place in the economy. But over the years some major developments have taken place. The only important economic activity at Independence was agriculture, mainly cattle farming or ranching. Gradually, other economic activities took place. The drought ended in 1966. Good rains fell, especially between 1973 and 1978, and there were good harvests. The movement of the capital to Gaborone enabled the Government to spend money within Botswana. As imports of goods grew, the Government got more revenue from customs duties. That is money paid to Government by importers of foreign goods. Four major events took place in the late 1960s and early 1970s, which brought a lot of money to the country.

1 The discovery of diamonds at Orapa.
2 The development of the copper-nickel mine at Selebi Phikwe.
3 The successful negotiations with South Africa, which resulted in an improved Customs Union Agreement in 1969.
4 The increase of Botswana beef exports at good prices.

These developments increased Government revenues between 1969 and 1975. So from late

1969, the economy began to expand. The Government now had some money to pay for economic and social developments. Also it could pay the salaries of a growing Public Service (government workers). What follow are just a few examples of the many developments which have taken place since Independence.

Central Government

Under the Constitution of 1966, the Government consists of the President, the Vice-President, the Cabinet, a Legislature consisting of the President, the National Assembly, the House of Chiefs, and the Judiciary (law courts). All these branches of Government do their work under the Constitution. No arm or branch of government has power above the Constitution. The table below illustrates the structure of government.

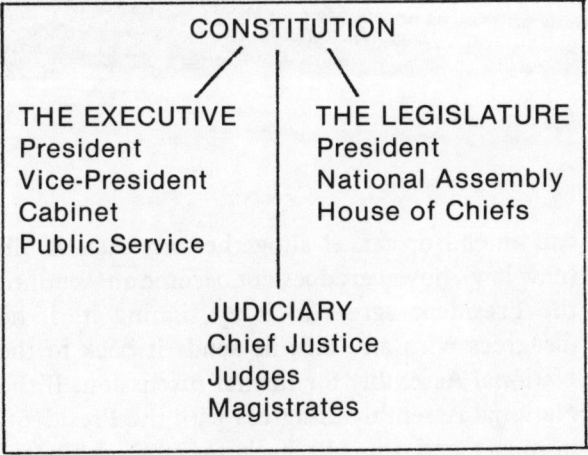

The Constitution

The Constitution consists of the laws which say how Botswana should be ruled. Among many other things it states how elections should be held, what the rights of the citizens are, the powers of each branch of Government etc. In this way it is expected to control the power of Government and to protect the people. Under the Constitution the government is not supposed to do whatever it likes. If it violates (breaks) the Constitution, any citizen can take it to court. The 1966 Constitution has not changed much since Independence. However, it can be changed whenever necessary, and there are rules which state how this should be done.

Under our Constitution the Government has three main parts: the Executive, the Legislature and the Judiciary.

The President

The President is the Head of State and represents Botswana in all respects. He is also the Head of the National Assembly and the Executive (Cabinet), and is Commander-in-Chief of the armed forces.

The President has several powers among which are the following.

1. He appoints certain top officers in all the state organs such as the Public Service, the army, the Judiciary and the police department.
2. He has the prerogative of mercy, which means that he can pardon criminals.
3. He can convene (call) or dissolve Parliament.
4. He must sign all bills before they can become law.
5. He can declare a state of emergency by suspending the Constitution.

It is clear from the above that the President has a lot of power.

The Legislature

The Legislature is the branch of Government which makes the laws. It consists of the President and the National Assembly. From 1965 to 1973 the National Assembly consisted of 31 elected members. In 1972 the Constitution was amended or changed to add one more member. So, after the 1974 general election, there were 32 elected members. In 1983 the Constitution was further amended to add two seats to bring the total to 34 seats for the 1984 election. Until 1973 the President had his own constituency (electoral district). The 1972 amendment meant that the President had no constituency. This was done

Fig. 171 The opening of the National Assembly

because it was felt that the President represents the whole nation and not just one area of the country. In addition to the 32 members, there are four members nominated by the President; the Attorney-General (Government's Chief Law Officer), who is not a Member of Parliament (MP) and has no vote, and the Speaker (Chairman) of the National Assembly (Parliament). The Attorney-General's main duty in Parliament is to give legal advice to the National Assembly when it makes the laws. The Speaker, who may or may not be an MP, is appointed by the President. His main job is to guide the debates in Parliament. Dr Merriweather was the first Speaker.

The function of the National Assembly is to make the laws or Acts which govern Botswana. Once an Act is made no person, even the President, can change it. Only the National Assembly can amend or cancel altogether any Act. A bill (new law), however, does not become an Act until the President agrees to it by signing it. If he disagrees with any bill, he sends it back to the National Assembly for further discussion. If the National Assembly disagrees with the President, it must send the bill back to him within six months. If he still disagrees, he must dissolve Parliament and call for new elections.

The National Assembly also decides how much money Government can spend each year. It does this by approving the budget which is prepared by the Ministry of Finance and Development Planning and presented to Parliament by the Minister in charge of that Ministry. Parliament also authorises the Government to raise loans (borrow money). The budget debate is one of the most important debates Parliament undertakes every year. Another function of

Parliament is to approve the Government's National Development Plan for the next five years. These are the main functions of the National Assembly.

The House of Chiefs

During the Protectorate days a start was made to reduce the powers of the *dikgosi*. However, the *dikgosi* remained fairly powerful. They controlled nearly all aspects of the activities of the *merafe*. This was mainly because the Government itself was not interested in ruling the *merafe* directly.

After Independence, the *dikgosi* lost a lot of their powers. There was now a new Government which wanted to rule the entire country directly. It wanted to create a feeling of attachment to the nation Botswana rather than to the individual *merafe*. This would ensure national unity. The way to do this was to have everybody within Botswana under one central government whose power spread throughout the country.

During the Lobatse constitutional talks in 1963, there was already a struggle for power between the *dikgosi* and the young educated politicians. The question was how much power to give to the *dikgosi* under the new democratic Government. Kgosi Bathoen II was the articulate (spoke well) spokesman of the *dikgosi*. In the end, it was decided to give some recognition to the *dikgosi* but with reduced powers. It was recognised that the ordinary people in Botswana still respected them. So they could not just be done away with. The BDP had won the election because of the support of the rural areas where the *dikgosi* also had strong support. In fact, some *dikgosi* supported the BDP. So it would have been unwise for the BDP Government to destroy its support by treating the *dikgosi* badly.

The *dikgosi* were recognised by the creation of the House of Chiefs. It consists of the *dikgosi* of the eight *merafe* considered to be the main groups since the colonial days. They are: Bangwato, Bakwena, Bakgatla, Bangwaketse, Balete, Batlokwa, Batawana and Barolong. There are also four members elected by the junior *dikgosi* in the Chobe, Francistown, Ghanzi and Kgalagadi Districts, and three other members nominated by the President.

The House of Chiefs is not part of the Legislature, and it does not have any power to make laws. Its main duty is to advise the Government on *merafe* and customary matters. Bills before the National Assembly dealing with such matters must be sent to the House of Chiefs for its advice. The National Assembly can ignore such advice. This could cause friction between the two Houses. So the advice is usually taken seriously.

In the early days of Independence, the *dikgosi* tried unsuccessfully to use the House of Chiefs to gain more power for themselves. They were led by Kgosi Bathoen II and Kgosi Linchwe II. Unhappy with the powerlessness of the House of Chiefs, Bathoen II resigned from the *bogosi* and joined politics in 1969 in time for the general election. He later became a member and leader of the Botswana National Front (BNF). He used his family name Gaseitsiwe from then on. He stood for election in the Ngwaketse constituency, and defeated the then Vice-President, Dr Quett Masire in that election. Bathoen II's movement from *bogosi* to politics showed the Government that if they did not treat the *dikgosi* carefully, they might join opposition parties and win because the people still strongly supported them.

Reduction of the powers of the *dikgosi*

In spite of this, however, the BDP Government passed Acts to reduce the powers of the *dikgosi*. An example of such Acts is the Tribal Land Act of 1968. It took away from the *dikgosi* the power to hold land on behalf of the *merafe* and to allocate such land. This power was given to the Land Boards. The Chairman of the Land Board who may or may not be a *kgosi*, is appointed by the Minister of Local Government and Lands. The Matimela Act of 1968 transferred power over *matimela* (stray) cattle from the *dikgosi* to the District Councils. The District Councils were created by the Local Government (District Councils) Act of 1965 passed just before Independence.

Fig. 172 A *kgotla* meeting in session in Mochudi

The powers of the *dikgosi* have been greatly reduced since Independence. Their former powers have been taken over by the Central Government and several branches of the local administration such as the District Councils, the Land Boards and the District Development Committees. These branches of Local Government, rather than the 'Chief's Administration', are mainly in charge of planning and implementing (putting into practice) district development programmes. The *dikgosi* are now regarded by the Government as being under the District Commissioner. However, the *dikgosi* still preside over customary courts which try cases according to Setswana custom.

The *dikgosi* have not accepted quietly and willingly the reduction of their powers. In particular they dislike being regarded as public servants. Kgosi Linchwe II of the Bakgatla and Kgosi Seepapitso IV of the Bangwaketse have been particularly outspoken about this. The *dikgosi* still consider themselves as the leaders of their *merafe*, and therefore different from public servants.

The Executive

The Executive is the branch of Government that is responsible for seeing that the laws are carried out. It consists of the President assisted by the Vice-President, the Cabinet and the Public Service. The Public Service under the direction of each Ministry does Government work. Each Ministry is headed by a Minister. The Minister is advised by a Permanent Secretary who supervises the work of the Ministry. The Cabinet consists of the President, Vice-President, the Ministers and the Attorney-General. It meets regularly to take government decisions. It then instructs the Public Service to carry out these decisions within the laws of the country. The Public Service includes the Civil Service and the Police. The leader of the whole Public Service is the Permanent Secretary to the President. Members of the Public Service are not elected, but are appointed by the Public Service Commission on the basis of their qualifications. Although the politicians lose their jobs if they lose elections, public servants can continue to serve any party which comes into power.

The Judiciary

The Government's powers are controlled by laws which the Government must obey. Anyone who breaks the law has the right to be tried in a law court. A person is considered innocent until proved guilty by the court. The Judiciary is that branch of Government which upholds the law. Its job is to see that offenders are tried and freed or punished. It is also expected to explain and interpret the law freely without Government interference. This is why the Judiciary is separate and independent of the Legislature and the Executive. Even the President should not interfere with the work of the Judiciary. The President, however, can exercise the prerogative of mercy, but he can only do this after the courts have passed their judgement. Also, if Parliament is unhappy about the way the courts apply a certain law, they can amend it. This is how Government can get around the powers of the courts.

The Judiciary consists of several levels including the Court of Appeal, the High Court, the Magistrates' Courts and the Customary Courts. A person can appeal from one level to the next. This ensures a fair trial.

Local Government

The Central Government cannot be everywhere and do everything in the country. It gives some of its work to the Local Government. But Local Government acts under the supervision of the Central Government. Local Government refers matters it cannot deal with to the Central Government. A system of local government means that decisions can be made faster. Also it enables the local people to participate in their own government. It enables people to make decisions which affect them.

In 1966, Botswana was divided into nine Districts, each run by a District Council. The towns of Gaborone, Francistown, Lobatse and Selebi Phikwe have Town Councils. District Councils are responsible for primary education, public health, supply of water and maintenance of district roads. Town Councils have similar duties in towns. More District and Town Councils can be created if necessary. Their functions can also increase as more and more developments take place. Local Councils are assisted in carrying out development work by District and Village Development Committees.

Elections and political parties

Botswana has a democratic system of government. The main characteristic of this system is that it allows the citizens to change their leaders from time to time. In Botswana this is done through general elections every five years. Botswana is a multi-party state, that is, it has

Fig. 173 Political rallies like this are common at election times

more than one party. These parties are free to compete to be the Government.

For the purposes of elections the country is divided into electoral districts called constituencies. The number of constituencies can increase as the population grows. Each constituency elects one Member of Parliament. During elections all parties are free to compete to win constituencies.

From time to time, at intervals of between five and ten years, a Delimitation Commission is appointed by the Judicial Services Commission. The Delimitation Commission is an impartial group of people which decides whether any new constituencies are needed. If they are needed it draws their boundaries. The Commission can also divide, abolish, or join existing constituencies. The aim is to ensure that as population increases, or moves, people in all parts of the country are represented in Parliament as equally as possible.

The party which wins the majority of the constituencies, wins the general election. The winning party forms the Government. The other parties which win some constituencies become the Opposition in the National Assembly. The Opposition is led by the Leader of the Opposition. This is the leader of the party with the most members within the Opposition. For several years the leader of the BPP, the late Philip Matante, was Leader of the Opposition. The main function of the Opposition is to see to it that the Government rules well. It is supposed to do this by criticising the Government both inside and outside Parliament, and by making suggestions for improvement. Since Independence, however, the Opposition has had very few members in Parliament. So it has not been effective enough.

A new political party, the Botswana National Front (BNF), was formed in 1966. Its founder, Dr Kenneth Koma, was a well educated man who had returned to Botswana just before the 1965 election from studies in Russia. The first leaders of the BNF were K. Koma, Secretary for External Affairs; Daniel Kwele, Vice-President; R. Molomo, President. Although the other two have now left the party, K. Koma is still its leading figure. The BNF aimed to replace the BDP as the Government. It argued that under the BDP Botswana did not have full control of its resources. This, they argued, was because the BDP encouraged private enterprise rather than state control of the economy. Private enterprise means the running of the economy by private (non-Government) companies. The BNF, therefore, stated that it would introduce Government control of the economy. It wanted to introduce socialism. A socialist form of government is one which directly runs the major economic activities of a country. The BNF also criticised the BDP for what it considered conservative domestic and foreign policies.

In order to defeat the BDP, the BNF tried to unite all the opposition parties. This failed mainly because the different parties did not have the same political ideals. The BNF, however, was joined by some members of the former K.T. Motsete wing of the BPP, some labour groups, and some civil servants. Kgosi Bathoen Gaseitsiwe later left the *bogosi* and joined the BNF. The party hoped that Kgosi Bathoen II would effectively challenge Seretse Khama since both were of royal birth. Bathoen was a man of great influence among the Bangwaketse.

In the first three elections since Independence the BDP retained a large majority in the National

Fig. 174 Kenneth Koma, founder and leader of the Botswana National Front (BNF)

Fig. 175 Seretse Khama campaigning at a BDP rally

Assembly. The table below shows the number of seats obtained by each party.

Seats won by each party 1965-79

	1965	1969	1974	1979
BDP	28	24	27	29
BPP	3	3	2	1
BIP	0	1	1	0
BNF	—	3	2	2

How many seats did all the opposition parties have in 1969? In 1974? In 1979?

An interesting feature of the elections is that the Opposition has not increased its seats but the number of people voting for the BNF has increased. In 1969, 10 041 voted for it and in 1979 the number increased to 17 324. By comparison the BPP numbers fell from 19 964 in 1965 to 9 983 in 1979. The BNF has its main support in the towns whereas the BDP is supported mainly in the rural areas. For example in 1969 in Gaborone the BNF got 51 per cent of the votes and the BDP won 48 per cent. But Ramotswa was also in the Gaborone constituency at that time. So the BDP won the seat because most Ramotswa people voted for the BDP.

The table below shows the number of people who voted for each party between 1965 and 1979.

Number of votes for each party 1965-79

	1965	1969	1974	1979
BDP	113 168	52 518	49 047	101 098
BPP	19 964	9 329	4 199	9 983
BIP	6 491	4 601	3 086	5 813
BNF	—	10 410	7 358	17 324

A major feature of Botswana politics is that there has been free expression of ideas by all parties. There has been no imprisonment of opposition party members for their political beliefs. New political parties continue to be formed. In 1982, Daniel Kwele, a former Assistant Minister, and founding member of the BNF formed the Botswana Progressive Union (BPU). It is still too early to judge the performance of this party.

Questions

1. Using one sentence for each, list the main functions of the National Assembly.
2. List the names of the Acts which reduced the power of the *dikgosi*, and say briefly what each of them did.
3. Say briefly what the Executive and Judiciary are.

26 Economic and Social Developments

The Economy

The new Botswana Government inherited a very poor country which was not able to pay for running its affairs. It relied on British grants-in-aid (financial help) to pay for its needs. Social facilities such as education and health were very poor. Botswana was an extremely poor country and had few educated people to run it. Other problems were caused by the geographical location of the country. Botswana is land-locked, that is, it has no sea coast. It was surrounded by powerful racist neighbours. The new Government, however, faced these problems and tried to find ways to solve them.

From the very beginning, the Government's main aim was to improve the economic situation of the country as soon as possible by carrying out development programmes. Indeed, the economic picture has changed a lot. For example, in 1966 the Gross Domestic Product of Botswana (the value of all goods and services produced in the country) was P37 million. By 1979, it had risen to P650 million. Botswana has made some progress since Independence towards improving the lives of its citizens. But there is still a long way to go in raising the standard of living of all Batswana, especially those in the rural areas. There are still many poor Batswana in both urban and rural areas. This is mainly because there are not enough jobs and many Batswana do not own much property. This is particularly true in the rural areas where a few rich people own most of the cattle.

The aims of development

Since Independence the Government's main concern has been to reduce or end poverty. Each National Development Plan (NDP), states how the Government plans to do this. From the very beginning, the Government's economic planning has been guided by the following aims.

1. It wants rapid economic growth to bring more money to the country so as to improve the standard of living of all the citizens. Livestock, minerals, manufacturing and arable farming are seen as the main activities that can bring wealth to the country.
2. It aims at economic independence. This can be achieved through having more goods produced in Botswana. Then the country does not have to import too many things it needs from other countries.
3. Social justice is the other aim of development. All citizens must benefit from development. The Government is trying to provide jobs and social services such as health and education.
4. The Government also aims at sustained (continuing) development. This means that the country should use its wealth wisely so as not to destroy it.

The Government has not succeeded in achieving all these aims, but it continues to try.

Because it had not got enough money, Botswana borrowed funds from other countries for its development projects. This money came in the form of loans or grants (gifts). The number of donors (lenders) has increased over the years as Botswana has become better known internationally. Because of its political stability, peace and good management, Botswana has been able to attract foreign aid.

Funds were also raised internally by various means. One of the early sources of revenue was the Southern African Customs Union (SACU) formed in 1910. It consisted of the Union of South Africa, Botswana, Lesotho and Swaziland. Southern Rhodesia was a member, but withdrew later. SACU was formed to encourage free trade among these countries. This meant that goods travelled from one country to another without customs duty. The member countries had the same customs rules and shared the revenue earned by charging customs duty on goods from outside the customs area. Each got money from the customs revenue pool according to the value of the goods it imported. So the more goods a country imported, the higher the revenue it earned. The main weakness of SACU was that South Africa decided by itself how much money each country got. After Independence, Botswana complained that the old SACU agreement favoured South Africa. It asked that new negotiations be undertaken so as to give Botswana, Lesotho and Swaziland (BLS), a better share of the customs revenues.

A new customs agreement was reached in 1969. Since then Botswana has received much higher revenues. The revenue has continued to increase over the years, especially because of imports of large machines used in the newly opened mines in the early 1970s. These revenues partly enabled Botswana to balance its budget for the first time in 1972/73. This meant that Botswana was now able to pay for running its affairs (recurrent budget), every year without British grants-in-aid. This was an important step towards self-sufficiency. The 1969 agreement also made it possible to protect young industries in the BLS countries from the competition of larger South African industries. So Botswana can now prevent certain South African goods from being imported if similar goods are made in Botswana.

Transport and communications

No country can develop fully without a good infrastructure or communications system. This is why the new Government concentrated on road building from the very beginning. It tarred nearly all major roads and improved gravel ones. When the Francistown to Plumtree road and the Nata to Kazungula road are completed, there will be tarred roads linking Botswana to South Africa, Zambia and Zimbabwe. Some rural roads have also been built. They link major villages to the main road and railway systems. In the 1970s the roads within most major villages were tarred. There are still many remote areas, however, which have poor roads or have no roads at all.

The Department of Civil Aviation was created to develop and control air services. Air Botswana runs air transport. Since Independence, air transport has grown both internationally and inside Botswana. Air Botswana has links with international flights through Lusaka, Johannesburg and Harare. There are several landing strips in the country, but most of these are for small aircraft. The larger airports are in Gaborone, Francistown, Selebi Phikwe, and Maun. But these cannot take very large aircraft. In 1982 the Government began to build an International Airport near Gaborone. It will handle more aircraft, and enable larger aeroplanes to land in Botswana.

Fig. 176 An Air Botswana aeroplane at the old Gaborone airport. Expanding communications of all forms are essential to development

Fig. 177 A Botswana Railways locomotive. Following the Independence of Zimbabwe plans for Botswana to take over the railway were put into operation

The railway is still the most important means of transport. It carries both people and goods. In the colonial days it was run by the Rhodesia Railways. Since the Independence of Zimbabwe in 1980 it has been operated by the National Railways of Zimbabwe. In 1974 the Botswana Government decided to take over the portion of the railway inside Botswana. Preparations are being made and the takeover is expected to take place in the late 1980s. The Government has begun buying rolling stock such as engines and trucks, and training railway workers such as engineers, drivers and others. Work has begun to build a railway headquarters in Francistown.

The postal and telecommunications (telephones, telegrams, telexes), services have greatly expanded since Independence, especially in linking main towns and villages. The remote areas, however, still have a poor telephone and postal system. Many do not have a telephone service at all. Before 1957 the postal system was a branch of the South African postal system. In 1957 the Protectorate Government controlled it from Mafikeng. By 1963 the system operated from Lobatse, and later it was transferred to Gaborone. In 1980 the Botswana Telecommunications Corporation was formed to run the telecommunications, leaving the Post Office to be in charge of the postal services and a savings bank. A further improvement was the completion of a satellite station at Kgale Hill in 1980. This makes it possible to communicate with the outside world without going through South Africa.

Cattle farming

Cattle were the main agricultural activity which brought revenue. The good work in cattle health begun by the Colonial Government continued after Independence. The Government took further measures to control and eradicate foot-and-mouth disease. More cordon fences were erected and the Veterinary Department carried out more vaccinations. More spraying was carried out to destroy the tsetse fly. See Fig. 178. The Government expanded the Veterinary Department by training more Batswana. In 1982 a Motswana became the head of the Veterinary Department. The Government also realised that good animal health care would improve the quality of beef. The Ministry of Agriculture extended its services to many parts of the country. It distributed officers to advise cattle owners on animal health care. Radio programmes were devised and a newsletter was started to spread information about livestock care.

As a result of these measures cattle numbers, which were very low after the drought of the 1960s, increased. There were about three million in the 1970s. But most cattle are owned by only a few Batswana, and the majority do not benefit much from cattle. The Government is, therefore, encouraging more Batswana to own more cattle. They can do this by borrowing money from the National Development Bank (NDB). This Bank was created by the Government in 1965 in order to give loans to Batswana.

After successfully controlling foot-and-mouth disease for several years, the disease reappeared in 1977. The Botswana Government built more cordon fences. It also created the Vaccine Institute which now produces a strong vaccine against the disease. Because of the disease Botswana could not sell its beef to Europe for some time.

Some new developments took place after Independence. Because the Lobatse Abattoir has

Fig. 178 Vaccine being prepared at the Botswana Vaccine Institute. The Institute makes many of the vaccines needed in Botswana and exports some also

become too small, the Government has started to build another slaughterhouse at Maun in Ngamiland. A third abattoir is planned near Francistown for the northern areas. These new abattoirs will enable Botswana to export more beef. Batswana in far off areas will not have to drive their cattle to distant Lobatse.

Tribal Grazing Land Policy (TGLP)

As the number of cattle increased, it became clear that they would destroy the land through overgrazing. This would lead to soil erosion. So the Government introduced the Tribal Grazing Land Policy in 1975 to deal with the problem. The new policy aimed to control grazing by reducing the number of cattle in the communal areas and to increase production. This would be done by opening up new grazing areas in regions generally not used by anyone. The new areas would be turned into commercial farms. These would be leased to individuals or syndicates for a 50 year period. To be allowed to rent such a farm the person or syndicate must have at least 400 livestock. Arrangements were made for those interested to borrow money from the National Development Bank. The policy also aimed to protect the interests of the many Batswana who do not own cattle or have few cattle. These are largely the people who live in the remote areas. This would be done by safeguarding their land or by getting large cattle owners to move out of communal areas to commercial farms. In this way it was hoped that the gap between the poor and the rich would be narrowed.

TGLP divided *merafe* or 'tribal' land into three zones or parts: commercial areas, communal land and reserved areas. Commercial areas would be divided into farms. Communal areas would continue to provide grazing for *merafe* cattle as before. Reserved areas would provide more land for those with few or no cattle at all. The Government gave the Land Boards in each district the power to allocate the new farms.

Results of Tribal Grazing Land Policy

The Government had expected to allocate about a thousand ranches by 1980. In fact, only very few leases, about 17, were signed by that date. So progress has been slow. There are a number of people interested in leasing farms, but there are not enough of them. This is because so far, the Government has not been able to find sufficient new grazing areas. In some districts the people are not willing to implement the new policy because they have doubts about it. But the main reason for the lack of new grazing land is that areas which were thought to be vacant (empty) are in fact occupied. In some cases large cattle owners with boreholes in commercial farms areas are unwilling to lease farms. The crowding

Fig. 179 The success of the cattle industry depends on good grazing like this....

Fig. 180 .....while overgrazed land impoverishes the industry and overgrazing in communal areas has not lessened. This is because in general large cattle owners have not moved out, and there is no law to force them to do so. Some cattle owners have moved into commercial areas, but still retain their grazing rights in communal areas. This gives such people an advantage over other communal area dwellers. In some cases commercial ranches have been allocated in areas where remote area dwellers live. There is a danger that commercial farmers might expel these people from their farms. If the government is unable to resettle them, then they would become landless people. Another problem is that Batswana are not yet used to the idea of syndicates in cattle farming. And yet poorer people need a syndicate in order to have the 400 livestock required. The result is that generally only the already rich cattle owners are able to lease ranches. This further increases the gap between the rich and the poor, which is against the Government policy of social justice.

Arable farming

Like the previous Colonial Government, the new Government did not pay much attention to arable farming until recently. Until 1973 the Department of Agriculture concentrated on assisting the small group of master farmers. After 1973 the Department thought of new ways to teach more Batswana modern methods of farming. This was done through radio programmes and lessons given to farmers by agricultural demonstrators. The Government built the Botswana Agricultural College at Sebele to train demonstrators. In 1967 a research station was established to study new and better methods of farming. By 1976 some of these methods were being tried. At the same time a new kind of plough was invented (made) in Botswana. It is called *Makgonatsotlhe*, the (conqueror of all machine). It is light and can be pulled by four donkeys. The machine, however, is not yet used by many Batswana.

One problem faced by Batswana was that there was no good market for their crops in the country. They sold surplus crops to traders who sold the crops to the South African Maize Board. In years of drought the Batswana bought back the food they had sold earlier, at much higher prices. This discouraged Batswana from producing more crops. In order to solve this problem, the Government established the Botswana Agricultural Marketing Board (BAMB) in 1974. BAMB buys grain at fairly good prices and stores it. Some of this grain is exported. The rest is sold to Batswana at reasonable prices during times of need. The Government assists BAMA financially to carry out this process. This is encouraging Batswana to produce more food crops. Some Batswana are also producing cash crops such as groundnuts and sunflowers. Cotton is grown at such places as Talana Ranch in the Tuli Block, Mabadisa in Bangwaketse area, etc. Citrus fruit growing has been going on in the Tuli Block since 1944.

But until the late 1970s, the Government did not help the poor Batswana farmers much. Only people who had oxen and donkeys managed to benefit from farming. In 1979 the Government introduced a new programme aimed to help the poor small farmers. It is called the Arable Land Development Programme (ALDEP). Its main aims are to increase food production by enabling more Batswana to farm, and to create self-employment. In this way Batswana will not rely on food imports and more Batswana will get money by selling their produce. This will, it is hoped, reduce rural poverty and unemployment. The farmers are assisted by loans from the NDB to buy donkeys or oxen to plough with and to buy ploughing equipment. These loans are subsidised by the Government. They are given mostly to poorer Batswana who have few or no cattle at all. Loans are also given for fencing, buying tractors and for developing water resources. It is too early yet to judge how successful ALDEP will be.

Another major development was the introduction of rice growing in Botswana. In 1978 the Government asked the Government of the People's Republic of China to teach Batswana how to grow rice using water from the Okavango

Fig. 181 Growing rice near Maun. Diversification from traditional arable agriculture helps to expand the arable sector of the economy

Delta. The aim was to grow enough rice to feed Batswana and to export. Research now aims at investigating the possibility of large-scale production.

Mining

At Independence in 1966, Botswana was one of the poorest countries in the world. Today it is no longer classified as one of the poorest nations. It is now among the richer developing countries. This is because of its minerals, mainly diamonds. See Fig. 182. Botswana has large deposits of diamonds, coal and soda ash as well as small quantities of asbestos, gold and manganese. More minerals may be discovered in the future as more mineral exploration is carried out.

Before Independence, minerals belonged to the different *merafe*. Soon aften Independence the new Government successfully persuaded the *merafe* to give all mineral rights to the state. This was important because it enabled the Government to make a common policy for mining throughout Botswana. It also enabled Government to use mining revenues for the development of the whole country instead of just those areas with minerals.

DeBeers Botswana Mining Company was formed in 1969 to mine diamonds at Orapa. Production started in 1971. In 1977 mining started at Letlhakane. In 1976 DeBeers discovered a very large diamond pipe at Jwaneng. Full production began in 1982, and a large town is developing around the mine. Copper-nickel mining at Phikwe was started by the Bamangwato Concessions Ltd (BCL) in 1973/74. The mine had several problems. This together with the low prices for copper and nickel all over the world made the mine unprofitable. A second mine was started at Selebi in 1979/80. Coal mining at Morupule began in 1973. The main user of the coal is the mine at Selebi Phikwe. There are plans for further expanding coal mining in

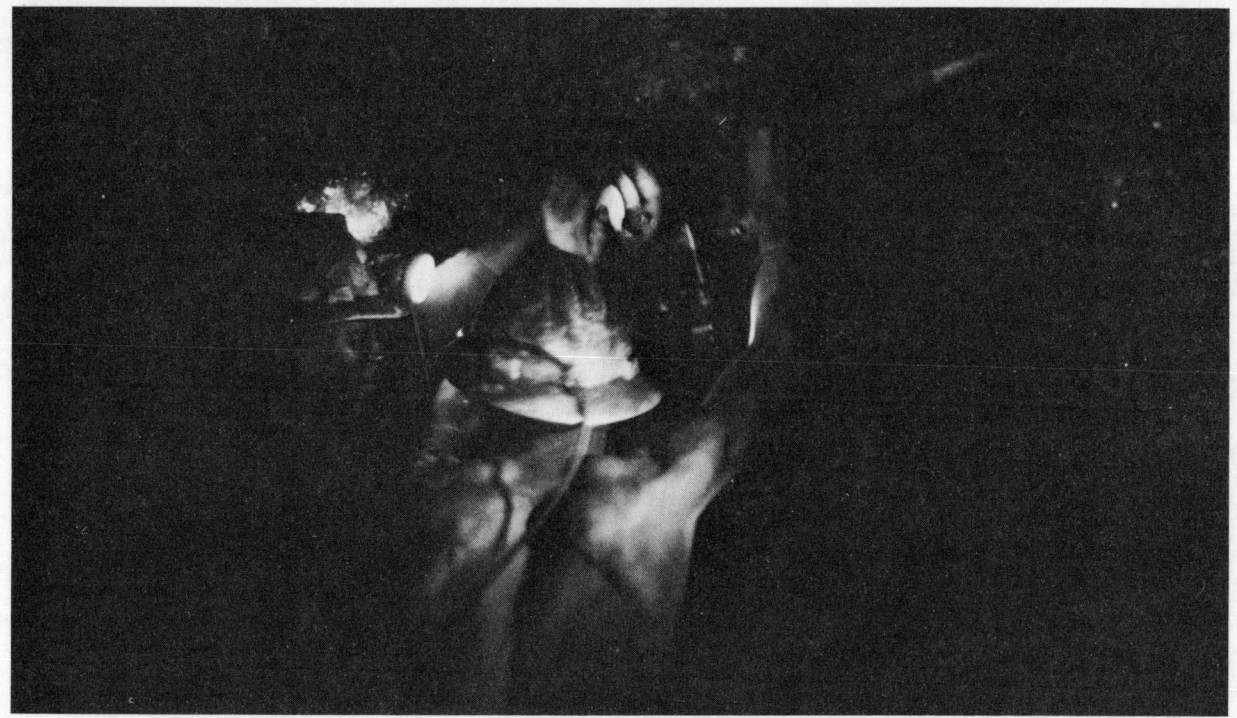
Fig. 182 A miner underground in the Selebi Phikwe copper-nickel mine

order to export coal to other countries. Also a power station will be built at Morupule. It will use coal to produce electricity. Shell Coal is intending to open a large coal mine at Kgaswe, near Morupule.

The Government does not do the mining itself. It encourages private companies to do so, but it makes laws to regulate and control mining activities. For example, the Government has negotiated with each company what share of the mining profits the Government should get. The most important policy is to use mineral revenue to develop rural areas especially. So far the results of the policy are small because most development has occurred in the towns. In order to create employment and get higher profits, the Government has decided that, where possible, minerals should be processed (prepared) in Botswana.

Advantages of mining
1 Mining has brought Botswana more money. This money is used for all kinds of development.
2 Mining has led to the building of more roads, and even railways such as the stretch of railway from Morupule to Selebi Phikwe. There is now talk of building a railway to link Botswana to Walvis Bay in Namibia. This would transport coal and other minerals for export.
3 Batswana have learned new skills from mining.
4 New towns have developed around the mines and new businesses and industries have been established there.
5 Mining has given employment to many Batswana.

The main disadvantage of an economy which depends on mining is that minerals can become exhausted (finished). Then the towns around the mines die out. Mineral prices can also fall and force a country to lose money.

Mining has created some social problems. The

Fig. 183 The mine at Selebi Phikwe. Unless controlled, smoke and fumes from industry can damage the environment of Botswana

water used for washing mineral ore sometimes flows into nearby rivers and makes them dirty. The fumes or smoke from mines can also dirty the air. This is pollution of the environment. It can be harmful to people, animals and vegetation living around the mining areas. Ways have been developed to reduce the danger of environmental pollution.

Wherever mining has developed, towns have sprung up where miners and people doing business in these towns live. Many people moved from the rural areas to seek jobs at the mines. But not all these people found jobs. Instead of returning to the villages, they settled around mining towns. These settlements, such as Botshabelo in Selebi Phikwe, are called squatter townships. Quite often these settlements did not have facilities like schools, clean water, clinics, a sewerage system. Children often had to walk long distances to school, and they had to go to the main town for shopping and health care. There was high unemployment. In such circumstances crime increased. The squatters cannot be forced back to their villages. So attempts are now being made to improve their lives by providing some facilities such as clinics, shops, schools, etc. The squatters themselves have found many ways to survive. For example, they sell traditional beer or they start *Shebeens* where they sell non-traditional beer and spirits illegally. Some become barbers or sell firewood, etc.

Manufacturing

At Independence, there were hardly any industries in Botswana. The few small ones that existed were in Francistown and Lobatse. These were a bone-meal factory and leather tannery in Francistown, and a small meat cannery and maize meal factory in Lobatse. Gaborone had

none. The main reasons for this situation were that:
1. Batswana did not possess enough money to start industries or businesses,
2. Batswana lacked industrial skills and knowledge of running industries,
3. Botswana's small and scattered population did not provide a profitable market for manufactured goods,
4. there was competition from large South African industries which made cheaper goods,
5. because of the Southern African Customs Union, Botswana could not prevent competition from South Africa,
6. there was a problem of scarce water and few natural resources.

These problems still exist, but some progress has been made. Industrial and commercial activities remain less developed than mining or agriculture.

Starting in 1968 the Government decided to expand commerce and industry. In 1973 a Ministry of Commerce and Industry was established to develop industry. Between 1973 and 1978 some progress was made in industrialisation.

From the beginning, it was realised that foreigners controlled industry. The Government tried to find ways to help Batswana to participate in industry. Government also found ways of encouraging foreign investment especially in industries where Batswana were not active. Botswana's economic policy is that of free enterprise. This means that the Government does not itself engage in producing things or in running businesses. It encourages individuals and companies to do this. Because there were few Batswana in industry, the Government has sometimes created parastatal bodies or Government companies to run businesses. The aim was to stop foreigners from running all businesses. Often these bodies run enterprises (businesses) jointly with foreign companies.

The Government took the following steps to promote industry. It negotiated a new customs agreement (see page 239), which enabled the Government to protect new industries.

A Government-owned public company called the Botswana Development Corporation (BDC)

Fig. 184 A furniture factory in Gaborone. Industrial growth is important for the development of the nation

was formed in 1970. The Corporation enabled the Government to participate directly in industrial and commercial development. In this way, the Government was able to compete with foreign companies and to create revenue. The BDC also aimed to work in partnership with foreign companies as long as such companies did business which created employment and trained Batswana. The BDC aimed to:

1. assist in the establishment of enterprises which could create employment,
2. train Batswana,
3. produce products which could replace foreign imports,
4. exploit Botswana's resources,
5. create new business opportunities for Batswana.

It has become involved mainly in the areas of transport, tourism, hotel business, brewing, property development, agriculture and financial services. The Corporation has made some progress in these areas. BDC, however, has not succeeded so far in starting development projects which can employ many Batswana, especially in the rural areas.

In 1973 the Government created the Botswana Enterprises Development Unit (BEDU) within the Ministry of Commerce and Industry. Financial assistance for BEDU came from the Swedish International Development Agency and the United Nations Development Programme. BEDU aimed to encourage and train Batswana to run businesses of their own. A number of BEDU premises were built at places such as Gaborone, Pilane and Francistown. Batswana ran businesses in these facilities. BEDU and the National Development Bank provided loans to poor Batswana who could not start in business on their own. The NDB was given more funds to enable it to serve Batswana better. BEDU has faced such problems as competition from large manufacturers in neighbouring countries, lack of properly trained people especially at technical and managerial levels, and the lack of local raw materials. However, some progress has been made. Some Batswana have been successfully trained, and BEDU projects have created some employment. But BEDU has not yet started operating effectively in the rural areas.

As a result of these measures and the general growth of the economy, a number of industries have developed. Examples are meat canning, tanning and leather works, weaving, clothing, wood and steel furniture, light engineering, mineral processing such as diamond cutting, etc. Most of these are in urban areas. Very little

Fig. 185   BEDU workshops provide opportunity for the small-scale businessman

Fig. 186 Weavers at Odi. Production cooperatives also play a part in the economy. At this cooperative fine tapestries (like the one on the cover of this book) produce export earnings

Fig. 187 Clean water, pumped from thousands of boreholes throughout the country, is a key to a healthy population and to rural development

industrial activity takes place in the rural areas. There are still very few Batswana owning and running industries. Most Batswana who own businesses have small retail shops.

An area in which Batswana have succeeded is the cooperative movement. It began in the 1960s and has Government support. The cooperative movement has supermarkets and shops in all towns and in many villages. The consumer cooperatives are the most successful. Producer cooperatives, such as the cattle marketing ones, are small but growing.

In 1982 the Government introduced the Financial Assistance Policy. This was to help Batswana engage in productive employment (job) creating projects. This is an important step because lack of finance has always been one main reason why Batswana have not carried out large projects.

Water development

The water development programme started in colonial times was expanded. More boreholes were drilled. A major new development was the provision of clean water to nearly all villages of reasonable size. Water pipes provide water to various parts of the village. This has removed the burden of women carrying water from long distances. Clean water has resulted in better health for the villagers.

The development of mining, industry and large towns made it necessary to provide even more water sources. So dams were built for these purposes. Examples are the Shashe and Mopipi dams which were built to serve the mines.

The growth of the economy has resulted in the rise and growth of towns. Before Independence, Lobatse and Francistown were the only urban centres. To these were added the new towns of Gaborone, which was a small camp until it became the capital, Selebi Phikwe, Orapa and Jwaneng. The populations of these towns are rapidly growing as shown on the table below.

Urban population 1964-81

	1964	1971	1978	1981
Francistown	9 521	19 903	36 000	31 100
Gaborone	3 855	18 436	47 000	59 700
Lobatse	7 613	12 920	17 000	19 000
Selebi Phikwe	—	4 940	28 000	30 200

Gradually a new generation of urban people is growing up. Traditional customs practised in the villages are disappearing in the towns, and a new industrial culture is developing. The growth of wage employment has led to the growth of a labour movement, which is gaining in strength. It plays an important part in protecting the interests of the working class. It promotes better wages and working conditions.

Social developments

Health

The social services which were very poor in colonial times have been greatly improved. The Government concentrated on education and health as the most important services. The aim was to make these services available to more people throughout the country and as cheaply as possible.

Before Independence, health work was done almost entirely by the missionaries. After Independence, the Government took over most health care work. Rather than build expensive hospitals for the urban areas alone, the Government has built rural health centres and clinics in nearly all villages. The Government also aims to prevent rather than just to cure diseases. So public health officers are trained and sent to the villages. They teach people how to avoid disease by living clean lives. Family planners teach mothers how to plan the size of their families, how to space their children and how to feed and care for children. These measures are meant to ensure that both mothers and children are healthy. The Government also provides immunisation for children against common child diseases. This is done free of charge.

The Government has built the National Health Institute to train nurses. Scholarships are provided to train Batswana doctors abroad. Recently a degree course was started at the University to train better teachers of nurses. All these measures have resulted in a healthier population. More recently the Government has begun to turn its attention to the care of the handicapped. Until recently only churches and some private organisations had cared for these people.

Education

At Independence there were few well educated Batswana. The Government decided to expand the education system quickly so as to provide manpower to run the country. So a lot of money was spent on education at primary, secondary and university levels. Several new primary and secondary schools were built. Bursaries (funds) were provided by the Government to enable Batswana to study both at the local University and abroad. The Government's aim was to provide at least primary education for all who needed it. So primary school fees were abolished in 1980. The problem is that not all children who complete primary education can find places in the fewer secondary or vocational schools. So there are many young people with primary education who want to, but who cannot continue with their education.

The question then was what to do with children who could not go on with their education. How could they be made productive and useful

Fig. 188 Expansion of education has been one of the Government's top priorities since Independence

citizens? In 1963 Patrick Van Rensburg started a new kind of school at Swaneng Hill in Serowe. He was at that time a political refugee from South Africa and is now a Botswana citizen. He used money from private overseas organisations to start the school. The Swaneng Hill School would give a different kind of education from the other schools. Normal secondary school courses would be taught, but there would be some practical subjects too. This would encourage Batswana not only to receive academic training but also to develop manual work. It was hoped to create a spirit of self-reliance in the students. However the School could not provide education for all the primary school leavers who wanted it.

Van Rensburg realised that it was unlikely that more secondary schools would be built for the

Fig. 189 Patrick Van Rensburg, founder of Swaneng Hill School and the Brigades movement in Botswana

Fig. 190 Shashe Builders' Brigade at work. The idea of combining education with production is still one of the central issues in education in Botswana today

many Primary School leavers. There was no employment for them. In 1965 he decided to start the Serowe Brigade near Swaneng Hill School. The brigade was separate from the secondary school. The first brigade was the Builders' Brigade. Later other brigades followed, such as those in metalwork, weaving, carpentry and so on. As time passed, other places such as Shashe introduced their own brigades and gradually the idea spread throughout the country. This came to be known as the Youth Brigade Movement and it became more widespread after Independence.

The brigades aimed to turn primary school leavers into productive citizens who relied on their own labour to make a living and to get education. This was done through a combination of work and training. The students learned skills on the job. They spent a lot of time learning by doing things with their hands together with their teachers. Only short periods were set aside for lessons in a normal classroom. The students built their own classrooms and dormitories. They earned money from their work to pay for running the brigade schools. Brigades aimed to cover all their own costs. They were a good example of self-reliance. Brigades produced goods which had been imported before. In this way they created wealth for the nation and contributed to the development of Botswana. They created jobs for many. They used local materials such as wood and leather to produce goods. Above all brigades produced young men and women who were confident, proud and useful citizens. The brigades were so successful that the Government decided to help by giving them financial assistance.

The main problem faced by the brigades was that students found it difficult to do manual work while students in non-brigade schools did not do any such work. There were also some problems caused by poor management. This caused some brigades to close. However, brigades still exist and some changes are being decide to change the education system in Botswana. The Government wanted education which would make Batswana more productive by doing things with their hands.

So in 1975, a Commission on Education was appointed to examine the education system in Botswana and to make recommendations on how to improve it. One of the recommendations is that practical work should be introduced in the schools.

All schools face the problem of lack of trained teachers, especially in the science subjects. The Government uses expatriate teachers while Batswana are being trained. Teachers are trained in the Teacher Training Colleges and at the University of Botswana.

Vocational or practical training has remained the weakest branch of the education system. There are hardly any vocational training schools. Many of the practical skills are obtained from such government departments as Public Works, courses in welding, electrical work, painting, carpentry, refrigeration, plumbing, etc. The courses are taught at the lower and advanced levels. The Automotive Trades Training School in Gaborone trains motor mechanics. The brigades, as stated above, also do a lot of vocational training. The Botswana Institute of Administration and Commerce teaches courses in such subjects as accountancy, commerce, business management, secretarial practice, typing, shorthand, etc.

Non-formal education: education outside school

In 1973 the Botswana Extension College (BEC) was formed with the aim of providing Junior Certificate and School Certificate courses for students who could not normally enter formal secondary schools. Teaching was done by correspondence (post), books and instruction being

Fig. 191 The University of Botswana from the air. The University became fully independent in 1982

Fig. 192 The University produces high level manpower for the country. Here a student teacher is in practice

sent to each student. Each student then sent work completed back to a teacher or tutor, by post.

In 1978 the BEC was absorbed into the new Department of Non-Formal Education (NFE) and about 4 000 students were studying at one time. In 1979 NFE started a huge literacy programme to help the large numbers of illiterate adults in the country to read and write. Assistants were appointed in each district to carry out the programme. By 1984 the programme is due to be completed. The Institute of Adult Education at the University of Botswana also provides non-formal education. It trains adult educators and teaches many other courses.

University education

For degree education, students go to the University of Botswana, which was established in July, 1982 when the University of Botswana and Swaziland (UBS) was closed by agreement between the Governments of Botswana and Swaziland. The UBS itself was formed after UBLS broke up in October 1975. The break up took place because Lesotho pulled out of UBLS and took over the University at Roma. Botswana and Swaziland were forced by this action to expand their own University Colleges quickly. These Colleges became full-grown, independent Universities in July 1982. The University of Botswana teaches certificate, diploma and degree courses.

For courses or training not offered in Botswana, the Government sends students to study abroad. There are now many more educated Batswana at all levels than there were at Independence. They provide much needed manpower to develop the country. Many of these mains to be done in training more Batswana, a great deal has been achieved in the field of education.

Questions

1 Write briefly and in your own words about the improvements in communications since Independence.
2 In no more than five sentences describe what
3 What has been the general ...... Tribal Grazing Land Policy? Was this what the Government intended?
4 Draw a sketch map showing the position of the mines in Botswana.
5 Hold a class discussion about the meaning of the statement, 'Botswana's economic policy is that of free enterprise.'
6 What are parastatal bodies? Discuss their role in Botswana's development.

27 Botswana and the World

Foreign policy

Every state has what are called a foreign policy and a domestic or internal policy. Domestic policy means all the things a state does inside its own boundaries. Foreign policy means what a country does outside its borders. It means how a country deals with problems of the world. It also means how a country works with other countries to solve world problems. The way in which a country relates to other countries is called international relations. No state can exist in isolation. States are interdependent. This means that they cooperate or work together. When a country makes its foreign policy, it makes sure that this policy will not damage its own interests. Thus any country's foreign policy is guided by self-interest. States usually recognise each other's self-interest when they deal with one another. Nations exchange ambassadors who look after their countries' interests abroad. Nations also form international organisations where they exchange views from time to time.

Botswana's foreign policy

Botswana became independent on 30 September 1966. Some people thought that it could not have an independent foreign policy because it was so economically dependent on (tied to) South Africa. Indeed South Africa expected Botswana to follow a foreign policy that would not criticise it. But Botswana has worked out an independent foreign policy which has won the country praise and respect in the world. The policy did not seem quite clear in the early years of Independence. President Khama clarified the policy at the Organisation of African Unity (OAU) summit in Lusaka in 1969. He said:

> 'But we are not deterred by our present economic weakness from speaking out for what we believe is right. We have made no secret of our detestation [dislike] of *apartheid*. We have condemned the theory and practice of the racial policy of *apartheid*... Botswana does not endorse [agree with] the denial of self-determination, human dignity and equality to people anywhere on the face of the earth.'

Later that year he stressed this policy at the United Nations General Assembly.

Foreign policy is made by the President with the advice of the Cabinet. The Minister for Foreign Affairs heads the Department of Foreign Affairs which carries out foreign policy. Botswana's ambassadors carry out the policy in foreign countries. Botswana's foreign policy can be looked at in terms of how the country deals with regional problems and with problems of the wider world.

Botswana and Southern Africa

The geographical location of Botswana has influenced its foreign policy very much. At Independence the new Republic was surrounded by Southern Rhodesia, South Africa and Namibia. All these countries were ruled by small groups of white people who oppressed black countries to be independent or to participate in politics. They all practised racial discrimination. The only link with independent African countries to the north was a small point across the Chobe-Zambezi Rivers at Kazungula. Botswana also depended on the transport and communications systems of Southern Rhodesia and South Africa. Her economy was also heavily dependent on South Africa for many reasons.

Because of all these factors Botswana had to be careful not to offend her racist neighbours. Botswana's foreign policy, therefore, aimed at criticising the White-ruled states, but being careful not to cause them to attack her. Similarly, Botswana assisted the oppressed people in these countries, but was careful not to provoke the white minority governments there. This careful policy was not always successful. For example in 1977 the white government of Rhodesia attacked Botswana several times.

Racism and *apartheid*

From the very beginning Botswana made no secret of her dislike for racial discrimination. President Khama publicly criticised Rhodesia and South Africa for their racial policies. This is why even though Botswana's economy was so dependent on these countries, she did not establish diplomatic relations with them. There is no Botswana ambassador in South Africa, and there was none in White-ruled Rhodesia.

Botswana's policy towards South Africa is to have minimum political contact with that country. The contacts which exist are mainly economic ones. Most of the goods Botswana uses are made in South Africa. She exports goods to South Africa or through South Africa to other countries. Her imports come through South Africa. The South African Government however, sometimes prohibits some Batswana from entering South Africa, usually for unknown reasons.

Botswana's relations with White-ruled Rhodesia were the same as those with South Africa. The economies of the two countries were interdependent. More importantly, Botswana relied on Rhodesian trains while they ran. Free movement of Rhodesians into Botswana was stopped when Rhodesia continually attacked Botswana during the liberation (freedom) war. So in 1978 all Rhodesians required visas (permits) to enter Botswana.

The liberation struggle

Botswana, like most countries, prefers to use peaceful means to solve problems. This is the method preferred by the Organisation of African Unity (OAU) to solve the problems of Southern Africa. The OAU declared this policy in 1969 in Lusaka in a document (paper) called the *Lusaka Manifesto*. But the OAU also stated that if the white minority governments refused to free the people of Southern Africa, it would support armed struggle (fighting) by the liberation movements.

Botswana supports this OAU policy regarding liberation. She emphasises that she prefers peaceful means, but she understands why people have to fight to free themselves. But Botswana also realised that she could not allow liberation movements to fight from her soil because she feared that she would be attacked by the powerful white governments.

Even though Botswana follows this policy, she recognises (accepts) liberation movements and helps people who are oppressed. She recognises the liberation movements recognised by the OAU, such as the South West Africa People's Organisation (SWAPO) of Namibia, the African National Congress (ANC) and the Pan-Africanist Congress (PAC) of South Africa. Before Zimbabwe became independent, Botswana recognised the Patriotic Front of Zimbabwe.

Botswana assists the liberation struggle and the oppressed people in the following ways.

1. Botswana has an open policy towards refugees, and accepts all true refugees. These are people who flee from their countries because of oppression. Botswana settles them, feeds them, allows them to run

Fig. 193 Seretse Khama as President addressing the UN General Assembly in 1969: the speech that clarified Botswana's foreign policy, particularly with regard to South Africa

businesses, gives some of them work and admits some of them to her schools and the University. Those who qualify for citizenship are allowed to become citizens if they should want to.

2 Botswana gives diplomatic and political support to the oppressed. This means that she speaks out against oppression at international conferences such as at the OAU and the UN.

3 Botswana takes part with the other Front Line States in assisting the liberation movements to negotiate a peaceful settlement. They helped the Patriotic Front to negotiate with Britain in the late 1970s. They are now helping SWAPO to negotiate for the Independence of Namibia.

4 Botswana, together with liberation movements, believes in and insists on true Independence for the whole of South Africa. For this reason she rejects 'Bantustans' such as Venda, Transkei, Bophuthatswana and so on because they are not independent countries.

Policy on sanctions

In order to force South Africa to end *apartheid*, the OAU and the United Nations have asked states to apply economic sanctions against that country. While Botswana does not oppose sanctions, she is unable to apply them because they would damage her own economy. She cannot stop trade between the two countries because she relies on South African goods. In addition South Africa could punish Botswana painfully by preventing her imports and exports from passing through. Botswana does not, therefore, apply sanctions because of her own self-interest. However, her policy is that she would not oppose those who wanted to apply sanctions so long as her interests were protected.

In the case of Rhodesia, however, Botswana applied some sanctions against the illegal (unlawful) white government after Ian Smith unlawfully declared Rhodesia independent in 1965. For example, in the early 1970s she banned Rhodesian goods such as tobacco and beer from the whole of Botswana, except for the on Rhodesian goods. Rhodesian construction companies were not allowed to work in Botswana. Oil and weapons were not allowed to pass through Botswana to Rhodesia.

The Front Line States

In 1974 a group of African States consisting of Angola, Botswana, Mozambique, Tanzania and Zambia formed a regional group called the Front Line States. They were so named because they were closely involved in helping those fighting for freedom. Their main role was to support and advise liberation movements in all negotiations. They also tried to unite these movements. For example they helped to unite Joshua Nkomo's Zimbabwe African People's Union (ZAPU), and Robert Mugabe's Zimbabwe African National Union (ZANU) into the Patriotic Front. They advised the OAU, the UN and other organisations about the liberation struggle. The Front Line States concentrated on Zimbabwe and Namibia. Sir Seretse Khama played an active

became independent and became a ... the Front Line States.

The response of the white governments

Starting in 1977, Rhodesia attacked Botswana on several occasions. She claimed that Botswana had freedom fighters' camps. But there were none in Botswana. The northern and north-eastern parts of Botswana were in great danger. Some Batswana and refugees were killed and property was destroyed. For example the ZAPU office in Francistown was destroyed. In 1978 15 young Batswana soldiers were killed at Leshoma.

Botswana replied by appealing to the UN which sent a team to Botswana to recommend ways of helping the country. The UN appealed to states to assist Botswana. Various states and the UN through the High Commission for Refugees assisted in caring for the refugees. Other countries helped in such projects as

Fig. 194 President Khama receiving the Nansen Medal in Geneva for the care Botswana has given to refugees

Fig. 195 A scene at Leshoma following the disaster in 1978 when 15 young Batswana soldiers were killed by troops from the Rhodesian army

Fig. 196 BDF soldiers demonstrating modern weapons to President Masire

building oil storage tanks. Botswana also created the Botswana Defence Force in 1977 to defend the country against Rhodesian attacks.

South Africa has not attacked Botswana yet. But from time to time South African soldiers have entered Botswana. Sometimes there has been some shooting between Botswana and South African soldiers on the borders. Sometimes the South African Government has protested against speeches made against it by Botswana. At times she has made difficulties for Botswana in transport, for example by not supplying sufficient railway trucks.

Southern African Development Coordination Conference (SADCC)

Origins of SADCC
SADCC was formed by the Front Line States.

decided to cooperate in economic development as well. Most of the planning for the establishment of SADCC was done by the Botswana Government. The President of Botswana, Sir Seretse Khama was the Chairman of all the major preparatory meetings. The first meeting was held in Gaborone in May 1979 by the Front Line Foreign Ministers. The next meeting was that of the Front Line Economic Ministers in Arusha, Tanzania in July 1979. All these meetings prepared for the 1980 Lusaka meeting to which the other independent countries of Southern Africa were invited and asked to join SADCC. This meeting was chaired by the President of Botswana, Sir Seretse Khama. In all these preparatory meetings Botswana officials,

swana, Lesotho, Malawi, land, Tanzania, Zambia and Zimbabwe.

Aims of SADCC
The main aims are as follows.
1. To reduce economic dependence on South Africa in particular, but also on other countries outside the SADCC area. All the SADCC countries except Angola and Tanzania are economically dependent on South Africa.
2. To promote trade between SADCC countries.
3. To unite SADCC countries in getting foreign aid for development projects.
4. To develop joint projects which benefit SADCC countries.

Fig. 197 Lusaka, 1980: the birth of SADCC; Sir Seretse Khama, founder and first Chairman of SADCC, seated right, with President Kaunda of Zambia seated left

In order to carry out development projects, SADCC set up commissions (committees) in each state to deal with different projects. Botswana is, for example, in charge of animal health because of its experience in this area. Botswana is the headquarters of SADCC, and the Secretariat is based in Gaborone. Since 1980 the President of Botswana has been the Chairman of SADCC and Zimbabwe has provided an Executive Secretary.

It is still too early to judge whether SADCC will succeed. But some results are already seen, such as the roads which are being built or improved to link SADCC countries.

Some of the problems SADCC may face are as follows.
1. The different economic and political systems of the SADCC countries could cause disagreements.
2. In order to protect their own industries, some SADCC countries could make it difficult for regional trade to develop.
3. Lack of sufficient funds could slow down certain projects.
4. External forces, such as South Africa, which fear competition from SADCC, may try to weaken the organisation.

Reducing dependence on South Africa

Even before the formation of SADCC, Botswana had tried in a small way to reduce dependence on South Africa, and to some extent on Rhodesia. With regard to Rhodesia, Botswana decided to take over the railway line inside Botswana. The Nata-Kazungula road was built to link Botswana to other African countries to the north without going through Rhodesia.

To reduce dependence on South African airports, an international airport is being built near Gaborone. A telephone system which links Botswana to the outside world without passing through South Africa has been established. In 1976, Botswana introduced its own currency (money), the *Pula*. Botswana hopes to use SADCC to further reduce its dependence on South Africa in the future.

Botswana and the wider world

Although Botswana's foreign policy focuses mainly on Southern Africa, Botswana is also interested in dealing with countries outside its region.

The Organisation of African Unity (OAU)

Botswana is a member of the OAU and plays an active role in it. The roots of the OAU are found in the Pan-African Movement. This movement developed throughout the world wherever black people lived during the 19th century. Its earlier aim was to unite all black people throughout the world against racial discrimination. Young Africans studying in Europe learned the ideas of Pan-Africanism there. They brought these ideas to Africa after the Second World War. In Africa, Pan-Africanism now aimed to decolonise all Africa. The cry everywhere was 'Africa for Africans'. Kwame Nkrumah of Ghana was the chief spokesman for the movement. He wanted Africa to unite because through unity it would be strong enough economically and politically to compete with other continents. In 1957 Ghana became the first African colony to gain Independence. After many more colonies became independent, a conference was held in Addis Ababa, Ethiopia in May 1963, to establish the OAU. Its headquarters is in Addis Ababa.

The main aim of the OAU is to work for a strong Africa through cooperation among African states. This cooperation can be in the economic, political, and military areas. One of the ways to ensure unity is for the OAU to solve disputes among African states. Another aim of the OAU is to help to liberate those parts of Africa which are not yet free. The OAU has not succeeded in achieving some of its goals. But it has succeeded in helping to decolonise Africa.

The problems of the OAU are generally caused by:
1. differences between African states caused mainly by their different political views and self-interests,

Fig. 198 The Botswana delegation led by Seretse Khama at an OAU summit

2 interference by outside powers,
3 the difficulty of so many countries in such a big continent being able to work together.

Botswana supports the OAU by supporting its aims. It cooperates with other OAU members at the UN and other international meetings to defend African interests.

Botswana benefits from the OAU in some ways. For example it gets some financial assistance in times of trouble such as during the Rhodesian war. It also gets loans from the African Development Bank which is supported by the OAU. The OAU gives Botswana political support against South Africa.

Other international organisations

The Non-Aligned Movement

Botswana is a member of the Non-Aligned Movement. After the Second World War the great powers, the United States of America (USA), and the Union of Socialist Soviet Republics (USSR) or Russia, competed for control and domination of the world. They wanted to do this by creating spheres of influence. This would divide the world into blocks or groups. One block would be led by the USA, and the other by the USSR. They are sometimes referred to as the Western block and the Eastern block. This competition led to the 'cold war' between East and West. The world feared that real war might break out.

Some leaders of the Third World (developing countries) decided to establish a movement that would work for world peace by not aligning with (joining) the East or the West. This was the Non-Aligned Movement whose first conference was held in Belgrade, Yugoslavia in 1961. It was started by Tito of Yugoslavia, Nehru of India, Nasser of Egypt, Soekarno of Indonesia and Nkrumah of Ghana. The movement aims to work for world peace by helping to end the cold

Fig. 199 T. Tlou, Botswana's former Ambassador to the UN, being received by the Secretary-General, Kurt Waldheim (January 1977)

war. It also opposes interference in the internal affairs of other states, especially by the big powers. It opposes the division of the world into spheres of influence or blocks. It expects its members to follow an independent foreign policy without dictation (being forced) from the big powers.

Botswana plays an active part in this movement which has supported the OAU in the struggle to liberate Southern Africa. Between 1977 and 1979, Botswana was a member of the Bureau (executive committee) of the movement. To show that it is a non-aligned country, Botswana has established diplomatic relations with countries from different political systems. There are embassies from the capitalist countries such as the USA and Britain, and socialist countries such as the USSR and China.

The United Nations

Botswana belongs to the United Nations and benefits from it in several ways. UN agencies such as the United Nations Development Programme grant funds for various development projects. The World Food Programme gives food in times of starvation. The World Health Organisation helps in health care. The United Nations Childrens' Fund feeds school children and other vulnerable (weak) groups. The High Commissioner for Refugees cares for refugees in Botswana. The UN also gives Botswana political and diplomatic support in times of need such as during the Rhodesian war.

The Commonwealth of Nations

Within the Commonwealth of Nations Botswana helps to solve problems facing other member countries. These are mainly political and economic problems. For example, in 1980 the Commonwealth took part in helping to solve the problem of Zimbabwe. Commonwealth countries also discuss how to cooperate in

Fig. 200 President Masire at the EEC headquarters being met by Botswana's Ambassador to the EEC, G. Garebamono (extreme right)

economic development, education, health, sports, etc.

The European Economic Community
An international organisation from which Botswana benefits a lot economically is the European Economic Community (EEC) consisting of countries of Western Europe. When Britain joined the EEC in 1972, her Commonwealth partners were allowed to export to the EEC some of their products needed by the EEC countries at favourable prices. In order to promote this cooperation and to get better prices, in 1975, some African, Caribbean and Pacific (ACP) countries joined to form an organisation to negotiate with the EEC. Botswana exports its beef to the EEC. The EEC also helps Botswana in its economic development by granting it funds or loans. The problem with the EEC market is that it is not always dependable.

It is quite clear from this chapter that although Botswana is a small country whose economy is tied to South Africa, it has followed a fairly bold foreign policy with regard to Southern Africa. It has also played its part in world affairs. This has won the country some respect internationally. The main focus of Botswana's foreign policy is Southern Africa because what happens in that region affects the country directly.

Questions

1. Explain what we mean when we say Botswana is 'non-aligned'.
2. Name the Front Line States. Why do we use this name?
3. Name the members of SADCC. Write a brief essay on SADCC using the following headings.
   (a) Aims (b) Results (c) Problems
4. List the other international organisations to which Botswana belongs.

Selected Bibliography

Botswana Society, *Proceedings of the Symposium on Settlement in Botswana: The Historical Development of a Human Landscape*, Heinemann, 1980

Chirenje, J.M. *A History of Northern Botswana, 1850-1910*, Associated University Presses, 1977

Colclough, C. and McCarthy, S. *The Political Economy of Botswana. A Study of Growth and Distribution*, OUP, 1980

Dachs, A.J. *Khama of Botswana*, Heinemann, 1971

Inskeep, R. *The Peopling of Southern Africa*, David Phillip, 1978

Lee, R.B. and De Vore Irven (eds.), *Kalahari Hunter Gatherers. Studies of the !Kung San and their neighbours*, Harvard University Press, 1978

Lye, W.S. and Murray, C. *Transformations on the Highveld: Tswana and Southern Sotho*, David Phillip, 1980

Parsons, N. *A New History of Southern Africa*, Macmillan, 1982

Sillery, A. *Botswana, A Short Political History*, Methuen, 1974

Sillery, A. *John Mackenzie of Bechuanaland. A Study in Humanitarian Imperialism 1835-1899*, Balkema, 1971

Vengroff, R. *Botswana Rural Development in the Shadow of Apartheid*, Associated University Presses, 1977

The following will also be of interest to younger readers.

Chirenje, J.M. *Chief Kgama and His Times, the Story of a Southern African Ruler*, Rex Collins, 1978

Lichtenstein, W.H.C. *The Foundation of the Cape: about the Bechuanas* translated O.H. Spohr, A.A. Balkema, 1973

Thomas, E.M. *The Harmless People* hardback Alfred Knops, 1959, paperback Random House, 1965

A number of articles of interest may also be found in *Botswana Notes and Records* and *Pula: Journal of African Studies*.

Since 1976 fourth year students of History at the University of Botswana have produced theses which are available at the National Archives and at the University Library.

Abbreviations

AAPC	African Auxiliary Pioneer Corps
ALDEP	Arable Lands Development Programme
BBP	Bechuanaland Border Police
BAMB	Botswana Agriculture Marketing Board
BDP	Botswana Democratic Party
BIP	Botswana Independence Party
BNF	Botswana National Front
BPP	Botswana Peoples' Party
BEDU	Botswana Enterprises Development Unit
BDC	Botswana Development Corporation
BSAC	British South Africa Company
BWCC	British Westland Chartered Company
EEC	European Economic Community
HC	High Commissioner
LMS	London Missionary Society
NDB	National Development Bank
OAU	Organisation of African Unity
RC	Resident Commissioner
SACU	Southern African Customs Union
TGLP	Tribal Grazing Land Policy
UN	United Nations

Terminology

It is necessary to explain the use of certain names in this book. We have tried wherever possible to call the various people mentioned in this book by the names they use to refer to themselves. For example, the Amandebele and not the Ndebele or the Matabele as they are called in many books; the Bakalanga, and not the Bakalaka or the Makalaka, and so on.

For the people generally referred to as the Basarwa or 'Bushmen', we use the name San to refer to the whole group of people who speak a variety of San dialects. But where we speak of one particular group of San, we use the name they use for themselves. For example, the !Kung. the symbols !, / and // represent click sounds.

Similarly we have used the name Khoe for the *Bakgothu* who others often call 'Hottentots'. Some modern books call them Khoi but this is more correctly spelt Khoe. The name Khoesan is used to refer to the Khoe and San together.

In many books the names of people are used without the prefix, for example, the Tswana, the Sotho and so on instead of the Batswana, the Basotho. But the people concerned never drop the prefix. So we too have not dropped the prefixes from peoples' names.

In some cases we have retained certain names such as 'Kalahari' which the Batswana call 'Kgalagadi'. This is because Kalahari is the name commonly used.

Glossary of Non-English Terms

Bakgothu: Khoe
Bantu-speaking: people who use African languages which use the word stems 'nt', 'th,' 't' for persons, e.g. 'batho' (Setswana)
Basarwa: San
Boer: White South African farmer of mainly Dutch, French or German origin
Bogadi: cattle (usually), bridewealth given to parents of the woman by parents of the man on marriage
Bogosi: kingship
Bogwera: male initiation
Bojale: female initiation
Difaqane: troubled times associated with the rise of Shaka's Zulu state
Griqua: Khoe living on Orange River who had some white ancestry and spoke Dutch as their home language
Khoe: *Bakgothu* or 'Hottentot'
Khoesan: a collective word describing all Khoe and San people
Kgosi: king or ruler
Kgosing: king's ward of a village or town
Kgotla: meeting place; court
Lekgotla: ward of a village or town
Letsholo: regimental game hunt
Mafisa: cattle lent out to secure service in return
Malata: serfs or semi-slaves
Mambo: king
Mokoro: canoe
Mophato: regiment
Morafe: nation
Motlhanka: servant, sometimes used to mean serf or semi-slave
Muslim: Trader from the east Coast who practises the worship of Allah
San: *Mosarwa* or 'Bushman'
Sebilo: specularite
Sehuba: tribute (literally 'chest')
Setswana: language of the Batswana
Trekboer: Boer (op.cit.) who stays in one place for only a few months or years before moving on

Index

Abattoir: First, 191; BMC, 241-2
Acheulian Culture, 12-13, 19
Agriculture: see also Cattle and Crops; introduction, 22, 30-3; new methods, 141; Colonial period, 189-92; modern, 242-3
African Advisory Council (Native), 171, 182-3
African Auxiliary Pioneer Corps (AAPC), 210-1
African Civil Service Association, 220-1
African National Congress (Native), 171, 209
African Teachers' Association, 203, 221
African Treasuries, 186
Afrikaners, see Boers
Aluwi, see Balozi
Amahlubi, 103
Amakhumalo (Amandebele), 73, 85, 108-13, 170
Amangwane, 103
Amanguni, 57, 85, 102, 103
Andersson, C.J., 3
Anglican Church, 133
Angola, 39, 41, 99, 259
Apartheid, 146, 170, 257
Archaeology, science of, 2-3
Archell, J., 136
Arden-Clarke, C., 186
Army: historic, 75; BDF, 260; see also War
Ashton, Rev. W., 136
Australopithecines (Early Man), 5-6

Babirwa, 73, 85, 167, 199-200
Babolaongwe, 60, 64-5, 68, 103
Badighoya, 60
Bafokeng, 60, 61, 63, 103

Bagaseleka (Baseleka), 117, 167
Bahlakoana, 103-5
Bahlubi, 103
Bahurutshe, 60, 61, 64, 71, 72
Bain, A.G., 3, 106
Bakaa, 67, 68, 73, 85
Bakakhwe (Khoe subgroup), 93
Bakalanga, 5, 46, 73, 81-8
Bakgalagadi (includes many subgroups), 57, 68-70, 73-4, 91, 200
Bakgatla, 60, 61, 64, 66-7, 73, 145, 169
Bakgwatheng, 60, 64, 65, 68, 75
Bakhurutshe, 67, 85, 98
Bakololo (formerly Bafokeng), 78, 98-9, 104-6
Bakwena, 60-2, 64-7, 73, 77
Balala, 200
Baldwin, W.C., 3
Balete, 79, 85
Balozi (Aluwi), 73, 93-5, 102
Bamangwato Concessions Ltd., 195, 244
Bambandyanalo (S. Africa), 47-51
Bambata (pottery type), 37, 41
Bangologa, 60, 65, 68, 70, 90, 98-9
Bangwaketse, 5, 62-7, 71, 77
Bangwato, 62-7, 71, 73, 77, 213-19
Banoka (Khoe subgroup), 22, 24, see also Bateti
Bantu-speaking Peoples, 22, 26, 29-33, 35, 40, 53, 57, 60
Bantustans, 171, 258
Bapedi, 60-1, 64, 68, 85, 104, 166
Baphaleng, 65, 68, 90
Baphofu (Phofu Confederacy), 64-5
Baphuting, 103-6
Barolong, 60-8, 71, 77, 85, 90, 105-6
Bashaga, 68, 91, 103

Basimane ba kgosi, 117
Basimane ba mafatshe, 118
Basotho, 53, 62, 85, 102
Basubiya (Bekuhane), 89-90, 93, 95
Batalaote (Bandalaunde), 73
Bataung, 104-6
Batawana, 64, 71, 78-80, 97-100
Bateti (Khoe subgroup), 32, 53, 75, 91
Bathoen I, K. of Bangwaketse, 136, 153, 159-61
Bathoen II, (Hon. B. Gaseitsiwe, CBE), 173, 186, 214, 217, 221, 233, 236
Batlhanka (Servants), 74, 75, 80, 99-100, 185
Batlhaping, 3, 65, 68, 71, 104-5
Batlharo, 60, 64, 68, 71, 77, 90
Batlokwa, 64, 71, 80, 103
Bavenda, 57, 68, 85
Bayei, 70, 89, 93, 95-6, 98-100
Beads, glass, 40, 44, 46, 48, 50, 55, 83, 87
Bechuanaland Border Police, 176
Bechuanaland, British, 152
Bechuanaland, Protectorate: Declaration of, 146-52, Early years, 152-3, Administration of 175-228
Berlin Conference, 143
Bethell, Cristopher, 147
Bewlay, Charles, v
Biddulph, J.R., 106
Boabile, Tepo, 147
Boers: 113, 116, 133, 143-5, 149-53, 165-74; see also Great Trek
Bogosi: traditional, 72, 75-80, 115-17, 124, modern 185-7; loss of power, 233-4; see also House of Chiefs
Bome, son of K. Makaba, 115
Bosman, John, 163
Bosutswe Hill, 39

273

Boteti River, 21, 22, 31, 37-8, 53, 91
Botha, Louis, 170
Botlhapatlou, 60
Botswana Civil Service Association, 220
Botswana Development Corporation, 248
Botswana Enterprises Development Unit, 248
Botswana Teachers' Union, 221
Botswana Vaccine Institute, 241
Boundaries, Colonial, 177-81
Brigades, 252-3
British South Africa Company, 154-65
British Westland Chartered Company, 162-3, 181
Broadhurst, 68
Brockway, Fenner, 217
Broederstroom (S. Africa), 36-7, 42, 57-60
Brooks, Alison, v
Burchell, W.J., 3
Bushman Mine, 194
Bushmen (*Basarwa*), see San

Campbell, Rev. J., 129, 136
Canoes (*mekoro*), 95
Caprivi Strip (in Namibia), 181, 209
Catholic Church, Roman, 205
Cattle: Introduction of 22, 31; Customs relating to, 72-4; *Mafisa*, 73; Kgamelo, 117; in modern economy, 190-1, 240-3
Central Government, 231-3
Chamberlain, J., 147, 160-1, 166
Changamire, 84
Chiefs, see *Bogosi*
Chikaranga Language, 81
Chishona Language, 46
Chobe River, 31, 37, 39, 89, 94
Christianity, see Missionaries
Churches, Independent, 135-6
Cilliers, 113
Civil Aviation, Dept. of, 239
Climate, past, 8
Cloth: Introduction of, 49, 50, 55; local manufacture, 48-9
Collins-Hooper, Jerry, v
Colonial Development and Welfare Fund, 188, 192
Colonialism, 143, 154-5, 188, 199, 220-1
Commerce & Industry, Min. of, 246

Commonwealth Development Corporation (formerly Colonial), 191
Commonwealth of Nations, 264-5
Communications, modern, 239
Concessionaires, 154-6
Concessions Commission, 158-9
Constitution (of Botswana), 230-1
Cooke, John, v
Cooperative Movement, 249
Copper: Early mining of, 35, 42; modern mining, 194-5, 230, 244
Crops: Introduction of, 34-6; traditional cropping, 78-9, 87, 97; in the modern economy, 190, 243-4
Crown Land (State Land), 181

Dambe, Amos, 225
Danangombe (Dlhodlho, Zimbabwe), 84
Daniell, Samuel, 3
Dating (Archaeological), 2
De Beers Botswana Mining Company, 195, 244
Denbow, James, v
Diamonds, 230
Difaqane, 71, 85, 101-13
Dikgatlhong (S. Africa), 65
Dimawe, 116
District Councils, 233-4
District Development Committees, 234
Dithakong (S. Africa), 105
Dithejwane, 62, 65, 70
Dithubaruba, 78, 106
Diyei (Caprivi Strip), 93
Dumbrell, H.E., 203
Dutch, 3, 21, 26; see also Boers
Dutch Reformed Church, 133

Eastland, Clare, v
Economy, modern, 188-198, 230-1, 238-50
Education: *For* traditional see Initiation; Missionary, 136-41; Colonial 201-7; Modern, 250-5
Edwards, W., 129
Elections: First 227, 230; Analysis of, 235-7; and Delimitation for, 236
England, Russell (Sir), 190, 221
Environmental Change, 4-11, *see also* Climate
Ethiopianism, 135
European Advisory Council, 183
European Economic Community, 265

Evans, Admiral E.R.G.R., 184
Evolution, 4-7
Executive of Government, 234

Fawcus, Sir Peter, 220-1, 223, 226
Fertile Crescent, 34
Financial Assistance Policy, 249
Firearms (guns), 75, 115-17, 123-4
Fishing, traditional, 24-5, 95-6
Flag and Anthem, National, 224, 227-8
Foot-and-Mouth Disease, 191, 240-1
Foreign Policy, 256
Forest Hill Farm, 205
Fourie, Gideon, 178
Francistown, 31, 37
Front Line States, 258-63
Fuller, Capt. James, 163

Gabamukuni, 94, 99
Gabane, 51
Gaborone (Capital), 228
Gaborone, K. of Batlokwa, 228
Gaborone Farms, 165
Gaborone Secondary School, 217
Gaseitsiwe I, K. of Bangwaketse, 150
Gcwi (San subgroup), 40
Geological Survey, Dept. of, 188, 192, 194
Germans, 209
German S.W. Africa (Namibia), 148, 209
Germany, 148
Ghanzi, 8, 11, 70, 90, 99, 164, 200
Glossary (Meaning of Non-English words), 271
Goats: Origin in Africa, 30, Introduction into Southern Africa, 37-40
Godisamang, Elizabeth, 138
Gokomere (Culture), 37, 38
Gold: Early mining, 43, 44; early trade, 47-50; Discovery by Whites, 145, 194
Goshen, Republic of, 148
Gould-Adams, Lt-Col. H.J., 167, 180
Grahamstown (S. Africa), Ivory Sale, 120
Great Trek, 111-3
Great Zimbabwe see Zimbabwe Town
Griqua, 105, 121
Grobler, P.D.C.J. and widow, 177
Gumanye, 47
Gundwane, Lt of Mzilikazi, 85
Gxana (San subgroup), 40

Hamashi, 94
Hambukushu, 90, 93
Hamilton, R., 136
Hankusi, *K*. of Bayei, 93
Harragin, Sir Walter, 215
Harris, H.R., 160-1
Harts River (S. Africa), 65
Haskins, J.G., OBE, 221
Health Facilities, 207-8, 250
Hepburn, Rev. J.D., 132-3
Hermannsburg Mission *see* Lutheran Church
Hertzog, Gen., 172-3
Hicks, 162
High Commissioner, 175
High Commission Territories, 171, 177, 207
History, Sources of, 1-3
Hitchcock, R.K., v
Hitler, Adolf, German Dictator, 210
Homo see Australopithecines
Hottentots (*Bakgothu*), *see* Khoe
House of Chiefs, 226, 233
Houses, Traditional, 26, 37, 46, 79, 81, 95
Huffman, T., v
Hukuntsi, 70
Hunting, traditional methods, 23-4, 77-8, 91, 96-7, 116
Huru, son of Mangava, 92

Ikaneng, *K*. of Balete, 159, 161
Imperialism, 143 *see also* Colonialism
Independence, 1966, 227-8
India, 40, 48, 51, 55, 82
Indian Ocean, 40
Indirect Rule, 175-85
Industrial Revolution, 142-3
Initiation (*Bogwera* & *Bojale*), 1, 70, 75-7, 134
Iron, introduction of, 30, 31, 37
Iron Age: Early, 31, 33, 34-41, 46-8; Later, 46-114
Iron Smelting, 34-5, 42-5, 87
Irrigation, 190
Itenge, Land of Basubiya, 93
Ivory Trade, 48, 75, 82-3, 121-2

Jameson, Dr L.S., 159, 161, 164-5
Jameson Raid, 164-5
Joint Advisory Council, 183
Judiciary, modern, 235
Jwaneng, 244

Kaditshwene (S. Africa), 104

Kang, 70, 77
Kanye, 8, 51
Kapako (Namibia), 40
Katima-mulilo (Caprivi), 93
Kaunda, K. (President of Zambia), 261
Kazungula, 89
Kedia Hill, 98, 106
Kenya, 5, 31
Kgabo, *K*. of Bakwena, 62, 65
Kgafela, *K*. of Bakgatla, 67
Kgakgwe Hill, 106
Kgamane, Keaboka, 131
Kgamane, Rasebolai, 217, 219
Kgamanyane, *K*. of Bakgatla, 145
Kgari, *K*. of Bangwato, 106, 117-18
Kgari, Step-brother of Sebele I, 178
Kgasa, M.L.A., 221
Kgaswe, 245
Kgosidintsi, Brother of Sechele I, 152
Khama II, *K*. of Bangwato, 98
Khama III, *K*. of Bangwato, 73, 86, 118, 131, 145, 149, 159-61, 171, 176-7, 184, 199, 292
Khama, Brigadier Ian S.K., 218
Khama, Lady Ruth (Miss Ruth Williams), 213-19
Khama, Sekgoma, *K*. of Bangwato, 184, 199
Khama, Sir Seretse (First President), v, 184, 213-19, 221, 224-8, 261
Khama, Tebogo Jaqueline, 217
Khama, Tshekedi, Regent of Bangwato, 173, 184, 186, 205-6, 210, 212-19, 221
Khami (Zimbabwe), 56, 81-4
Khoe (*Bakgothu*), 17, 20-8, 31-2, 53, 57, 64, 80, 90, 103, 200-1
Khoekhoen, 21
Khoesan, 21-2, 57, 89
Khunwana, 105
Khwebe Hills, 70, 98
Kilwa (Kenya), 51
Kimberley (S. Africa), 128, 147
Kingdoms, early, 41, 46-56, 81-8
Kobe, K. of Bagaseleka, 176-7
Kok, J.M., 129
Koma, Dr Kenneth, 236
Kopong Conference, 152-3
Kruger, Paul, 148, 166
Kuando River, 94
Kudumane (Kuruman, S. Africa), 129-30, 137-8
Kwele, Daniel, 236-7

Kwena, son of Malope, 60, 62, 65
Kwenaitsile, son of Gaseitsiwe, 136

Land Boards, 233-4
League of Nations, 209
Legislative Council (LEGCO), 221
Legislature, modern, 231-7
Lehututu, 109, 136
Lephepe, 60
Lesoma, 259, 260
Leswingo, 83
Letlhakane, 244
Letlhakeng, 11, 75, 109
Letlogile, *K*. of Barolong, 157
Letsholathebe, *K*. of Batawana, 99-100, 131
Lewanika, *K*. of Balozi, 181
Liberation Struggle, 257-62
Limpopo River, 37, 39, 40, 41, 48, 65
Linchwe I, *K*. of Bakgatla, 153, 159, 169
Linchwe II, *K*. of Bakgatla, 233-4
Linyanti River, 93, 99
Literature, early Setswana, 136
Livingstone, Dr D. & Mrs M., 3, 131, 137
Lloyd, Rev. E., 133
Lobatse, 37, 68
Lobatse Constitutional Conference, 226
Lobatse Farms, 165
Lobengula, *K*. of Amandebele, 177, 180
Local Government, 235
Loch, Sir Henry, 177, 180
London Constitutional Conference, 227
London Missionary Society, 129-41, 201-2, 217
Lotsane River, 83
Lusaka (Zambia), 261
Lutheran Church, 131-2
Luze (Dutle), 109

McIntosh, Phineas, 184
McNeill's Farm, 199
Maalola Regiment, 169
Mababe, 93
Mabuasehube, 65, 68
Machechele Regiment, 204
Macheng, *K*. of Bangwato, 145
Mackenzie, Rev. J., 133, 146-7
Mafikeng (Mafeking, S. Africa), 167, 175
Magogwe (S. Africa), 67
Maguire, J.R., 156

275

Mahalapye, 83, 190
Majojo, 84
Majwanamatshwaana (S. Africa), 65
Makaba, K. of Bangwakwetse, 104-5
Makgadikgadi Pans, 8-9
Makunga, M., v
Malema, K. of Babirwa, 199
Malope (Ancestor of Batswana), 60, 65
Mambari, 94
Mambo, 47, 82-5
Mambo People, 47, 49, 51, 52, 81
Manchester (U.K.), Cotton Mill, 142
Mankurwane, K. of Batlhaping, 148
Manufacturing, modern, 245-6
Manyane, R., v
Mapungubwe (S. Africa), 53
Marapong, 213
Maribe, A., 225
Marico River (Madikwe, S. Africa), 64-5
Maritz, G., 113
Mashango, Mumbukushu rainmaker, 98
Mashi (Caprivi), 98
Masilo (Ancestor of Batswana), 60
Masire, Dr Q.K.J. (President), 224-5, 233
Mason, R., v
Masvingo (Zimbabwe), 54
Matante, Philip G., 222-4, 236
Matebele, J., 189
Mathiba, K. of Bangwato, 98
Matimela Act, 1968, 233
Matiwane, K. of Amangwane, 103
Matlapaneng, 38, 39
Matopo Hills (Zimbabwe), 39
Matshege, K. of Bakgatla, 67
Matsheng, 11, 65, 70, 90
Matsieng/Lowe, 60, 62
Matsitama, 48, 51
Maun, 38, 39, 53
Mbolawe, K. of Babolaongwe, 68
Mebalwe, 137
Melita, 51
Melville, J., 105
Meroe (Sudan), 34
Messina (S. Africa), 51
Metsemotlhaba River, 71
Metsimaswana Bridge, 168
Mhalatswe River, 52, 56
Mhondoro, 56
Migrant Labour, 124, 128, 197-8, 246
Migrations, early, 31, 46
Millet, 31, 37, 53, 97
Milner, S. A. (later Lord), 166, 169

Mining: Ancient, 34, 42-5, 46, 47-8, 51, 52; Colonial, 194-6; Modern, 244-6
Missionaries, 129-41
Mmadinare, 52
Mmamabula, 195
Mmamagwe, 53
Mmanthatisi, Regent of Batlokwa, 103
Mmashoro, 38
Mochudi, 62
Mochudi National School (now museum), 203-4
Modisaotsile, Headman of Bobonong, 199
Moeding College, 202
Moeng College (Bamangwato College), 206
Moffat, Rev. J.S., 163
Moffat, Rev. R. and Mrs Mary, 3, 105, 130-1, 136
Mogalakwe, Regent of Batawana, 99
Mogale (Ancestor of Batswana), 64, 73
Mogale, K. of Bakgatla, 67
Mogodi, Khukhu, 133, 138, 163
Mogopa, K. of Bakwena, 65
Mohurutshe, daughter of Malope, 60, 65
Mokgosi, K. of Balete, 217
Molalatau, 199
Molema, Dr Silas M., 186, 221
Molema, Sebopiwa, 186
Molepolole, 37, 40, 64, 65, 68, 91
Moletsane, K. of Bataung, 104-6
Molomo, R., 236
Molopo Farms, 191
Monarch Mine, 194
Mongologe, K. of Bangologa, 65
Monnyelatsela, 92
Montshiwa, K. of Barolong, 145, 147-8, 161
Mophuting, K., v
Morafe (Group or Nation): 73-80; traditional organisation, 117; reconstruction after 1840, 117-18, 124-5
Moremi I, K. of Batawana, 98-9
Moremi II, K. of Batawana, 100, 132, 162, 178
Moritsane, 40, 51-2, 68
Moroka, K. of Barolong, 113
Morolong, K. of Barolong, 60, 62, 63
Moruakgomo, Regent of Bakwena, 75
Morupule, 195, 244-5
Mosega (S. Africa), 109, 113, 143
Mosetlha, daughter of Matshege, 67

Moshaneng Asbestos Mine, 194
Mosiemang, B., v
Mosinyi, Goareng, 224
Mothibi, K. of Batlhaping, 129
Mothoagae's Church, 135-6
Motloutse River, 32, 38, 46, 83, 85
Motsete, Dr K.T., 205, 223, 226
Motswakhumo, son of Mathiba, 98-9
Mozambique, 46, 259
Mpanga, Leader of Basotho group, 85
Mpangazita, K. of Amahlubi, 103
Mpapho, Levuna, 213
Mpho, Motsamai M., 222-4, 227
Mphoeng, brother of Khama III, 159
Mphoeng, Oteng, 213
Mugabe, R., Prime Minister of Zimbabwe, 259
Mukuru, the first Omuherero, 92
Mulambwa, K. of Aluwi, 95
Murray, M., 131
Muslim (traders), 51
Mwanambinyi, Mulozi *kgosana*, 93
Mwari, 56, 86
Mynhardt, Louis, 226
Mzilikazi, K. of Amandebele, 85-6, 104-9

Naletale (Zimbabwe), 83
Nama (Khoe subgroup), 92, 93, 170
Namibia (South West Africa), 22, 23, 40, 91, 148, 259
Nareng (S. Africa), 85
Nata River, 21, 22, 77
Natal Colony, 166
National Assembly, 226, 231-3
National Commission on Education, 253
National Development Bank, 243, 248
National Development Plan, 238
National Health Institute, 250
National Party (S. African), 170
Native Administration Proc., 1934, 185
Native Fund, 181, 203
Native Recruiting Corp., 1912, 197
Native Tribunals Proc., 1934, 186
Nchabe River, 39
Ndumba, Mukalanga *kgosana*, 85
Ngalama, Mulozi *kgosana*, 94
Ngami, Lake, 39, 71, 77, 90, 98, 106, 131
Ngamiland (N-W District), 99, 121, 149, 161-4
Ngasa, Land of Bayei, 93
Ngoma, 93

Ngombela, *K.* of Balozi, 94
Ngotwane River, 66
Ngwaketse, son of Malope, 62, 65
Ngwamamaseko, Leader of Amangoni, 85
Ngwato, son of Malope, 62, 65
Nicholls, 162
Nigeria, 30, 34
Nilotic languages, 31
Nkgaraganye, *K.* of Bahlakoana, 104-5
Nkomo, Joshua, 259
Nkrumah, Kwame, President, 262, 263
Non-Aligned Movement, 263-4
Noto, son of Morolong, 63
Nswazwi, J.M., Mukalanga *kgosana*, 212-3
Nswazwi People, 205, 212-13
Nunga, 93
Nurses Training Centre, 207
Nwako, M.P.K., 224
Nyamazana, Leader of Amangoni, 85
Nyambi (Ancestor of Hambukushu), 97

Odi River *see* Marico River
Odi Village, the weavers, 249
Okavango Delta, 35, 90, 161
Okavango River, 40, 90, 94
Olduvai (Tanzania), 12, 19
Omaweneno, 92
Openshaw, J., 222
Oral History, 1, 60
Orange Free State (S. Africa), 65; Republic of 165
Orapa, 195, 230, 244
Organisation of African Unity, 257-9, 262-3
Oswell, W.C., 131
Ovaherero, 89, 91-3, 103, 170
Ovambanderu, 73, 91-3, 98, 103
Ovambo, 92
Ovimbundu *see* Mambari

Palapye, 39
Pan African Movement, 262
Panzera, Maj. F.W., 181
Parsons, N., v
Persia, 34, 40, 55, 82
Phetlhu, S., 184
Phuduhutswana, *K.* of Batlhaping, 65
Pilane I, *K.* of Bakgatla, 145
Pilane, Bogatsu, 186
Pilane, Isang, Regent of Bakgatla, 145, 183, 204
Pilane, Molefi, *K.* of Bakgatla, 217

Pilane, T., 184
Pim Economic Commission, 185, 188
Pitsanaphotlokwe, 161, 164
Pitsane, 106
Political Parties: Early formation, 221-6, 235-7; Federal Party, 222; Peoples Party, 222, 227; Democratic Party, 224-7; Independence Party, 224; Peoples Party No 1, 224-6; National Front, 233, 236; Progressive Union, 237
Price, Rev. R., 180
Prospecting: Ancient, 42-3; modern, 193-4
Public Service, 234
Public Service Commission, 234

Queen's Commissioner, 226

Racism, 111, 146, 171, 214, 256-7
Raditladi, L.D., 222
Raditladi, brother of Khama III, 159, 180
Railways: Introduction of, 156, 161, 165; Colonial Period, 195; Walvis Bay, 196, 245; Modern, 240
Ramatlabama Veterinary School, 191
Ramokate, P., *K.* of Bakhurutshe, 184
Ramokgwebane River, 48
Rasesa, 60
Rathantang (S. Africa), 65
Ratsebe, Leader of Baphuting, 104
Ratshosa, Obeditse, 184
Ratshosa, Simon, 140, 184, 221
Read, James, 136
Recruiting for mines, 197
Refugees, 103, 222, 257-8
Refugees, High Commissioner for, 259
Religion: Traditional, 25-6, 56, 86, 92; *see also* Bogosi *and for* Christian see Missionaries
Rensburg, Patrick Van, 251-2
Resident Commissioner, 175
Rey, Sir Charles, 184-6
Rhodes, Frank, 161
Rhodes, Hon. C.J., 147-8, 154-65
Rhodesia (Zimbabwe), 156, 171, 258-9, 262
Riley, C., 157
Rinderpest, 191
Road to the North, 146-7
Robinson, Sir Hercules, 148, 161, 175
Rock Paintings, 31, 33, 40
Ruare (Okavango R.), 98

Rudd, C., 156

St Joseph's Mission, Kgale, 206
Sabe River (Zimbabwe), 48
Salt, 49
San (*Basarwa*, Bushmen), 17, 20-8, 31, 37, 40, 41, 51, 53, 57, 73, 90, 200-1
Sanctions, Policy on, 258-9
Sand River Convention, 144-5
Sargant Report, 202-3
Scholtz, Commandant P.E., 116
Schulenburg, Rev. H. 131, 137-8
Scramble for Africa, 143
Sebego, Regent of Bangwaketse, 78, 92, 106-9, 178
Sebele II, *K.* of Bakwena, 150-3, 158-9, 178
Sebitwane, *K.* of Bakololo, 98-9, 105-9
Seboni, M., 186
Sechele, *K.* of Bakwena, 75, 116-17, 131, 145, 150-3, 159-61
Sechele, Kgari, *K.* of Bakwena, 217
Sedie, D. 224
Seepapitso IV, *K.* of Bangwaketse, 234
Sefunelo, *K.* of Barolong, 104
Segokotlo, Mokwena *kgosana*, 75
Segotshane, Regent of Bangwaketse, 115
Sehuba (trad. tax), 41, 51, 52
Sekgoma I, *K.* of Bangwato, 117, 133
Sekgoma Letsholathebe, *K.* of Batawana, 100, 133, 152, 163-4, 178
Sekgoma, Peto, 216-7
Sekwati, *K.* of Bapedi, 104
Selborne, Lord, 171
Selebi-Phikwe, 195, 230, 244
Seleka, son of Kobe, 176-7
Seoke, 68
Serondela, 39
Seronga, 94
Serowe, 37, 38, 71, 77, 85
Serowe Public School, 140
Serule, 83
Setswana Language, 60
Seventh Day Adventist Mission, 207
Shaka, *K.* of Amazulu, 103
Shakawe, 39, 100
Shashe Builders' Brigade, 252
Shashe River, 37, 39, 41, 46, 85
Sheep, 22, 26, 37, 40, 70, 80, 89, 92
Shells, sea, 40, 48, 50, 52, 54, 55, 67, 81, 83, 85
Shepstone, Theophilus, 166

Shippard, Sir Sidney, 152-3, 161, 175
Shoshong, 32, 37-9, 52, 67, 68, 85, 90, 125
Slaves, 49, 145
Smith, Dr A., 3
Smuts, Jan, 170
Somolekae, 133, 138
Sorghum, 31, 53, 70
Sotho-Tswana Peoples, 60, 64, 68, 102
South Africa: Before Union in 1910, 165-70; During Union, 170-4; As Republic, 1961, 173, 256-63
South African Native Labour Contingent, 209
South African Republic (Transvaal), 154, 157, 164
Southern African Customs Union, 230, 239, 247
Southern African Development Coordination Conference (SADCC), 260-2
Specularite, 40, 42, 47, 79
Spindle-whorl, 48
Steesma, Moruti, 204
Steinberg, B., 225
Stellaland, Republic of, 148
Stone Age: Early, 12-16; Middle, 16; Later, 16, 33, 37, 39
Strombom, 162
Sung, 52
Surmon, W.H., 167
Swaneng Hill School, 251-2
Swaziland, 85

Tati Area 55, 64, 145, 180, 194
Tati Company, 200
Tati Concession Mining and Exploration Company, 180
Tati Training Institution, 205
Taung (S. Africa), 5
Tawana, K. of Batawana, 98
Tax, modern: Introduction of, 181-2; Education, 140, 181, 203; War, 212
Terminology (Use of Names), 270
Thabane, K. of Bakgatla, 66
Thamaga, 43
Thamalakane River, 22, 31, 39, 90
Thaoge River, 99
Thogo, Mokwena guide, 98
Thompson, F.R., 156
Tiger Kloof College, 1904 (S. Africa), 201-2
Tin, 42, 46
Tjikalanga Language, 46, 81-4
Tobane, 39, 44

Toromoja, 53
Torwa State, 81-4
Toteng, 39
Toutswe People, 39-41, 47, 49, 51, 52, 53, 64, 81
Toutswemogala, 29, 39
Trade: Traditional, 31, 40, 44, 46, 47-8, 51-4, 120-1; wagon trade, 35, 100, 115-16, 121-8; modern, 42, 125, 173, 197
Transfer (Proposed incorporation of Bechuanaland, Basutoland and Swaziland in Union of S. Africa), 149, 171-3, 183, 186; and with Rhodesia, 156-65, 172, 210
Transportation, modern, 195-7, 239-40
Tribal Administration, 185-7
Tsetse Fly, 30, 31, 85, 89, 92, 241
Tshabong, 92
Tshane, 77
Tsheko Tsheko, 224
Tshesebe, K. of Barolong, 65
Tshwane, Leader of Baphuting, 104
Tsienyane, 37
Tsodilo Hills, 32, 37, 39, 40, 42, 53, 90, 97
Tsoebebe, A.M., 224-5
Tswapong Hills, 85
Tuli Farms, 165, 199-200

Uitlanders (White non-Boers in Transvaal), 157, 166
United Nations Organisation, 264
United States of America, 209, 263
University: UBLS, 207; UB, 254-5

Varozvi, 81-8, 102
Vashona, 53, 170
Vegkop (S. Africa), 113
Vereeniging, Treaty of, 166
Veterinary Dept., 1905, 191
Village Development Committees, 235
Villages, ancient, 46, 48, 51, 81-2, 86
Voortrekkers, 110-3 see also Boers
Vukwe, 83

Waldheim, K. Secretary-General of U.N.O., 264
Walshe, A.E., 164
War: ancient, 103; Anglo-Boer, 166-170; First World, 209; Second World, 209-10, 222
Warren, Sir Charles, 147-52
Water Development: Colonial Period, 191-2; Modern, 249-50
West Africa, 30
White Settlers, Early, 103
Williams, Rev., 169
Williams, Sir Ralph, 178
Willoughby, Rev. W.C., 159-61
Wookey, Rev. J., 133, 163

Xau, Lake, 37
Xhumo, 98

Yellen, J. v

Zambezi River, 55, 89, 97
Zambia, 31, 39, 40, 41, 99, 113, 259
Zimbabwe (Town), 51, 52-6, 81, 84
Zwangendaba, Leader of Amangoni, 85